SUSAN MYRICK OF *GONE WITH THE WIND*

An Autobiographical Biography

Copyright © 2011, 2020 by Susan Lindsley, all rights reserved. No portion of this book may be reproduced, stored or transmitted in any form or by any means without written permission from Susan Lindsley and/or ThomasMax Publishing. An exception is granted for brief excerpts taken for review purposes.

ISBN-13: 978-1-7334044-1-9
ISBN-10: 1-7334044-1-4

Front cover and second title page photo: Clark Gable with Susan Myrick on the set of Gone With The Wind, picture courtesy of Daniel Selznick and Selznick Properties Limited.

First hardcover printing, February, 2011
First paperback printing, February 2020

Cover design by ThomasMax

Published by:

ThomasMax Publishing
P.O. Box 250054
Atlanta, GA 30325
404-794-6588
www.thomasmax.com

SUSAN MYRICK OF *GONE WITH THE WIND*

An Autobiographical Biography

SUSAN LINDSLEY

ThomasMax

TM

Your Publisher
For The 21st Century

Susan's Other Books

Southern historical novels
- The Bottom Rail
- When Darkness Fell

Memoirs
- Blue Jeans and Pantaloons in YESTERPLACE
- Possum Cops, Poachers and the Counterfeit Game Warden

Biography: The Lindsleys of Westover

Collections of works edited
- Myrick Memories
- Margaret Mitchell: A Scarlett or a Melanie?
- Luther Lindsley: His Literary Works

Poetry
- When Yestertime Was Now
- Christmas Gift
- O Yesterplace and other poems (out of print)

Short Story collections
- Finding Bigfoot
- Whitetails and Tall Tales
- Emperor of the United American States

Wildlife
- Wildlife in Persimmon Paradise

DVD: MYRICK DISCUSSES PEGGY and GWTW

For Lil and Thulia

ACKNOWLEDGMENTS

Numerous people have been involved in the production of the biography.

First and foremost, I wish to thank Reg Murphy for his tribute to Sue, which opens this book. Reg knew both me and Aunt Sue when he worked for *The Macon News* back in the 1950s.

Special thanks go to the three persons most important in my life: My life partner Gail Cabisius and my two sisters Thulia Lindsley Bramlett and Lillas Lindsley James. They all provided moral support and hours of help in gathering, organizing and correcting materials. Thulia nominated our Aunt Sue into the Georgia Women of Achievement and she made that material available. Lil, who lives in Macon and spent many hours weekly with Sue, contributed her memories and many details of events and of Sue's friends, and guided me to many resources.

Sue's sister Allie gave me many documents and oral information over the years that have been priceless in preparing this book.

Several of the *Gone With The Wind* pictures from the sets are used with the permission of the heirs of David Selznick, and I thank Daniel Selznick and Selznick Properties Limited.

I received help from Muriel Jackson and her staff of the Washington Memorial Library and the Middle Georgia Archives in Macon, from the Special Collections of the library of the Georgia College and State University in Milledgeville, and from Emory University Special Collections. John Jones of the Macon Little Theatre provided information on Sue's activities with the Theatre.

Thanks also are due various individuals for their help: Patricia Blanks, Valette Jordan Adkins, Sara Landry, Joe Popper, and Sibley Jennings.

Most of all, I must thank Sue herself, for giving me many of her papers and photographs, not just from her days in Hollywood, but also her diary and personal letters. And of course *The Macon Telegraph* for allowing me unlimited quoting of articles by Sue and about Sue.

TRIBUTE TO SUSAN MYRICK

Reg Murphy
Reporter: *The Macon Telegraph*
Editor: *The Atlanta Constitution*
Kidnapping victim 1974
Editor & Publisher:
The San Francisco Examiner
The Baltimore Sun
CEO: The National Geographic Society
President: U.S. Golf Association

July 10, 1957

In broiling 98-degree Georgia heat, a graying, Southern-talking gentlewoman last week looked for boll weevils on cotton, complimented a farmer on his good corn, and spent two hours watching another farmer plant soy beans in grainfield stubble with a new machine.

Then she went back to an air conditioned office, sat down to a typewriter and wrote a believable, authenticated story on how the new machine works.

The lady, Miss Susan Myrick, farm editor of *The Macon* (GA) *Telegraph and News* (circulation 61,000), has been writing farm stories for Georgia readers for 15 years—and winning prizes for her efforts.

Farm editing "just comes naturally" to one of the very few feminine agricultural editors in the nation. "I always say I was born and bred in the briar patch, and the first thing I can remember is riding two-on-a-horse across the fields with my father," she said in a soft Dixie drawl.

With no qualms about digging a story from the dirt, "Miss Sue" has decided farming is a good enough vocation to enter for herself. She operates a 315-acre tree farm of her own ("loblolly pine") on the old family estate at Dovedale, Georgia.

Fortunately a tree farm takes little time. In addition to conducting a weekly farm page of features and turning out almost daily farm stories, she contributes editorials on agriculture, writes the well-read advice-to-the-lovelorn column under the pseudonym Fanny Squeers, and counsels

Telegraph-News readers on etiquette. As a catch-all title, she is listed as associate editor on the masthead.

One of her co-workers said, “Doesn’t matter who you are or what your problem is, she’s got the answer. Youngsters in love, farmers making a cash crop, college classes studying literature and writing, or the director of a community theater casting a play—they all look to Miss Sue for advice.”

She finds her farm features through hundreds of sources she has cultivated for the past 15 years, particularly soil conservation district supervisors (non-salaried farmers who joined together to promote land-saving practices) and professional agriculturists.

“I’m not attempting to educate the farmer, or teach him or instruct him,” she said. “I’m not a graduate of any agricultural college and I don’t attempt to act like an agronomist. Instead, I’m trying to tell the success story of a farmer and let other farmers see in his success a method of improving. The story of Farmer X who has made a better living because he has followed sound conservation measures and applied modern methods to his farming may influence other farmers to improve their agricultural practices.”

Explaining the popularity of a farm page in a Southern newspaper, she said, “Curiously enough, 90 per cent of our businessmen are farmers at heart or are trying to get ready to retire on a little farm.”

From providing background data on agriculture to retired Senator Walter F. George (D-GA) of nearby Vienna to counseling young married couples on their problems, her career has flitted through several stages.

She came to work at *The Telegraph* 28 years ago for Mark Ethridge, now publisher of *The Louisville Courier-Journal.* “I was teaching physical education at the local high school and kept seeing things I thought would make news,” she recalls. “I kept dropping into the newspaper office to tell him (Ethridge, then *Telegraph* editor) about them and he kept saying ‘sit down and write it.’ Finally, I started working full-time. I’ve done everything on the newspapers except polish the cuspidors.”

Working in a rich agricultural area where farm buying income is up 23.5 per cent over five years ago, Miss Sue is the chief writer of more than 150 solid pages of agricultural news which *The Telegraph-News* publishes each year, or better than one million words annually.

She roams through lespedeza patches, woodlots and pastures to get material, chatting all the time with farm friends. Then she writes the copy, edits it herself and figures type size for makeup purposes.

One of her typically acid editorials against government farm policies last week said: "It looks as if Mr. Secretary Benson is getting an assist from old Jupiter Pluvius. Floods and cloud bursts (in Kansas' rich wheat belt) have done more to settle the surplus problem, it seems, than all Congress could figure out."

"Out in the fields, farmers aren't reticent about talking to her," *Telegraph-News* executive editor Bert Struby said. "She has an advantage with the backwoods farmer because she is a woman, rather than in spite of it. She can get them to talk because she knows their idiom. If a man farm editor comes around, the farmer doesn't know whether he's an income tax man come to check on his income. The natural instinct is to be a little close-mouthed around other men about yields and cash crops. But she often talks to the farm wife first, getting an entrée with the husband when he comes home to lunch. Her femininity is a distinct asset."

Testifying to that, staff photographer Talmadge Veal, who accompanies her on many of her feature-hunting jaunts, said, "We're always getting invited to 'dinner.' And people are always giving us peaches or country ham or something."

Miss Myrick became farm editor 15 years ago when the papers, deciding they needed a coordinator for all the farm news they were printing, selected the person who was doing most of the agricultural coverage. She stuck to her other duties and they multiplied.

"She's really phenomenal," Publisher Peyton Anderson said. "Sue is one of the most versatile and capable newspaper women I have ever come in contact with. Her assignments have included every type and she has wound up in her first love, the farm section."

Although there has been a recent trend toward male editors of women's sections, almost all women were relegated earlier to society and home news. When Miss Myrick crossed the line into a seemingly male-only department, she found it fun.

Pretty soon she was earning titles such as Miss Lupine Queen for daily promotion of planting a winter cover crop called Blue Lupine. "Now they're saying I'm a queen almost without a kingdom, because a bitter cold snap in 1955 killed almost all the lupine."

She won first prize in 1956 in the National Editorial Associations' (NEA) contest for agricultural coverage, one of the top prizes in the nation for service to agriculture. That same year she won *Progressive Farmer* magazine's title as "Woman of the Year in Agriculture." Other prizes include numerous ones from the Georgia Association of Soil Conversation District Supervisors.

Other *Telegraph-News* reporters frequently find they have a conversation-starter with sources who said, "*Macon Telegraph*? Oh, yes, how's my friend Sue Myrick? Give her my regards, will you."

The circulation department reported her Sunday farm page is one of the first stops for agriculture-minded Middle Georgians, and she is a frequent speaker on the civic-club-farm bureau-school assembly circuit.

Two years ago, when a heart attack slowed her momentarily, she rested for a couple of months, then went back to work. That seizure took away one of the prime joys of her life, "spading my garden." One tiny concession is an air-conditioned automobile to take her to and from the farms.

One of the few other times she has been away from work was a leave of absence to teach Vivien Leigh how to speak with a Southern accent for *Gone With The Wind,* being filmed in Hollywood. As technical advisor, she also stopped the show long enough to get actors to chop cotton in the right season.

Away from the office, she found time to help organize the Macon Little Theatre 25 years ago and has averaged at least one part per season since.

As director of the Macon Art Association for the past 10 years, she also authored a book called *Our Daily Bread* for use in the third grade "to teach children that everything we eat and everything we wear comes from the soil and to give them an understanding of protecting and replenishing the soil's fertility."

Now, she has begun developing another hobby for retirement, which comes in four years—painting water colors. "I'm not as good as Grandma Moses, but I am better than President Eisenhower."

Editor's Note: A graduate of Mercer University, Reg began his newspaper career in the city of his alma mater at the Macon Telegraph and News. *There, as a young reporter, he met Susan Myrick.*

Reg became editor of the Atlanta Constitution, *editor and publisher of the* San Francisco Examiner, *publisher and CEO of the* Baltimore Sun, *and president and CEO of the National Geographic Society.*

NOTE TO MY READERS

A large portion of this book is autobiographical, that is, taken from Sue Myrick's own letters, diary and columns. She used words, such as "fey," "laught" and "stopt" that are no longer commonly used, and at times violated grammar for emphasis. These words are retained to keep the flavor of Sue's works.

Her words, *and those of others who wrote about her or to her,* are given in a different type face to avoid confusion as to whose words you are reading. These quotes will be in these type faces, larger than the regular text.

Table of Contents

PART I The Dovedale Years 1
Birth of a Legend 2
Sue's Family 4
Sue's own Stories of Childhood 20

PART II The Academic Years 49
Georgia Normal & Industrial College 50
Sue in Society 71
Early Teaching 73
Graduate Studies 75
Superwoman 80
Charles Deets 82
Teaching in Hastings, Nebraska 93
Summer School 94
Almost Military 95
Back to the Classroom 97

PART III At *The Macon Telegraph*: The First Ten Years 104
The Beginning 105
Solid Friendships 113
Macon Little Theatre 116
Georgia Press Institute 122
Aaron Bernd 126
Other Adventures 126

PART IV *Gone With The Wind* 130
The Road to Hollywood 131
Sue's Diary 133
Hollywood 171
The SMMA 293
Sue's Return to Macon 298
Premiere's: Atlanta and Macon 306
GWTW in Later Years 313
GWTW Friendships 322
The 1967 Premiere 325
The Tara Ball 328
GWTW on TV—1976 333

Did Rhett Return? 335
Sue's Sequel to GWTW 335

PART V After GWTW 338
Expanding Duties 339
Politics 350
Farm Editor 350
Blue Lupine vs. Kudzu 356
Other Duties 357
Another Promotion 357
Our Daily Bread 359
DAR 360
Equality for Women 361
Smoking Challenge 364
Awards 365
Greatest Honors 371
Fun Awards 372
Women's National Press Club 374
Speeches 376

PART VI Retirement 393
Headlines 394
Painting 395
Travelling 400
Writing in Retirement 405
Sue's Unpublished Manuscript 406
Letter from a Yankee 409
A Margaret Mitchell Movie? 410

PART VII Memories of Sue 412
The Three Lindsley Girls 413
Susan Lindsley's Memories 413
Memories of Dr. Lil L. James 422
Thulia L. Bramlett's Memories 425
Euri Belle Bolton 427
Mrs. James (Dee) Shelburne 427
Sara G. Landry 428
Cecile Humphrey Hardy 429
Senator Sam Nunn 429

Milledgeville Friend 429
Ann Rutherford 429
Herb Bridges 430
Other Authors 430
Mollie Haskell 430
Michael Sragow 430

PART VIII Exit, Laughing 431
Her Death 432
Sue's Reflections on her Life 433

Appendix I Sherman 437
Appendix II Layout of Myrick Home 438
Appendix III Home-Churned Ice Cream 439
Appendix IV A Teacher's Friday Night Dream 439
Appendix V The Well 440
Appendix VI Little Theatre Roles 441
Appendix VII Shows, Books and Frocks 442
Appendix VIII Hollywood People 447
Appendix IX GWTW Documents 450
Appendix X Reference Materials 459
Appendix XI Bibliography 460
Appendix XII Westover Plantation 462
Appendix XIII Other Awards 463
Appendix XIV Cotton Chopping 467
Appendix XV Cammie King 468

Index 470

PART I

THE DOVEDALE YEARS

BIRTH OF A LEGEND

Kate Myrick gave birth to her fifth child on February 20, 1893, and called her Susan. But the real Susan Myrick of newspaper and *Gone With The Wind* fame actually came to life about five years later on the counter of a Milledgeville dry goods store. Miss Kate took Susan with her on the 12-mile carriage trip from their Dovedale Plantation home to Milledgeville to do some shopping. While Miss Kate looked over fabrics, lace and threads to make her girls new dresses, the child wandered off.

Laughter pulled Miss Kate to the back of the store and she paused at the sound of Susan's voice. The child stood on another counter, facing away from Miss Kate and toward several ladies and other children. Her right arm was extended forward, and her little hand was balled into a fist.

"Brer Rabbit, he seys, seys he, 'You le' me loose, your hear. Er I's gonna bust you wide open wid my other fist.' "

Miss Kate stood back, watched, and listened as her child spoke in the inflections and dialect of one of the hired men at Dovedale.

" 'I ain't telling ya agin,' Brer Rabbit seys, seys he. But de Tar Baby, he ain't saying nut-in', and Brer Fox, he lay low."

Susan swung her left fist forward and stood frozen, leaning slightly forward, both fists now buried in the unseen Tar Baby. "Brer Rabbit, he done whomped de Tar Baby again. He seys, seys he, 'You let me go.'"

Laughter rose again. The children slipped closer.

When Brer Rabbit had kicked the Tar Baby with one foot and was ready to kick with the other one, Susan realized she couldn't lift both feet and looked down as if puzzled. But she kept her balance on one foot and continued the story. "'I tells you, you le' me go, er I'll butt you cockeyed,' Brer Rabbit seys, seys he. But de Tar Baby, he don't sey nuthin' and don't let 'im go. And Brer Fox, he lay low. Brer Rabbit, he butted up on de Tar Baby, and dere he was, all stuck up. And Brer Fox, he couldn't lay low no mo'. He laughed and he laughed and he laughed till he couldn't laugh no mo'.

"And he pulled Brer Rabbit off de Tar Baby and told 'im, 'I'm gonna eatcha up.' And Brer Rabbit, he looked at Brer Fox and he seys, seys he, 'You kin eat me up, Brer Fox, but please, oh please, don't tho' me in de briar patch,' he seys, seys he.

"And Brer Fox, he threw Brer Rabbit right smack dab in de briar patch dar on de side-a de road and laughed and laughed and laughed till he couldn't laugh no mo'. 'Cepting bout den Brer Rabbit, he laughed and he laughed and he seys, seys he, 'Thank 'ee, Brer Fox. I was bawn and bred in de briar patch.'"

Susan curtsied, the children and their mothers clapped, and Susan smiled and curtsied again.

She had found the self she would become, and her first public appearance became a family legend.

SUE'S FAMILY

THE FAMILY

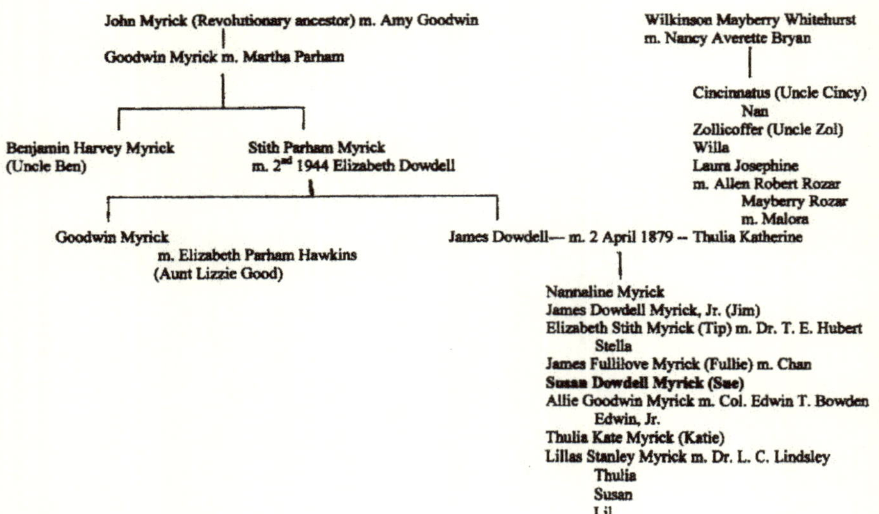

This chart is not a complete list of family members, but serves as an aid to the reader in understanding family relationships.

"Uncle Ben," brother to Stith Parham Myrick, was Sue's great uncle. He served as a colonel in the Confederate Army.

Martha Parham Myrick, Stith and Ben's mother, was sister to Sarah Parham, wife of U. S. Senator Benjamin Harvey Hill. Sue's library held a copy of the Senator's biography, written by his son; the book is believed to have been in the library of Sue's parents.

Sue was grounded in time and place by her life at Dovedale, by the close association of her family with the tenants, both black and white, and by the stories they all told. She learned the Negro culture and language from Sherman, a plantation worker whose influence eventually became a factor that led her to Hollywood. Nightly, he entertained the Myrick children with stories of African lore that had been modified to fit the animals of America. Passed down through generations of slaves, these tales eventually reached the white culture. (See Appendix I.)

From her family, she learned about The War Between The States (*The War*) and the strength of Southern women who kept the families intact during the hard times. These family history stories were told and retold at the dining table and in the evening when Grandma Whitehurst came for the summer or when one of Miss Kate's brothers' family came for a week or two-week visit.

Both parents told stories about their ancestors. Sue's mother, Thulia Kate Whitehurst Myrick, told about the courage of her own mother (Nancy Averette Bryan Whitehurst) when the Yankees under General Sherman arrived at the Whitehurst home in Wilkinson County. Nancy was alone except for four small children and several old Negroes—Miss Kate herself was still in diapers at the time.

The soldiers chopped up the furniture, burned the cotton and the gin houses, mixed salt into the ground, dragged the bedding and clothing into the yard, shredded the mattresses, poured the kegs of molasses onto the furniture and clothing and burned it all. They took all the food, the cows, the chickens and the corn crop. They then told Nancy to get out of the now empty house because they were going to set fire to it.

A small woman whose eyes appeared black when she was riled, Nancy drew herself up tall as she stood in the front doorway and said, "This is my home and I'll leave it only when the fire drives me out."

They must have admired her spunk because they did not burn it.

The day was cold when Sherman's army ransacked the home and plantation. But after they destroyed everything, a Yankee soldier gave a sweater to one of the children. When Miss Kate told her children about the event, she added, "Perhaps they were not all bad."

Miss Kate told them that Nancy had never done any type of work before *The War*—she did not even comb her own hair. She managed, however, to milk the cow a neighbor gave them, and was able to provide milk for the children and butter for the table. She treated her hands, which became red and raw from work, water and harsh soap, by rubbing tallow on them at night.

Sue's father, James Dowdell Myrick, told her about his great-grandfather John Myrick, a Revolutionary War veteran who acquired vast holdings of land in northwestern Baldwin County. James went on to tell how these holdings expanded so that his own parents—Stith Parham and Elizabeth Dowdell Myrick—had great wealth when he was a boy. The family lands included 3200 acres at the River Place (birthplace of James and his brother); 2600 acres at the Homestead (also called the Summer Place, in northwest Baldwin County, about 10 miles from Milledgeville), 3700 acres at Myrick's Mill in Twiggs County; and 23 acres at Midway, the location of the Rockwell Mansion, where the family lived at the time of *The War*. Stith added to his lands during *The War* by purchasing, at public auction, a tract of 972.5 acres called the Hurt Place. James told his children, "He paid for it with Confederate treasury notes, all $19,000 of it." Better, he would say, to have spent it on land, which never goes away and can feed you forever, than lose it when the Confederate notes became worthless.

Sue heard about the grand parties her grandparents held at the Rockwell Mansion before *The War*, when the landed gentry and their ladies visited their home in Midway, an estate once home to a Georgia governor.

Her grandfather had been a general, not in the Confederate Army but in the Georgia Militia, appointed to that rank at the age of twenty-nine by the governor of Georgia. Although this military position exempted him from service in the Confederate Army, Stith had outfitted the Myrick Volunteers—a troop of about 75 men. Stith had provided them with horses, weapons and uniforms, and while they were on active duty, he had also supported their families.

James's adventures in *The War* began at the age of eighteen, when he and other cadets from the Georgia Military Institute in Marietta, Georgia, were called to active duty by the governor. Off he marched, armed only with his cap-and-ball pistol and a Joe Brown pike, to fight the Yankees. Unlike James, his brother, Goodwin, never saw action—he was captured by Yankee soldiers soon after he ran away from home to enlist, at the age of sixteen. He spent his war time in a Yankee military prison.

Before *The War* ended, the Myricks' fabulous parties were over—Stith had lost his wealth. He had loaned money to friends during the hard times, and when *The War* was over, the borrowers were unable to repay the loans. Stith himself had converted his "Union" cash into Confederate bills, bonds and notes during *The War*, and these papers no longer had any value.

* * *

Because Sue's grandfather had to tend to family business and had not had an opportunity to go to college, he had insisted on his children becoming educated. Shortly after *The War* ended, James's mother, Elizabeth, had written to General Lee, president of Washington University in Virginia, to ask him about sending James there. The great general had written back—James would carefully unfold the letter for them to see Lee's neatly penned words strongly urging Elizabeth to ensure that her son "continue the study of Latin. He will soon recover all he has lost by application and advance rapidly; no matter what occupation he may follow it will be beneficial. It will improve his knowledge, diction, style, taste, judgment."

Lee added, "Wisdom is the only investment we make in this world which pays us tenfold."

* * *

Rather than go to Virginia to college, James chose to stay closer to home and attended East Alabama College, now know as Auburn University. On his return home after graduation, he was considered the area's "most eligible bachelor" in spite of the declining wealth of the family. It was not a local girl that caught his eye, but a young lady, Thulia Katherine ("Miss Kate") Whitehurst, who lived in the adjacent county.

James and "Miss Kate" married on April 2, 1879 and moved to one of Stith's plantations, Myrick's Mill. Their first two children, Nannaline and James, Jr., were born there.

When his father, General Myrick, died in 1885, James and his family left Myrick's Mill and moved back to the family home at Midway (the Rockwell Mansion) to help his mother and to settle his father's estate. He had to sell off large tracts of land to pay off his father's debts. They kept the family home at Midway and also retained two of the plantations: The Homestead, where Goodwin and his family lived, and the Hurt Place.

The Homestead lands extended from a dirt road (now paved and called Nelson Road) northward to the south side of Potato Creek. The Hurt Place ran from the north side of Potato Creek northward to the north bank of Little Cedar Creek. James Dowdell and Miss Kate built their own home here and changed the name from the Hurt Place to Dovedale, a name derived from James's middle name—Dowdell, which was also his grandmother's maiden name.

James moved his family to Dovedale after his father's death and his mother remained at the Rockwell Mansion in Midway. After her death in 1889, he sold that house.

Although Dovedale was a plantation, with a fairly large acreage and many hands to work the land, the house was single story, without the high columns of antebellum mansions. James had been as practical with his house as he was in business and farming, and built a home for comfort and economy. (See the layout of the house in Appendix II.)

Ahead of his times, some fifty years before electricity reached the countryside, James devised a system to pump water into the house from a nearby spring, so the family had a bathroom with running water—many years before even Delco systems came to the country. The hydraulic ram provided water only for bathing. Water for drinking and cooking came from the well and was hand-drawn and hand-carried into the house.

By 1900, the family had grown by another six children: Elizabeth Stith (Tippie); James Fullilove (Fullie), Susan Dowdell, Allie Goodwin, Thulia Kate, and Lillas Stanley, the youngest, born in 1900, and referred to by her sisters as "the spoiled one."

Miss Kate said that Susan was the biggest and strongest of her eight babies and called her "robust." Her younger siblings admired Susan for her energy and intelligence, and said that from early childhood she loved an audience and would "act" for them.

Although the Myrick children, like the tenants' children, ran barefooted, Dovedale was considered a wealthy plantation at the time. The family owned a pair of horses for the carriage (Bill Nye and Lady), one for the buggy, one that only Papa rode, and one for the children to ride—bareback. The family had only one saddle, Papa's. They had countless mules for plowing and a pair for the wagon that hauled supplies and ice from Milledgeville, several yokes of oxen, as well as hogs, sheep and a variety of poultry.

A story of Susan's childhood was written down by her sister Katie and is still being passed down in the family:

Miss Kate walked into the kitchen where Manny, the Negro servant who tended to all of the children, was feeding Susan. The child sat in the wooden high chair.

"What are you feeding her?" Miss Kate asked.

"Rice and gravy," said Manny.

"Don't you think she's big enough to have a little meat?"

"Lawd, Miss Kate, dis here chil's been eaten rabbit a long time."

"Rabbit? Where in the world would she get rabbit?" Miss Kate asked.

"At my house. Alf (her son) kills 'em, I cooks 'em, and Susan eats 'em."

* * *

The family considered itself "land poor" (rural words meaning all the cash goes back into the land), and when Susan's friend Margaret Mitchell recommended Susan to be an advisor on Southern matters for *Gone With The Wind*, she wrote: *Being poor as Job's turkey, Susan was raised up in the country and she knows good times and bad, quality folks and poor whites, Crackers and town folks. And good grief, what she doesn't know about Negroes! She was raised up with them.*

Which was true. The children adored Sherman, as well as many others who worked for the family, both household servants and farm workers. Sara Lou, who worked as their cook, failed to show up for a few days, and then Susan and Allie learned Sara Lou had had twin girls, named Susan and Allie.

Allie wrote: *I was jubilant! My mother said she would take us to see the babies soon.*

Next day, she took Susan and me with her in the carriage into town, which was twelve miles away. Our favorite horses, Bill Nye and Lady, pulled the carriage. In town, we went immediately to the dry goods store to purchase two little white baby caps, all lace and ribbons, for our namesakes. Next day, we walked with Mama to Sara Lou's house (we were never allowed to go to a servant's house alone), to take the presents to the little girls. Sara Lou tied the caps under their chins. I was rapturous; the little black faces in the pretty lace caps were more beautiful than anything I had ever seen. Susan was the larger of the two and Allie was quite fragile, but Sara Lou promised that next time she would let us hold the babies very carefully.

* * *

Various hired men tended to the garden and the livestock, did the milking and butchering and gathered the eggs. One of Hezekiah's jobs was to keep fresh well water in the house for drinking and cooking; Will Collier curried the horses, and young Mattie played outside games with the girls. Playing in the yard, in and around the barn, and in the wagon yard, the children encountered these folks daily.

Sherman's duties kept him closest to the house—he filled in when Will or Hezekiah was elsewhere, and toted in firewood for the kitchen stove and fireplaces. He also slopped the hogs and tended to the chickens and other fowl. In summertime, he led the children to the fields for strawberries, blackberries, and plums. If the youngest child "got wo' out," he would sit her on his shoulders on the way home. Family tradition says sometimes the younger children ate more than they brought home.

Year-around, the Dovedale lands provided food, both wild and domestic—peaches, pears, apples, walnuts, scuppernongs, muscadines, persimmons, pecans and scaly barks (hickory nuts). The garden yielded abundant vegetables—including some that were not common in middle Georgia, such as artichokes and egg plants—and the fields grew corn and wheat for both the people and livestock. Dovedale provided everything except clothing and a few staple goods.

* * *

At Dovedale, as on most plantations, the farm bell was rung to signal the beginning of the work day, noon dinner break, and quitting time. Any other time of day, anyone who heard it clanging knew help was needed immediately—the hired men and neighbors would come to help out.

All of the children wanted to be allowed to ring the bell. It hung high on a post, with the pull rope hanging down low enough that the children could reach it before they entered their teens. Susan was thrilled the day she was first told to clang the bell.

She seized the rope and heaved with all her weight—and the rope broke. Down came the bell, onto Susan, and she and the bell hit the ground. Bruises did not mean send for the doctor, however. After the rope was replaced, Susan was again allowed to ring the bell to call the hands from work at suppertime.

* * *

The children lacked for nothing and never went hungry—barefooted, but not hungry. Breakfast meant eggs any style, biscuits, waffles, battercakes and Georgia cane syrup made at home, ham and bacon, and grits. Dinnertime (at noon) was their major meal, with chicken and pork, garden vegetables, and always biscuits and cornbread—sometimes hoecake (thin cornbread cooked in a skillet on top of the stove instead of baked). Supper, the light meal of the day on the farms, usually consisted of hominy and either biscuits or battercakes.

The Myrick table was never set for fewer than ten. The older of the eight children were leaving home as the younger ones came along, but the family always had visitors. Miss Kate's mother spent every summer with them after her husband's death. Others who came to stay, sometimes for weeks, were Miss Kate's sister Willa and her two children; and Miss Kate's brother Zollicoffer with his wife and three children. If more than ten were there at a meal, adults ate first and Sara Lou gave the children a sweet potato to hold them over until there was a place at the table for them.

The children were given a ten-minute notice before mealtime, and they had to wash their faces and hands, and comb their hair before they were called to the table. Papa was strict. Being late was just not allowed.

After supper, their major preparation for bed was to wash their feet on the back porch, where Sherman had filled up the wash tub (not a "bath tub" but what we would now call a No. 10 wash tub).

And then it was to the kitchen to listen to Sherman's stories again.

As a special treat, the family would churn ice cream. The churn at that time had to be cranked by hand. Ice was always kept at Dovedale, but was brought out in 200-pound blocks by a mule-drawn wagon and stored in a large box on the back porch where it was covered with sawdust. The oldest child used an ice pick and hammer to chop off chunks of ice, which then had to be crushed to fit into the bucket around the churn. The easiest method available to crush the ice at that time was to put in into a croaker sack and beat on it with the hammer.

When the ice cream was frozen, everyone wanted the pleasure of "licking" the dasher. Home-churned ice cream seems much colder than store-bought ice cream because it melts more rapidly and cools off the eater quickly. The family had home grown peaches and a variety of berries from their fields and woods for flavoring.

Their recipe (in Appendix III) called for raw eggs, now avoided because of the fear of food poisoning. Country people, knowing the problem of disease from dirty eggs and raw fowl, were always careful to wash eggs, not to leave any raw meat "off the ice," and to clean all knives and other items that touched the raw meats.

The major "social" events for the children were church and school. Church was "just down the road a piece" (maybe two miles). Goodwin's family also attended the Old Bethel Church, a one-room wooden structure with two front doors: One for the women and children (the younger boys and all girls) and one for the men. A divider ran down the middle of the pews from the front wall to the altar. Allie said she could look over this divider and just see the top of her papa's head. Church records show that Susan was baptized on April 18, 1896 and joined the church by profession of faith in August 1902, together with her sisters Allie and Katie.

When someone who did not know the children well would see Susan away from her parents, perhaps in the church yard at "dinner on the ground," she would get the question: "Honey, are you Mr. Jim Myrick's child or is Mr. Goodwin your papa?" Or, "Is your Mama Mrs. Jim Myrick?"

Susan said: "Such questions asked of me when I was 10 or 12 years old used to make me angry; I thought I was important enough to be known in my own right, without regard to my ancestry."

She described the family men:

My father wore a bushy mustache and a Van Dyke beard, though he was always meticulous about a morning shave. I remember he shaved with a straight razor and we children admired the way he held the razor in his right hand to shave the right side of his face, and swapped the razor over to his left hand to shave his left cheek. We didn't know the word "ambidextrous," but we did know we could not do much with our left hands.

My Uncle Good and my (Great) Uncle Ben, age about 60-odd as I remember them, wore beards down to their waists—well, almost, anyway. I shrank from being kissed by the uncles, and to this day I wonder how their wives liked all that brush.

Goodwin's wife, called "Aunt Lizzie Good" by Susan and her siblings, taught Sunday school to the children, who gathered around her by the organ. For Susan, the highlight of each Sunday was the little cardboard cards that Aunt Lizzie passed out to the students. The shiny cards bore pictures of Jesus and the prophets, the apostles and Mary Magdalene and the healing of Lazarus, as well as the boy David playing his harp, the Ark and its animals. Susan said, "The cards enchanted me. To my country child eyes, they were the most beautiful things in the world."

Formal education began less than a mile down the road from home, in a one-room school heated by a pot-bellied stove and built by their father on Dovedale land. All the white children in the neighborhood, including Goodwin Myrick's children and those of other neighbors, attended the Dovedale School. Each child toted her own dinner bucket, which usually contained a sweet potato and a sausage and biscuit. A spring near the school provided water for teacher and children.

School children chanted a rhyme that led them to think that school was really not supposed to be held on April Fool's Day: "Fool, fool, April fool, you learn naught by going to school." In a column years later, Susan told on herself and her classmates.

> We giggled all the length of the mile walk to the school house, thinking of how we would fool the teacher and take off at recess, and of how we had fooled our mother by our pretense of going to school in the normal fashion. Came the early recess and off we went. It wasn't difficult. It might have been if the teacher had not quietly remained inside the school room, making a great pretense of writing something on the blackboard.

The eldest of the four youngest Myrick girls, Susan was probably the ring leader of these escapades.

The teacher, who boarded with the Myrick family, knew the children's plans to sneak away—the children made a habit of playing hooky every April Fool's Day. It also gave the teacher a day off, which she probably needed—since she boarded in the household, she likely had to ensure that the children did their homework.

Each Friday, every student had to recite a poem memorized that week, a routine in almost every school at that time. As a result, a poem grew that bore the title "A Teacher's Friday Night Dream." The poem was a jumble of lines from various poems, in an order that was almost totally nonsense. All of the Myrick children not only learned their weekly recitation, but memorized the teacher's nightmare and could recite it even in their sixties and seventies. (See Appendix IV.)

A course no longer included in the lower grades' curriculum, Latin was required at the Dovedale School, perhaps because of General Lee's letter to James's mother.

After school when the children returned home, Sara Lou had a platter of freshly baked, thin "ginger cakes"—cookies—ready for the children, to hold them over until suppertime.

As the children grew, they were free to pursue their own activities when they were not in school or doing their chores. Susan's sister Allie said their play included cards (Flinch), hopscotch, dolls, paper dolls (cut out of the *Ladies' Home Journal*), and reading.

Allie also said that Susan would almost fight to be the first to read *The Youth's Companion*, and that Sue was enthralled by "The Five Little Peppers" and the "Little Colonel" books. When not reading these childhood books, she read the classics, over and over.

When Susan was ten, she became the envy of her younger sisters because she was allowed to go with her father when he made rounds on the plantation. She rode astride, her bare legs poking out from under her skirt tail, and sat on a croaker sack behind his saddle. She learned about farming, crops, soil fertility, and fertilizer. James told her how rain washed away the earth, and how crops would suck all the nutrition from the soil—he had seen how rainwater carried the soil downhill, along plowed furrows, into the streams and colored the creeks dirt-red. Her father would not let his tenant farmers follow the old customs—instead he had them build terraces; he taught them to plow with the contour of the land so soil could not easily escape downhill, and he had them rotate crops annually to revitalize the soil. His farming techniques were some 40 or 50 years ahead of common practices.

Sue absorbed everything her father showed her. His love for and knowledge of the soil soaked into her blood and would never leave her.

Her younger sisters also longed to drive the two-horse team that pulled the carriage—until the day Susan had the reins and they met a car, the first one the horses had even seen. The horses reared and bucked and dumped the four girls onto the ground. Susan held onto the reins, even while lying on the ground, and then got up, controlled the horses, and the group went on.

Unable to abide laziness, Miss Kate pushed her children to success. She remembered what her own mother had endured after the Yankee soldiers destroyed everything useful the family owned, and she drew strength and courage from those memories. Through either inheritance or example, her children carried that gumption throughout their lives, especially the four youngest daughters. They left home for school—alone—on trains, on boats, and by car, and travelled to schools and jobs at Harvard and Columbia, and in Battle Creek, California, Colorado, Montana and Minnesota without fear or hesitation—adventures like these were rare for young women of the time.

Thulia Kate Whitehurst Myrick 1933

Myrick's Mill about 1960, painting by Katie Myrick Lowerre

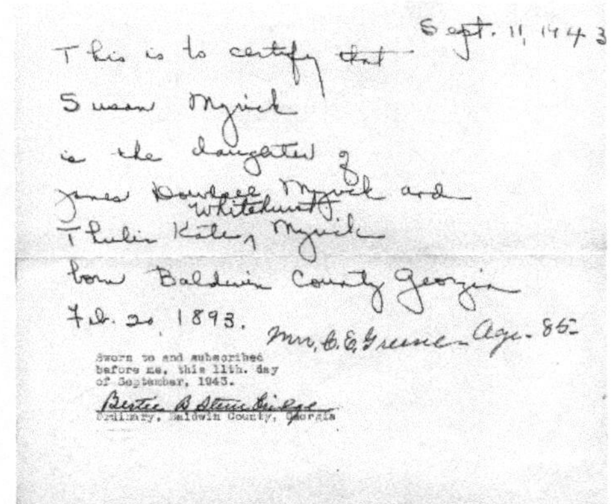

Sept. 11, 1943

This is to certify ~~that~~
Susan Myrick
is the daughter of
James Dowdee Myrick and
Thulia Kate Whitehurst Myrick
born Baldwin County Georgia
Feb. 20, 1893. Mrs. C. E. Greene Age. 85

Sworn to and subscribed
before me, this 11th. day
of September, 1943.

[illegible]
Ordinary, Baldwin County, Georgia

Sue's birth certificate

Allie, Sue, Lillas Myrick, c.1904

James Dowdell Myrick

Elizabeth Dowdell Myrick

General Stith Parham Myrick

James Dowdell Myrick

Myrick store and post office, Dovedale, Georgia, as it appeared in mid-1950s

Rockwell Mansion, 2000

LANDLORD'S LIEN. FORM No. 26. Louisville, (Ga.,) News & Farmer Job Print.

STATE OF GEORGIA, Baldwin **COUNTY.**

THIS AGREEMENT, Made and executed this 6 day of July 1900 189..
between James D Myrick Landlord, and
Jessie Freeman his tenant doth witness, that in consideration of the said
James D Myrick Landlord, furnishing the said
Jessie Freeman supplies, money, farming utensils, or other articles necessary to make crops; clothing, medicines and articles of necessity to supply a family, or any of said articles, during the year 1900, not exceeding Ninety five Dollars
he hereby obligates himself to pay the same on the 15th day of October 1900
And in order to secure the said James D Myrick Landlord, or assigns, in making the said advances, I, the said Jessie Freeman hereby create and give to the said James D Myrick Landlord, and his assigns, a full and complete lien on my entire crop of corn, cotton and all other produce growning or to be grown by me during the year 1900, on the land in said County whereupon I farm during said year. I further affirm that this is the only lien given by me on said Crop.

I AGREE, that should this lien have to be enforced by law, to pay ten per cent. Attorney's fees and Court costs.
As against this debt I waive all my rights to Homestead or exemptions allowed under the Laws of Georgia.
IN TESTIMONY of all all of which, I have hereto set my hand and seal, the day and year first above written.

Executed in presence of:

John Henry Calhoun — Jessie his X mark Freeman [SEAL.]

[SEAL.]

Tenant lease at Dovedale, 1900

Stith Parham Myrick

James Calhoun, "Sherman"

Thulia Kate Whitehurst at time of marriage to James Dowdell Myrick

SUE'S OWN STORIES OF CHILDHOOD

In later years, Sue often wrote about her childhood in her columns on *The Macon Telegraph* editorial page. These columns—spanning some 20 years—provide vivid pictures of Sue's life on Dovedale Plantation and show the sources of her love of dialect.

Bats in the House

Our house had a long hall—a sort of breezeway running from front door to back door, with rooms on each side. The front hall was separated from the back hall by portieres, of velour with fringe and little balls hanging off the edges. The portieres hung from a wooden rod, and to my childish mind were about the most elegant things in the nation.

The front and back doors were often left open. If not wide open, the doors swung too and fro with the goings and comings of children so often that they might as well have been left open all the time. And once in a while, a couple of bats would fly into the hallway. Whether they flew in by chance or by echolocation, I don't know, but they came in, to the horror of all the family. Children ran screaming to Mama that bats were in the house, and I, in particular, was torn between fright that a bat would be tangled up in my hair, and the excitement over the coming broom-fight with the flying critters.

Some three or four children, each armed with a broom, ranged the hallway and swung at the flying menaces, yelling the while at each other and the bats. Mama disappeared into her own room. I have never known whether she was afraid the bats would get in her hair or whether she just couldn't stand the yelling and the flailing brooms.

Sooner or later, the bats would be swatted to the floor and swept out into the open air. All of us were too chicken-hearted to kill the bats.

The Fireplace

The open fire is lovely to look upon but the heat it gives out is often insufficient to warm the sissified bones of one accustomed to a warm house. You sit before the burning logs, happy in the beauty of the firelight, but warm only in the front; often, too warm in the front, with your legs turning into a fabric design what with the blood vessels swelling and making red patterns on your skin where the fire heats them so.

Your back, meanwhile, is freezing.

Of course, nothing is more delightfully sensuous than the fine warmth on your rear when you turn your back to the fire, stand on the hearth with your skirt hiked up and rub yourself gently to keep the heat from becoming too much.

But unless you are a pointer dog, you have no right to usurp all the space on the hearth and keep the fire from warming the others in the room.

I can hear my mother now: "Don't stand in front of everybody; how can we keep warm if you stand on the hearth and keep all the warmth away from us?"

So, while there is pleasure in a wood fire, there is also unpleasantness associated with the house that has only a fireplace to warm it. I remember how I used to dress in bed in order to keep my teeth from chattering out of my head. Papa always rose at an early hour, made the fire in Mama's room, and went about the chores of early morning on the farm. Mama dressed by the fire and went about her tasks. And when breakfast was well on the way, she called us to get up.

The frosty air made patterns of my warm breath; the "Little Room" where my sister and I slept had no fireplace. We could jump out of bed and run to Mama's room to dress, but the rugless floor was icy to bare feet and the glacial air was too much to bear when one wore only a cotton nightie.

So my sister and I evolved a plan for dressing in bed. When we got undressed the night before we put our clothes into bed with us. That kept them warm through the night—that is, after we had warmed the icy sheets with our bodies.

Next morning, pushing the covers up to form a sort of deflated tent, we struggled out of our nighties and into our underwear and petticoats and balmorals and stockings.

Then we hurried out of the covers into our shoes and into the starched, cold calico frock we were to wear to school. We grabbed our sweaters and thence to breakfast.

Wash our faces? Well, we made a pass at it. Would YOU have washed yours in the pan on the back porch shelf when the water in the bucket had little flakes of ice on it?

Books

In my childhood, out in the country, with no library in miles and miles, and with few magazines coming to the home, I read books which today's city child would probably consider far too "grown-up," books which were in the family bookcases and provided all the literature we had access to.

Fortunately for us, the books were "classics"—*David Copperfield, Ivanhoe, Rob Roy, Great Expectations, Alice in Wonderland, Alice through the Looking Glass*, Lamb's *Tales from Shakespeare, Tales of King Arthur's Court*, some Thomas Hardy books, Poe's stories, and Louisa Alcott, Washington Irving, and so on. I wondered when I read *David Copperfield*, what had happened to Little Emily that caused her to drown herself. That gives some indication of how youthful and naïve I was at the time of reading some of the grown-up books.

There were three volumes called "Heart of Oak Books," filled with short stories, famous poems, certain chapters of famous books and some nonsense verses. Over these I poured with joy, time and again. It was in that series I learned of "Horatio At the Bridge," thrilling at the sound of my own voice as I lay on the back yard grass and read aloud—just for myself: *And how can man die better than facing fearful odds for the ashes of his fathers and the temples of his gods,* and "*Curse on him" quoth false Sextus, "will not the villain drown, but for his stay, ere close of day, we could have sacked the town."*

As a child I often plagued my mother by whining "Mama, tell me something to do," to which she often replied in her exasperation: "Oh do pray!" Not meaning for me to say my prayers; just meaning "Oh for goodness sakes," or "Do go jump in the lake. I've got to get dinner for ten people."

Now and then, I sneaked out to the book case in the hall (the one with glass shelves and a lock in which the key always stayed) for a "dime novel," brought home by my oldest brother from the wicked city of Atlanta where he went to college. I read with vast emotion and great delight, such stuff as Helena Rivers and other yellow-back, trashy novels.

Magazines

At Dovedale, the magazines were not legion, I'll admit; still, they provided many a pleasant recreation hour.

The Southern Cultivator, the *Saturday Evening Post*, *The Youth's Companion*, the *Delineator*, and the *Ladies Home Journal* are the ones I remember, chiefly. The LHJ of that day carried up near the front a page of jokes. These were the delight of our childish lives (probably a nuisance to our parents, who had to hear us tell the jokes a few dozen times a week).

The *Saturday Evening Post* of that era was the favorite reading for the grownups, who admired Harrison Fisher's drawings and the stories written by Robert Chambers. They could scarcely wait for next week's issue of the "continued story," which managed to "continue" almost as long as today's TV soap operas.

As for me, my favorites were the *Delineator* and *The Youth's Companion*. The first, I admired mostly because of the fact that Mama would let me have it for paper dolls when everybody had read it and she had ordered the dress patterns that appealed to her and to my older sisters.

The Youth's Companion, I read from cover to cover, with special affection for what was called "The Children's Page," where the stories were of the sort second graders could master, and rebuses, a form of simple puzzle, made me feel so brilliant when I had mastered one.

Papa or Mama often read the stories to us evenings, especially in summer when it was possible to read in the waning light of evening as we sat on the front piazza, Papa and Mama in big rocking chairs and the children gathered on the front steps.

The Southern Cultivator was hardly considered suitable reading for a girl of 10 or so, but I read it, just the same. There was little else to do on the farm save read, and everything in print was my meat. I remember my father's telling about something called "the Williamson Plan for Stunting Corn," and my struggle with trying to understand what the *Cultivator* said about the plan. It was something to do with applying fertilizer of a certain sort at a certain time, then withholding fertilizer to stunt the corn stalk's growth. All this to produce extra large ears of corn and more of them.

I'm sure today's magazines are all right; the trouble is with me—I feel as if I've already read the stories.

The Glide

We had a glide at Dovedale, which was made by Papa. We never had money enough to buy one brand new, even if one had been advertised in *The Union-Recorder*, the weekly newspaper that Papa subscribed to. Our glider sat on the front lawn and it was the loveliest swing in all the world. The giant oak trees shaded it; the seats, which faced each other, were made of wooden slats and the arm rests were comfortable, though children didn't care a whit about comfort. That was for the grown-ups, who occasionally took over the swing.

Alongside a couple of sisters, I'd sit in one seat, while a few more of the children, either my sisters and brothers or some of the scores of cousins who were always visiting us during the summer months, sat opposite. On our side, we'd push gently on the floor of the glider, causing it to swing slowly forward; then, the opposites would push with their feet and the glider would swing back. Sometimes we'd sit quietly, rocking the swing slowly and gently back and forth. At others times, the energy of youth (or maybe it was all inspired by the devil) would take hold of us and we'd push violently, causing the glider to swing rapidly and almost jump out of its balance, the while we screamed and giggled and had a glorious time, though Mama was not so happy about it.

My father, like most men of his generation, could do all sorts of things with his hands; he made not only the glider, but he made us a barrel swing, which hung between two poles beneath the elm tree. A barrel swing (for the information of the younger generation) was made by boring holes in the staves of the barrel, threading the staves with a "plow line," then taking off the barrel hoops, thus providing a long "hammock" of sorts which was a resting place we promptly gave up to Papa when he asked for it.

In addition to doing useful things like making swings for the children, putting up shelves for Mama, fixing the well pulley when it needed it, and doing whatever needed to be done about the household affairs, Papa could whittle the most delightful and exciting things for us. He made whistles from the shoots of the shrubs, and pop-guns for us from the elder bush, and oh, fabulous joy, he made finger rings from dried peach seeds for his small daughters.

The Goat

Nothing he ever did for us was quite so fine as making the glider. Except my brother—and Papa, who let him have it for his special possession—thought his Billygoat was downright marvelous. It was not what I call a creature suited for a pet. He was meaner than a hornet, could butt harder than a tractor could shove, was sneaky about slipping up on you to get a chance to butt you half way across the farm, and if he had a kindly bone in his body, it never took possession of his manners.

My long suffering brother built a "little wagon" to which he aimed to hitch up the goat. He spent long hours sawing out the wheels from an oak log, and nailing together the axles and the body of the wagon, which was an old pine box that had once contained some products to be sold in the country store my father owned. Hickory withes made the shafts for the wagon. Oh, it was a wagon to be proud of.

But did that Billygoat have any pride in pulling it? Not

hardly. He bucked and butted and raised hell in general when my brother tried to get him to act like a horse and back into the shafts.

And it was not just a Billygoat that acted ugly about association with humans. One of my mother's brothers had a sick baby and the doctor had recommended goat's milk. In those blessed days when families stuck together in times of trial, the sick baby and its mother and father and a couple of older brothers and sisters came to stay with us, on the assumption that Papa could supply a Nannygoat to provide the baby's milk. Papa was a farmer, he owned goats as well as mules and horses, cows and calves, pigs and dogs and chickens and guineas and turkeys, and goodness knows whatall.

Papa, being a kindly in-law and a man of good heart, brought up a Nannygoat from the back pastures, a Nanny whose kid was only a few weeks old, and, therefore, a Nanny who produced a modicum of milk.

Poor Sherman! He was the-man-of-all-work about the house, and naturally it was he who was expected to milk that goat. As all the children stood at a respectable distance and watched, he wrestled with that goat for half an hour to get a half cupful of milk.

If you think goats aren't ornery, you've never met the common ordinary plantation style goat.

I had my own pet, a beautiful yellow kitten, when I was about six years old, and for some reason I know not what, I called the kitten "Flossie." I loved Flossie with a great love, and it was mighty sad when "she" turned out to be a tom cat and was always walking out at night, often returning home after three days or so, with many scratches and cuts and places where "her" pretty fur coat was torn.

I saw an ad the other day (August 1972) for a new health drink to be added to a pet's water. Flossie lived to be 14. I fed her table scraps and just plain well water from the chicken trough.

Unusual Lessons Learned

As children, we were not permitted to drink coffee. When I cried for some, my grandma told me coffee would turn my skin black.

I believed, well, more or less, that the sure cure for backache was: Turn a somersault when you hear the first whippoorwill in the springtime.

The forecast calls for a cold winter when the persimmons are so thick on the trees, everywhere, that the limbs are bending down, and the berries on the holly trees, the haw trees, and sugarberry trees are thicker than peas in a pod, and the corn shucks are thick.

Mama always used to say Christmas comes but once a year, so let the children overeat if they want to. They'll "throw up the hash," and, when their stomachs are emptied, they'll go to sleep.

Papa's Whittling

I doubt that my father ever knew the word "HOBBY," but I think he had one, just the same. He loved to whittle—when he found any spare time to devote to the pursuit. What with running a farm of some 1,500 acres, supervising the tenants' attention to the livestock, keeping accounts of their purchases of seed and fertilizer and such, looking after the garden (which provided vegetables for a family of ten), taking care of the orchard where he grew peaches, plums, apples, figs and whatever else the *Southern Cultivator* advised, he had little spare time.

He would sit on the front porch after supper on summer evenings, while the children gathered on the front steps, watching with awe and wonder as he shaped a dried peach seed into a finger ring, or made it into a miniature basket which one of the children would stow away with her most precious treasures, a possession to be taken out only now and then to be touched, admired, and showed off to Grandma when she came to visit.

I remember one evening I saw him carving—or whittling—on a piece of white pine, shaping a hand-fitting handle to a two-pronged something, the like of which I had not before seen. To my question "What is it, Papa," he replied, "A catapult."

It was several nights later when he had finished the piece, complete with a wide rubber band attached to the forks, that I realized he had made a "sling shot." I'd seen my brothers shoot dried peas or young chinaberries or an occasional small stone from sling shots, but I didn't know they could also be called catapults.

I imagine many a song bird escaped death because the boys in my neighborhood never managed to master the catapult. Or, perhaps it was because the boys could not afford to buy BB's for their weapons; they only had berries and dried peas.

Mama's Lemonade

Hot muggy days, which make your appetite call for something cool and, particularly, for something flavored with lemons, remind me of the days of my childhood at Dovedale. Did you ever roll lemons for Mama? It was a great honor to be invited to help with the lemonade making and it was a joy to smell the lovely aroma of fresh lemon juice, along with the slightly bitter smell of the lemon peel.

On a hot afternoon, Mama would say it was time for a picnic on the lawn and that meant lemonade—except maybe it meant, instead, homechurned ice cream made on the back porch with much beating up of hunks of ice, taken from the sawdust-protected, 200-pound cake of ice down in the cellar. But ice cream was usually served for Sunday dinner; lemonade and ham-and-biscuits and jelly-biscuits were the fare for afternoon picnics.

We did not go off in the carriage to a spot in the woods, nor did we have a large basket for carrying the family silver and china and linens to the site of the picnic, nor did we drink from silver goblets as did the wealthy families such as the Roosevelts or the English lords and ladies.

Nor did we have paper cups. We took the glasses (we called them "tumblers") out on the lawn and carried out a large bucket of cracked ice. The trip to the front lawn was not a long one—the dining room was right near to the little spot, which was always freshly mowed with a hand mower (no power mowers in that day) and separated from the rest of the large sweep of grass by a picket fence. There were eight children, Grandma always spent the summer at our house, and there were usually an aunt and uncle and their five or six youngsters. There were only a few chairs available. Most of the younger set sat on the grass, while the grownups sat in the kitchen chairs fetched out on purpose for the picnic.

Various children had various tasks. My specialty was rolling the lemons so the juice squeezed out easily. And I had another job: getting the ice from the cellar, washing off the sawdust, putting the hunk of ice into a clean flour sack and beating it up with a hammer to the desired size of small hunks and some smashed-up tiny pieces.

I wonder what lemons cost in the early part of this century. I think lemons must have been about 10 cents a dozen or we should not have been so generous with them. We were a family that raised a lot of our "vittles," and spent comparatively little on bought things. Peaches and watermelons and cantaloupes Papa grew. Strawberries, blackberries, dewberries and plums from the field and hedgerow were plentiful in summer, and we gathered them for pies and canning and jellies as well as eating "as is." But, somehow, lemonade was a "special treat" and the afternoon picnic was a big event, far more important than the morning gathering to eat fresh peaches or melons, standing around a big table out in the shade of the huge oak tree in the wagon yard. Often, after eating watermelon, skeeting seeds at one another, and making "false teeth" of a bit of melon rind, we'd have a serving of fresh figs from the dozen fig trees Papa had planted along the fence around the chicken yard.

But sitting on the grass in the yard, leaning against the picket fence and drinking homemade lemonade, savoring its flavor and sucking on a bit of ice—man, that was livin'.

Medicines

Man (including woman) has been seeking easement for ills—real or fancied—since the time when memory of man goeth not back to.

Some psychologists say the medicine man's potions and his dances often "cure" ills because of the psychological effect.

La me! I remember the magic lantern show with the medicine man's pitch. With a hoarse voice, "Excuse me, folks, I have a cold," he'd spell the values of the medicine he had to sell—good for coughs, colds, sneezes, shortness of breath and that sore throat accompanying. Then, he'd pour out of his bottle a dose of the elixir of life, toss it down, and in a loud, non-husky voice exclaim:

"Now folks, you can see how effective this medicine is."

And everybody shelled out his money for a bottle of the cold cure.

* * *

Since I was knee-high to a grasshopper I knew warts could be cured in several ways—sure and certain cures, too. Bury a string in which you have tied three knots was one cure, but best of all was to "conjure" off the wart—scratch it with a sharp pointed something to make it bleed, then, dip a grain of corn in the blood, throw the corn out for a chicken to eat, and the wart will leave you and to go the chicken.

The country doctor we had in our family (Tippie's husband, Dr. Terrell Hubert) never said the conjurin' of warts was not good; he had too much respect for psychological behaviorism, but he did tell Mama when she asked him on meeting him at some social occasion like, say, all day church with dinner on the ground, that rubbing the wart, each day for a week, with freshly cut leaves from the snap bean vines would do the trick. It did, too. Took off a big wart from my middle toe.

Turpentine was the most important article in the Myrick medicine chest. We used it to cure stumped toes, sore throats, any sort of wound, including a nail stuck in the ball of the foot, and to rub on a piece of flannel cloth, along with beef suet, kerosene and camphor, to make a poultice for croup.

Papa kept Sloan's liniment in the barn, where it was often used to treat ailments of "Ole Bill Nye" and "Lady," the horses, and also to treat mules and cattle when they got some sort of ailment. I don't know what the ailments were. It was, as Prissy said, "Papa wouldn't let me 'round when he was doctorin' animals."

Mama's treatment for a cold was, at the time, considered the "cure"—a dose of castor oil. Various rubbings, too, were considered necessary—camphor, turpentine and mutton suet were used as ointments. For a sore throat, you got a drop of kerosene on a teaspoonful of sugar. Ugh! Did you ever taste kerosene?

Old fashioned remedies also included calamus root for the stomach-ache. Vitamin pills and visits to the doctor's office and anti-tetanus shots and penicillin are commonplace today (1971), but not so in the days of my childhood.

Dr. Hubert lived three miles from our house and his horse was slow and so was ours. We had no spare cash to hand out to a doctor unless somebody was about to die. Sticking a nail in your foot was no reason for "sending after" the doctor and anti-tetanus was something we hadn't heard about.

My mother had an idea that when a child was cross there was one of two things wrong: Either he was hungry or he needed a dose of calomel. So, Papa kept a bottle of calomel on hand, a dark blue bottle with a wide mouth and a big stopper, and when one of the children got so cross nobody would live with him, Mama mentioned the fact to Papa and he got out the calomel bottle.

He seated himself at the desk with the bottle of calomel and a box of Arm and Hammer Brand soda in front of him, and he took a sheet of writing paper (it was slick and ruled in pale blue lines) and carefully tore little three-inch squares from it and laid three of them in a row. Then, with the smallest blade of his pocket knife, he lifted from the bottle a "dose" of calomel and placed it on a slip of paper, to which he added about three times as much of the soda. He fixed three doses, folded the paper up so none of the stuff would spill, and the horrors of dosing began.

Not that the calomel tasted bad; it didn't. You stuck out your tongue and Mama carefully spilled the dose upon it. Then you drank some water. Four hours later, the business was repeated. Next morning, you got a dose of Epsom Salts. THAT was the awful taste.

Awful, too, perhaps worst of all, was the feeling that if you so much as tasted anything acid—such as a wild plum or some blackberries or lemonade you'd salivate and all your teeth would fall out.

* * *

Sassafras tea was a springtime drink. It thins your blood and gives you more pep than a gallon of vitamin pills. Some unfortunate children had to take sulphur and molasses for spring-time complaints. I missed that unhappy experience. In my family, sassafras tea held the upper hand as the panacea of all ills which winter had induced. I used to think of my blood as thick, thick, thick. I could see it trying to run through my veins (I had never heard of an artery) and being slowed down to a crawl because it was as thick as the starch Aunt Minerva used to make to starch the petticoats.

Making Ourselves Sick

We made a record swallowing such items as pins, pennies, small nails, nickels and even a bullet. That bullet, a loaded cartridge to fit a revolver, caused quite a commotion. My brother swallowed it, came running to Mama, and told her what he had done. Well, in those days nobody called the doctor. (To call him, you'd have to saddle the horse and ride to his house—no telephones.) But Mama would not let my brother stand near the open fire lest the bullet explode inside him. No harm was done. Matter of fact, that bullet swallowing was great; it provided a topic for conservation for months.

I was sitting on the floor pinning clothes on my doll, one day, and suddenly I began weeping and when Mama asked what was wrong, I said I had swallowed a pin. What kind? A black headed pin, I said. Mama took me up to comfort me, and there on the floor where I had been sitting was the black headed pin. Seems I tried to find it, I had failed, and got scared I'd swallowed it.

My younger sister swallowed a penny, in spite of the fact that Mama had always told us not to put money in our mouths. It was dirty, she avowed, and might make us sick, and besides we might swallow it. Though we would have qualified for the Poor People's March, back then, nobody got much upset over the penny's being swallowed. Nobody, that is, except the sister who had swallowed it. She had planned to spend the penny for some candy.

The Seven Year Itch

The "seven year itch," as we used to speak of that disease, was not just hysteria; it was a matter of "germs" spreading—or so we thought. That is what the graduate nurse at GN&IC told us. As did the health teacher, who warned us to wash our hands when we had borrowed a pencil from somebody or studied the lesson from a fellow student's book, or played basketball with the ball that a lot of others had played with. The "germs" of the Itch (known medically then as "scabies") were mighty powerful and one that had settled on a pencil from the hand of an "Itcher" would grab you faster than you could say "Itch."

I was brought up to consider "The Itch" a complaint that belonged to the underprivileged who might not be as clean of habits as they should be, and that "the best people" did not have the Itch. My poor mother was mightily embarrassed to have to admit that I had the "Po-White-Trash" disease.

Sewing

There seems to be a great upsurge in home sewing (1969); mothers of today are beginning to act like mothers of yesteryear, when money was scarcer than it is now, and Mama made most of the clothes for the children, as well as an occasional frock for herself.

Ads for "yard goods" appear often, now. Splendid words beckon the women: "Sew the summer jersey-knit, fashion fabrics that follow today's soft body lines"; and "Supple, flowing, graceful clinging—make dresses, wide-leg pants that you can pack in a flight bag—romantic coats, suits, midriff-baring separates that refuse to wrinkle".

La me! I remember my childhood days when Mama sewed and sewed but could not keep up with the needs of eight young'uns, and a lady we called "Miss Mat" came and stayed a week to sew up a mess of clothes, "drawsbodies," pantalets, petticoats for the girls; underpants, jackets, undershirts for the boys. I can still hear the whirr of the old foot-pedaled Wheeler and Wilson as Miss Mat stitched up little gingham dresses quicker than you can say "calico shirtwaist."

Mainly, I recall how bitterly I resented being sent out "to play" instead of hanging around the sewing room and listening in on the gossip. For Miss Mat, who sewed here and there in the neighborhood, knew all the goings-on, especially when somebody was "in a family way," with or without benefit of clergy. I wanted to hear the talk, and I hated to go out to play dolls or swing in the barrel swing or make little houses under the big oak tree.

In that day sewing was not as easy as it is today. Nowadays you can stitch up a sleeveless shift mighty fast; in my youth sleeves had to be gathered and set in, waist lines had to be established, and hems had to be pinned up with a yard stick for measuring the proper length.

Nobody ever heard of a zipper in my young days; buttonholes were not made on the machine, as they are today. Grandma spent endless hours working buttonholes in our clothes.

And nary a word did we hear back then about packing

in a flight bag a dress that would not wrinkle. We sewed on cottons, ginghams, calicos, Fruit of the Loom, madras, and sometimes, osnaburg. Only we of the establishment have any idea what "osnaburg" is. You under thirties can just go hunt for the word in the dictionary if you care to know what it is.

I do recall a friend who was sewing on a handsome gown of satin, shiny and slick and elegant. Said she: "This stuff keeps slipping off my lap. I'd just as soon sew on a chitlin'."

When Mama tried to teach me to do "neat" scalloping, using mercherized cotton floss and a fine needle and taking close-together stitches of the button-hole variety, she made me practice on an old piece of cloth until I learned to keep the stitches close together so that they made a firm, tight, smooth edge of scalloping. I "laid off" the scallops with a pencil, using an empty spool of the size number 60 cotton came on, so the scallops would be even and regular.

I had in mind the lovely dress I saw in *The Delineator*, the fashion magazine of the Butterick Publishing Co—a frock of one-piece design which buttoned all the way down the left side with the opening decorated with scalloping. Miss Mat would make the dress when she came for her week's stay, and when it was properly put together I'd do the scalloping.

"Practice makes perfect," my mother quoted to me and I kept at the practicing until the scalloped edge was firm and smooth. Though I was not truly "perfect," I was good enough that Mama bought the linen for my dress and ordered the pattern from Butterick.

I wore it to Sunday school one Sunday that spring, and in my mind's eyes, I was the best-looking girl in the house.

The Well

I remember gourds used for dippers at the well at my home in the country. The gourd had a long handle, which had a hole in it, and a convenient nail on a post that held the shed over the well served as a place to hang the gourd.

The well bucket was black with age and the effect of

constant dampness. It was in truth the old oaken bucket, iron-bound. But the bucket that sat on the shelf on the back porch, alongside the wash pan and the piece of homemade soap, was made of cedar, bright and shining as any modern housekeeper's polished maple chest, and the brass bindings were bright as a summer's midday. Though, so far as I know, nobody at our house ever polished the brass on the bucket.

See Appendix V for more on the well.

Guineas

My father raised guineas, and I can still hear in my memory the sound of the pot-rack of the guineas at dusk, when they had settled for the night in the tree where they roosted.

I remember going with my father to a guinea nest in the field near the house. The guineas lay in community nests, and Papa liked guinea eggs better than hen eggs, so we visited the nest many times to take home a few of the brown-speckled eggs to be soft-boiled for Papa's breakfast.

Once, I found that a bob white had laid eggs in the guinea nest. If I had climbed Mt. Everest, I'd have been no more pleased with myself.

Lightning

One event at Dovedale in my childhood will linger in my memory for the rest of my days. My father, as did many plantation owners in my time, had a store of sorts from which he sold fertilizer, seed, kerosene, tobacco, snuff, sugar, meal, syrup, side meat, cheese, calico and other items to the tenants on credit. This was a double-pronged business—the supplies bought at wholesale prices provided a little profit when he sold them to the tenants who paid when they sold their cotton in the fall; and also enabled Papa to purchase supplies for his family at wholesale rates.

One day a tenant was seated on his mule (barebacked) in the side yard in front of Papa's store, when a violent clap of thunder followed a brilliant flash of lightning. The lightning hit the mule, killed him instantly. The rider was shocked a little but otherwise unhurt.

The episode caused much consternation among the children of the household, you may be sure, and from that time on, we firmly believed that lightning was much more likely to strike anything with four legs than something with only two.

I was not old enough, then, to realize what a catastrophe a dead mule was to a farmer. The animal cost $250 and neither the tenant nor my father could afford to lose the mule or the money. And in the early part of this century it was seldom that any farmer carried any sort of insurance on his belongings.

Laundry

I remember the wash tub—it was wooden with wide steel hoops around it, and I remember the homemade lye soap and the rubbing board. Goodness knows nobody could wish to have the return of those.

I enjoyed the fire in the fireplace and I treasure the memory of standing in front of the fire to warm my back before I ran to jump into the bed in a cold room with the sheets like iced blankets. I'll swap the open fire for a warm room and an electric blanket, any old December night.

One thing of "the old days" I'd like to see return is the clean smell of fresh air in the house; no odor of trash fires or garbage or any sort of "pollution." Living in the country where the nearest neighbor was a mile away was a different state of affairs from today's living where there are "so many people" and so much industry and so much pollution of the air.

During my childhood in the country nobody had a washing machine; such a thing was probably not even invented yet; surely, farm dwellers had no such luxury. Instead, the washing was done in huge wash tubs, with a rubbing board to get out the worst dirt, and for some reason, another pot in which some of the clothes were boiled.

"Aunt Jennie Tough" was the washer woman for our family, and a good one she was. I considered it a boon to be allowed to visit with her while she did the wash. The tubs and the boiling pot were near the spring, beneath the shade of a giant oak tree. The rubbing board got out hard-to-remove spots, and the soap used was homemade—yellow hunks of soap made from the leftover fat and the lye gleaned from the ash hopper.

Water dripped through the ashes made the lye, which was put into a huge iron pot with fat from hog-killing and cooked to make soap. Soap could be made only on "the increase uv de moon"; otherwise, it would "swink up ter nuthin'."

Grits and Hominy

Having been bred and bawn in de brier patch, I feel I should be able to explain the difference between "hominy" and "grits." But there is a marked variation in the terminology of people—Southerners or not. In my own family, the word "grits" was unknown. We ate "hominy."

I'll say we did. We ate it for breakfast 365 days out of the year, and we had it for supper about that many days. And for company dinner (or maybe for supper), we often had baked hominy, a delicious food made of left-over hominy combined with beaten eggs and plenty of rich milk and butter.

Breakfast in the days of my childhood was a real meal—no ready-to-eat cereal with skim milk, but hot biscuits and hominy and scrambled eggs and either ham or bacon or hash made of leftovers back then. Often "battercakes" accompanied the breakfast too. But hominy we had.

Hominy for supper was a staple in winter. When summer days came, our supper often consisted mainly of a large bowl of clabber served with sugar and rich milk. We had a Jersey cow and the cream would rise half an inch thick on the large pans of milk that we kept cooled in the "dairy"—a small wooden house on stilts that stood beneath a large tree where it was shady and cool.

Our hominy was waterground, from white corn my father had raised, at Mr. Skelton Napier's mill operated on Big Cedar Creek about a mile from our home. I was the proudest girl in the world the first time my father let me take the corn to the mill to be ground into hominy. I rode Bill Nye, a gentle, plodding old horse, and the corn rode in a croaker sack behind me on the horse's back.

And what a delight it was to watch while Mr. Wes Hawkins poured the corn into the hopper; then, to go with him to see the meal pour out into the huge trough, smelling better than anything I can think of, and looking powdery and soft and beautiful as he poured it into a sack. I didn't quite understand about the "toll," but I knew he took his pay for the grinding in meal—never in cash.

For some people, "hominy" is what used to be called "lye hominy," to designate the kernels boiled in a lye solution. Lye hominy was once produced in the back yard of many Southern homes; it now comes in cans. Grits is bought in paper sacks and is produced by the millers—the best grits being waterground.

Milking

The time when just anybody could be a milker is long gone. In the past, all the job required were strong fingers (for that last stripping), a three-legged stool, a bucket to hold between the knees, and the ability to dodge fast when Old Bossy switched her tail.

The three-legged stool and the milk bucket were the usual when I was growing up out in the country. My father's five-gallon Jersey, a beautiful little reddish-brown cow that always looked thin, was important in the Myrick family where eight children, a grandmother and the boarding teacher made a big family to feed.

The foaming white milk was strained, set in large white enamel pans in the dairy. There was no refrigerator in our house, only a box in the cellar where sawdust protected the 200-pound block of ice from the melting heat.

We drank skimmed milk; the cream was reserved for

whipping cream, for adding to the home-churned ice cream, for topping for the apple pie, and mainly, for making butter. We never heard of cholesterol and nobody bothered about animal fats; we just ate cream and butter and loved it.

I was the daughter chosen for the chore of churning. I rather enjoyed it. And I've always been thankful I was not a boy and therefore never had to milk. I know little of cow psychology.

Butter

We had whipped cream as part of most desserts, and our cakes were all made with butter. We never heard of oleo.

Our churn, in the first years of my life, was one of those crockery jars, whitish in color with a blue-gray overcast. My earliest recollections are of the fireplace in Mama's room where the churn sat on the hearth in fall and winter, so the warmth helped the milk to "turn."

As the churn sat beside the fire, it was covered with a clean white cloth; the crockery top with its hole for the dasher handle topped the cloth and the whole shone pleasantly in the light of the kerosene lamp.

Now and then, the job of churning fell upon me and I enjoyed the slow up-and-down working of the dasher for a while. Then, growing impatient, I'd pout and mumble about howcome Mama wouldn't put some hot water in to help the butter come faster. She always refused. Hot water made the butter puffy, she said.

In later years we acquired a barrel churn, the sort with a handle to turn. It was considered quite modern and held the status of today's' automatic dishwasher, I'd say. There was a stopper to take out when the churning was over, to allow the buttermilk to run out of the barrel-like container into the big white pitcher.

I'd like to have some good, fresh, newly churned, country butter on a stack of battercakes, right this minute.

Note: Sue's sister Allie said that Sue did not like to give up her books when she churned and soon learned to crank the barrel churn with her foot so she could read as she churned.

Lard

At Dovedale, Mama made lard with the help of "Aunt Minerva," who knew you must always stir the pot in the same direction and who knew by the way the mixture felt, as the wooden paddle stirred it, whether it was about right.

All she did, so far as I can remember, was cut up the pork fat in pieces about the size of a thumb, put it into the pot not too hot, just enough heat to keep the fat cooking and not burn.

Curds and Whey

Growing up on the farm, I was mighty familiar with curds and whey. There was more milk available than our family needed in the guise of liquid milk, so Mama often skimmed the cream off, let the pan of milk sour, then strained it through a cheese cloth sack to get rid of the whey. She then poured the whole panful of clabbered milk into the sack, tied it up with a twine string (it was carefully saved from one time to the next) and hung the sack to a branch of a tree in the shade. When all the whey had dripped out, we ate the curd for supper, with plenty of sugar and cream on it.

Hogs

I don't know what people said in South Georgia to call a hog, for I was raised on a Middle Georgia farm, but I assure you that when somebody yelled "Souie" or "Souiee" at a hog on our farm he meant for that hog to "git"—to take a sudden leave—to high-tail it away. To yell "Souiee" at a hog meant the same as yelling "Scat" to a cat.

To call the hogs to come get their feed, we'd yell "whoop-pig-pig!" And repeat the "who-o-p" over and over.

Some farmer, now and then, would tell his pigs to feed by knocking on the side of the trough with a stick—"rap-rap-rap" he'd go, then "whoop-pig-pig!"

Church

When I was seven or eight and went to Bethel Church on the third Sunday to hear the circuit riding preacher tell of hell fire and brimstone (the wages of sin), Uncle Good, Mr. Jones and Mr. Harper sat in the amen corner. Mrs. Humphries played the organ with the tremolo stop wide open, and the choir sang loudly.

The men sat on the left hand side of the church and the women on the right. It was only at protracted meeting time after the crops were laid by that an occasional boy brought his girl to the evening service and sat on the "ladies" side with her.

In summer, the bees and dirt daubers buzzed in through the open windows; in winter the wood burning stove kept us from freezing, but didn't quite bring what you would describe as "comfortable heating" to the people on the back seats.

Trash

We didn't have anything to throw away. There was no such thing as a milk bottle; we milked the Jersey cow into a milk bucket, strained the milk into pans, set the pans in the dairy, and after the cream was skimmed, poured milk into pitchers to fetch to the table for mealtime.

Mason jars we had, all right, but Mama used them over and over again. Home-cooked jellies, jams, pickles, preserves and other such delicious stuff was put into jars, large or small, which were carefully washed and stored for next year's crop. The few that ever got thrown out were broken. We children treasured those pieces of broken glass—we used them in our playhouses beneath the big oak trees or to make peep shows.

As for soft drink bottles, we never had any soft drinks. We made our own. We'd combine sugar and water to make a "sweetened water" drink; then, we'd add a little vinegar and soda to produce the bubbling action. The bottle from which we drank we used over and over again.

It wasn't IN to have soda pop when I was a child growing up on the farm.

Fire Engines

My father had brought me, along with some others of the many children at our house, to the Macon Fair, when I was a little girl, maybe seven or eight. As we rode the street car toward town, Papa rang the bell for the car to let us off, and led us, wide-eyed, into a fire station. That was a long time ago when fire engines were pulled by big, fat, beautiful white horses.

Some of the firemen at the station were grooming the horses, others wiped the shining brass of the engine, and one of them, the chief I suppose, showed us about the place. Most thrilling of all was the pole down which the firemen slid when they were called out to a fire at night. I am certain that I could have slid down that pole but Papa didn't think well of the idea.

It didn't matter, however. It was enough thrill to pat the friendly horses which looked so huge in comparison with our Bill Nye and Lady, and to be permitted to smooth my hands over the shining brass and the bright beautiful red of the engine. The Fair's exhibit, its rides, its excitement faded to nothing by the side of a visit to a fire engine.

Games

Few persons born after 1930 have even heard of "cotton bagging"—or even the boll weevil. When I think of "Bagging-and-Ties," I always think of them in capital letters, for they were an important symbol of fall and a little money coming in for the farm family.

Bagging is the coarse, woven, heavy stuff which is used to wrap up the bale of cotton. That bale is "tied" together, the bagging held in place by "Ties," strips of metal which wrap around the bale in four or five places to hold the cotton firmly until it got to the mill.

At our house, Bagging-and-Ties appeared about the middle of September, for before the boll weevil, cotton was not picked as early as it is today (1967). Cotton picking went on until after Christmas, and little cotton was picked until "frost fell," back in the early nineteen hundreds.

My father's tenants paid their rent in cotton—a bale of cotton for a one-horse farm, I think. He furnished the Bagging-and-Ties which the tenant took with him to the gin house when the cotton was ready. Meanwhile, extra Bagging-and-Ties lay in the wagon yard. I suspect my father was not happy to have us play on the rolls of bagging, but he never told us not to, so we did. The rolls were about a foot in diameter and about six feet long, and each roll made a fine plaything. You'd stand on it, get it rolling by shifting your feet rapidly, and wave your hands and scream happily as the bagging rolled across the sandy yard and you maintained your balance. It was even more fun when you fell off.

Later in the fall, as tenants paid their rent and bales of cotton were set in the wagon yard, our chief pleasure was in hiding back of the cotton bales, or in running and jumping from one bale to another.

La me, I feel so sorry for today's child who has no wagon yard to play in.

* * *

A game I played on the front lawn with my brother was mumblety-peg; he always beat me at the game, and then I had to draw out the peg from the ground with my teeth. It was a game played with a knife.

The knife (in case you are too young to have ever played mumblety-peg) must be tossed from various positions so that it lands upright with the blade stuck in the ground. I can't remember half of the more-than-a-dozen positions we used, but I do know that the hardest one for me was swinging the knife by its blade just beneath my nose and flipping the knife as I tossed it out to make it stick up on the ground.

It was easy to place the knife on the four fingers that had been folded into the palm, and, by twisting the arm over as you threw the knife, make it stick into the ground. And it wasn't hard to make the knife stick into the ground when you held the tip of the blade between thumb and the first finger, swing it over, and let it go. But I never could learn to make the knife work right when I held the tip of the blade against the heel of my hand and flipped the knife over to make a complete circle in the air on its way to the ground.

I recommend that any father who can find a little spare time and a not-too-sharp jackknife, take his 10-year-old son or daughter out on the lawn and teach him or her how to play mumblety-peg. It's a good way to enjoy some of the vacation time and a fine way for Papa to gain favor in the eyes of a child.

* * *

Going to pick blackberries, or wild plums, was a fine way to entertain yourself, only you had the itching that followed because of the red bugs (or chiggers) that you always got from the blackberry bushes.

It was more fun to go with Papa to the peach orchard and pick peaches that we brought home in a basket, which we set on a long rustic table under the big oak trees where the family gathered around for the morning feast. The peaches were picked in the early morning while they were cool. Hot peaches, picked at noon, didn't taste so good, and we had no refrigerator at Dovedale.

There were no movies, no radios or televisions anywhere when I was a child. So looking though a viewing device at a card that bore right-eye and left-eye images of a single view gave the looker a three-dimensional picture that was exciting every time you had a session of viewing.

The session was not often; it was reserved for a special occasion, a sort of reward for good conduct, or for a birthday, or some great event such as the arrival of Grandma for her spend-the-summer visit.

The stereopticon and the 24 cards we had were kept carefully "put away" in the parlor, along with such heirlooms as the daguerreotypes of great-grandparents, ancient aunties and small children (long since dead), and officers in Confederate uniforms. Other genealogical treasures, such as the tissue-paper-wrapped silken shawl that belonged to Great-Grandma Myrick and Great Aunt Kittie's white satin wedding slippers, were kept in the chest at the foot of the four-poster bed. The satin slippers were size three, and they never lost their interest for us, but even they could not compete with the stereographic views.

Niagara Falls was the crème de la crème of the views to me. The vast expanse of the rushing torrent of water, the sight of a pleasure boat below the falls, the thrilling thought that some day I'd be grown up and get to go to the real falls—ah! What joy. When I did actually see Niagara Falls, it was not so thrilling as was the view on the stereopticon.

There were views of the Mormon Temple at Salt Lake City, of the Grand Canyon, of the Great Desert of the West, of Androcles and The Lion, of Daniel in the Lions' Den—oh, the views were "educational" as well as "entertaining."

There were six "comics"—slides that showed scenes almost as funny as the circus clown we saw when the show came to Milledgeville and Papa took us to see it. My favorite view was of an old man with his feet in a tub of hot water, curing his cold. He wore an old-fashioned flannel nightshirt, and on his head, a tasseled cap, which I guessed was his son's toboggan cap. (The reason I knew about a toboggan was not—goodness knows—that I had ever seen one, but because we took *The Youth's Companion*, published in Boston, and it often had pictures of Yankee children sliding down hill in the snow.) The steam from the hot water in the foottub rose up and made a cloud around the old man's head. Why I thought it was so funny, I don't know. But I'd always hold onto the viewer long past my turn, to laugh at the old man with the bad cold.

The view of the city of San Francisco after the earthquake of 1906 almost scared me to death. So did the scene of the battleship Maine as she sank beneath the waves.

I wonder what ever became of our stereopticon. Maybe Uncle Ben, who had fought for four years with Marse Robert, found a picture of President Lincoln in the set and we threw it away.

NOTE: The stereopticon eventually went to Tippie whose children were only slightly younger than Sue and her siblings.

* * *

Reared thus in the lengthy shadows of the War Between the States, in a South that was still changing from large plantations to smaller farms operated by tenants and sharecroppers, Sue spent her youthful hours equally split between the educated whites and the black tenant farmers and house servants, many of whom could not read or write. With so much exposure, she became as comfortable in one setting as in the other, as fluent in one language as in the other, as knowledgeable of one culture as of the other, as adept at repeating the histories of one culture as of the other.

Born to educated, cultured and loving parents who taught by example, and reared in this multi-racial atmosphere, Sue enjoyed a unique childhood. Her years at Dovedale provided a foundation for the mature, self-confident, productive and creative person she was to become.

PART II

THE ACADEMIC YEARS

GEORGIA NORMAL AND INDUSTRIAL COLLEGE

The Georgia Normal & Industrial College (GN&IC), located in Milledgeville, some 12 miles from Dovedale, stated in its catalog: "A student is admitted on what she knows, not on what she has at some time and in some manner studied." Such a statement might have frightened some hopeful students, but not Sue although she was only 14 when she took the exam in 1907.

The entrance exam questioned the prospective student on her knowledge of Latin, science, literature, grammar and mathematics.

Allie recounted Sue's response to the question: "What is your favorite book?"

Sue wrote: "*David Copperfield* by Charles Dickens, because of its continuing wit and constant pathos."

Allie said that Sue's answer gained the attention of Mr. Powell, chairman of the English Department, who guided her in elocution and writing, thereby providing her a strong foundation for her later work with the Little Theatre, with the newspaper and with the movie *Gone With The Wind.*

Sue passed the examination and was admitted into GN&IC, although her formal education had been limited to the Dovedale School, basically an elementary school. Founded in 1889, GN&IC was Georgia's first state-founded college for women.

For the first three and a half years at GN&IC, Sue lived on campus, at first on the second floor of the former Governor's Mansion, and later in the Mansion Annex. Students had several roommates, sometimes as many as five. The Mansion is still a part of the college. It became the residence for the college president and now has been renovated and is open to the public as a museum operated by the college.

Students attended classes six days a week. Some met Monday, Wednesday and Friday, and others on Tuesday, Thursday and Saturday. Students were not allowed go home for the weekend, nor could they have visitors on campus.

Sue began to focus her dreams on becoming a teacher of physical education, and she majored in "physical culture." She later wrote about her classes at the college:

Back in the dark ages when I was at school in Milledgeville, at what is now known as the Woman's College of Georgia, I had classes in Physical Culture. Later, these became known as Physical Education, shortened by most girls to Phys. Ed.

We wore bloomers and middy blouses to the classes, which we were required to attend twice a week, and for all the games we played—volley ball, sack races, potato relay races and the like.

Those bloomers were made of serge, and during fall and spring days were about the hottest bits of wearing apparel ever required of girls. I don't mean "hottest" in the sense of sexy and sporting and gay and fashionable. I mean "hottest" in the sense of making the wearer of the woolen bloomers sweat.

Girls at today's gym classes, wearing shorts and cool shirts, are blessed and don't know it.

The bloomers were pleated and full and bloused below the knee. It was considered scandalous enough that girls would show their legs almost to the knee and the thought of showing the knees—well, it just wasn't done. Our skirts reached about to our shoe tops.

In our physical culture classes we did calisthenics, mostly. Not because the teacher thought them the best forms of exercise. It was because the gym was about big enough for a class of 30 and there were always about 65 or 70 girls on hand. About all the teacher could have us do was march to the tinkles of an old upright piano or do deep knee bends and jump up and down, clapping our hands over our heads in time to the music.

The teacher lectured us at intervals on how to be healthy—brush your teeth regularly, eat lots of fruit, get plenty of fresh air, don't read in bed, take plenty of baths, and such like.

Since the teacher was a handsome, slender woman who was witty and liked to make us laugh, we all believed every word she spoke. I was convinced that an apple a day would keep the doctor away, and believed implicitly in throwing open all windows even in the coldest nights of the hardest winter.

I believed the teacher when she told me exercise would

keep me healthy. Now, I am certain I can get the pneumonia even if I walk a mile a day, and that exercise won't keep me from getting arthritis anymore than taking a bath every day will make me live to be 100.

* * *

Required courses included not only physical training but also home economics—cooking, sewing and nutrition. Sue recalled making a camisole in her domestic science class—"a bit of wearing apparel."

She described another sewing project:

...A bridge table cover of linen, all cross-stitched in fancy patterns at each corner, with a decorative vine-like sort of design to tie the whole together. I made it when I was about sixteen or so. I made it for a Christmas present for my mother—who never played a game of bridge in her life.

Sue also took piano lessons, but decried her inability to learn to play well.

I could play Chopsticks on the piano, and I did, to the screaming horror of my family, but doing scales was an intolerable chore which I avoided as often as I could get away with. Consequently, I never learned how to play anything more than "Over The Waves" and "Kiss Waltz." And I am sure the ears of a real pianist would have been sick at the sound of my playing those.

I tried mighty hard and unsuccessfully to play "The Lost Chord." I was coaxed and admonished by my mother who reminded me that playing the piano was a ladylike accomplishment that I should strive to attain.

My brother came home for his summer vacation from Georgia Tech, strumming on a banjo, and setting me wild with envy. If Mama would just buy me a banjo and forget about those piano lessons.

The grand piano from Dovedale would not fit into the new house when the family later moved to Milledgeville, and family lore says it was sold to the Cline family, who were neighbors and family friends in Milledgeville. Daughter Regina Cline became the mother of Flannery O'Connor.

Although Sue made light of her piano lessons, she learned to read music. Her siblings said Sue was the only family member who could read music and was the first member of the family to join the glee club at GN&IC. In later years, Celestine Sibley described her voice as a "raspy baritone."

* * *

When Sue was sixteen, her elder brother Jim began her introduction into a social life not available at Dovedale or at the college. He took her to his first business banquet as an employee of Westinghouse. He came home to escort her by train, which gave him time to coach her on how to conduct herself at the hotel and at the banquet—how to sit when he pulled her chair out, how to use the finger bowls, how to turn down her wine glass when the waiter approached to pour the wine.

Allie said, "Susan seemed so grown up. It was an education for her and showed in what esteem her older brother, older by almost seven years, held her and how our mother encouraged them both."

Later that year, Sue travelled by train alone, to visit relatives in Dublin, some 50 miles from Milledgeville.

In my young days, what with eight children in the family and the era being far from an affluent one, my vacation was more likely to be spending a week with the girl I had roomed with at school, or going to visit Aunt Pauline or Uncle Cincy for five or six days.

When I was 16, riding the train to Gordon was an event that set a girl apart from the usual. A trip to Dublin for a visit was big doings. The train ride was only a few hours but the visit was to far places and you grew important in the eyes of the less fortunate ones who stayed at home.

* * *

Life for the entire family took a sudden change when Sue's father died in late 1910, while Sue was still in college. He had known death was approaching—at the time, diabetes was not treatable—and had discussed with Miss Kate that she should move into Milledgeville after his death. If the boys did not want to return home and run Dovedale, Sue would be invaluable help to Miss Kate.

Nannaline, Sue's eldest sibling, had died the year before. Others had left home: James, Jr., had completed college and worked out of state; Tippie was married with children; Fullie had enrolled in Georgia Tech in Atlanta.

Fullie dropped out of college for a year and stayed at home to help the family re-settle in Milledgeville. Miss Kate rented a house on Columbia Street, and Sue then moved into the house with her mother and sisters. She then saw her college friends only when on campus.

As a "town girl," Sue was still subject to the same rules as the dormitory girls, however. She had to wear the brown serge skirts (which soon became slick in the back), long-sleeved and high-collared white shirtwaists, black ties and brown belts. Allie said the belts were necessary to cover the row of safety pins used to fasten the skirt and waist (blouse) together. For church and special occasions, they wore a brown fitted coat suit until spring, when white waists and skirts replaced them.

Town girls were also under the same restrictions as the students who lived on campus as to dating, or even speaking to boys—such associations were not allowed.

In September 1911 Miss Kate purchased and moved into a house on Liberty Street with her four daughters, and Fullie returned to college.

Liberty Street was so named because it was the way to freedom for the prisoners jailed on the government square—it ran from the prison to the graveyard.

In spite of the restrictions imposed by the college, Sue was much like a teenager of the late twentieth century—concerned about looking good and about socially acceptable behavior. She told of two of her self-applied beauty treatments.

I spent hours putting on and taking off mud packs which I fondly hoped would make my skin fresh, lovely, pink-and-white, girlish—everything desirable in a girl's face. I applied hot towels to my poor face to open the pores and rubbed it with ice cubes to close them. I got my skin to the place the pores would open or close on command.

Mercy sakes alive. When I was about sixteen or so I used to soak my scalp in hot oil for an hour at a time, my head wrapped in a towel and the towel dripping oil all over the place. Mama was a kind and understanding mother; she never once fussed about oil on the back of the chair or on the rugs. She remembered, I supposed, when SHE used to be a girl and soaked her hair in stuff to make it curly. Flax seed, they used in HER day. She told me: Wet your hair with a gooey substance made from flax seed steeped in boiling water; roll small humps up on a strip of folded paper and, presto, you had a more-or-less perm.

And you have no idea what a mess I could make when I decided that my face was getting wrinkled and I looked every day of twenty-four when I was really only eighteen. The magazines told me that hot mud packs would keep my skin soft and smooth and unwrinkled, and if I'd just put on mud packs, once a week, I'd be as lovely as the reigning beauty of that era—maybe I'd get in the movies.

I certainly did not have much of an allowance when I was 18, so I can't imagine how I saved up enough money to buy mud packs. But I did. All I had to do was add warm water to the stuff that came in a package, spread the gooey mess in a thick paste over my unhappy face and neck, and wait around for an hour while the stuff dried to a hard film. You could pick off little flakes of the paste from your face like picking plaster off the wall that the rain had fallen on too often.

I am certain, as I think back on it, that I left plaster flakes all over the house. Though I carried out the beauty rite in front of my mirror in my own room (which I shared with three sisters) I was never one to be careful of where the chips fell.

In my youth, I had no perm and no electric curling iron, nor any blower for my hair. But I did have "curling tongs." They were called "curling irons" by some but at my house they were "curling tongs," and you heated the "tongs" by sticking them down into the heat of a lighted kerosene lamp.

Everybody in town knew when you curled your hair on the "tongs." The smell of burning hair polluted the air like the exhaust from a worn-out old automobile.

Some things change. But the efforts of the female to be beautiful go on forever.

* * *

One of Sue's tennis games caused her some trepidation—she feared she might have violated some social code. She wrote:

Today's tennis players will probably weep to read my

saga of tennis in Milledgeville back in the early 1900s. I had a wonderful time playing tennis, in spite of the lack of good courts and no instruction whatever, but moderns will probably either die laughing about the lack of sophisticated equipment, or will declare I am exaggerating.

Growing up in the country, I never played tennis, devoting my athletics to a form of baseball, played with a ball made of raveled socks and a bat of good willow stick. But when we moved to Milledgeville I saw my first tennis game and fell in love with it. The tennis courts were in an old field at the edge of the campus of the woman's college (GN&IC), and the clay courts were seldom if ever rolled; the lines were marked with a crooked streak of lime; the nets often sagged; there was no referee; and nobody taught the neophyte anything about backhand strokes or double-handed returns.

Tennis shoes cost about a buck and a half; balls cost—I don't remember just what, but even the cheapest ones were pretty costly to us—and we used a pair of balls until all the bounce wore out. My first racket cost $1.50 and I considered my mother a most generous soul to let me have it.

Tennis was more than a game for me; it was an aid in getting to know the boys in the neighborhood. After I had played a set or two with a neighborhood boy I felt he was my friend and I was free to call him up on the wall telephone and invite him to come have a few games with me.

One chap, who lived about a block from our house, was a little older than I and was a sophisticated chap who had travelled and been away from Georgia to school. To get a date with him was a most desirable matter. Finally, I got into a game of tennis with him and was emboldened to ask at the set's end: "How about a set early tomorrow morning before the sun gets so hot?" He agreed and we set the hour at 7 a.m.

Well, at 7 a.m. I was all done up in my tennis shoes and a white middy blouse and white skirt, sitting on my front porch waiting for my date to come. At 10 minutes past seven, no date. Don't think I was going to let that engagement go to pot. I picked up my racket, walked up to his house and began tossing bits of rock at his window. The scattering of gravel awakened him and he yelled out the window he would be down in a minute. He was, and I won the set that morning, 6-4, 6-4, 6-3.

However, I never lived down the ribbing I got from all over town about waking up a fellow to get a tennis date.

On porch of Liberty Street house, with brother's banjo.

Lois Barnett Josie Sibley

Sue Myrick Isabelle Allen Josie Sibley

1.
2
3
4
GNIC
1 Minnie Barnett
2 Sue Myrick
3 Josie
josie
4 Lois Barnett

Minnie Barnett
Lois Barnett
Sue Myrick
Josie Sibley

UNIFORM SUITS: 1. SENIOR CAP AND GOWN. 2. WHITE DRESS. 3. SERGE COAT SUIT. 4. SCHOOL SUIT. 5. COOKING UNIFORM. 6 ATHLETIC SUIT (with Sweater).

APPLICATION FOR ADMISSION
TO THE
Georgia Normal and Industrial College.

N. B.—Before filling out this blank it is exceedingly important that you and your parents or guardian should read very carefully the articles in the catalogue on "Government" and "Business Regulations." These rules will be strictly enforced in every instance. Please do not come to this school unless you mean to obey them.

____________________ 190

Name ____________________ Age ________

Post-office ____________________

County in which you live ____________________

Did you attend this College last session? ____________

What course of study will you probably take? (See Catalogue, page 46.)

____

For what class do you think you are prepared? ____________

____

Will you probably take music? ____________ Art? ________

Have you read very carefully the articles in the Catalogue about "Government," "Business Regulations," and "Class Entrance Examination?"

____

If admitted to the College, do you promise to make an earnest endeavor to be a diligent student and to obey all the rules and regulations of the School? ____________________

Have you ever been successfully vaccinated? ____________

When will you probably reach Milledgeville? ____________

Not only new applicants, but also students of last session who expect to return, are requested to fill out the foregoing blank.

Do not make this application unless you really intend coming to the College.

If you have never attended this institution, I should like to have from you, in addition to this application, a letter telling me fully of your advancement, your purpose in attending the College, and asking me any questions that you may think proper.

I shall also be glad to have letters from former students concerning their work for the next session.

Send this application in a sealed envelope to

J. HARRIS CHAPPELL, President,
Milledgeville, Ga.

UNIFORM DRESS

Students are required to wear a uniform dress on all occasions while in attendance on the College. The several suits devised for this purpose, while inexpensive, are exceedingly pretty and becoming. Illustrations on different pages of this catalogue will give some idea of their appearance. They are as follows:

No. 1. Every-Day Suit

The material for this suit is brown serge of a beautiful shade and excellent quality, and makes an elegant and becoming dress and one that will wear well. The suit consists of a skirt of brown serge, to be worn with shirt-waists. Eight white percale waists are necessary. These waists are worn with white standing turndown collars, and at all times a brown leather belt and black grosgrain ribbon tie must be worn. This suit should in every case, if possible, be made up before the pupil leaves home, and should be worn as a traveling dress in coming to Milledgeville.

A circular containing full and explicit directions for making this suit will be sent to every prospective student of the College before the middle of July. The circular will also contain an itemized price-list of the goods required and the addresses of Milledgeville merchants from whom they may be obtained. Students must not undertake to make up this uniform or to buy any part of it until after the circular is received. (See illustrations.) This suit will be worn for every-day throughout the year.

No. 2. Sunday Dress

The Sunday dress, during the warm months, is the percale waist, collar, and tie of every-day worn with a white linene skirt and belt. In the winter months the brown coat suit is worn.

Note—An inspection of uniform will be made shortly after the students reach the College and all uniforms found made other than according to specifications in every particular, will be condemned and the student will be required to purchase a new garment.

67

Inspections will also be made at certain intervals during the year and any uniform considered by the Matron unfit to be worn will be condemned and the student will be required to purchase a new garment.

Kindly see that all waists are provided with buttons and buttonholes and all skirts with hooks and eyes on belts and plackets.

No. 3. Winter Dress

After the middle of November and during the winter a coat suit is worn on Sunday and all formal occasions. (See illustration.) This suit must be tailor-made and ordered as directed in the circular on uniforms. Each year by means of competitive bids from merchants and manufacturers a high grade suit can be obtained at a very low price, quality and workmanship being considered.

Measurements will be taken at the College about the middle of September and orders will be taken at this time and not before. Both the coat and skirt are made of a fine quality of serge and finished in good style. By means of the large contract, the suits have been furnished during the past year at the very low cost of $11.00. Students coming to the College in September should be supplied with this amount of money to pay for the suit.

Seniors are not required to buy the coat suits as they wear the College cap and gown on Sunday and formal occasions.

No. 4. Physical Culture Suit

Every-day white shirtwaist, bloomers of brown serge. No corset or other binding or cramping garment allowed. Gymnasium shoes. The entire cost of this suit will be about $5.00.

No. 5. Senior Cap and Gown

The regular members of the Senior class are expected to be provided with caps and gowns. This costume is worn to church, on public occasions and to receptions.

Other Items of the Uniform

CAP—The Oxford Student's Cap is worn on all occasions when the students appear on the streets, at church or in any public place. The cost of the cap is $1.50, and one cap lasts throughout the session of nine months.

GLOVES—Dressed kid, dark tan color, costing about one dollar.

COOKING DRESS—White cooking apron and hand towel must be furnished by each girl in Domestic Science.

SWEATER—A plain white sweater may be worn during the fall and winter. This must be of specified length and quality as described in circular on uniform.

Remarks on Uniform Dress

In most colleges where a uniform dress is attemped it turns out to be a little better than a sham or pretense. Such is not the case in this Institution. The rules in regard to the matter are most rigidly enforced. Any attempt at evasion or partial violation of them by pupils will be in every instance promptly and positively put down.

2. All uniform goods are made by the manufacturers expressly for this school, and are sold to pupils for cash by Milledgeville merchants at an exceedingly small profit, and for the most of the articles at a less price than they can be bought anywhere else. Pupils must not attempt to buy them elsewhere than in Milledgeville, as it is impossible to exactly match them elsewhere, and no other goods, however similar, will be permitted.

3. Pupils are required to wear full uniform on the cars in traveling between the College and their homes.

4. Pupils are not allowed to give or sell their cast-off uniforms or any part thereof, to servants or other persons about Milledgeville.

5. Pupils are requested not to bring any other dresses to the College than the uniform suits. A kimono or two (of any material suitable) to wear around the house will, however, be allowed.

69

AT SCHOOL — AT TENNIS — IN THE COOKING SCHOOL

SUNDAY UNIFORM.

S

THE MANSION DORMITORY, ERECTED 1838. THE RESIDENCE OF THE GOVERNORS OF GEORGIA, 1838-1868

Sue's dormitory when she first entered GN&IC.

Senior-Junior Basket Ball Game

FALL UNIFORM.

DRESSED ACCORDING TO OCCASION

ATKINSON HALL LAWN

* * *

Miss Kate was herself an astute business woman, having operated the family store and the post office for a number of years, and she realized that in spite of the restrictions placed on a woman by law and custom, her daughters, as well as her sons, needed to be prepared to support themselves. She ensured that each of them could.

When both sons' interests turned to engineering, Miss Kate realized neither would be returning to Dovedale or Milledgeville to live. She also knew that she herself lacked the knowledge of farming necessary to properly manage all aspects of Dovedale, but that the plantation could provide funds to educate the children as well as support the family. Therefore, when Fullie returned to college, although Sue was still a fulltime student and only seventeen, she was the eldest child at home and thus took over much of the responsibility for Dovedale.

The long days of riding behind her father, her bare legs poking out from beneath her dress as she perched on a croaker sack, had stayed with her.

She had learned farming from his discussions with the tenants and the hired men. He encouraged building terraces, rotating crops, planting cover crops for the winter months, and the need to keep the fertilizer (the farmer's greatest expense) from washing down to the creek along with the top soil.

She had seen farmers struggle to grow enough food to feed the family, enough corn to feed the mules, and enough cotton to pay for next year's fertilizer. She knew that a farmer's yield often lay beyond his control—weather determined his profit. Too much rain late in the late fall meant fewer bales of cotton; a dry summer lowered the yield for corn.

Sue knew how to squeeze a handful of dirt to see if it was too wet or too dry to plow—not so wet it would clod when plowed or so dry it would blow off the fields with the wind.

Cotton was still King in the South, and as Miss Kate foresaw, the cotton of Dovedale continued to pay Sue's and Fullie's college expenses and eventually paid for the other three children—Allie, Katie and Lil—to attend college. Dovedale provided family income for many years after the children were adults, and those lands that have remained in the hands of Miss Kate's descendents still provide income—from sportsmen and from timber rather than from crop farming.

But Sue's life was more than plantation work and studies. Living at home, she enjoyed going back to Dovedale with her mother, and she wrote of their trips to make arrangements with the sharecroppers for the coming planting season.

They took along sandwiches for lunch. They also took the old tin coffee pot and the ground Arbuckle's coffee, and made boiled coffee over a fire of sticks, out in the wagon yard.

Sue said:

If I ever saw anything hot, that coffee was hot. We drank it from the cups and a hot tin cup is about as hot as anything I know of. I don't know which was worse the awful taste of boiled coffee or the inconvenience of burned lips from trying to drink from a hot tin cup. Maybe the coffee was not quite as bitter as quinine, but it didn't miss far.

When Sue completed her studies at GN&IC in the spring of 1911, she was graduated with a diploma. Students who did not complete the four years of study, but did qualify to become teachers, received a certificate. At that time, the college numbered the students in order of graduation; Sue was the 497th student to be graduated with a diploma.

SUE IN SOCIETY

The local paper reported the comings and goings, as well as the social events, of the "upper crust" of society in Milledgeville. As early as August 1910, "Susan Myrick of Dovedale" was mentioned in the society pages. Her activities also were front page news in the local *Union-Recorder*.

Because of the family's social position in Milledgeville, Sue's arrivals from and departures to teaching positions as close as the next county, as well as from hundreds of miles away, were announced in the paper. Her dramatic readings and her participation in dramas made front-page news. She told Sherman's (Uncle Remus) stories at the local elementary schools; she directed *The Miser's Dream*, and she gave a reading at the local Methodist Church. Many of her "readings" were actually recitations of the stories she learned from Sherman. The play *Microbe of Love* was labeled a "howling success," and the reviewer stated that "Susan Myrick, in her role as president of The Spinsters, is one scream after another."

The family's position in the 1920s also shows in the guest list for Floride Allen's party for the "As You Like It" club. The invitees included many of the future leaders of Milledgeville and Baldwin County:

George Carpenter (Superior Court Judge)
Richard Binion (physician; owner of Binion Clinic)
Furman Bell (banking)
Charlie Conn (banking)
Dawson Allen, Jr. (physician)

Russell Bone (businessman)
Jesse Bone (businessman)
Culver Kidd (businessman)
Bertie Stembridge (county ordinary; now called Probate Court Judge)
And others.

At a garden party with some 400 guests, hosted by Mrs. E. R. Hines, the entertainment included Sue telling one of Sherman's (Uncle Remus) stories.

Sue was much in demand at local schools to present readings of the Uncle Remus stories. She presented two different tales in one day at the Scottsboro School, and a day or two later, told students at another school how Brer Rabbit got his wife. As her niece I well remember hearing her tell the tales in dialect.

A notice about one of her readings appeared in the *Union-Recorder* (the weekly Milledgeville paper) on June 18, 1912:

The children who attend the "Story Hour" on the campus of the Georgia Military College Wednesday afternoon will have a picnic in connection with the stories and the play.

Miss Susan Myrick, who fascinated the children last Wednesday, has consented to tell some more stories Wednesday.

All of the children of the town, twelve years old and under, are invited to be present promptly at six o'clock Wednesday. The mothers may come also, should they care to do so.

Sue wrote in one of her columns:

Brer Rabbit and Sech

The rabbit is a hero; the tales of his prowess are great folk stories as are the legends of Greeks and Romans, the tales of the Norse gods and heroes, the stories of King Arthur and his court, and the stories of the Rhinegold and Valhalla. But there is one difference which is important when you consider the heroes of the Trojan War or those of King Arthur's court. Brer Rabbit carries no sword or lance, he is not the brave, hard hitting warrior; he is, instead, the most harmless and helpless of all wild creatures and he wins his contests by his wisdom, his slyness, his ability to outsmart everybody else.

EARLY TEACHING

Sue was chosen to return to GN&IC for the school term 1911-1912 as "scholarship teacher," one of the highest honors offered graduates. Not only would the graduate gain a year's experience, but she would have the comfort of being "at home," and working with people she already knew. For Sue, the position meant she could live with her family on Liberty Street, only two blocks from the campus, and continue to help her mother supervise Dovedale Plantation. So she accepted the position as Assistant Physical Director for the monthly salary of thirty-five dollars. She worked under the supervision of Miss Ruena G. West as she made plans for her career.

The next year, she accepted a position in an adjacent county and moved away from home. Although she had taught for a year, she considered this her first real job.

My first job was at Round Oak, a little place in Jones County (Georgia), where three teachers took care of the schooling of children from first grade through high school.

I had first, second and third grades. A man who had just been graduated from Emory University taught the high school girls, and somebody named "Miss Rosa" taught the intermediate grades. We had wood-burning stoves to stoke and cracks in the walls of the rooms through which wind whistled mightily in the winter months. Children from the fifth grade or maybe sixth and seventh went to the spring for buckets of drinking water and we all drank from the same dipper on the shelf at the corner of the porch.

The state had not gotten around to furnishing books for the children, back then, and often there would be second graders who had no books at all. Students would borrow back and forth from other children when reading lesson time came. As for spellers, nobody could spell (even I wasn't so hot at it), and I wrote words on the blackboard for the children to copy down and take home to study. Incidentally, the black boards were planks that had been painted black and nailed to the walls. I can't remember who provided the chalk, but I do remember we used pieces of somebody's old undershirts for erasing the chalk marks on the boards.

Unlike Mr. Wiggins, who rode 20 miles to school in a Model T, I walked to school. Not 20 miles; but about 15 blocks (or what would be called blocks in a city). There was no paving, and the "blocks" were knee deep in dust in dry spells and sloppy with mud when the rains came.

The children were expected to sweep the room, but among children of the first, second and third grades, there were few who could wield a broom, so the job was mine. I never was what you'd call a good housekeeper and it's a good thing the Health Department never came to examine our school room.

There were several very pretty high school girls, so it did me no good to hang around, late in the afternoon, sweeping floors; the good-looking principal always had half a dozen girls hanging around him, so there was no chance for me. Somehow, the high school boys didn't care enough about the primary teacher to come in and help me clean up, though the principal did require them to tote in my stove wood.

And for all the work I did at the Round Oak school, reckon what my wages were? Forty dollars a month. Still, I only paid $15 a month for a lovely big room and three meals a day, at my boarding house.

Sue moved back home the next year to serve as a Critic Teacher for the fifth grade at the Training School of GN&IC for the term 1913-1914. The Training School, later called Peabody School, was a local grammar school and part of the college. It provided an opportunity for education students at the college to gain classroom experience for one quarter while having the supervision of the regular classroom teacher.

GRADUATE STUDIES

Sue learned about Dr. John Harvey Kellogg's Battle Creek Sanitarium and his emphasis on nutrition as a basis for good physical conditioning—the Sanitarium was becoming a world famous treatment center. Dr. Kellogg had also gained recognition, along with his brother, for the Battle Creek Toasted Corn Flakes Company, the first national company to produce whole grain dry cereal. Five years after he founded the Normal School of Physical Education (N.S.P.E.) in Battle Creek, in 1914. Sue applied for admission.

The School, like the Sanitarium, emphasized nutrition, and Sue's interests included nutrition as well as exercises, games and dance. She had few choices for advanced education in both fields of study at that time, and the N.S.P. E. was her logical selection.

The distance had to have seemed great to Sue. Only her older brothers had travelled so far from home. Sue took the train from Milledgeville, which presented her with both challenges and excitement. She wrote:

I rode the train all the way to Chicago, taking a Pullman and riding in the lower berth, though the lower berth cost a couple of dollars more than the upper. My mother thought it would be safer in the lower berth. Goodness knows why—or for that matter, safer from what.

I had been carefully warned not to talk to strangers on the trains, and I'd been informed about the dining car where I would read the menu card from the "Price" side, to check the prices before I ordered food. Trouble was that after finding an item priced reasonably I'd discover it was celery or something else that would not satisfy my appetite.

I was scared to death of the sleeping car porter and even more afraid of the dining car waiter. Scared of making a boo-boo and of having him find out I'd never ridden on a Pullman car before. To see the steward bow and show the passengers to seats at the little tables, to watch the waiters in their polite fashion offer menus, spread napkins (the napkins were NOT paper), serve everything with an extra plate under it—that was about the last word in elegance so far as my young eyes knew.

But the trip was ever so gay and pleasant. I spent the night with a cousin in Macon, caught the train here early next morning, rode all day and all night. A slow trip compared with today's jets.

But no flying machine can compare with the old Pullman train for excitement. I feel sorry for today's youngsters who never get to sleep in a sleeping car, though they have money enough to fly to Europe.

In her two years and three summers at Battle Creek, she became a school leader. In November 1915, she was elected president of the Normal Club, which organized all social functions for the students. She supervised and organized numerous events, including a roller skating party at Lake Gognac, the school reception on campus, and float day—an annual event held in the Battle Creek River, in canoes.

The Normal Club arranged programs for chapel, and the school annual (The Blue and White), states that "Miss Sue Myrick has favored the students with several readings which were fully enjoyed." Some of the readings she retained in her files were in the dialect of the country Negro of her childhood, and the sounds were probably new and enthralling for the other students.

The Battle Creek school was the first to organize a scholastic honor society for physical education students. Analogous to Phi Beta Kappa, Sigma Sigma Psi was organized on May 25, 1916. Sue, one of the eight charter members, was elected vice-president.

Sue excelled in athletics. Her basketball team won first place in intracollegiate competition, as did her field hockey team, which she captained. Sue took the first place medal in individual swimming and diving competition.

In the 1916 May Festival in Battle Creek, Sue played an attendant to the Queen of Spring in a presentation before some three thousand people. Her experience with this pageant aided her in later years when she supervised similar May Day pageants for an entire school system.

Sue worked on the college annual as assistant editor and joke editor and wrote the class prophecy for her class of 1916.

In the joke section, called "Chuckles," Sue listed some of the "students" at school, including "Billy Rubin," "Perry Cardium," "Polly Morphonuclear," "Polly Peptide" and "Polly Saccharid." She advised the Juniors that if they are not familiar with these "students" they will meet them all in Senior Physiology.

She also drafted an examination for hockey students, which apparently included inside jokes for her fellow students:

1. Draw a picture of the field with picture of each player.
2. Describe a scrap between Misses Austin and Wright.
3. Show Miss Burton making a goal at the rate of a mile a minute.
4. Why does Miss Blake wear shin guards in the middle of the

field?

5. What have you derived from hockey games with reference to your pedal extremities?
6. Why is Mrs. Jones like a sieve? If so, where?
7. What has the game of hockey to do with Thumb Nails? (References Myrick and Exley.)

Sue titled her class prophecy "The Autobiography of a Golf Ball." The ball began its journey when it was purchased at a local pharmacy and carried to a Battle Creek golf club where it overheard the gossip about all students—except for one. Sue ended the article with "There remains one member of whom I have heard nothing. I have no doubt, however, that she is living a happy married life—and her name is Susan Myrick."

Sue (1914) at Liberty Street House; man is unknown

SUSAN MYRICK . . . . Georgia

Sober on occasion, yet ready for fun;
Mighty captain in hockey—made the Juniors all run.

Vice-President, Sigma Sigma Psi
Assistant Editor of YEAR BOOK
Joke Editor of YEAR BOOK
Class Prophet, '16
Captain Senior Hockey
Senior Basketball
President, Normal Club

In Blue And White, the annual at Battle Creek

Honor society at Battle Creek (Sue, back row, left)

Probably in Battle Creek

In Milledgeville

On the road again on the job

In Battle Creek

Job application picture, taken in Battle Creek

Sue's swim medal, in possession of niece Lil James

SUPERWOMAN

Dr. Kellogg, as president of N. S. P. E., aroused Sue's interest in eugenics, the study of hereditary improvement of the human race by controlled selective breeding. The idea was to select your mate on the basis of physical condition (strength and health) and mental acuity to ensure a stronger and healthier next generation. In 1915, Dr. Kellogg established the Eugenics Registry, and she signed up for this registry in

1916. She made national news.

This story appeared in the *Detroit Free Press*, August 2, 1916. It was carried nationwide.

This Superwoman Awaits Superman
Dateline: Savannah, GA, August 1

Susan Myrick, beauty and athlete, the first superwoman of America to enroll in the well known eugenics registry, which was organized by the national conference, comes from Milledgeville, Ga.

From this auspicious start of the registry it is now up to a superman to step forth and make his bow to the public. There are quite a few in Milledgeville, so it is said, but their natural modesty when it comes to signing their names as a confession of perfection may deter them from enrolling before at least a man steps forth from Atlanta.

Of course, the idea of the registry is to get a list of human thoroughbreds, tested for physique and mentality. Beautiful boneheads do not count and high foreheads on puny physical specimens are equally out of the running. Miss Myrick qualified with a high average on the list as the first to aid in building up an aristocracy of health in the United States.

Miss Myrick is a graduate of the Normal School of Physical Education at Battle Creek, Mich. She is now a physical director and next year will be a supervisor of physical training in the public schools of Hastings, Neb., where she is director of physical training for girls in the high school. She is a firm believer in the theory of practical eugenics.

The *Detroit Free Press* carried a picture of Sue that appears to be one of her school pictures.

For Sue, "practical eugenics" meant select your spouse not only for love but with logic. Sue was perhaps one of the most non-bigoted persons of her generation—she cared not about a person's color, origin, nationality, or sexuality.

Her sister Katie wrote about another article, which appeared in the Atlanta paper shortly after GN&IC students began classes in 1916.

Nan Whitehurst (Uncle Cincy's daughter), who had stayed with us to go to school for several years, was staying in the dormitory. She stopped me in the hall one day to tell me that a girl had seen a picture of Sue, in the Atlanta paper. The picture was of her in pajamas, a one-piece flannel affair with feet.

Nan wondered if we should tell Mama. I said no, she would only be upset and there was nothing she could do. About a week or so later, Great Aunt Lily, who lived in Cincinnati, Ohio, wrote Mama and sent the picture, voicing her disapproval. Mama was upset and I had to tell her the Atlanta paper had printed it too.

She phoned Uncle Cincy, and he came from Dublin, and advised her to say and do nothing. We took the Macon paper, which did not carry the story.

The pajama picture might have been taken in the college dorm at the Battle Creek school and obtained from another student. With her love of drama, Sue might have posed in pajamas for a picture, but not to be published, especially if her family might see it. She would never embarrass her mother.

CHARLES DEETS

With her high-honors class standing at Battle Creek and her previous teaching experience, Sue easily obtained the position of Supervisor of Physical Education for City Schools in Hasting, Nebraska, for the school term beginning the autumn after her graduation from Battle Creek. She remained there for two school terms, 1916-1918. In Hastings, she entered her first serious courtship, with Charles Deets.

With the World War going on, Charles and his friend Harry Schutlz signed up for naval service, and Charles and Sue courted by mail, starting in April 1918 when he was stationed at Great Lakes for training. They continued to write through World War I, while he was in France and after his return. When he was stationed in New York City, Allie and her cousin Nan were students at Columbia. Charles and a sailor friend escorted them around town and took them to shows.

We have a copy of only one note from Sue to Charles, written on a cost-estimate form for a brick and stone contractor and sent to him by Harry Schultz, when Charles was sick.

My dear,

Harry told me at noon you were feeling just rotten and I want you to know I am awfully sorry. I just want to tell you that if you get so sick I have to come and nurse you that you'll have to sing to me "I don't want to get well."

Hoping you'll be all right soon and with much sympathy and love, Sue

Charles's letters to Sue reveal the innocence of young love and the dreams and hopes of a sailor away from home. Excerpts from a few of his letters given here also reflect Sue's personality and daring.

April 23, 1918, from Chicago

Be sure, dear, and let me know about your going thro Chi. I can't tell, dear, I may leave this station inside of three weeks. They are going to send 1,000 men here every day for the next 12 days. Some of us may land in France. But don't worry, I am not going to.

May 1, 1918, Great Lakes

No matter what happens, I always love you. I wish I had been there the other eve to cheer you up but I suppose we would have scrapped, so I am glad I was not there.

You can go riding with that Dennis guy in his Stutz, but please, dear, don't tell me about it. I don't care to have the blues.

Right now is the first time I have felt home sick and I believe it was your letter. I think I ought to be there to take care of you.

Today you gave your May festival. I hope it was a grand success. I am more than sorry that I was not there to see it.

May 8, 1918, Great Lakes

Love, I do remember when we used to ride together, I wish we could tonight.

Sat May 18th 10:00 a.m. Phil. Pa.

You people don't realize what is happening in this country. There are more men being shipped to France and other foreign service than you have any idea.

If you could see where I am writing you would under stand the scratching. I am sitting on the ground and using a suit case for a desk. Some class. I had some ice cream last evening. I didn't know exactly how ice cream ought to taste but that tasted good anyway.

Well, dear, I can't write much and I can't tell you where to send mail. I guess you will have to quit writing until I send you an address. I realize more and more every day how dear you are to me, Sue. I miss you more than I can tell. But I will see you --- "When my ship comes sailing home."

Yours forever, Cha'les.

Sat May 18, 1918, 5 p.m. Jersey City

Just arrived here from Phil. I don't know when we will leave but soon I suppose. We are at a pier awaiting a ship for some place that is about all I know.

I wrote you a letter before leaving Phil. But didn't get a chance to mail it. I threw it out the car window about twenty miles from here. I don't know whether you will ever get it or not.

There was a crowd of people standing at the station but the train went so fast I couldn't see where the letter went. I never took such a fast ride in my life outside of one night when we rode in a big Paige.

It makes me sore to see these big birds running around here selling peanuts and candy around in this bunch of sailors. You should hear how we bawl them out. They ought to be over in France doing their bit.

I am getting more patriotic every day. I see things that would make any one patriotic.

All along the way people ran out and cheered and waved at us. Old men, children and all. It is great to see those things.

June 25, 1918, Great Lakes

My dear, tell me about your plan to see me. I am anxious to know about it. Will you please tell me. Your letter was written May 16th after you had received word that I could not see you in Chi. You felt no worse than I did about that.

Aug 2, 1918, Pauillac, France, sent to Sue in Milledgeville

I hope that you have been having a good time during your stay in Battle Creek, and I hope that your sister has been a good chaperon.

I think I shall have to write her a letter and give her a few instructions. Ha. Would she receive them?

Oct 18, 1918, France

I received only two letters today. The second was from Beulah. She said the High School girls were making life miserable for the new physical training instructeress by telling her how Miss Myrick did things. Ha

Oct 25, 1918, France

I can use a pair of socks if you must knit. But if you don't want to knit don't bother on my account.

Oct 28, 1918, France

I am glad you are enjoying yourself. You may have my share of enjoyment also until I get back where I can use it myself.

Nov 26, 1918, France

I must tell you that I expect to spend Xmas in the dear old States if nothing happens. I know nothing of when we are leaving here but rumor has it some time in the near future. It may be possible for me to see you before Xmas if it is your wish that I should.

Feb 14, 1919, Pelham Bay

Dear heart, I received two letters from you today. You are the dearest girl in the world to write to me—and such nice letters. I got your Valentine. It was real cute and I think—I am quite sure it represented the truth.

Sue, dear, I'll bet Harry and Bennett are framing up to kid the life out of me when I get home. You know how they will fuss at me don't you?

Oh! I saw my name posted at the Receiving ship for discharge Monday. Isn't that great? I will sure get out next week if some of my blooming records aren't lost. I will probably start for home Tues. Gee! I wish you were in Hastings. I can't think of going so far away from you. If it were not foolish for a young man to cry I could almost do it. But it is as you say, we will see each other again some day. I feel it in my bones, as the sayin' goes.

I wrote Allie a short letter yesterday. I expect to see her on my way home. I want to see her before I leave for good.

I say some of these soldiers and <u>sailors</u> take the cake. I saw a soldier and a girl on the train coming from Atlanta. They were quite a pair. I am wondering if we appeared as they did when we were riding on the train. I don't think we did but I suppose we did to other people.

Feb 19, 1919, Pelham Bay

My little darling—I guess I am the happiest fellow in forty eight states this evening.Ho-o-----------------rah.

I received my pay this afternoon. Just enough to take me home. I will leave for home on your birthday (February 20). That must be some good omen. Superstitions—that's me all over Mable. I drew my pay and came back to the barracks and there was a letter from you and Oh! how you said you love me.

I make so much noise once in a while I nearly get my self put out of the barracks—can you blame me?

Do you still think you will see me in six months?—surely not if I go home. I hope you do however. Only one thing could make me happier than I am now and that would be to see you – to be with you again. You don't love me any more than I love you, little girl.

I am going to sleep in my hammock one more night and then I am going to turn it in in the morning and get my final papers.

My dear, tell me about your plan to see me. I am anxious to know about it. Will you please tell me.

You can send my letters to Hastings hereafter. I will have my headquarters there in a few days.

I will call Allie in the morning as soon as I get the little paper that says I am a civilian or words to that affect and will probably see her tomorrow after noon.

Good bye my darling for the last time at Pelham and I will write you later.

With love
Your
Cha'les

Feb 20, 1919

My Darling,

I received your letter this morning, the one you wrote when you were "sitting, as usual, naked as a jay"—as usual. "How do you get that way?" Oh, just take your cloths off, eh?

I received a short letter from Allie. I guess she is pretty busy. I will go to see her before I leave.

My darling, I must close or this will be a book.

Write often to
Your
Chas.

Monday, March 3, 1919, Hastings Nebr.

My Darling,

I received your letter written at Tifton, Feb. 28. I was very glad to hear from you sweetheart but your letter was awfully short, but I know you are busy so I will excuse you.

Sue, I'm a blue old baby. But I guess I'll get over it. I am going to work in a Grocery store. Ha—can you "beer" it? It's not a case of what you want to do it's what you can get to do. I want to go to school and I am going to, or bust.

Well, I must close. Please, my love, write me a nice long letter. I love you so—if you should "go away" I would melt into tears—there would be naught left but a fountain, in your memory.

With all my love enclosed and a kiss for every bit of love that is big enough to deserve a kiss, I send this "old blue letter" to you.

Your,
Cha'les

In 1920, Charles came to Milledgeville and met the Myrick family; Sue's sister Allie reported that the family expected them to marry.

A letter from Sue's friend "Daf," who lived in Atlanta at the time, said in part:

How did all the indignant cats like sweet little Sue's beau? I bet every last one of them right now have their heads together, saying something wicked about him, for that is certainly typical of a little town. But I know who cares, tho.

I hope that this 1921 that is slowly snooping in will be full of thrills for you, love affairs, marriages, divorces and everything that is good and sanitary, cause darling you deserve it."

May Day festival in Hastings

May Day in Hastings

Sue in Hastings

Sue in Hastings

Charles Deets with Sue

Unknown friend, possibly Harry Schultz

In Hastings

Charles Deets early 1917

As Reconstruction Aide

Hastings, Nebraska, ______________ 191__

M______________________

To **FRED. BUTZIRUS**, Dr.

Brick *and* Stone Contractor

Estimates Furnished on Short Notice

Residence, 322 West 1st St. P. O. Box 123

My dear,

Harry told me at noon you were feeling just rotten & I want you to know I am awfully sorry. I just want to tell you that if you get so sick I have to come and nurse you that you'll have to sing to me "I don't want to get well".

Hoping you'll be all right soon & with much sympathy & love

Sue

Note to Charles when he was ill. The only letter we have from her to Charles.

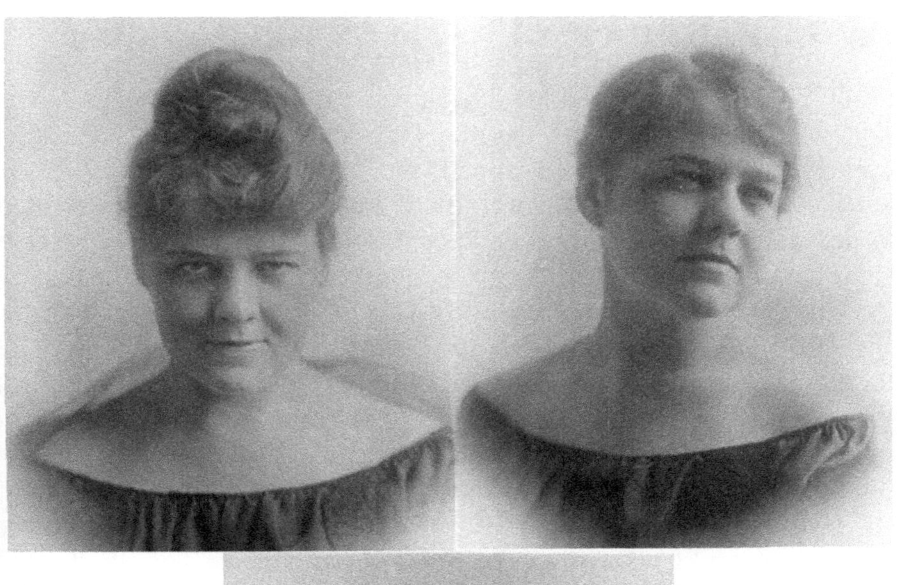

TEACHING IN HASTINGS, NEBRASKA

While Charles penned his letter to Sue from Great Lakes, on May Day of 1918, Sue supervised the May Day pageant for the school system in Hastings, and as Charles hoped, the pageant was successful. *The Hastings Daily Tribune* declared the "Crowning of Queen a Brilliant Scene," and the "Ceremony in Prospect Park Wednesday Wins Universal Approbation."

Under Sue's direction, the May Day celebration for the Hastings City schools included all grades, from elementary on up, and some 300 students participated. The Queen of Spring, borne to her throne in a palanquin by bearers in deep purple, was escorted by sunbeams and flowers—violets, buttercups, lilies and daisies (all students).

The Queen came to be crowned and to unseat the King of Winter. His elves gamboled around before he was dethroned and she was crowned by the Lord of May. The South Wind danced. The sun danced. Sixteen girls performed the "Farmer's Country Dance" in quadrille formation, and the Spring Fairies danced. The high school cadets marched.

The *Tribune* reported that the magnificent generalship of the director—Susan Myrick—was very apparent throughout the whole program.

Each event followed the other without a single delay. Children watched for their cues and came on at once. The teachers in all instances cooperated with Miss Myrick.

Miss Myrick will leave the Hastings schools at the close of this year, but by universal acclaim she may bear with her the satisfaction of knowing that in the opinion of many hundreds who witnessed yesterday's ceremony, it was the best managed ceremony of its kind that has been seen in the history of the Hastings schools.

That she was indeed missed is shown from a letter of recommendation supplied when Sue was seeking another position a few years later:

Adams County
Young Women's Christian Association
Hastings, Nebraska
Feb. 10, '22

Mrs. Lulu B. Carr,
Y.W.C.A. Greensboro, North Carolina

My Dear Mrs. Carr:—

I understand that Miss Susan Myrick is a candidate for the position of physical director of your Association. I would like to tell you in her behalf, that she was the physical director here in our public schools and during that time, she conducted our classes in physical education in our Association. We consider her the very best physical director who has ever been in Hastings, and I almost envy the Association that secures her. Miss Myrick is a whole souled sort of person, who beams with optimism and good health all the time, and spreads it among people with whom she comes in contact. She is a reader of some ability, too, and her services were much sought by every organization in town when programs were to be given. She works well with everybody, and knows how to put on big pageants. Everyone likes her, but they couldn't help it. She is a delightful personality and in the years I knew her, I never saw her any different. She is not the kind of person who is easily offended, and this also makes her easy to work with. She is fine in committee work.

Miss Myrick is a member of the Methodist Church and was a very faithful member. The only reason we could not keep her here, was that we couldn't pay her enough salary. She can command so much more than our schools here would pay. You would find her a most excellent young woman in every way and exceedingly efficient.

Very Truly Yours,
Mabel M. Dixon
Pres'd Y.W.C.A.

SUMMER SCHOOL

Sue attended summer school every year—three at Battle Creek (summers while she was a student there), two at Harvard (1917 and 1920), and one summer at Columbia to take advanced courses. Following is a copy of one of the exams given at Harvard summer school.

SUMMER SCHOOL OF HARVARD UNIVERSITY

PLAYGROUND

The quality of your English and the general appearance of your book will affect your mark.

1. Give the names of the six theories explaining the play instinct in children and give short explanations.
2. Explain the Schiller, Spencer and the Atavistic theories.
3. Give some of the physical, mental, social and moral elements in games which give us pleasure and delight.
4. Why do we have to make play a part of the school education of children ?
5. Of what importance is the environment of children from the physical, mental and social training aspect ?
6. What would you do if you needed greater loyalty and more capable leaders among your people ?

July 28, 1917.

Her summer school session in 1920 began with a sail aboard the S. S. Ontario, a ship of the Merchant and Miner Transportation Company, to Boston. She probably sailed from Savannah. Aboard, Sue directed some "exercise classes" on the deck for other travelers. At Harvard that summer, her courses included preventive medicine, teaching methods, marching tactics, public school games and clubs, dancing, and gymnastic apparatuses.

Her grades averaged B to B+.

ALMOST MILITARY

At the end of the school term in spring of 1918, Sue returned to Battle Creek for the summer to teach calisthenics and swimming at the Normal School of Physical Education. That September, while she was still in Battle Creek and Charles was in Europe, Sue volunteered to the Surgeon General to serve as a Reconstruction Aide (equivalent to a physical therapist). In reply the surgeon general directed her to report to Detroit, Michigan, for a personal interview and for Practical

Demonstration, and to submit three letters of recommendation. This letter reached her after she had returned to Milledgeville.

She then took her physical and practical at Ft. McPherson in Georgia, and received a letter dated October 31, 1918, stating that her paperwork was in order and she was "therefore, eligible for appointment as a Reconstruction Aide and assignment to duty when and where needed."

On January 13, 1919, the Surgeon General appointed Sue a Reconstruction Aide in the Medical Department of the U. S. Army and ordered her to take the oath of office.

Unlike modern-day inductions into military service, her oath was a printed form, to be filled out and signed before a notary public "or other official authorized to administer oaths." A return envelope was provided. The letter warned that if the form were not properly completed, "complications may arise respecting your right to pay and travel allowances."

As a Civilian Employee of the Military Service travelling under orders, Sue was to be given travel expenses for going from her place of appointment to the first duty station and travel from the last duty station to home.

Travel orders were included with the letter of appointment; she was to proceed without delay, after having taken the oath, to Base Hospital, Camp Jackson, South Carolina. Also included were transportation requests that, when presented to the local railroad, would gain her passage on a Pullman car. She also had a request for excess baggage.

The letter ended with an all caps statement advising her to order her uniforms immediately.

We think that Sue did obtain her uniform because of the photograph of her in what seems to be the uniform.

But we know that she did not report for duty, for only ten days after her orders to report to duty, she received this notice:

WAR DEPARTMENT
OFFICE OF THE SURGEON GENERAL
WASHINGTON

ORDER

So much of order from this office dated January 13, 1919, as directs Susan Myrick, Reconstruction Aide (Physical Therapy), Medical

Department, U. S. Army, now at Milledgeville, Georgia, to proceed without delay after having taken the oath of office to Columbia, South Carolina, and report to the Commanding Officer, Base Hospital, Camp Jackson, for assignment to duty, is hereby revoked.

By order of the Surgeon General:

F. K. Strong
Lt. Col., Medical Corps

BACK TO THE CLASSROOM

She was in Battle Creek over Christmas 1919, as we learned from her letter home, postmarked Battle Creek, December 23, 1919. Her job application, however, does not mention this stay, but it must have been brief, perhaps a special teaching or learning experience. The trip was probably not for social purposes because the letter indicates she could not be at home for the holidays. Close-knit, the Myrick family's girls gathered at Liberty Street for the holidays until marriage took them away.

To my dear Mother and the rest of the family. Wishing you each and all a very Merry Christmas and a New Year full of joy. I am thinking of you all the time these days and of course I'd like to be with you but don't feel bad that I can't. Just think what a grand time we'll have when I do come home. Don't forget any thing that happens so you can tell me all about it

With all the love that's ever been from long ago til now,
Sue

Sue worked as Teacher of Physical Education and Health for the Extension Department at GN&IC for the school terms 1918 through 1920, with summer months spent elsewhere, teaching or as a student. This position, although associated with the college, was also under the supervision of the State, and it carried her into several counties and many schools. She sometimes spent several days at one school helping establish courses in physical education as well as helping select proper equipment for the students. Letters from Charles and others were addressed to Georgetown, Ellaville, and Fort Valley.

A letter from one school district spells out some of her work and also asks that she be allowed to return:

March 28, 1919
Dr. M. M. Parks, President
Georgia Normal & Industrial College
Milledgeville, Georgia

Dear Sir:

Some time during last Fall Miss Catherine Turner and Miss Susan Myrick, who are doing certain field extension work for your college, visited our school, each at a different period, for a few days.

At the time of their visit we were just passing through a severe epidemic of Spanish Influenza; our school attendance was low and conditions generally demoralized, and for these reasons we do not feel the whole school received the full benefit of their visits.

We are writing to ask if it would be possible for you to allow Misses Turner and Myrick to return to us for a few days. We are deeply interested in the work they are furthering; they are both experts in their line, and the benefits we did receive from their former visits, even under such trying conditions, lead us to believe that a visit from them at this time will mean a great deal to our school.

Miss Myrick, when with us, made certain recommendations as to our putting in playground equipment, and acting upon such we have purchased a considerable quantity of playground apparatus, which is now on the road, and we would like very much to have her here when it arrives to superintend the installation.

This is a proposal which is altogether new to us, and as we have invested quite a bit of money in same we are very anxious that we get it started off right, and for this reason it seems almost necessary that we have Miss Myrick with us for a few days.

We want to thank you for your courtesy in allowing these splendid young ladies to visit our school last Fall. They seem to be well up in their respective lines, full of energy, enthusiastic and very capable. They are a credit to the Institution they represent and the State of Georgia at large.

We sincerely trust that you will give this your most favorable consideration, and advise us at what date we can again have the pleasure of having Misses Turner and Myrick visit us.

Yours very truly

(initials J. C. M)

Secretary Trion School Board

Trion Public School

The map below shows the counties and the number of schools in each county that she visited during the 1918-1919 school term.

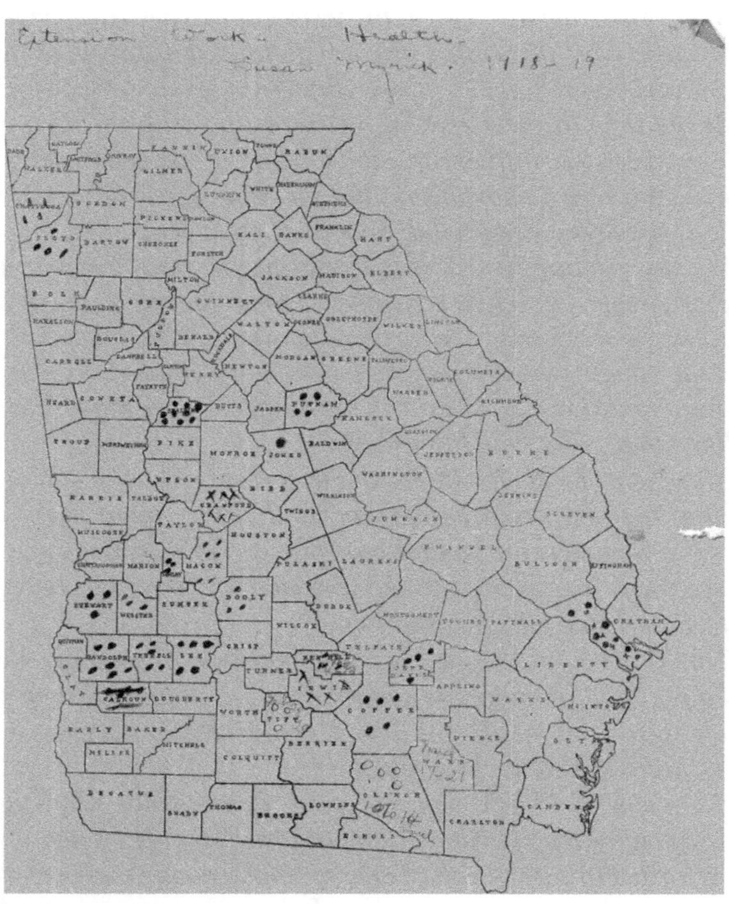

Sue was not fond of the travelling she did during that time. Most of it was on a train.

In my horror ridden past, there was a year in which I

served as a sort of aide to the late Mr. Fort Land, who was an assistant state commissioner of education. We travelled from one county to another, spending a week or maybe only three days at rural school work. Just what we did takes too long to tell. What I mainly remember is the awful meals we had to take on.

The state paid certain of our expenses, such as train tickets and boardinghouse costs, but back in those dark ages the state made no provision for automobiles for their employees; at least, not for lesser ones such as Mr. Land and me.

We'd catch a train out of Macon at 10:30 p.m., ride on the day coach for five hours, change trains somewhere and ride on until breakfast time. Meanwhile, he and I had drunk innumerable cups of sorry coffee, eaten dozens of soggy sandwiches, and half rotten apples or bananas or whatever the "butch" had to sell.

And that late breakfast we'd catch at the railroad station, now, that was usually pretty terrible. The hominy grits would be cold and stiff; the eggs (none too fresh, to start with) scrambled in rancid grease, the toast soggy with yesterday's butter, melted and poured over it. The less said about the coffee, the better.

Sue's sister Allie said that Sue received her Ph.D. shortly after this work with the extension service, but the rest of the family has no knowledge of such a degree and believes Allie was perhaps referring to a Master's Degree or the completion of course work for a doctorate.

Sue decided to sever her associations with GN&IC when the college president opposed all types of dancing. Her classes had included various forms of dancing, such as ballet steps, that she felt should not be excluded from a physical education curriculum.

She applied for a position with the Y.W.C. A. in Greensboro, North Carolina in 1920. Her application listed not only her education and experience, but also her "personal qualifications":

Height 65 inches, weight 160 pounds
Member Methodist Episcopal Church
Born in Georgia
Winner—All round championship girls' Swimming and

Diving contest, N.S.P.E, Battle Creek, Michigan

Captain—Girls' hockey team, N.S.P. E., Battle Creek, Michigan

Guard—Senior Basket Ball team, N.S.P.E., Battle Creek, Michigan

Member—Sigma Sigma Psi (High Scholarship Society) N.S.P.E., Battle Creek, Michigan

With the application she sent several letters of recommendation, including the one given earlier sent from the Y.M. C. A. in Hastings, Nebraska, as well as another four. One from the pastor of her church stated:

In reference Miss Sue Myrick as physical director in your Georgia Normal and Industrial College, I wish of my own accord to speak to you because I know I cannot misplace a word in her behalf. As a community member & church member & professionally she easily makes herself the idol of all by her pleasing personality and her pep and readiness. She is sought for all construction work in the community and with her every movement succeeds. She will leave the community to the regret of everybody. In saying these things, I realize that we will be the loser here, but in justice to her as she seeks more ambitious and useful work I feel that I have not said enough.

From her alma mater's YWCA came the statements that:

...It is useless for me to repeat what has already been written you concerning her splendid training and experience in Physical Education.

Undoubtedly she is one of the most optimistic, glad-hearted people I ever knew. She has a keen and never-failing sense of humor. Yet along with this happy disposition, one immediately sees and feels wholesomeness and strength in her personality and power in her ability to do the thing in hand. She is "everybody's friend," and can quickly adapt herself to any group. I believe she would be thoroughly tactful and successful in working with your Board.

In the College Y.W.C.A. here, Miss Myrick very gladly and helpfully advises and cooperates with the head of our athletic committee. She never does a thing half-heartedly, and would, I believe, be a valuable asset to your Association work in Greensboro.

Other letters included one from the Director of the Department of Education of Harvard University, and a strong letter from the Georgia

Department of Education that highly praised her work with the Extension Service which stated:

There is nobody in Georgia—if anywhere in the South—who has had more or better training, or greater success in her work, or finer personality for just this work. I regard her as foremost in her profession, very attractive, and most efficient. If what I had said sounds in the least extravagant, let me add that it does not begin to express my deliberate opinion of her.

* * *

Sue received mail addressed to her in Greensboro, but apparently did not remain there for the school term. In January 1923, she was in Macon, Georgia, where she took a position teaching physical education at Lanier High School for Girls, and on January 19, 1923, she had a food column entitled "Saner Eating" on the Women's Page in *The Macon Telegraph.* The column appeared on an irregular basis and provided not just menus, but information on a variety of healthful foods.

In later years, Sue wrote a column about her teaching experience at Lanier High school:

When I first came to Macon, I was director of physical education at the girls' high school (Lanier High School for Girls). There was literally no playground of any sort. A gymnasium of sorts existed, a dark, mouldy, smelly basement room, about half big enough for the class.

I recall my request to the Superintendent of Schools for some playground space for the school; he sent me to Mr. Wallace Miller, member of the Board of Education, who listened understandingly to my report of conditions. Later on, shacks at the back of the school building were bought by the city-county, torn down, and a small space provided for a playground.

I was permitted a tiny budget for buying six basketballs, six softballs and six softball bats. We used stones to mark bases; the basketball hoops were pretty unsteady. But we had an outdoor place to play.

Even such provisions are a far cry from the playthings provided for my set at the country school I attended as a child in Baldwin County. Papa's old hand-knitted socks were raveled out and rewound into balls for our "baseball" games. We had not slides or swings, no rings, no trapeze bars. If we wanted to climb, we could climb the old trees growing beside the gulley at the edge of the school yard, or run down to the nearby woods, climb a small pine and "ride it over" to the ground.

As for trapeze bars for skinning the cat or hanging by the knees, there were limbs on the elms or the hickories.

When I taught in the high schools in Macon, it was my habit to mark down on the calendar those happy days which were set up as vacation days—a day for The Fair, a day for GEA meeting, Washington's birthday, Thanksgiving Day (we had only Thursday, not a whole weekend), and if the calendar was in our favor, almost two weeks at Christmas.

It was a good thing I had only a little holiday time then. My income wasn't good enough for me to take many trips, and vacation would have only meant staying at home and cleaning out the closets.

In early June 1928, Miss Kate wrote her youngest child, Lillas, (then in Colorado) that Sue "is 'cuckoo' over reporter's work and would love to quit her profession and take up journalism."

That year Sue's teaching career fell before the power of the press as she took a full-time position at *The Macon Telegraph.*

PART III

AT THE MACON TELEGRAPH

THE FIRST TEN YEARS

THE BEGINNING

As director of physical education at Lanier High School for Girls in Macon, Georgia, Sue supervised the students' athletic activities and taught them about nutrition. The girls' questions about food, diet and cooking led Sue to extend her free-lance writing from physical education journals to the local paper. She approached Mark Ethridge, editor of *The Macon Telegraph*, about a food column. In 1923, Sue's newspaper career began.

Her by-line for the column "Saner Eating" indicated that she worked for the Macon Food Clinic. The first column was very clinical, a straightforward listing of foods. Sue stated that "Whole Grain Wheat" was the "complete food," and that it "contains the entire sixteen elements comprising the human blood, the bran furnishing necessary bulk in addition."

In a short time, readers queried her about diets and recipes, and she provided menus filled with the foods now recommended by the Public Health Service.

In these early years "back home," Sue influenced her younger siblings; for example, Lil, the youngest, became interested in nutrition and went on to Columbia University to work on her Ph.D. in nutrition.

Sue continued to teach, and continued to advise her students on a variety of matters that the girls did not want to ask Mother about—including social and "courtship" issues. From her brother Jim, when he took her on his first business conference, she had learned many social "do's" and "don't's." Life on the plantation, at GN&IC with its strict social rules, exposure to life in larger towns and cities, and her long relationship with Charles Deets, gave Sue the confidence to provide answers to the students.

She presented the idea of a social/manners/lovelorn advice column, similar to her "Saner Eating" column, to Mark Ethridge, and Fannie Squeers was born.

On March 17, 1928, the front page of *The Telegraph* carried this announcement:

Life in a Tangle
By Fannie Squeers

This is the title of a new feature that The Telegraph *is beginning Sunday, to be written and managed by a well-known woman writer. As the title indicates, the department will undertake to discuss intelligently and helpfully the many problems that confront human beings in their every-day affairs. Inquiries are invited from all readers of* The Telegraph, *and comment and criticism will be welcomed.*

Miss Fannie will undertake to tell mother, if she asks, just what to do with the unruly daughter, or how to get daughter a beau and make her popular, to make the correct answers to the questions by the children in order that they may grow up in the way they should go, whether or not they should be spanked, to tell daughter or son solutions for love and life problems—in short, to untangle life for everybody who has it in a snarl.

Miss Squeers is a philosopher, a strategist, a woman of wide experience with humanity, analytical, practical, human, and sympathetic. Like the illustrious character from whom she derives her name, Miss Squeers will prove not only helpful and interesting, we hope, but resourceful in the "pinches." Telegraph *readers are urged to watch for it as a daily feature, and to make use of the department in the solution of their social problems.*

The next day, Fannie Squeers, who took her name from *Nichols Nickleby,* made her debut in *The Telegraph*—with a lengthy back-and-forth about whether or not a disobedient child should be spanked. Fannie stated, "This is a question that has never been answered satisfactorily and probably never will be. The tendency of the time is to let children run wild, to obey or not to obey, as they choose."

She then quoted several people—including a school superintendant and a mother—some of whom supported spanking and some who opposed. She ended the column with examples of inconsistency on the part of parents in disciplining children and went on to conclude:

> If mothers will be patient and loving, but above all firm while the child is still very young; if she will make it a rule not to "lay down the law" unless she is going to stick to it; if she will make no exceptions to her rules; if she will unendingly and everlastingly keep faith with the child; then punishments of any kind will never be necessary. And a child of 10 years will not need a spanking, either a mild one with a palm or a more severe one with a coat hanger!

There was no photograph with the column, and readers had no way to know Fannie's real name. Sometime later, a drawing of "any woman" was used in the header, and later, a photograph of Sue. By the time the photograph appeared, most of Macon knew who Fannie Squeers was.

Sue herself wrote:

My 40-year career with *The Macon Telegraph* began with a sort of Dear Abby-Emily Post column for teen-agers: "He has been going steady with me for six months; now, another girl is breaking us up. How do I get him back?" "Should I let him kiss me goodnight on the first date?" "Tell me how to order lunch at a big city hotel." There were usually 50 letters a week, but in the springtime, the number would double.

Sometimes Sue used the column to editorialize about some event that made the paper as a news story or that someone related to her personally. This is one such column—written from her own teen-age experiences.

What a shameful thing it is to make fun of a person! To hurt feelings of another, to look down upon another, to feel superior to others! It is bad enough when one is superior, but when he is not, such an attitude is sickening.

The other day, there came to my attention a case of "snootiness" which is of the sort I mean.

A young woman who was without money for a college education had the good fortune to have relatives offer to pay her way. She accepted with happiness that amounted almost to exaltation. Her reaction was one that the sheltered, protected petted girl can scarcely appreciate. To her an education meant more than anything in the world. College training was the star of her existence, the supreme chance.

She entered college. Shortly after arrival she found that some of the girls had an opportunity to help pay their expenses in the dining room. She applied at once for a job and got it. She wrote the relatives, with great delight, that they need send her only half of what they had been sending as she had a position that enabled her to help pay expenses.

She counted as nothing the hours of work, the time spent serving and clearing tables. It was a glorious opportunity.

But girls who had lived sheltered lives, who had always

gone to Dad for every penny they spent, who counted a dollar thrown away as nothing, who were not worth the powder and shot it takes to shoot them, began to snub the "waitress."

Girls, who had at first considered the "waitress" attractive, interesting, worthy of having as a friend, began to look the other way when she passed by. They began to ignore her when there were little confabs. They stopped dropping into her room for a good night chat or a gab fest and they did not invite her to skate with them or to go town with them.

The "waitress" is miserable. But she stifles her tears and pockets her loneliness. She holds up her chin and looks the other way, herself, when the girls who were once her friends pass.

That situation is the sort that provokes an honest, sane, thinking person to exasperation.

One of the things that makes me view the modern generation with considerable pessimism is the lack of courage, of independence and of initiative and the tendency to take everything as easy as possible, to demand all and give nothing in return. Seemingly the traits which enabled our pioneering ancestors to make a home in the wilderness and triumph over difficulties are long lost. All we want is to take the easiest way, whether it involves laziness, lack of principles, or what not.

Luxuries and soft living make weaklings of us. Rugged individualism seems to be a thing of the past. It's "Let the government take care of us" or "Let Dad do without and give to me" or "Let the aunts and cousins pay my way through college. It is too much trouble to work and help pay for my education. The world owes me a living and a chance. Somebody owes me an education."

Then: to the young lady who waits on tables to help pay for her education I say? All honor! I wish I could erect a monument to her and inscribe it:

"To a girl who is willing to do her part in the world, who has courage and leadership, who refuses to be a leaner and who doesn't mind work."

Someone told me that this girl, whom I honor, was unhappy because of the way she was treated, that she suffered a great deal, that she was developing a feeling of inferiority. That is hard to believe. A girl with courage and ability enough to do what she has done must also have the character to overlook slights, the personality to gain friends who are worth while, no matter what sort of work she does.

It is hard for me to see how any girl should look down upon the one who works. Perhaps I was not clever enough to know that I was being slighted when I was waiting on tables at college. So far as I know, nobody looked down upon me. Perhaps it was because I thought it was fine to work. A lot of trouble—yes. But cotton was down about eight cents a pound and there wasn't money in the family to pay all my expenses and I was proud that I could earn the rest of the needed money for my year's schooling.

To you, young lady, earning your way and working for an opportunity to get an education, I make a deep obeisance. To you, I do honor. To you, I offer congratulations and the hope that you will carry on bravely and finally achieve your heart's desire. I know you are forming character and I am sure that you will find happiness.

Readers are invited to ask questions concerning their problems. Address Fannie Squeers, care *The Telegraph*.

Mark Ethridge suggested she come to work on the paper full time at the end of the school year. Jokingly, she told people that she was just getting too old to be a physical education teacher, and besides, "teachers in those days didn't make a nickel. Of course as a newspaper reporter you didn't make a dime, but it was a percentage change."

Sue's assignments were not limited to the Fannie Squeers column when she went to the paper full time but included the duty assigned to new reporters: Obituaries. She soon advanced to cover the police, courthouse and the hospital beats.

Whether she was assigned specific feature stories or she went on her own to expand her responsibilities, we don't know; but Sue was never one to wait around to be told what to do. Shortly after her feature stories carried her by-line, she got tips from readers about stories waiting to be written, and she wrote them.

Sue covered every kind of event imaginable—the Ocmulgee River flood, the organization of the World Bank, opening night of the opera, murder trials, teas, flower shows, fashion shows, farm shows, livestock shows at county fairs, horse shows, political events.

Sue wrote about families in central Georgia, about the "little people," about historic homes and historical events.

"Though I was famous in my neighborhood for the smell of burning toast that wafted from my kitchen of mornings, I wrote a food column," Sue said. That assignment was only a step to becoming food editor.

"Georgia peaches!" she wrote July 7, 1938. "Well might poets write odes to their beauty or ballads to their juicy delights!

"The nectar of the gods, themselves, could not be sweeter than the ripe, tender, luscious Georgia peach; beside it the ambrosia of Mount Olympus grows insignificant."

In that one column, she gave health benefits of the raw and cooked peach, as well as sixteen recipes for preparing them.

She wrote book reviews for the Sunday supplement, "although most of my knowledge of literature came from reading novels of Walter Scott and Charles Dickens and the poems of Longfellow."

In 1929, barely a year after joining *The Telegraph* staff, she became editor of the women's page in the Sunday magazine section of the joint issue of *The Telegraph and News*, and immediately moved up again, to become editor of the Sunday supplement, for which she also did much of the writing. The supplement was discontinued during the depression because of the cost of paper.

She still covered widely diverse stories, such as the annual soap box derby in Indianapolis, and construction and launching of the U. S. Navy's dirigible "Macon" on July 4, 1932—in Akron, Ohio. As the sponsor of the dirigible, Sue blew the whistle to signal the lifting of the nose cone to attach it to the body.

Old homes in Middle Georgia became topics for her feature articles and stirred up more interest in local history. People, from farmers to politicians to the "tea" set to "the common individual" found themselves profiled in *The Telegraph*. For a "travel story" while she was in New York, she took a flight up the Hudson River in 1929. A visit to her sister Allie in Hawaii in 1934 provided a portrait of the dream vacation for her fellow Maconites.

When she quoted anyone, she quoted not words but sounds. Some might be offended today by the dialect of a former slave, but to Sue the language held beauty and the sounds of her youth.

In October 1931, she wrote a feature story about a five-generation family living in Macon; the matriarch was grown, married and had children when she and the other slaves were set free. Asked if she were born there, in Macon (Bibb County), the lady replied:

"Naw'm, I come from Lee County, but I wazen't bawn there. I wuz bawn in Putmon County. I belonged to de Newsomes in Putmon. Old Man Johnnie Newsome was my old marster. We live twixt Sugar Creek and de Oconee River."

Also in the 1930s, she interviewed a group of white sisters who had lived during The War Between the States. The youngest was in her seventies, and the sisters had maintained the farm, alone, since their father had gone off to *The War*.

"We hain't needed no man. I kin plow good as any man or split rails or do anything else that's needin' to be done. Least ways, I could before I got sorter old. I hain't so much account now. I can't do no plowin' much, jest a little in my garden."

For Sue, the music of the voices painted a portrait of the people.

She often spoke of the time she and Franklin Roosevelt were columnists together. Roosevelt, then governor of New York, spent months at Warm Springs, and W. T. Anderson, publisher of *The Telegraph*, became a close friend of the governor. In a conversation between the two men about forestry methods, soil erosion and race relationships, Anderson suggested that Roosevelt write a column for the Sunday edition. "You'd have a good-sized audience, your words would carry much weight and a column from you in our paper would bring us great prestige," Anderson told him.

Thus Roosevelt became a fellow columnist with Sue on *The Telegraph*.

Sue reported that Roosevelt, when asked how the democrats would get power back after Hoover's landslide election, told Anderson, "Bill, pray for a panic."

Sue said, "I don't know whether Mr. W. T. Anderson prayed, but Lawd knows we had a panic; only we called it a depression."

* * *

In the fall of 1932, Miss Kate died suddenly of a massive heart attack, and the family gathered at the Liberty Street home. Sue and the youngest sibling Lillas were the only unmarried children at the time. A letter from Fullie's wife Chan, who was unable to come to Georgia from their home in Maryland, to Sue and Lillas shows how much the in-laws cared for Miss Kate.

I wanted to come home and do what I could for you all and help bear the great burden of your grief. Perhaps if I try to tell you a little of how I think of your Mother it will be a little comfort.

A finer, dearer or more noble woman never lived. She was the inspiration of every one of her children, myself, and I am sure many others, and I cannot think of a higher tribute than that. She has left this world having lived a full life, having done her duty, and at all times been kind, sweet and understanding.

I am filled with regret that we did not come home last Christmas. At the time it seemed impossible, but we should have done so at all costs, for that I cannot forgive myself. And now I want to send you both my tenderest love and sympathy. Try to be brave and go on in such a way as would make Mother proud of you.

Most lovingly,
Chan

* * *

In 1933, when Sherwood Anderson came to Macon to visit his friend Aaron Bernd, then a columnist for the paper, Sue and Aaron were dating. Sue and Anderson became friends, and she wrote:

"Carrying a blackthorn cane and looking like a movie star, he came into the city room of *The Telegraph*, causing near-fainting spells for all the women reporters overcome by his masculine good looks."

He visited Aaron several more times. Sue took him riding through the peach belt of middle Georgia "when the trees were in full bloom and he talked and talked of the red soil—not of the pink peach blooms, the early growth of small grains in the fields, nor of the effort the farmer had put forth to improve impoverished lands."

While in Macon, Sherwood spent a lot of time visiting with the Negro shop owners on 4th Street, listening to the Negro music. His favorite song was one with the line "take soap and water fer to keep it clean."

Sue wrote:

The grand entrance to the city room of the newspaper, the unruly shock of black hair tossed back, his face alight with smile, his warm brown eyes melting every woman's heart, he'd called out to me, "Sue, take soap and water fer to keep it clean."

I have two treasured autographs of Sherwood's. One is in *Puzzle America*, the other in a book he picked off my bookshelf one evening in my apartment and wrote, "To dear Susan, from the author—Sherwood Anderson." Trouble is, that book is Andersen's *Fairy Tales*.

In a letter to Aaron Bernd, who was his host, he wrote: "You and Sue kept me in Macon. You are so damned Southern and you know I am a South lover."

* * *

Sue's training in elocution paid her in good stead when she was assigned to substitute for Mr. W. T. Anderson, publisher, when he had a conflict and could not attend some meeting of a social or fraternal or business organization. These speaking assignments sent her over most of central Georgia. At first, her topics were about "Health and Sane Eating" and "Etiquette for the High School Girl," both subjects of her by-lined columns. Her topics quickly expanded to include a wider range of subjects as her audiences also expanded from women's clubs to male-oriented organizations.

She attended events in the black community as the representative of *The Telegraph*. The leaders and the "average Joe" of that community welcomed her as a reporter who presented them and their society in her stories with the same courtesy she gave members of her own race.

SOLID FRIENDSHIPS

Sue was quick to make friends. When she lived in the Fredonia Apartments in Macon, from the mid-thirties to mid forties, she and her neighbors became friends: George Dole Wadley Burt (managing editor of *The Telegraph*) and his friend Hamilton Napier; Del and Fran Kenyon, and Jimmy Shelburne and wife and son; and Fred New and his wife Betty. They partied together while they were neighbors and even later, and they stayed in touch for life.

Sue did not forget people. Some she met briefly and years later, upon their deaths, she fondly recalled the relationships and wrote about the lost friends.

When Sue got the call to come to Hollywood, she was out to dinner with friends. Selznick Studios could not reach her, so they called *The Telegraph* and reached George Burt. He called every friend of hers that he knew, but no luck. When Sue returned to the Fredonia, well after 10 p.m., the stairs to her third floor apartment were filled with friends—and fellow dwellers at the Fredonia.

After Sue called Hollywood, the party began:

"Burt brought up all the eggs in his refrigerator; the Kenyons fetched their newly bought pound of bacon; various ones robbed their refrigerators of cheese and crackers and other goodies. And 'bathtub gin'—bootleg—flowed freely."

Sue said that her apartment entertained the most important visitor Macon had since the Marquis de Lafayette (or perhaps President Taft) came to Macon—Margaret "Peggy" Mitchell.

Another visitor, a private at Camp Wheeler, would come down to her office, to borrow her typewriter to write his column—he was known in the literary world as Henry McLemore. His wife and Sue also became close friends. One evening, Henry showed up at her door with three fire extinguishers, because she had no fire escape from her third floor apartment.

Later—in the 1940s, with food and shoes rationed—a fire did break out in the attic. Friends Delmar Warren and Gus Kaufman rushed in and saved two pairs of her shoes—the old ones, not the pair she had just bought with her ration ticket.

These apartment neighbors later declared social life in Macon dead when Sue left for Hollywood, and formed the Susan Myrick Memorial Association, to mourn her absence.

She herself said that no one liked to be the center of attention more than she did. And she knew that to be the center of attention you must give attention to others. She loved fun and laughter, which, combined with interest in other people, expanded her social life; and as her social life expanded, so did her contacts in the community. She had on hand an ever widening source for newspaper stories. Friends would say, "I know about so and so. He (or she or it) would make a great story." And so Sue would turn the person or event into a news or feature article.

Sue and her prize winner horse, 1935

MACON LITTLE THEATRE

Sue's interest in drama, begun on that counter in Milledgeville when she was a preschooler, led her to join others—some were her friends who also lived in the Fredonia apartments—to form the Macon Little Theatre.

Sue was one of forty-seven people who assembled on January 14, 1934, to organize the Macon Little Theatre. Within six months, the organization put on its first show, and Sue appeared on stage in *Wedding Bells*, described as a "joyous comedy."

The playbill for the next play, *Hay Fever*, presented in March 1934, shows that many of Sue's friends who are mentioned in her diary were involved with the Little Theatre. Fred W. New was Theatre president; Frank Hawkins of *The Telegraph* was on the press staff; Eddie Nims was a regent; Virginia Hall, Robert Quinlan, and others made the masks that decorated the walls; Miss Sally Aiken was a member of the board of directors, as was Sue; and business manager was Joseph W. Popper.

At that time, all married female cast members were listed as "Mrs. Husband's name" rather than by their given names.

In the years that followed, Sue performed in more roles than any other member of the Theatre. John Jones of the Theatre staff wrote in 2008:

> *She worked tirelessly with Mrs. Piercy Chestney to guide the theatre through the Depression and World War II. Miss Myrick contributed to the theatre's development through numerous newspaper articles that she wrote for* The Macon Telegraph. *Her support through news articles, human-interest stories and announcements was very important for the early growth of the Theatre. Also, as chairman of the casting committee, she worked diligently to contact the public and provide a steady supply of potential community actors. Her work was most appreciated during the war when a shortage of men created a hardship on directors in casting male roles. Her efforts in providing qualified male actors helped the theatre through some difficult times. After Mrs. Chestney stepped down from her 13-year reign as theatre president, Miss Myrick served as president during the 1947-1948 season. She provided a vital transition of leadership that led Macon Little Theatre to many successful years.*
>
> *Not only did Miss Myrick provide support to the organizational front, but she also lent her acting talents to many productions. Most often reviewers singled her out for her outstanding performances.*

Susan Myrick was a key force in the formative years of Macon Little Theatre. Her talent, hard work, devotion and love for the arts were gifts that she gave freely to make Macon Little Theatre the force in community theatre that it is today. In our 76th season, we still benefit from the spirit that she shared in our history.

In the year that Sue was president, she performed the roles of Lady Bracknell in *The Importance of Being Earnest*, and of Amanda in *The Glass Menagerie*. That same year, her duties at the newspaper expanded—again.

Having been a charter member and having served on the board of governors since the Theatre was founded in 1934, she was eligible to be a Life Member. When that honor was offered, she at first objected. She feared that such a position would deprive her of a vote at board meetings. Only when assured that Life Membership gave her a continuing vote on the board, as well as a continuing seat on the board no matter what election results might do to other members, she accepted, and in 1948 she was presented a "lifetime membership." Hers was one of only five such honors ever presented in the history of the theatre.

Joe Popper, Macon attorney, served as pro bono counsel for the Macon Little Theatre for a time while Sue was on the Board of Directors. He called her "the voice of reason in a sea of theatrical people. When she spoke, everybody listened."

The Little Theatre presented the play *Relatively Speaking* less than a month after Sue's death, and the printed program was a tribute to Sue. Also as a tribute, the Theatre displayed in the lobby many of Sue's favorite watercolors for the duration of the play (September 30-October 7).

The program stated: "The Macon Little Theatre lost its last life member, one of its best actresses and one of its staunchest supporters when Susan Myrick died on September 3."

The Theatre also exhibited two portraits of Sue, both in her role as Lady Bracknell in *The Importance of Being Earnest.* The oil portrait was painted by Lucille Blanche, Sue's friend who taught her painting and who was an art professor at Macon's Wesleyan College. It is now hanging in the home of Sue's niece, Lil James, in the place of honor, over her mantle.

The other portrait, a charcoal and crayon, was done by Macon artist Houser Smith as a gift to the theatre on its silver anniversary; it hangs permanently in the lobby of the theatre.

A playbill from the 1940s stated "for activity alone her record is impressive but it commands respect on other grounds. Each role she has essayed has been added proof of her ability, which, added to her enthusiasm, is a tremendous asset to any play."

Even during World War II, when she was too busy with her newspaper work and her defense work to continue as publicity chair for the Citizens' Defense Committee, she continued to work with the Theatre. Since she reported on activities of the military, she knew many of the soldiers at Camp Wheeler, and encouraged them to participate in Little Theatre activities as relief from their military duties. They not only participated, but one of them helped write and produce a musical, *Good Buddies*, for the theatre. Sue played in it.

As the demands of her work on the paper increased, her participation on-stage decreased; most of her performances were in the "old" building downtown, on Riverside Drive. Because of her devotion to the Theatre, at her death the family requested no flowers, just donations to the Little Theatre.

A list of the plays she acted in is given in Appendix VI.

Wedding Bells" (L-R) Billy Methvin, Susan Myrick, R.H.Casson, Henry Kendall, Kathleen Harper Jaques, James Shelburne, Katherine Gustin, Betty Alexander, Elliot Dunwody, Jr

Sue (second from left) in *Wedding Bells* (1934)

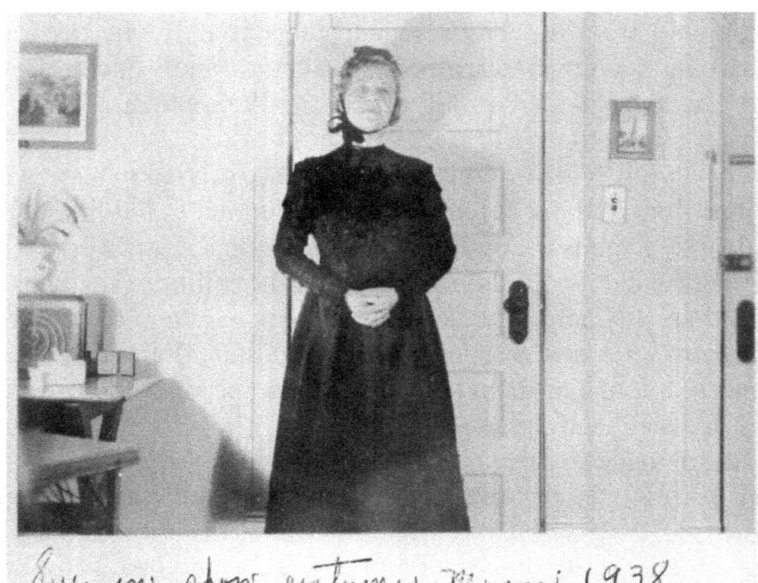
Sue in show costume Macon 1938

In costume as Christina Linden in *A Doll's House*, February 1938

Sue as Mrs. Bracknell in *The Importance of Being Ernest (1948).*
This portrait is on permanent display in lobby of the Little Theatre.

Original Little Theatre Building.

Sue (middle) in *The Royal Family*

As Carrie Nation, 1953

Sue as Mrs. Higgins in *My Fair Lady*

Sue in *Therese Raquin*, December 1952

GEORGIA PRESS INSTITUTE

Sue joined the Georgia Press Institute in 1928 shortly after she went to work for *The Telegraph.* At the first meeting of the Institute, she met Margaret (Peggy to Sue) Mitchell; they were two of the many news people of Georgia who attended the inaugural meeting.

Sue wrote of that meeting:

These days, the Georgia Press Association holds its annual summer convention at Jekyll Island, but back in the 30s they chose a different place for each meet, often staying in a small town where hotel accommodations were pretty short. Nevertheless the newspaper people were always on hand for conventions. It was at my first press convention that I met Margaret Mitchell—not a celebrity then, but a charming, petite former member of the *Atlanta Journal*'s Sunday magazine staff. She was married to John Marsh, public relations director for the Georgia Power Company. She liked to say she and John were the "Marshes of Atlanta, not Glynn."

Reams have been written about Peggy Mitchell, most of it accurate, but some of it written since her death would have made her furious if she'd read it. She couldn't bear publicity about her personal life. "When I have to go downtown in Atlanta for something, I am filled with dread," she told me the year after GWTW was published. "Somebody jumps out from behind a telephone pole and asks me if it is true that I am blind or that I have only one leg."

Peggy's talent in exaggeration was one of the things that made her popular with everybody who ever knew her; her wit and gaiety, her ability to listen to what you said and her generous, friendly manner all made her a loveable and delightful woman. But best of all I like what her husband said about her when a reporter asked him to describe his late wife.

"She sho' was a heap of fun," he said.

Long before the movie, or the book, Peggy Mitchell and her husband were the most sought-after persons at the press meets. I remember Peggy's description of an evening in their room at the old Georgian Hotel in Athens (Georgia) when the Georgia Press Institute was underway.

The people sitting on beds you wouldn't believe. As more people came into the room, those farthest back on the beds moved still farther back until somebody was sitting on the floor; by 11 o'clock, goodness only knows how many more were on the floor. And the spray from ginger ale bottles and sparkling water mixers was as thick as that over the Maid of the Mist at Niagara Falls.

On the floor sat young reporters, gray-haired editors of small-town papers or metropolitan dailies, city editors, state editors, society editors, editors of cooking columns and bridge columns, even University of Georgia professors and journalism teachers—all eyes fastened on Peggy, everybody listening raptly to the riotously exaggerated stories she told. Waves of laughter rolled over the room, splattered against the walls and swept out into the hallway through the open door. John Marsh sat beside his wife, looking admiringly at her as she talked, laughing with the audience and giving the word to all that she was the funniest thing in the whole wide world.

* * *

Sue and Peggy put on a skit at one of the Institute meetings, "acting the fool" as Sue herself would say. The photo of the two of them performing is the only one the family has of Sue with Peggy.

The friendship lasted. Sue's respect for her friend's desire for privacy led her to destroy 69 personal letters from Peggy.

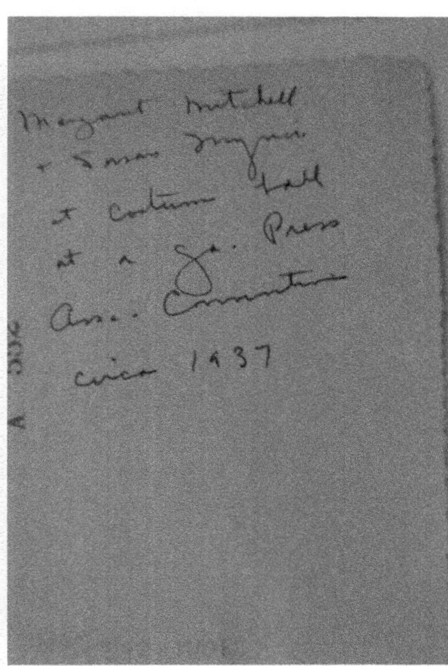

Caption in Sue's hand on back of photo of her and Mitchell in costume

Margaret Mitchell

Sunday

Sue, I wondered if yall had seen this. Who did Alicia Patterson visit in Macon? I think its a lure & ponder over "Elephants & Georgians never forget.

Love
Peggy

Note attached to news article by Alicia Patterson that Peggy sent to Sue.

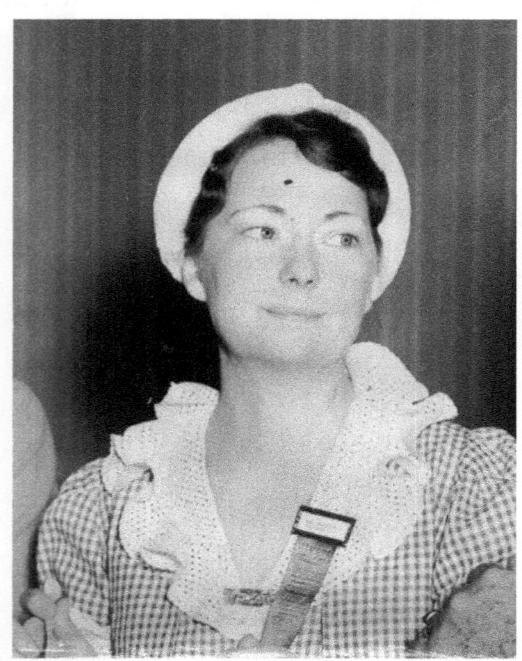

Photo of Peggy Sue kept framed in her home

AARON BERND

Sue lost Aaron Bernd when he died of complications of pneumonia and influenza on February 11, 1937. To give Sue emotional support, her friend Peggy Mitchell came to Macon and stayed with Sue for a few days. Aaron was only 42.

He had begun his work with *The Telegraph* in summers while in school and continued after graduation. With the outbreak of the First World War, he went overseas with the American Expeditionary Forces, and after the war, became a publicity agent for Fox Pictures, Inc.

Aaron returned to Macon when his father died, and took the positions of vice president and treasurer of his father's company, the G. Bernd Company, one of Macon's oldest. The long-established company dealt in leather and harness and hides in its early years and later with meat products. Aaron's brother served as president.

He also returned to *The Telegraph* as literary editor and editorial page columnist. For ten years, he authored a column called "Coleman Hill," ending it in 1933.

A graduate of the University of Georgia, class of 1914, he was a member of the Gridiron Club, Sphinx, Phi Beta Kappa, and other organizations. He obtained a post-graduate degree in literature from Columbia University.

Aaron was active in community social and business affairs, and was a charter member of the local Lions Club and served as an officer for several years.

Aaron's obituary in *The Telegraph* stated that "he was widely known in literary circles."

In her diary, written only for her eyes, Sue on several occasions referred to how much she missed Aaron.

Allie said that the Myricks expected Sue to marry Aaron, although at the time persons of Jewish heritage and Christian heritage seldom married. Aaron gave Sue a diamond ring of several carats, which is still in the family. Sue told her niece that the ring came from a "serious" boyfriend. The family thought of it as an engagement ring.

OTHER ADVENTURES

Sue loved fishing, and one of her fishing trips brought her lots of laughter later, when Roland Ellis told his version of the "scandalous" events to others. Sue recorded his story in her diary in 1937. Four went on the trip: Sue, Mr. W. T., Ruffin Chestney, and Roland Elllis.

We visited some people down there. No, I don't know who they were. I don't think anybody in our crowd knew them. I was introduced to them and they said how do you do and never spoke another word to me—or to any of us the rest of the visit.

They were three old ladies, about 50, who were old maids and wore spectacles; the house was a big shack on the bay and there was only one room.

The beds were ranged about the room and we all undressed before each other and slept together. Sue and I slept together. There was a bed apiece for the old maids and for Ruffin and Mr. W. T.

It was the funniest thing you ever saw. We had been out fishing the first evening, gigging flounders. About ten-thirty Sue and I decided we would go on to bed. All the lights were on and the three old ladies were in bed with their specs on, lying up on their pillows in high-necked long-sleeved night gowns, with the covers pulled up close around their shoulders and just watching us like Walter Winchell.

Sue didn't seem to mind. She just stripped off and put her pajamas on and got into the lower deck of the single bed. I tried very hard to put my pajama tops on and let them hide me while I put on the britches but didn't succeed very well. Then I said to Sue:

"Move over," and she said, "Roland, don't be a fool. Get on up top."

She giggled but she was embarrassed to death—because of the old ladies of course, not for any other reason. And she whispered to me to shut up, couldn't I see I was shocking the women to death, but I didn't care. I wanted them to have a good time. They were having the time of their lives already watching me undress and I thought we just as well give them some real fun.

So I said to Sue, "Very well. I'll get up in the top deck but I'm coming down after a while."

Then Mr. W. T. and Ruffin came in. Mr. W. T. serenely turned his back, stripped down to his skin and got into his pajamas. But poor Ruffin! He tried to hide behind the bed post and since he weighs 200 pounds it wasn't very easy. It took him half an hour to get undressed, trying to decide whether it was better to turn his back or his face toward whom. The beds were in a circle around the room. So far as I could see there was no need for Ruffin's dilemma. He looked just as bad in the rear as he did in the front. There was only a minor difference of where he was fattest.

Finally we got the lights out and I whispered to Sue, "I'm coming down in a minute," and all the old ladies sighed and sat up in bed.

Sue whispered, "Don't be a fool, Roland." But I had her worried. Every time I turned over all night the bed would creak and Sue would say, "Roland, don't you come down here," and wake everybody in the room.

Sue did not limit her life to her close friends, colleagues, Aaron, her nearby family, and her work. She owned a horse, competed in horse shows, and took a blue ribbon. Joe Popper of Macon stated that before his birth in 1932, his parents were "horseback buddies" with Sue and were in the same riding club. Joe recalls his parents telling him that they rode with Sue every Saturday and Sunday. They kept their horses in the same stable, operated by Wade Stepp and located across from Wesleyan College.

Joe laughed that his parents had to sell their horse when Joe was born—it was the middle of the depression, and the family could either keep the baby or keep the horse. His sister always said they should have kept the horse. Although the sale of their "Big Red" ended Joe's parents' riding with Sue every weekend, the friendship remained. In later years, Joe provided pro bono legal work for the Macon Little Theatre.

Sue later judged horse shows, as well as flower shows, beauty pageants, and diving competitions. She was uniquely qualified to judge the diving events, having herself won the gold medal at Battle Creek.

And she travelled. One of her favorite trips in those years was to New York City to see the Broadway plays. Usually some of *The Telegraph* staff would go, too, so they could split the cost of gas.

Sue travelled to France in 1936 and met Ernest Hemingway while there. She obtained his autograph, which he gave her to be pasted into one of his books.

In August 1939, after her Hollywood adventures and before the premiere of *Gone With The Wind*, Sue went to New York City to attend several plays, one of which starred Tallulah Bankhead. Sue wrote:

...*Little Foxes*—a dramatic and moving play that shows a very bad group of Southern capitalists at their worst, with Tallulah Bankhead in the role of what is probably the meanest woman in the world.

Sue had sent a note backstage, asking to speak to the star, and using the name George Cukor as a mutual friend. Tallulah agreed to see her.

And she had also agreed to see several other individuals. Right behind Sue entered several men—whom Tallulah greeted as "Darling" this and "Darling" that. Then she turned to Sue.

"You are Miss Myrick, aren't you? I am so glad to know you. Any friend of George Cukor's is a friend of mine, too."

She gave Sue no time to reply but turned to another man with "Darling…"

Tallulah's attention stayed with the men the whole time Sue was there, but, Sue said, "There was much chatter and gay laughter, and in a little while I said I must go."

Tallulah encouraged Sue to stay awhile longer, and when Sue said that she did have to leave, Tallulah said, "It was wonderful of you to come back to see me. Please pardon me for not getting up. I have gotten so used to that corset (worn in the play) during the last three hours that it makes my back weak to take it off. I have bad manners, so do pardon me."

Then Tallulah laughed a throaty, husky laugh: "Anyway, I am just a lazy Southern gal, you know."

Sue left, but said, "I felt sort of dazed but I know now why Tallulah Bankhead has made such a hit both in London and in America. She is a glamorous creature and a wonderful actress."

As Sue's career advanced with the paper, she became "entangled" in the world of Southern writers. Her cousin was married to William Faulkner's best friend, Philip Stone. From her talking to her nieces about various women writers, such as Eudora Welty and Carson McCullers, the nieces think that she knew them. She knew the famous—Peggy, of course, as well as Celestine Sibley, and Flannery O'Connor, and the lesser-famous, such as Harry Hervey.

We know of her friendship with Marjorie Kinnan Rawlings from a letter Ms. Rawlings wrote Sue:

Bless your heart for your good letter about "Cross Creek."

It is such a queer book that I had no way of knowing whether it would be liked or not, and it is good to have applause from you.

My husband and I had a brief visit with John and Peggy Marsh when we were in Atlanta recently. Peggy was in high spirits, as usual, and enchanting all the visiting firemen. Best wishes and lots of thanks.

(signature) Marjorie Kinnan Rawlings

PART IV

GONE WITH THE WIND

THE ROAD TO HOLLYWOOD

I had the good fortune to be a good friend of Peggy's. As almost everybody knows, it was through her friendship with me that Selznick International Pictures hired me to serve as a technical advisor on the movie *Gone With The Wind*.

In 1936, Sue was chair of the casting committee for the Macon Little Theatre, and that fall she received a telegram asking her to arrange some auditions for possible performers in the upcoming movie *Gone With The Wind*. Margaret Mitchell was one of the four who came to Macon for the auditions. At the time, David O. Selznick was still prodding Mitchell to come to Hollywood to advise on the movie. Katherine Brown (Selznick's representative in New York, variously called Kay and Kath), David O. Selznick, and Anton Bundsman (a New York director) arrived on December 7, with Mitchell, for the auditions. Sue had arranged for thirty local hopefuls to try out.

As well as helping with the auditions, Sue took the GWTW group on a driving tour of middle Georgia for them to see the winter-barren fields of Georgia's red soil. She constantly reminded them that the plantation houses they were seeing in middle Georgia were not typical of those in North Georgia at the time of The War Between the States.

At one point, she took—or sent—still photographers to Westover Plantation house, home of her sister Lil, where they photographed the boxwood gardens to have a reference for "building" the gardens at Twelve Oaks. No movie film, however, was shot there.

Margaret Mitchell refused to become more involved with the movie than her visit to Macon, and she repeatedly told Selznick that she would not go to Hollywood and would not select the actors and actresses for the movie or participate in writing the script. Mr. W. T. Anderson, publisher of *The Macon Telegraph*, wrote Mitchell and suggested that Mitchell recommend Sue to Selznick as an advisor on Southern matters.

Mitchell agreed with Anderson that Sue was suited to the job and would be the best the South had to offer. Mitchell then wrote Selznick, and her letter in part said:

Her grandpa, old General Myrick, had the biggest and whitest colyumned (sic) *house in Georgia, at Milledgeville. It's still there, a lovely place but no longer in Myrick hands. The family lost it due to hard times. Sue is the youngest* (Note: Sue was the fifth of eight) *child of a Confederate soldier and God knows she heard enough about the old days. Being poor as Job's turkey, she was raised up in the country and she knows good times and bad, quality folks and poor whites, Crackers and town folks. And good grief, what she doesn't know about Negroes! She was raised up with them. And she loves and understands them. Since going on the paper, she has been the paper's official representative at most of the negro affairs of her section (of the country). Mr. W. T. Anderson, owner of her paper, is strong for the colored folks and tries to get a square deal for them and the saying among the colored folks in the district is that "De Race is got two friends in dis County, sweet Jesus and de* Macon Telegraph.*" So whenever there's a colored graduation if Mr. W. T. can't be there to make a speech, Sue goes, and if the colored P.T.A. wants to be addressed by Mr. Anderson and he can't make it, Sue does the addressing—the same holds for funerals and awarding prizes.*

Moreover Sue is as competent a newspaper woman as we have in the section. She can-and-does-do everything from advice to the lovelorn and the cooking page to book reviews and politics and hangings. But the main thing that recommends her to me is her common sense and her utter lack of sentimentality about what is tearfully know as "The Old South." She knows its good points and she doesn't slur over its bad points. She knows her section and its people and she loves them both but she is not unaware of their faults or the charm of both people and section. In other words, she is a common sense, hard headed person with an awful lot of knowledge about Georgia people and Georgia ways, not only of the time but of times past.

Sue's experience on the paper with book reviews added to her qualifications for her work on GWTW. Her work with the Little Theatre and her attendance at many shows added to these qualifications. See Appendix VII for an insight to Sue's feelings for books, shows, and performers, as well as a description of a "frock" that she purchased for a special event.

Sue received a wire from Katharine Brown on March 27, 1937, to meet with George Cukor in Atlanta. W. T. Anderson notified The Associated Press of Cukor's selecting Sue to serve "in an advisory capacity" on the movie. On April 2, the AP sent out Sue's picture, noting only that "she is a member of *The Macon Telegraph* staff." The AP waited for *The Telegraph* to release the story first.

On March 29, 1937, Sue wrote on *Telegraph* letterhead to Margaret Mitchell to share the laughter she and Aaron Bernd had found in one more rumor about Peggy:

Peggy:

I don't know just what is the date of this but I am sure it was shortly after the publication of G with the W. One day when Arnold W. Little had been here and Aaron had talked to him, Aaron came to my office and brought me a scrap of paper on which Little had typed this:

Miss Mitchell took the title of her novel from a poem by Arnold W. Little, of Hampton, Ga., who is her favorite poet. The complete quotation, from which Miss Mitchell selected her phrase runs:

"—And buffetings, oh, little preciousnesses,
Are like last summer's leaf, gone with the wind,
The expansive wind, which rumbles as it goes."

Aaron dared me to send the thing to the A P or the *New York Times* or such and we giggled over it mightily.

Thought you'd like to have it.

Sue

SUE'S DIARY

Sue began a diary sometime before 1937 and continued it until spring 1939, when she became too swamped with her duties on the movie, with writing her twice weekly columns for *The Telegraph*, and writing Mitchell to keep her posted on the goings-on.

The diary and her letters to Mitchell and to others give us insight into the emotional swirl Sue felt in the months before going west and the early weeks of the movie production. We see Sue without her usual composure and self-confidence. On the other hand, the tone of her memos to Selznick and others reek with confidence—while showing great respect.

We don't know when she began her diary; the pages we have begin in October 1937. The earlier pages referred to in her first lines would have certainly contained details of her relationship with Aaron Bernd. We get only shadowy references to Aaron in the portion of her dairy that we do have.

While Peggy was in Macon for Aaron's funeral, Peggy stayed with Sue; probably to keep Sue's mind off of her loss of Aaron, Peggy kept Sue talking about the movie and what if this or maybe they'd do that.

Sue's diary entries given below are intermixed with letters she wrote to Mitchell, to family members, to GWTW personnel and to others, and are given in chronological order. Only excerpts are given for some of the memos. Letters from Mitchell to Sue are not included.

Diary October 9, 1937

It's been ten days since I wrote a line in this thing and plenty has happened. Spent the weekend with Peggy. The UDC (United Daughters of the Confederacy) held its convention here and brought the finest laugh in years. Had supper in the back yard with Eddie, Ken and Art.

About the Margaret Mitchell Marsh weekend. Peggy telephoned to come up and I was delighted of course. She is always kind. And she is more fun than anybody in the world. The only person alive who could take what she has taken and be completely unchanged. I knew her nearly eight years before she wrote GWTW and she is just the same girl now she was then, unspoiled, unchanged in every way. I couldn't have helped wallowing in excitement and riches and fame and I'd have accepted all the literary teas and acclaim and probably have made a perfect ass of myself.

We went to Lee Edwards' to tea. Enjoyed seeing Lee's painting, especially his red road and the deep cuts along the road with Georgia red clay well done and very good pines, all soft looking as they are in spite of the sharpness of the needles in reality.

Rushed home from the tea, guests for dinner. Peg changed in nothing flat. I took more time to put on a new greenish-gold, changeable taffeta frock. Always thought I'd like to wear a changeable taffeta. Makes me look a little fat, I'm afraid, but I AM fat, so what the hell! Lights make it look lavender and it is so elegant feeling and swishes divinely. Very full skirt with a little up-in-front-of-the ankles and touches in back. Peggy swore I stepped on the front of it and tore it and just cut it out to look like that.

The pretty and attractive Ann Cooper came to dinner along with Fannie Lou Harris and her husband Lloyd from the Marietta paper. Also Sammy Tupper, amusing cuss who thinks ladies should be ladies but is capable of delightful conversation, remembers everything he ever read and quotes entertainingly. Angus and Medora Perkerson dropped by on their way to East Lake Club. Angus, elderly, gaunt, Scotch-looking as his name, has gone nuts on the rumba! They brought me a book, *Scandals of Clochemerle*, translation from French, typical French novel, dirty and amusing. All about a quarrel caused in a little town by reason of a urinal erected by the mayor for political preferment. Grand illustrations. Angus reviewed it.

Sometimes I think I must be right cute for people ARE nice to me. But then I don't see why others don't take to me so there must be something wrong. Know I am growing more irritable as days go by. Maybe it is hard likker. Maybe it was Aaron's death. Maybe it is old age.

Most fun at Peggy's was Sunday when we slept late, ate leisurely breakfast, called on Mr. (Eugene) Mitchell, Peggy's dad, and spent the afternoon just talking. Nobody talks so well as Peggy and that slow sweet John is just grand. We talked about the medicines in our respective cabinets in our youth. All of us depended on turpentine and Peggy and I discovered a mutual interest in Darby's Fluid and John and I had mutual experience with taking two drops of kerosene on sugar for croup and all of us recalled that no doctors ever came to our houses. Cost too much, and doctors were too far away anyhow. Peggy told a wild story of sewing up the abdomen of a Negro cook who had been cut half in two by her jealous husband and who was back at work in a week!

Peggy has German edition which is very amusing. Mammy says "Ach Gott" instead of "Lawsy" and THAT'S funny. And the cover is amazing! Scarlett looks like Peggy. Melanie looks like a corpse, Rhett looks like something that never was on land or sea, and Prissy is as white as the others, with a round fat German face and kinks.

The Swedish (I think) edition is in three volumes. The Danish to be out next week has illustrations that are beautiful. Rhett would make any woman swoon with pleasure. Scarlett is beautiful. The Danish artist got the feel of the book well. Dutch edition is pirated and Peggy is suing so she has no copy!

Going to the Dunwody's dance Monday night with Bob Quinlan. I am delighted that Ken is going along with us, and the Albert Jelkses—Frank Hawkins, maybe, also.

So fine at Eddie's back yard party; only Ken and me; fried eggs, grand potatoes cooked in celery soup, baked ham, avocado and tomato salad, coffee. The starlight is so lovely. Saturn, Jupiter and Mars all in evening sky now.

Can never look at stars without thinking of Aaron.

October 20, 1937

Went to Bob Quinlan's Saturday night with Roland Ellis. Sunday afternoon, to the Library with Ken to the Art Association meeting which was not much. Pictures all lousy as I look at them. To dinner with Kenyons and Perry and Kenneth.

Sent receipt for spoon bread to John Winterich today and am sending him a peck of white meal. I think of Aaron always when I think of Winterich.

Wrote to Hobe Erwin, inviting him to eat dinner with me when he comes to Georgia. He is to do the interiors for *Gone With The Wind* and he was very nice to me when he was in Atlanta with George Cukor last spring. He tried to put me wise about things and was most delightful company. He is a big shot decorator but a gentleman and like a Southerner in many ways and very simple and unaffected and likeable. Hope he does come here.

I had a hope that the letter to Erwin might bring me some Selznick news, too. Not a word from Kay Brown since last July when she said she would let me hear again as soon as they settled on production date. I somehow have a sick feeling that I am strung and that George Cukor has forgot he asked me to take the job and now he doesn't care whether he has me or not since there is such a mess about it all. Fiddler said on radio last night that *Jezebel* with Bette Davis was going to take the gloss from GWTW and that Selznick had been a fool to delay so long. He bought the book in June 1936 and production was planned for last Spring, but no soap for some reason. They offer various ones but I don't believe anything they say any more.

Letter from Jerry Spiero yesterday. I wonder if Jerry considered it a bother to answer my letters. I think of him as a last link with Aaron somehow and hate to not write.

I wonder if I am going to have another thrill so long as I live. Just another man to take me somewhere. Yes, it's a kick being popular at a dance and getting lots of breaks and having friends, but what an awful empty feeling when I want to tell Aaron all about it and he isn't here. I think maybe the hardest of all is going upstairs in the evening after a show or party and missing the feeling of how it was when he was here.

I just listened to Richard Strauss' "Death and Transfiguration." The beat of the tympani was the beat of a man's heart, fighting for life, trying to keep on beating. It was so real to me, so reminiscent of the two days of agony when he (Aaron) died, that I had to fight not to weep before the group who were listening with me.

October 27, 1937

Letter from Gene Fowler, thanking me for the review of *Salute to Yesterday,* thrilled me to death. He writes: "The book is definitely not a woman's book yet you reviewed it so intelligently and so broadly that I bow from the hips. Young lady I am grateful."

November 20, 1937

A fine cold morning and the Chevy would not start!

Roland expressed himself as delighted with the fact that I have a ditch light on the Chevy. "Might have killed myself driving into a ditch between Fredonia and *The Telegraph.*" Said he lay awake nights worrying about me! Fool!

Sid and Marjorie, George and Blythe and Bob to supper

tonight. To dinner with Roland at noon tomorrow (Sunday). Some fun!

Don't let anybody tell you that oysters on the half shell are not worth what they cost at a hotel. We tried to open some last night.

To supper last Saturday night with Miss Florence Bernd, Roland Ellis and Mrs. Ellis and Bob Q. (Quinlan). Roland and Miss Florence made me furious they never let me talk at all! Seven times—I counted—I tried to get in my word when Miss F paused to grab a breath but Roland would grab the conversation. Then he'd stop and I'd try again and SHE'd grab the conversation. Mrs. E and I looked pleasant; Bob slept.

Note: Florence was Aaron's cousin and a long-time teacher in Bibb county, where a school bears her name.

On Wednesday this week drove over with Perry and Roland to hear Emile Baume at GSCW. Baume was marvelous. I felt sure Aaron was at the Baume concert to laugh with me when Emile crossed over his hands. We had so much fun laughing about crossing over hands when we played Gilbert and Sullivan.

Over to Sid's after the concert where Baume had the time of his life with Roland's French and that of Sid and Marjorie and Rose Capel. I could almost understand Baume for his eyes and hands are so expressive. He is enthusiastic and his smile is endearing. He's a honey. Hope he comes back here some time. Did a story for the paper about him. He says Georgia "remembers him of the Souzth of Franze."

Joe Popper asked: "If two trains left New York and Chicago at the same time, the one from Chicago running fifty mph and the one from New York running sixty mph, how old am I?" One man answered "Thirty-eight." Another asked, "How did you know?" Reply: "I have a nephew who is nineteen, and he is half-crazy."

Mr. W. T. just got back from a hunting trip near Darien. His first trip, he hunted in a CANOE and it turned over with him. This trip, he went with a guide who knew nothing about the marshes, to shoot marsh hens. Tide went down, they couldn't get home. Had to walk half a mile in marsh mud, sinking to his knees every step and the guide had to pull him loose several times when the mud sucked him down so hard he couldn't pull his feet out! He laughed. I would have been so mad I'd busted! I aint such a good sport, it seems.

Cold weather may mess up my party tonight; porch can get mighty cold but maybe it will warm up before night.

Ken has asked me to go to the Thanksgiving dance of Junior League. Pleased and flattered to be invited, but don't expect to have such a good time as the floor of the auditorium is hard to dance on. Hope a crowd goes with us so we can sit and imbibe and not have to dance too much.

Thursday, December 8, 1937

Snowed today, but all melted before ten. Nasty cold weather, the second spell of the year. Down to 21 Sunday and cold all week. No promise of rising temperatures, either.

Lunch with Sallie Aiken who suggested I write down the numberless rumors about Peggy Marsh.

From Allie, I heard the other day this new one. Al was at lunch with friends in Vancouver and another guest remarked that it was too bad Margaret Mitchell had lost her mind completely and was in an institution for the insane. Al said nothing, waiting to see what else would come. Hostess remarked, "Mrs. Bowden, your sister is a good friend of Miss Mitchell's isn't she?" Al said yes, and the guest began to apologize and said feebly that she had heard it.

Also, Al reports an acquaintance in Portland who said it was strange Georgia authors never wrote their own books. Caroline Miller's husband wrote *Lamb in his Bosom,* and Miss Mitchell's father wrote *Gone With The Wind.* Mr. Mitchell, it seemed, was for forty years head of Georgia's Department of Archives and did the research on the state's time and wrote the book and just gave the credit to this daughter.

Peggy long ago told me she had heard her leg was off,

first heard off to the knee, then to the hip. She is reported to be blind, feeble minded, to be divorced from John. Many persons have met her on the street and asked if she were not ashamed to have left her husband after he wrote her book for her and to have taken the twins from Mr. Miller. She says she is glad Caroline and Mr. Miller are both remarried—maybe now nobody will get them mixed up. John says, "No, my dear, Caroline will be pregnant in a few more months and everybody in Georgia will think we are having a baby."

With my Gert Stein mind, I jump now...

The trip to Philadelphia to the Army and Navy game was marvelous. Edwina and Arthur Nims are almost unexcelled as travelling companions. Of course, nobody could be more fun to travel with than was Aaron. Nimses are swell folks and Allie liked them and it was grand to see Edwin Sr. break down and laugh at Eddie's little whimsical remarks. They clicked just right with Edwin Jr. too.

NOTE: Sue wrote a by-lined article about the game.

December 10, 1937

Found my log of journey to New York in February 1935. ... Returning to Washington, spent second night at Sanford, NC, the 19th. Flowers for my birthday at breakfast table next morning.

Monday night, to *Children's Hour*. Tuesday, *Tobacco Road* in afternoon. *Romeo and Juliet* that night. Wednesday, Benton Murals and Brooklyn to see Cardini. Lobster house for dinner. *Anything Goes*. Al Frymir's, and then to Howdy Club. Clyde Beatty. Friday afternoon, Carnegie Hall, Toscanini conducting Brahms variations on a theme by Haydn, C Minor.

December 12, 1937

Saturday evening had guests for supper. Served ham slices with apricots which received wild applause. Had spoon bread, still popular in a big way. Eddie and Art, Fran and Del Kenyon and Roland Ellis. Queer coincidence;

during the evening a discussion of suicide went on and on while I tried to change the drift of conversation thinking that Roland's father had killed himself and it would be better not to bring it up. On Sunday, I said as much to Fran, whereupon Del remarked that his father committed suicide after the crash of 29. Then I recalled that Bob Quinlan's father also killed himself.

Saturday evening was QUITE an evening. Roland and Bob didn't want to go to bed at one when the others left so we started for the el Dorado—met Bobby Norris who drove us out. Danced a while. Home about 2:30 and Roland still refused to go to bed. George Burt's light on so we went down there. Ukulele, grand opera, hymns, scrambled eggs.

December 18, 1937

Going to Atlanta at noon to see *You Can't Take It with You.* Date with Peggy for dinner and bed-sitting session.

Found log of trip to Miami so recording it here: Leaving Macon 7:25 Jan 13th 1936, Tip, Aaron, Frank Hawkins and I. ... Went to Miami and stopt with friend of Aaron's sister. Caught boat that night to Cuba.

December 20, 1937

In Atlanta to show and dinner in Ansley with Peggy and John. They are nuts from lawsuits. The one against Billy Rose comes up in January. Peggy has been twice to see the State Department in Washington about the Dutch piracy of the book. Says they can't send a battle ship to Holland and demand her right and they've been grand to her. Trouble seems to be that the United States is not a member of the Berne Convention which all the rest of the world belongs to. So, any country can steal a book if it is copyrighted only in the United States. Some technicality about simultaneous publication of GWTW in Canada and the United States. Actually publication was simultaneous, but some of the first books in New York carry imprint of May while the Canadian books carry imprint of June.

Peggy told about Bessie's marriage. (Bessie was Mitchell's

maid.) Seems that Mr. Latham (of MacMillian) was down and Bessie told Peggy she wanted to get married but would postpone it because Peggy had company. But Peggy said no, the marriage was the most important thing in Bessie's life and they could take Mr. Latham out to dinner. And Mr. Latham would like to be invited to the wedding, too. So, Bessie had her choir of the Little Friendly Baptist Church to sing.

Seems when Mr. Latham came down that time to give Peggy the Pulitzer Prize, Bessie had the choir put on a song service for him and he was greatly intrigued. So Peggy and John and Mr. Latham and Ann Cooper and Malora went to the wedding at Bessie's house. Ann Cooper wore Juliet cap, low-cut evening gown of taffeta and swiped some of each of the seven varieties of perfume Peggy had as a gift from George Cukor. The white guests sat near the stove. The colored boys stoked the stove every few minutes. The perfume smelled to heaven!

The choir sang "Roll That Stone Away" and so on. The pianist, colored, struck a chord on the un-tuned piano and rose up and announced she would sing, "Didn't it Rain," And didn't it rain indeed, O Jonah, didn't it rain. O God how it rained.

Then the wedding. Congratulations from white guests and Peggy, who had presented the wedding cake, huge and towering and filled with rings, thimbles and so on, suggested to Bessie they'd have a piece of cake and go. The groom whispered to Bessie wasn't the white folks going to stay and get some ice cream. But Bessie started her wedded life off in the way a successful wife must and glowered at him and whispered back, "Shut up, nigger!"

December 27, 1937

Christmas was very fine. It's been the most wonderful weather for Christmas I ever saw.

Aunt Josie got the boudoir cap.

Back in about 1923, Lil was at Columbia and a girl who was going home for Christmas gave Lil a boudoir cap as a present. She gave it several days early because she was leaving. Lil, tickled because no one of our family EVER wore a boudoir cap, sent it home for a present for one of us. We were all amused and the next Christmas some bright member of the family—the name is lost in antiquity—suggested that we send it on to some other member of the family. We did, and the darn thing got started on what seems to be an endless journey. I remember one Christmas when Lil was enamored of some fellow, Al and I slipped out and wrapped the thing in a box that Edwin had sent roses in. We took it to the post office, mailed it special delivery. Almost before we got back to the house on Liberty Street in Milledgeville, the door bell rang. The postman brought the special package for Lil. Since it was obviously flowers, Mama consented to Lil's opening it, for she never let us open things until Christmas morning. Lil, agog over the box of roses which must surely have come from the admirer, opened the package to find the cap. One Christmas it went to Nan (a cousin). One Christmas, it went to me on the tree, in a package from Edwin, Sr., fooling me completely. It always manages to fool us. Maybe we are dumb!

Berry Rozar married a girl—Malora—from Chicago and brought her down for Christmas, so Lil and I put the cap on the tree for her. That poor girl, knowing nothing of the tradition, was a funny sight when she tried to look grateful but could not conceal the feeling of "What the hell! This old cap of broken lace and faded, worn lavender ribbon!" We explained, and she howled and said she felt she was really a part of the family. That spring, Lil married, and Malora sent the cap to her, in a large Marshall Field box, marked "fragile."

Well, Lil sent it to the boat for a going-away present when I went to Hawaii. I presented it to Allie as a visitor's gift when I arrived. It came to Thulia when she was born. It went to Al when she was very ill in Vancouver. Al sent it to Louise Green as a wedding gift, sending a letter a day in advance saying she had always felt Louise was a part of the family though she is only a fifth cousin. And she wanted

Louise to have something that was a Myrick heirloom.

So Louise sent it to Aunt Josie, marked perishable and open at once. It arrived Friday morning.

Saturday, Christmas Day, Aunt Josie gave it to Zoë Rozar Moore.

Several versions of the start of the boudoir cap's journeys have also travelled through the family.

January 3, 1938

Slept ten hours Saturday-Sunday, again an hour yesterday afternoon, and to bed before eleven last night. Am really starting the New Year today, for those two hectic days that came first in 1938 don't count. Parties and more parties!

Monday night at Bob's; Tuesday night Albert and Doris Jelks'; Wednesday night Margaret Haley's dance (but first to Bibb Manufacturing, where I did a reading); Thursday afternoon, to Red Dog Farm for supper. Friday night with Boots to see Marshal Daugherty's new sculpting. Then to Boots' house to see the New Year in; and to Len Berg's for sandwiches and to bed about two a.m.

Saturday evening to Perry's with Dave Probes. Dave took me to lunch Saturday and we listened to the football game Saturday p.m. Rice beat LSU and California beat Alabama.

Sunday to dinner with the W. T. Andersons—and the best roast beef I ever saw.

So sorry that Edward J. Neil, AP correspondent, killed while covering the civil war in Spain. Excellent reporter. The whole of Spain not worth the death of that one swell writer.

Sue's social schedule for the holiday week was heavier than a more routine week. Her diary indicates that she did, however, attend several social events every week—sometimes only supper "out" with some of the group of friends; sometimes supper "in" at a friend's home; other times she would go to supper and a show and afterwards a drink with one or more of the group; sometimes she was hostess; sometimes she and her date would go to supper and dancing. With her active social life, Sue seldom spent evenings alone.

Her friends apparently united to keep her busy to keep her mind off her loss of Aaron.

January 5, 1938

A letter this morning from Kay Brown indicates that I am not yet in the discard pile with Selznick. Shall have to get busy trying to put things in shape so if I get the call I can leave. Income tax to make out and must consult Mrs. Ellis and her friend about some things.

Wonder just what I shall be expected to do when I do—no, IF I do go to Hollywood. A colossal bluff is what I reckon I'll be. But even if I am ignorant I shall know more about the real South than they can ever read in books. I shall have to do a good job for Peggy's sake. She has been so very fine and so generous to me.

Everybody else seems to laze along much as I do and accomplish nothing much—yet they don't seem to even care. That's the worst of me! I don't DO anything about advancing. I just worry about it. I must begin doing more writing. I certainly do kill a lot of time.

Wednesday Jan 12, 1938

True, the thirteenth is not until tomorrow but today is—by the week—a year since Aaron, Frank, Tip and I set out for Florida. It was foggy and misty at seven a.m. when we left my front door. It misted all the way to Fitzgerald and we drove slowly but no weather could dampen the exuberance of our spirits! Will I ever forget it! I doubt it.

...On to Jax...and on down the coast where the water was so beautiful we nearly died. At Daytona I was driving and we rode down the beach and the setting sun cast colors from the clouds to the waters, making rainbows everywhere and bringing to the water's edge brilliant rose and pale green and soft yellow and gold that blended into the lavender from where the breakers curled over. Way, way out, where the sea met the sky the master artist had painted a blending of tints that were breath taking. O world, I cannot hold thee close enough! Particularly the world near the Florida coast.

On, then, to New Smyrna, where the streets jog and where we finally found Stella (Tip's daughter) and deposited Tip. Then at dusk, down an inland road, bumpy with tattered pavement but Frank and I never felt a bump. Poor Aaron, who was driving, was sober! But after dark, Frank took the wheel and Aaron and I sat together. Ah! Jane! Jane! You have only a faint understanding but you are about the only person who knows at all.

That night at Sanford. Next day—but why go on! I hope—I almost feel—that he is grinning that engaging and irresistible grin, chuckling to the angels (who are probably playing on Saxophones for him and maybe An Angel Duke Ellington is conducting!) and knowing that I am remembering and saying, "A year ago, today."

January 15 1938

Did a publicity bit for the polio foundation ball. It is pretty bad, but the story is the impossible sort of stuff anyway. Brought back vivid memories of Warm Springs trips we made so often. Wish I had been keeping a diary then.

Remember now, the trip over with John Winterish and the stop at Talbotton and his comments about peach blossoms and what fun we had. Weeks later, Aaron and I went over and from Talbotton wired John about the men who had been sitting on a bench in front of a Talbotton filling station. John was intrigued because the lazy looking chaps never even moved all the time we stopped there for a drink and a Rest. We wired "Bench warmers still here." The wire arrived "Berch warners still here." Caused much merry comment back and forth.

To lunch today with Ken who has told various ones the lunch is in honor of my going to Hollywood! He phoned Perry, "Come to lunch. I am having it for Sue who is going to Hollywood – Saturday." Perry thought he meant I was leaving Saturday! He told Eddie Nims the same tale and she said, "Shall I bring a gift?" He said yes, something suitable for Hollywood, and Eddie asked "A bed jacket?"

Somebody asked Frank Durham if we weren't planning to do Ibsen's *A Doll's House*, and he said, "We isben practicing it."

To Elliot Dunwody's tonight for supper at eight with Durhams, Hebe, Blythe and Marjorie Popper.

Peggy writes that Kay Brown writes Mr. Kurtz of Atlanta that things are worse than ever and nobody knows anything! More or less—Selznick deal with MGM seems to be off and no Scarlett yet. And if the MGM deal is off, no Clark Gable for Rhett. Maybe, says *Variety*, Gary Cooper or Ronald Coleman will be Rhett. I hope it is Gary if I go out. Katie writes that somebody told her George Cukor always gets whom he wants, so I hope he still wants me. He certainly did want me last spring when he was here. The old violet-scented rascal.

Did some excellent flash light pictures and feel very proud of them. Using them in *The Telegraph*—publicity for *Doll's House*.

January 19, 1938

Saturday Ken had a farewell luncheon for me. Says if I aint going to Hollywood, I should be—they are tired of hearing about it and now I HAVE to go. If I don't they get the presents back. Cutest of all was the poem from Blythe, who gave me a toy cannon:

"This is for Su
San Myrick, who
If she wishes may u-
Se it to start
With a bang, a heart-
Stirring career, a part-
Icularly thrilling
And glamorous billing
As an aide quite willing
To assist in producing
Peggy's grand and seducing
Story – to help in reducing
Errors in fact,

Blunders in tact
Whatever is lack-
Ing in the mind
Of those behind
Gone with the Wind.

Blythe also wrote: "There was to be more on the subject of using this cannon in the battle only if it looks Confederate enough. But I took sick—maybe on account of this. Anyhow, with things like they are with the Selznick outfit at this moment, maybe you'd better use it on the whole crew."

Louise gave me a Love Bug pin; Bob, perfume; Ken, perfume; P, handkerchief; the Kenyons, Drink A Bite to Eat when you get sick of Sunkist orange juice. Eddie threatens a bed jacket as the most useful gift for Hollywood.

January 20, 1938

Went to hear Angna Enters last night. No wonder they call her America's greatest artist of pantomime. What she does is present a dramatic sketch without words. Her "Field Day" almost killed Carrie Allen and me! The bloomers and middy looked so like GSCW (GN&IC's new name). Waving the flag at the end made me think of Nebraska and the Junior Red Cross pageant when we had—of all things—a FLAG DRILL.

The American ballet—1914-1916—was the opening number. The piano played *Dark Town Strutter's Ball, Too Much Mustard, Chicago,*" and so on. She foxtrotted and one-stepped and I loved it! But how Aaron would have enjoyed that number!

After the concert we went to Sid's and met the lady. Sid was very swell to me, insisted I should tell Negro stories to Miss Enters. When I thanked him for a lovely evening he insisted that HE thank me—I always contributed so much to a party, he said.

It pleased me greatly for I often wonder if I am still giving evidence of being shy and if I am sometimes loud and if people like me as much as I should like to be liked. And when Sid was so kind I was all ego and thrill.

January 27, 1938

The senate (Georgia) is still debating liquor bill and probably we are still going to be dry in spite of the fact that you can drive up to a score of places in down-town Macon, blow your horn and get curb service on rye, Scotch, or what have you and in spite of the thriving business done by native corn products. La me!

Pleased with myself today. George just came in and said the story I did about the Asher Ayers house was swell.

Have also finished the story of Papa and the gramophone and the feathers on the rooster. Am going to strike high and try *The New Yorker* and if it comes back shall try *In the Lion's Mouth*, and after that, *Scribner's*.

Note: The family has no record of this article.

Last night to Dempsey coffee shop for dinner. Martini, oysters on half shell, steak platter with string beans, carrots, green peas and French fries. Very nice indeed—85 cents for dinner, not including oysters or cocktail.

Note: This is one of the few times Sue does not mention sharing mealtime with someone.

January NO FEBRUARY 2, 1938

I wonder if the fact that I have written January instead of February three times this morning proves psychologically that I hate the month of February and carry in the back of my mind the tragedy the month held last year.

Note: The death of Aaron.

I started out to write about the fine week end I had with Jane Wilkes. She telephoned me from Atlanta to invite me to go to Cordele with her to see her granny and aunt. I went, and Granny is an inspiration! At 83, and slightly crippled by arthritis, she still is full of pep and interest in things, but doesn't get about well.

Born at the time when she met the Reconstruction Era right slap in the face, mother of half a dozen children, widowed when they were young, she has had nothing but hardships all her life. But she is happy, cheerful, patient, full of fun, completely adorable. Said she was glad she lived to see the time when it was decent for a woman to take a drink, and she encouraged Jane and me to have a drink before supper. She cooked the birds for supper herself—so they would be just right for her adored Janie and Janie's guest (me). They were grand too.

She said there was nothing to do in Cordele but eat and she wanted us to have good eats.

Doc, the hound that Jane loves so, kept us awake all night. If it had been anybody but Jane, I'd have been mad as hell but Jane is such a darling I merely thought it was funny.

February 14, 1938

For a Valentine I take my freedom from rehearsal and doing a show. "Free, Christina"—it feels swell to have hair pins out of my hair. I wore tight curls to look like the nineties and I slept in hair pins four nights and felt as if I were a dog with the mange my head itched so and hair pins stuck so!

I am pasting clippings to show that people thought we were good. I thought the performance was unusually good and was not amateurish which reminds me of a fine story.

Henry Kendall adores the Little Theatre and resents it when anybody takes a crack at it. Mrs. Odom, mother of Crockett Odom who is organist at the Methodist Church, came into his bakery and Henry said, "Mrs. Odom, how did you like the show?"

"It was very nice for amateurs. But I don't care for amateur productions," she said in her best condescending fashion.

"Well, some people are like that," said Henry. "Personally, I like amateur things; for instance I like very much to hear Crockett play. He's just an amateur, but I like him."

Mrs. Odom faded out.

But I was so pleased when a friend of Frank Durham's

(the director) from Columbia, S. C., told me I was the best in the show, that my performance was the most finished of any.

Jerry Spiero is such a nice person, wrote me a grand letter on the eleventh. I broke a rule or something and went to the cemetery (Aaron's grave) with Bert and Flora. Did me good, too, though I was a bit conscience stricken.

* * *

Spring is almost more than I can bear. The daffodils are all over town—have been for several weeks. The spirea is like snow piles and the grass is greening. For a week, now, I have watched the elm buds swelling and growing pinky-brown and showing each morning a faintly increasing trace of misty green. Today, there are definite greens veiling the pinky tans now and the riotously lovely color of the flowering quince is beginning to fade the least bit.

But wisteria blossoms will be too much to bear! Much harder even than the yellow bells or forsythia or whatever those little yellow things on long sticks are called.

Yesterday I worked in P's garden, pulling out chick weed and watching him fertilize and grub and water the pansies and tulips and plant some little blue things.

There is a pear tree at the foot of Coleman Hill that is dressed in white frills and the softest pink-green ever. In some back yards, there are already pink peach blossoms.

March 7, 1938

Just to kill time yesterday got to thinking of Lewis Carroll and did these as I drove to Milledgeville.

He thought he saw a cedar tree
A standing by the bank.
He looked again and saw it was
An automobile crank.
"Oh, dear," he said, "the fifteenth drink
I have myself to thank."

He thought he saw an engineer a lying by the track.

He looked again and saw it was the railroad on its back.
"O yes," he said, "the motor bus. I guess I'll take a hack."

He thought he saw a pen and pad beside the telephone.
He looked again and saw it was a governmental loan.
"O Mr. Morgantheau," he wailed, "will you leave me alone?"

He thought he saw a power dam a standing cross the way.
He looked again and saw it was a power dam okay.
"If you don't leave the house," he said, "I'll tell the T V A."

March 12, 1938

Letter from Peggy indicates nobody at Hollywood ever heard of me and Cukor doesn't know his own mind so it looks as if it were all a pipe dream about my going out.

Last Saturday night I went to Peyton's and Kat's to a cocktail party. ... And after the party Fran and Del and their guests and Bob and I "Tavern-ed" and it was pretty boring. I don't suppose I shall every completely enjoy another Tavern dance with no Aaron there.

April 8, 1938

Going to supper with Mr. W. T., John and Peggy and Jane, Ken and George B and Blythe. Then to a show and on to Bob's for a party, adding Hebe and Perry and Fran and Del. We'll have to sit on each others' laps, Bob's studio is so small.

Wrote Kath Brown that I am coming to New York on the 25th. She replied she was delighted and hoped to be able to give me some information but heard from David just today and he has no idea when production will start. Bobby Norris knows twins who are here trying out in the Sally League and they SAY they've been signed (an option) to take a test for the Tarleton twins in GWTW and the tests will be in September. Lawsy me! What a mess.

April 1938

Peggy and John came at four on the train from Jacksonville, last Saturday afternoon. It was cold and nasty, trying to rain and with a high wind that was chilling and horrible. We went to the Dempsey and Peggy said she just had to have a drink so she had hers straight and John and I took on a Martini. We gabbed until five when I had to go home to see if Jane had come. She had. She and George sat on the floor outside my apartment with Doc, their Scotty, on leash and with a bottle of rye in their laps. Crazy mutts! They pretended they were drunk and wouldn't speak to me for a spell. Then we took Doc to the vets and Jane parted with him without tears. Home and dressed.

Peg and John, Ken and Jane, George and Mr. W. T. and Blythe came along out to Fay's grill where we had fried chicken and just managed to get to the Little Theatre in time for the curtain. Vera got hold of poor Peggy in the lobby and we had a time getting her loose. That old fool can certainly set her teeth in you—the while she spatters you with droplets of saliva!

Sunday morning, breakfast with Fran; P and Bob and Peg and George and Jane and me. Then we played the piano and Jane sang the most marvelous country soprano—sounded just like Talbotton or Old Bethel Church. Eddie and Art and Blythe came along presently and we got John, and P took us to Fay's for chicken dinner. It was grand but we were tired to death when four o'clock came. Peggy had gone to see relatives and John and I talked and I almost went to sleep. At six, Peg called and we had a late supper and they caught the train at 8:00.

Had conversation with Peggy and decided to get a date for a talk with Wilbur Kurtz. Called him and made date for last night (Wed) and we all had dinner together at the Ansley. Wilbur was delightful and was cordial and helpful in a big way. Annie Laurie (Mrs. K) was bright and cordial and very pleasant. Wilbur's advice—in a nutshell—was

Just talk to Kath Brown as if you were sure you had the job and the only question was one of when you were expected out on the coast. You can't push that woman. Just act like the job is yours and it is all settled.

Well, here's hoping. I'll be seeing the Selznick front office in a short time. Leaving next Sat for New York and shall see Kath about Monday, I reckon.

May 3, 1938

On April 25th, Peyton and Katherine Anderson, George Burt and I started driving to New York. Stayed overnight in Richmond. Made good time except for Springtime but about ten miles from the Holland Tunnel encountered Springtime trippers, who blocked traffic more and more so that we made the last eight miles in little less than three hours!

Next morning, I called Kay Brown who had a date with me but she had flown to California responding to a call from Pappy Selznick. Well, business over, I had time to play.

That evening, attended *Mice and Men* and then to have a drink at the Waldorf. We started out about midnight and George Burt and I encountered Mark Ethridge on the stairs where we pretended not to see him and fell over him. He invited us to come have a drink in the Waldorf Bar. We had a number, and Mark and I danced. The orchestra stopped a 2 a.m. and he slipped a bill to the leader who obliged with 15 minutes more of "Melancholy Baby"! Mark, of all people.

Then to the 21 Club and it was just closing so we took Leon and Eddie's—a bawdy spot indeed my hearties but we had fun. To bed at daylight.

Next day I visited art galleries with Frank and Cat Herring. Lunched at the Russian Tea Room, then to Frank's studio to see his work, which is excellent. Water colors are bold and definite and although they conform to classic in a fashion, they are new.

Note: Some of Herring's work is in the permanent collection of the Smithsonian. He and his wife lived in Milledgeville at one time and were family friends.

That night, to Ed Winn's *Hooray for What*, and then to Belmont plaza bar and saw a good floor show. George and I snuck out and betook ourselves to the Stork Club, saw Broderick-Lennie and Claire Luce and danced and had drinks and later ate scrambled eggs with mushrooms that were grand.

Next morning, bought a white chiffon frock to wear in *Vinegar Tree* (a play at the Macon Little Theatre), and am I thrilled at doing the lead role! Then to lunch with Jerry and Elsie at Schrafts on 42nd Street.

To *Shadow and Substance* for the matinee with George and Kat. Sir Cedric Hardwicke is of the finest.

That night, to *Our Town* with Frank Craven—and no scenery and a funeral that would make anybody weep. God, it is gripping. Afterwards, we walked five blocks without a word and then George said, "Sniff, sniff! Don't you think we'd better have a drink!" Then we went to the Cotton Club and it is pretty sad, about like going to Lakeside to watch a dance! But at *Our Town* we saw Stuart Erwin in the gentleman's lounge.

Handwritten Note in Diary, dated *May 19* (1938)
From the desk of
P. T. ANDERSON, JR.

Sue—I think it a damn shame for you that George Cukor or Selznick didn't see your performance last night. Alice Brady and Billie Burke would have been put to shame—you were marvelous.

I always knew you were good but you even outdid yourself -

As much as I hate to admit it, I thoroughly enjoyed "The Vinegar Tree"—so much I think I will join the Little Theatre next year—but don't tell Kat yet.

Thanks a million for a most enjoyable evening—I humble myself before a truly great actress.

Peyton

Thurs. a.m.

Sue pasted Frank Hawkins' review of the play in her diary. On May 19, 1938, in *The Telegraph*, the article was headlined: BEST SHOW OF ITS HISTORY SEEN IN LITTLE THEATRE'S NEW PLAY. His review included such remarks as:

.....with top honors probably due Susan Myrick for a bang-up job as a scatter-brained woman romancing herself about a confused past. She virtually stopped the show several times.

Miss Myrick, as Laura Merrick, is as silly as a goose, probably because she has been confined for so long on the country estate of her aged husband.

May 24th 1938

Peggy writes that Selznick tells her production will positively begin in September or thereabouts.

Willie's book (*Twisted Yarn*) is really good, in spots. The love story is gripping. The social background bored me a little. The characters were so easily recognized that it is amazing she dared to do them. If I were Maggie Long I'd be maddern hell. And if I were Mark, I'd be embarrassed at finding myself on every page so vividly shown. I felt at times as if I were in the bedroom with Mark!

June 21, 1938

June 4 found Frank Hawkins and me in Brunswick for the re-opening of the King and Prince Club. Mr. W.T. came to Savannah and on Sunday he took several of us to Tybee. The ocean is magnificent there, such high waves and such effort to stand up and plenty of room in spite of big crowds. If it were not for the silt from the Savannah River that reddens the ocean for miles out, the beach would be divine. As it is, nothing in the world can compare with the sand and water and the loveliness and the memories of Sarasota.

Yes, there are other memories. There is Press Haven.

* * *

The next week end found me traipsing to Swainsboro with Peggy and John Marsh to the Georgia Press meet. At the Institutes in the winter, people listen to lectures and learn a bit of one thing or another, but the summer meets are just an excuse to drink and be gay and talk a lot and sit on beds and go to barbecues. To the shame of my Southern ancestry, I confess that barbecue leaves me plum sick—too-fat meat, heavy pork, wasp nest bread, no salads, sun hot as hell, probably flies and surely red bugs and mosquitoes, standing up to eat, loads of people pushing past – No thanks, if you please, Mrs. Pettibone.

But Peggy and I managed to skip two barbecues and to eat good meals at the little hotel in Swainsboro. And the bed sitting was pretty good, what with Edna Cain and Beth Williams and George Burt and Sara Lawson and Peggy and John and Willie Snow. Willie, by the way, told a grand story on herself. She says she was at the office in Louisville when the picture taker came in with some shots he had made of her speaking at a banquet. The picture showed Willie, head thrown back, the Eleanor Roosevelt teeth displayed to their widest, laughter written all over her countenance. She had obviously just told what she considered a good story and was vastly amused at what she had told. But the picture showed four or five men and women on each side of her and all of them wore the most lugubrious countenances. Two of them—nearest the speaker—were leaning over to look at her manuscript and the faces said quite plainly "How much longer is this going to last?" Willie's best trait is her ability to laugh at herself.

June 28, 1938

Today I read a poem (*A Song for Springtime*) that Don Marquis wrote when his little boy died back about '21. He wrote of the child's days as of spring time and then he said at the last:

Now I am one with trodden leaves and Autumn,
And all old broken things.

A lovely lovely poem and I remember that I too am one with old broken things.

August 5, 1938

I spent the past week end with Peggy Marsh and John. They had a cocktail fight (party) for me Sunday afternoon. The exciting guest was a young fellow name Lee (Harry, I think) who has just had a contract with McMillan for a novel. Peggy says McMillan thinks the book is a honey and predicts a great future for the boy and got the contract for the book the day he was fired from his WPA job because he married a girl working also for the WPA.

Peggy was upset as I departed and threatened to come to Macon with me because the phone kept ringing with the AP wanting her to say something about what she thought of Norma Shearer's resignation of the role of Scarlett.

Peggy told delightful tales of the Herschel Brickells in New York and Mr. Brickell's mother, who was a Vardeman of Mississippi, IF you please, and their visit to Isabel Patterson and Mrs. B's calling the Chablis "stump water" and Isabel's' serving them blueberry pie in soup plates with soup spoons and no napkins. It was all very delightful I figure.

Note: Herschel Brickell was a literary critic for *The New York Evening Post* and reviewed GWTW favorably when it was first released.

She also told me some fine low down on Lois Cole's story of the *Mingled Yarn* submitted for publication, and the changes made, all of which is better not written lest my children's grand children think I am catty! Or more to the point, lest somebody read this who talks too much!

Back to Peggy, to tell of going to the historical society with Peggy and how fine it was. I liked Mrs. Carter immensely; she is of Sears Lending Library and has good sense.

Wright Bryan of the *Journal* staff read excerpts from a diary kept in the late 1870s and early eighties. It was delightful stuff. One entry about a well caving on a Negro reminded me of Uncle Tom Thomas and the well at home—the time Tom went down after Papa's teeth and the well caved in on him. (See Appendix V.)

I must write that down some day. In fact, the experiences of my childhood are about as good as *Life with*

Father that Clarence Day wrote—only I don't write as well as Clarence! Maybe I shall some day. I found, long ago, that I learn slowly. That is strange, too, for I honestly think I have a good mind and I do so many things. I was slow with Indian clubs, with tap dancing, with getting hold of the main idea in anatomy, and with lots of things—skating for instance. Maybe I shall learn eventually to write well. I think one trouble is I am impatient and I **read** too hastily.

* * *

Have read *Madame Curie*, and it is so lovely it makes me cry. The death of Charlie Herty coming so soon on the heels of my reading that book made me feel as never before what a great man he was. So completely charming personally, so selfless, so grand, so brilliant, such a scientific mind, yet the ability to talk about his discoveries in terms the layman understood. Certainly he was Georgia's greatest son and I am proud to have known him and called him my friend. He always seemed glad to see me and we had such fun together. I shall miss him but not so much as the state of Georgia, I ween.

Unhappy days indeed! Our baseball team has lost a whole series to Savannah and our lead of many weeks standing is being cut down to the point where I am scared to death we'll lose the pennant.

I like lazy living and I shall hate it when we have to wear shoes and be big cities and have strike problems and be a big industrial country. Be it ever so selfish, I love creature comforts, lounging and lolling and dawdling and not hurrying and the way of living that Macon has—blow the horn for curb service, go to town bareheaded, quit work early, take plenty of time for lunch. The hell with bustle and ambition and hurry!

August 17, 1938

Kept the children for Lil to sleep a while last Sunday afternoon. They all have the whooping cough and she needs sleep! The cough has been worse on her than on them, for they have had comparatively light cases with not much loss of appetite and not much up chucking. Tip has had the whoops too, but is about over it.

August 22, 1938

Back last night from Jax. Impressions: Baby porpoise nuzzling her mammy, both of them grinning and happy; Fred falling on his puss when he got off the swing where George had twisted him round and round; Betty sick from the ride; the lady in the green skin slacks who told Betty she just needed a little tomato juice; Fred and me bowling; Fred and me slipping off from Betty and George when they insisted on going into that cold surf at three in the morning; the photographs we made—me with a match paper under my upper lip; the rye highball at the Dutch Tavern and the Negro offering to play Music Maestro.

To Jax with the Shelburnes in 34, Jimmie and Aaron in 35, Ken and Aaron in 36, Perry and Frank in 37, and this year with George (1938).

October 5, 1938

Last Saturday (Oct 1) Marshall Daugherty had his studio opening and exhibition. The boy has done magnificent things. I honestly think the finest bit of work he has is a small (about ten inches) head of a Negro, being burned at the stake. It is done in clay and glazed. The head is a dark brown, shiny; about the neck orange flames leap. There is an agony on the face of the black man and the work produces a feeling of vast sadness and of sympathy for a race long oppressed. There is a universality about it. One thinks also of the Jew in Germany today.

The new director of the Little Theatre is here. A Philadelphian, 26, unmarried, lovely voice, pleasant manner, name Harry Schofield. He and Burt and Ken to dinner with me tonight, then tryouts for *Penny Wise*, first Little Theatre production this season.

I shall miss Frank Durham (previous director); Kathleen will love his new work—Clemson College.

* * *

Sue kept in her diary a letter, dated October 10, 1938, that she received from John E. Drewry, dean of the Henry W. Grady School of Journalism at the University of Georgia, in which he invited her to speak to a feature writing class. Drewry was one of the founders of the Peabody Awards, originally for excellence in radio. He asked Sue to speak on the problems of feature writing; her time of fifty minutes could be split as she saw fit, for speaking and a round table discussion.

October 26, 1938

Day before yesterday, Marshall Daugherty asked my advice on how to get somebody to buy his bust of Harry Stillwell Edwards. We discussed it and decided the Library was a good place for it. Then we found out who was on the library committee. So, I telephoned Charlie Bowden, Mayor and member of the Board of Trustees of the Library, for an interview. Yesterday morning, I got to see Charlie, told him the whole story and asked if he didn't want to start a movement. He thought it was a fine idea, told me to quote him "just fix it up like you want to, Miss Sue, and whatever you say I said will be alright."

We got R. L. Anderson to act as treasurer and got a picture of the bust. I did a story which ran this morning. Before noon today, Charlie called me to tell me an unknown donor had just brought in a check for $500 and was giving the bust to the library. I am so pleased and proud at having had a hand in the pie. I feel like a Patron of the Arts, a sort of Mellon!

Note: Daugherty's bronze of John Wesley stands in Reynolds Square, Savannah, Georgia. The bust of Harry Stillwell Edwards continues to greet visitors to the archives of the Middle Georgia Regional Library, Macon.

Harry Schofield is enchanting me. He says such fine things to me and unaccustomed as I am to gentlemen, it is thrilling. Perry and Bob and George and the rest of my friends laugh at my new hat and say I ought to be ashamed. Harry says it is a smart hat!

Had a grand time fishing last week at Spring Creek, a river that rises in eleven springs and flows about five miles to the Gulf. It is some 50 miles south of Thomasville and when the cold weather comes again I hope to get back for red fishing. Ought to be swell then.

November 25, 1938, the day after Thanksgiving

Drove up to Atlanta with Boots Massee to see the Russian Ballet Wednesday night and stayed over with Jane Wilkes. We slept late, had breakfast about noon, and Peggy and John came to see us and we had a fine session.

Arrived back in Macon about eleven and went to Terry's to a party for Honey Chile Wilder, the daughter of a local fireman or cop, who has made good in radio and is now in movies. Introduced to Honey Chile, I say it was a pleasure, and so on, and she interrupted to say she was sooo glad to meet me, that she had heard George speak of me so often. Turned out she meant George Cukor.

She told me he said I was coming out to help with the picture and she is so pleased. Needless to say, I, too, was pleased.

Honey Chile turned out to be rather simple and unaffected and pretty decent. No act, just a gal.

Spoke to journalism class at University of Georgia on Wednesday, the 16th. Eddie Nims went up with me, and we had a fine time.

Have cast *Craig's Wife* at last. I wanted to do the role of Mrs. Frazier but was consoled when Harry said, "I don't want to waste you on that little part." May have been his defense because he didn't think I was right for it, but it flattered me as much as if I had been sure he meant it.

December 12, 1938

On Saturday morning I had a wire from Hollywood offering me the sum of $100 a week, on a weekly basis, to do technical advisor stuff for GWTW and saying please let them know at once—leave immediately—the deadline was practically here for hiring persons for that sort of business. I wired back about two in the afternoon that K. Brown had offered $150 and what the hell and I could come in five days if they'd meet Kay's proposition. Waited in vain yesterday. Have waited up to now (three p.m.) with constantly increasing jittering. Tell myself they close the office on Saturday and that it is now even only 11 in the morning in Los Angeles but that helps very little. If I don't hear something soon I rather think I shall pop.

If it isn't just like all the stuff I've ever heard about Hollywood. For nearly two years they have messed around, giving me no definite information, but sort of taking it for granted. Now they wire "leave immediately." Then I answer and they wait all these hours to answer back. Maybe they decided if I am going to be snooty they'll just hire somebody else.

Had been excited all last week over going to spend Christmas with Katie. Now I am all up in the air. If Hollywood calls I'll have to go. If they don't call, I'll be worried sick over it all and I wish they'd DO SOMETHING.

* * *

Sue received many letters and telegrams when the word got out that she was going to Hollywood. One of the many that she pasted into her diary came from Aaron's cousin Florence Bernd.

Dear Sue,

Sometimes I hear a song radio-wise that runs "You're wonderful," and now I want to join the chorus that's chanting that for you. The news of your honors and opportunities is just fine. Macon has been a good proving ground but now I feel about you as Philip the father of Alexander the Great did about him when he said, "My son, seek out other worlds to conquer. Macedonia is too small for thee."

How glad Aaron would be with it all. Wherever he is, I can picture him clapping his hands in great glee and giving his happy little laugh. I used to try to get him to go back to California, but he'd chuckle and say, "No, the flesh-pots have gotten me and I'm going to stay here."

If you do decide to stay on in what the natives say is all earthly paradise, don't forget us back here who will always remember you.

Faithfully,

Florence Bernd

Sue also kept in her diary two letters from the founder of the Sparta Agricultural & Industrial Institute, an all-black school in Sparta, Georgia: This one was dated December 17, 1938:

My dear Miss Myrick:

Words cannot express my regrets when I read in The Macon Telegraph *that you are planning to leave us for a while. I only wish that I were coming to Macon soon. I have some good jelly I would like for you to sample.*

I shall always remember and appreciate your friendship, and I wish to assure you that wherever you are you have a friend here in Sparta, Georgia.

Our school is still progressing and we are looking forward to a very successful term. We are very crowded and congested, however, in our class rooms, and we are trying to raise funds to add two rooms to the new brick-veneered building which we recently constructed. If you know of anyone who could help me in this project, I should appreciate it very much. Anyone who gives the money may have the honor of naming the new building. It may be named for some faithful servant or some devoted "mammy."

With sincere hopes that good fortune will follow you on your journey, I remain

Yours very truly,
Anna S. Ingraham

Christmas Eve 1938

Since I had the wire saying "could I leave immediately for Hollywood" I've been about nuts. Wired back and forth and finally Mr. O'Shea (imagine that name representing a Jewish organization) wired "OK It's a deal" and that he would let me know soon when they'd expect me and I know nothing yet!

Note: O'Shea is listed in some indices as "Shea."

Sort of sitting on my Frances waiting for the evening mail. Have studied and read a lot of stuff and spent hours thanking people and answering notes of congratulation. People have been so darn nice I have about wept half the time.

Malora Rozar gave me the loveliest party I ever saw. Bob and P., Harry Schofield, the Nimeses, Fred and Betty New,

George, Margaret and Blythe, the Albert Jelkses were there. A Christmas tree with all the presents for me to take to Hollywood.

Dark glasses, a little chair with my name on it,

Art gave me a puzzle that said "when will Sue and GWTW ever get to Hollywood." Eddie had taken one of those little puzzle things where you wiggle the contraption to get two small marbles into a certain spot. She had removed the cellophane from the round box, put a picture of Fannie on one ball and marked the other GWTW. The goal was marked Hollywood.

Perry gave me a card of weapons from the five and dime—a machine gun, pistol and revolver—with a poem that said:

Just as long as you are able
protect yourself from that man Gable
but when you see it's ineviTABLE
remember the old, old Chinese fable.

I got a pair of tiny roller skates, of a size to fit a baby doll.

Berry gave me a box of Southern accents. He had written "Honey child," "yo all," "shet my mouf," etc., on little slips and had them "guaranteed 99 44/100 percent pure Southern."

Malora, a bottle of corn likker.

Eddie, a watch from the dime store, with Fannie Squeers' picture pasted over the face and a poem saying:

Give a yell for Fannie Squeers,
At Little Theatre she leads the cheers,
She keeps it up all the time
Alas poor Fannie, gone with the wind.

George gave me a package of gay-colored things to powder the face with, laughing at the bow Dolly gave me with the dirty ribbon on it and the old flower in it!

Blythe brought me a Negro doll to be Prissy.

A priceless bit of writing from Harry. He brought a card on which were pinned two enormous celluloid ears, arranged like a museum card:

"Museum card—Year 2039

These curious artifacts are believed to be vestigial remains of the ears of one Clark Gable who submitted to a quaint Twentieth Century operation known as Slapping the Ears Down. Gable was a famous ham of his day.

The operation is believed to have been performed by the eminent surgeon Dr. S. Myrick at the request of many friends.

The remains of the doctor are buried in the Council Chamber at the Indian Mounds in Macon, in a characteristic pose—the index finger pointing to points of interest about the chamber.

Wednesday night to the Holt's for a party for the Baroness von Blumenthal who is visiting the Massees. Thursday night to the Bob Murray's for cocktails and then to the Clarke dance and then to Burt's to scramble an egg. Went with George and had a new amethyst colored frock and George sent an orchid and I was pretty gay feeling. The dress is princess style, square of neck, small sleeves, shirred across bosom, very slightly form fitting waist. Skirt flows out quickly below hips and is about five feet around bottom. (This is influence of my efforts to find out about clothes in period of the Sixties for GWTW.)

* * *

MESSAGES FROM FAMILY AND FRIENDS

Letter from her sister

Dearest Sue,

Not until your letter came did I realize that you were not going Saturday. We are all so delighted over the possibility of having you with us Christmas. We are feeling so sorry for Katie.

Ever since you first talked of going to Hollywood I have been so thrilled for you. Then when the paper carried the story, which I thought was very very nice, I felt so proud of you. But then I have always been so proud to say "Sue Myrick is my sister." I know too how proud of you and how happy Mama would have been.

We are going to miss you on all the Sundays that we can't have you with us. We'll look for you not later than around three Saturday.

Much love,
Lil

Wire from friend, wife of former editor Mark Ethridge

Susan Myrick, Macon Telegraph

Congratulations yourself. Your kind of production is much more unique.

Love
Willie (Snow Ethridge)

Letter from aunt

Milledgeville, Ga.
December 16, 1938

Dear Sue,

I do not recall any letter that so touched me as did yours this morning. The honor conferred on you was not unexpected; the newspaper notice only made certain what your family and friends have been looking forward to for a long time.

Your reference to your mother is so sweet it has brought more tears to my eyes than I have shed in a long time. They are tears of rejoicing for you and echo your feeling of sadness that Thulia cannot enjoy your success with you. Your letter makes me know what you feel, in a measure. I am as proud of you as she could have been, and am glad.

Nobody except her children know better than I do how fine she was. I have often said that nobody excepting my parents have meant so much to me as she did. I know of no finer spirit in the world than hers. Her children are very near and dear to me, almost like my own.

While I regret that Katie cannot see you Christmas, I am very glad you can be with us. I want Tippie, Lillas and the children to come Christmas morning as you have been doing and exchange greetings with us. Nanette will be here, and, maybe I can persuade Berry and Malora to drive over early to meet you. Lillas and I were talking a day or two ago and regretting that your visit to Katie would prevent your being with us. I am looking forward to having a Hollywood lady to visit.

I want to tell you how fine I think you are, and that you well deserve your success. The picture, I am sure, will be more as it should be because you helped make it.

Your own loving
Aunt Josie

Note: Aunt Josie called her sister, Sue's mother, "Thulia" but Dovedale personnel called her "Miss Kate."

January 1939

Party after party for the New Years. The most eventful comment came from one of Macon's premier ladies:

"I envy you. I have always wanted to go to Hollywood and meet Coral Gables."

January 5, 1939

Just A YEAR ago I was all hot and bothered about whether I was going to Hollywood. I still am.

December 11, I think it was, Daniel T. O'Shea (a Selznick executive) wired me "could I leave immediately" and here I still am, waiting for news, knowing nothing, laughing at myself, wondering what the hell and being kidded unmercifully.

Soooo much has happened. Letters and even wires of congratulations. Kind friends giving parties and everybody being so nice that I have been torn between the feeling that I had to weep and the feeling that I just as well give up and be swelled-headed. I try to be honest writing here so I admit I am about half way between thinking I am important and thinking "What have I done to deserve such kindness?"

Charlie Bowden's proclamation made my whole soul all warm inside me and some of the letters have made me cry and Malora and Berry have bowed me down with the feeling that I can't be worthy of what they seem to feel and altogether I am in a fog of pleasure and feeling I don't deserve any of it.

City of Macon, Georgia
Office of City Clerk
December 29, 1938

Miss Susan Myrick
Fredonia Apartments
Bond Street
Macon, Ga.

Dear Miss Myrick,

The following is a copy of a resolution, which was adopted by the Mayor and Council at the regular meeting, held Tuesday night, Dec. 27, 1938:

"We have noted with great interest the newspaper account of Susan Myrick's contract to assist in the motion picture production of the novel, "Gone With The Wind."

Because of the many ridiculous and "professional Southern" types to which we have been treated in the past, it was with some degree of anxiety that we learned that Margaret Mitchell's great work was to be filmed. We were fearful that the play, at least insofar as the characters and the customs of the South were concerned, might be counterfeit rather than counterpart.

Miss Myrick is a student who has looked closely into the life and manners of the South and has so learned to express and portray them with truth.

The absence of this charming personality will be a distinct loss but we are comforted with the thought that she goes as our ambassador and as an educator to the moving picture industry. As such, she can, and we are sure will, render a great service to that industry and an even greater service to our section of the country."

As Clerk of Council I was instructed to send you a copy of the resolution. Personally, I am glad you have been selected for this work, and feel sure that the moving picture industry had acted wisely in asking your assistance.

Yours very truly,

Viola Ross Napier
City Clerk

Colleague's Comments

Frank Hawkins wrote of her pending trip to Hollywood. He said that Cukor would want Sue at his side, "for she is as refreshingly Southern as a mint julep, as versatile and productive as her native soil."

He also reported that since she first talked to Cukor—eighteen months ago—Sue had been "engaged in intensive study of manners and customs of the Old South. She had a time trying to find out how pantalettes are made."

"But," he continued, "she had found time to continue her public appearances as a speaker before writer's clubs, journalism classes and PTA groups. Her talks before the Georgia Press Association in recent years have been notable."

HOLLYWOOD

When Sue arrived in Hollywood, she did not know the "characters" at Selznick International Studios. Some of the staff remained for the duration of the production—some did not. At times in her writings, Sue would refer to someone by a first name, another time that same person by the last name. Some of the people Sue mentioned as holding a position were sometimes fired and replaced, and sometimes credited with another title, as Selznick seemed to frequently fire and hire his staff.

Some of the people Sue met in Hollywood and mentioned in her diary or in her letters to Mitchell, together with their title or position or potential character role, are listed in Appendix VIII. It is not a complete listing of the GWTW staff and characters, but one of some of the lesser known people—those who tried out for roles or who were visitors on the sets or whom Sue met at social events. Appendix IX shows documents—cost estimates and call sheets, e.g., and Appendix X gives illustrations of some of the reference materials Sue took with her to Hollywood.

Jan 7, 1939, Culver City California

My ears are still buzzing from the noise of the motor on the plane and the 8,000 feet high flying we did between Dallas and Los Angeles, and my head is buzzing and my eyes are sticking out and my brain is whirling from the fast way things have happened today.

The plane arrived an hour late, 9:35, and when I alighted there was a wire for me from these angel fools who came to Atlanta to see me off. It read:

Social life died in Macon last nite. Lite of the party went out. No barbecue today; turnips and chitterlings. Crepe drapes Cherry Street today. Repeat aloud ten times and roll em baby. May the spirit of Southern chivalry hover over you wherever you may go—even to the Belles (not Watling) and Colonels of your set.

Mrs. Kurtz met me at the airfield in a studio car with a chauffeur and we came here to the Washington Hotel. Dreary but clean. (She is very sweet to fix me a place until

I can get settled.) I washed a little and went on to the studio. Just two blocks, where she showed me Scarlett Way (entrance to the studios) and her office and introduced me to Mrs. Leona, head of research, and showed me where she and Wilbur work. And then she took me to Mr. O'Shea, who had phoned me the night before to come on out there. He is business manager and very nice. Not like his voice sounded over the phone. He took me at once to George Cukor (dismissed Mrs. K) and George was very cordial, greeting me like a long lost friend. I HOPE I can remember this stuff as it happened. I am too tired to think with any degree of continuity.

George talked about my trip and how did I feel and stuff. He is VERY polite always. (Must remember later to quote as well as I can his telephone conversation with some mysterious Miss Leigh advising her about a secretary.)

We discussed dialect and he and I are in accord that people would prefer just ordinary stage English and not accent, with the South put in the mouth of Belle and Negroes.

He brought me a nice looking swell sort of young man, Mr. Price of Mississippi, who is head of speech department here. We agreed, too. I like them both! Mr. Price said Miss Keyes and Miss Stuart (I think) were here and George said, "Sue, would you just as soon listen to this?"

Of course I would just as soon; I heard Suellen and Careen do a scene where she is mad because Scarlett expects them to work and she tries to hold on to the old regime. They are both Atlanta gals and very nice indeed. Especially the blond one (Suellen) (Keyes).

Then George scared me pink by telling me he thought I'd belong to the art department and would I tell the gentlemen later how the sets ought to look about porch furniture and things. And he told his secretary to give me the Melanie office, right next to his own. Laughter about the Melanie Room which I didn't get.

Sometime later the secretary said Mr. Somebody was in the Melanie Office and George preemptorily said all right, get him out, he wanted me to have that office. Still later some man stopped me and said he wanted to put me in the office upstairs because he wanted Mr. Such and Such to have the Melanie Room. I shrugged my shoulders and said George said I was to have the Melanie Room. Don't yet know where I am to hang my hat. As George told me HOURS later to come to his office on Monday (and Mr.—, I forget his name, assistant director—said I should report there about ten).

Well, then in came—you won't believe me—William Farnum, who is to try for Gerald and probably will get it, too. He and George did a scene six times and then in came a Miss Martin (Marcella) who did the scene with him. She is pretty and looks like Miss X whose trial scenes I saw with Leslie Howard and with Doug Montgomery and with two Mammies.

Scared to even write down Miss X's name because it is a deep secret about the office. Think she is cast definitely though nobody ever told me so. (Hattie McDaniel is one Mammy's name. Just thought of it. She is cast—worse luck.)

George asked me if I would have lunch with him and the art department, and told the secretary to make the date. We then talked some more. I don't remember quite what happened then, except several women stopped him and finally we got to lunch at a place marked "Private." Every darn thing out here is, even the ladies room.

Mr. Platt is head art man, I mean head decorations man. Hobe Erwin is out. Assistant is Wheeler and there were some more whose names I can't remember, but just the four of us ate together. My lunch was marvelous, large green salad bowl with a roll and coffee. Mostly George talked about THE SOUTH, laughing at it and loving it at the same time.

We trucked over to the Art Department and George went to his office. And before the poor men had the sketches out for me to see, George phoned and would we bring them to Selznick's office to see.

I met David and he is charming, big, lanky, slightly Jewish, glasses, slouchy looking. Everybody here wears flannels and looks as if he slept in them. Fine, good-natured grin and completely disarming.

Tara is too grand but nice just the same. I hope I appeared decent and did a good job. I said the floors were too slick and there were too many decorations. When they showed Aunt Pitty Pat's house, I loved it but asked them to put in a lot of hassocks. George's face lighted up when I said Melanie and Aunt Pitty Pat were tiny and Southern women had to keep their feet together and these two needed footstools every where they sat down.

I also objected to a lot of statues of horses AFTER I had been told they were Selznick's pet idea. They are OUT.

George talked to David a lot about something and then promised to send me back to see David and some scenes in the projection room and took me over to his office again to see Miss Michael from Talladega. You won't believe me but she was doing a scene like Belle Watling. She is blonde, hussyish looking, beautiful, and wore the damnest frock all red and gold brocade and bosom showing. She was good.

More chit chat, then out to see Tara laid out in a studio floor. The men had put laths down to indicate shape, floor plan, and size of the house. Geo asked me if it was big enough and I said honestly I was so fuzzy headed from seeing so much I could not orient myself in California much less in that sound studio and I had no idea how big it all was. Geo was so kind and so sweet. He made one man stand at the front door and one at the back to show me and then outlined the parlor and the office and my gawd the house is about the size of the Governor's Mansion in Milledgeville!

Introduced me to Stacy, the assistant director whose name I had forgotten. He is charming, handsome, kind and gracious. Offered to help me find place to live and said Mrs. Stacy would be happy to show me where to shop and things. Stacy chased Geo all over seventeen studios to ask him about something. Then Geo told me good night, hoped I will sleep well, turned me over to Stacy, and Stacy took me in a car to Selznick's office where Marcella, a good looking brunette who is private secretary, said to please wait a bit. There were another secretary and a boy, Cecil. He is polite and gracious. There are probably six more but these are all I saw. I met fifteen more men and cannot remember who or what they are. Everybody is so damned efficient and all very polite and pleasant.

Marcella finally understood I was to see scenes shot and telephoned Set N. 3 and told them what to show me, and Cecil took me over and they showed them to me. Back to Marcella's to wait for David, and Marcella told me about betting a horse this PM, $2.00 to win and $2.00 to place and dogged if she didn't win $165.00. In came David and asked what I thought of scenes. Seemed disturbed that I didn't like Mammy and shows me another with a different Mammy which I liked more and he said unfortunately, they already had that one I didn't like under contract.

But he added couldn't I tell her the things I had told him and get her to do as I thought. Gawd! I am scared.

Then he said goodnight and at 6:30 I was back at the hotel. Chatted with the Kurtzes, had a sorry dinner at a joint and now in the room hard at it. To bed, now, with the script that Sidney Howard did and which is being redone by Mr. Garrett, whoever he may be. David told his secretary to send me new scripts as fast as they are done.

Jan 9, 1939 Monday

Whe-ew! So much has happened I don't know where to start. Well, I spent two hours of mighty hard work, suh, sitting in a chair that let me sink down to my neck in a beautiful room with a whole side made of mirrors and flowers all over the place and everything looking like something out of *House and Garden*, just talking and listening.

O, yes, AND drinking two cups of fine coffee from Spode china, poured from a silver pot by the hand of Miss X, who I feel sure is to be Scarlett, though tonight when I was leaving the studio at 6:30 somebody asked George Cukor if

Scarlett had been signed and he said, "I don't know." But his voice implied he did know and he couldn't tell!

Which reminds me. Wheeler asked if production would actually start on the 16th and George said, "I don't know," and then Menzies said, "Will it, George?" and George laughed and said, "You know goddam well it won't."

But back to this AM. I wandered into Mr. Cukor's outer office at quarter to ten and George doesn't get in till ten, it seems, and Miss Dorothy Dawson, pretty secretary, said my office was ready and she showed me to it and in came Will Price, who is a darling. He has already asked me to go to a show with him and he is taking me tomorrow to see about a new place to live and he and I have swapped lousy puns. He is definitely on my list of persons to like.

We talked about accents and we discovered we had met before. He had been with Federal Theatre in Atlanta and had once been to Macon to see a Little Theatre production and met me at Mamie's Dugout.

A bit later somebody said George wanted Price and me to come on over to Miss X's to hear her rehearse some and we went in a studio car to Beverly Hills to a beautiful house where we did as in first paragraph here.

MIGHTY hard work, suh!

She wore green slacks and green blouse, no hose, toeless slippers and she is beautiful—English and fiery and a fine Scarlett I think. Only poor Will Price has to teach her to stop saying some things in British fashion.

Most of the time Cukor talked and gave all of us the idea of the Scarlett he wants to put over. He loves to talk and he acts all the time, but he is the kindest person I ever saw and he is the brightest. And Boy-o-boy how he can use the right word in the right place. But he DOES love to tell about Tallulah Bankhead! And can he curse!

Finally he left us. We drank a second cup of coffee and corrected Miss X every time she opened her mouth, almost. Then she had an engagement and we left.

Back at the office, Cukor took me to lunch, and then we went to see Tara under construction. Only Saturday PM the men had laid sticks on a floor to show the size of the house and now by God here it was almost finished. If contractors would work like that for us in Macon!

Talked to Miss Florence Yoch about landscaping and found to my AMAZEMENT they made trees! I thought Only God Could Make 'em. She told the men what sort of leaves to get to look like oak leaves and how to manufacture dogwood blossoms and what to get for the branches of crepe myrtle, and it seems that before you can say Scarlett O'Hara they'll be growing in front of Tara.

Back to the office. O, yes, the Melanie Room is mine. Talked with Walter who never shaves and is head of costume dept, but before we got ten words said (and I somehow think he thinks I am phoney) Price called and would I come at once to Set 6 to see Miss X and some shots. Of course I had to go. Got back about an hour later, Plunkett of course again. Chap who does make-up called to talk about beards and hair doings. Secretary phoned that Hattie McDaniel was here. She is to do Mammy.

George brought Hattie in and he talked and I talked. I feel better about her as Mammy but not quite satisfied. She is an excellent actress. She said Yessum to me—she boasts of Southern ancestry and slave grandmother. She can perhaps get into herself the majesty and dignity of a real Mammy. I am troubled a little, however, about how much I should say and how far I should go lest it not be what George wants me to do. He says we are in accord, but I fear my idea of what she should do is not quite his.

Well—then Hattie left and I waited about and then George phoned could I come to Selznick's office where he had sketches of Tara and Aunt Pitty Pat's house. I went. Saw David. Asked about possible sketches for papers and he said let publicity department see. They would be told not to touch a thing unless it might be too early to release something they wanted kept hidden.

Home, supper (lousy), chat with Kurtzes, wrote story, washed things, now must wash face and to bed. Terribly tired.

Jan 10, 1939, Tuesday night quarter to 'leven:

Have written Jerry, Frank Hawkins (for the Tel gang), Peggy, Lil (for Tip too) and P. T. Jr. Must write Al to go to Katie tomorrow.

My! What a hard day's work! At the Melanie Room by nine thirty and over to Publicity to ask about stuff to mail. Secretary laughed at the idea of "the boys" being there so early. Somebody told me how to find Publicity and I walked to a bungalow (as they told me) and rang a bell. No answer. Man passed near. I yelped, "Is this the publicity department?" "No that's Miss Lombard's dressing room."

Left the stuff and the gal promised to call. Tried to impress her that the stuff is no good if it waited for a week! No report until I asked for it this PM and then all she said was Mr. Somebody would see me tomorrow. I think the head publicity man is all I heard he was – the sort of unfortunate child Frank Hawkins calls, "Revolving."

This term became one of Sue's favorites: A revolving, self-made bastard is one any way he turns, but his parents are not responsible.

Back to office anyway, about ten, chatted with Miss Dawson who is secretary to George, and is SOO kind. Asked how to get some stuff typed. She said always phone "secretarial" and ask for a girl. Did so, feeling very important with one of me and laughing at myself with the other one of me. All the time, here, there are two of me. One feels important and proud and puffed up and the other laughs her head off at the puffed up one and pinches her now and then to see if it is real.

Dictated stuff. Memo to Cukor and Garrett, that several errors in new script. Garrett is rewriting Howard's. I said no pine knots for lights at Tara, either candles or lamps. Said too many dogs in script. Said Prissy would not go barefooted into a lady's house. Said Big Sam might call Gerald "Marse" instead of "Mist Gerald." The steno went out. I twiddled my thumbs and wondered what the day would bring.

In came Billy the Price—a good egg I believe; saying he would be busy with That Woman this PM and could we go now to see about Santa Monica living quarters? I demurred, thinking I ought to ask Cukor. We chatted and he is bright and educated and charming. About eleven George came in, said "sure go on and find Sue a place to live," and he offered a studio car and told Price to find me a good place and see that I was happy.

We looked at a number of places, then decided on Apt 305, Georgian Hotel Apts, 1415 Ocean Way, Santa Monica. The hotel is about half a block from the Pacific and it is lovely. Maybe it is more than I should spend, but phooey! Let's live while we may. We'll be a long time dead. Price told the lady he wanted a commission for selling me and there was more laughter and stuff and then he said he'd take the commission in flowers that should be in my room tomorrow night when I arrived. I paid down five bucks and we got back to the lot in time for lunch.

After lunch, to see Platt who is going back to NY for a week or so. Seems Menzies is head man, next is Wheeler. Platt is just in for pix. Got things fixed about sketches. Then over to Wardrobe. I know he thinks I stink—not sure just why but he looks at me as if to say, "I'll be polite because George thinks I should. But she stinks. Who the hell is she, anyway? What does she know about pictures or clothes or art?" I'll win that guy over or die trying. Got to think of something.

Dawson called. George was not feeling well and he had ordered *In Old Kentucky* shown and he was going home and would I look at it. Of course it was hard to do such a dreadful task but I am not one to quibble with my boss. So I sank down to my eye brows in a plush seat on Set No 6 (I guess I should say Projection Room 6) and nothing happened. I remembered seeing Price telephone, so I tried. Operator said to use the hand set on the desk. I tried and nothing happened. I pushed things and still nothing. So I just walked outside and thank God I saw two men smoking on the top step. I laughed and said I was Miss Myrick and I was to see the picture and I could not manage that phone and how did it work, please?

So he showed me, push a button (the damned thing is hidden), pick up the phone, push a little thing in the phone and buzz it and then he'd answer. If I hear two buzzes, answer the other phone. Too complicated for my country brain!

So I saw the picture. Pretty nice. Grand horses but could do without Loretta Young. Some grand Negro men, but women lousy.

After that hard day's work, talked to Publicity, gabbed with Price a few minutes, and came home to get a lousy supper at a "jernt," talk to Kurtzes, and then to write letters, pack and now to bed.

January 11,1939, Memo to Eric Stacy

Suggest that little negro boy (or girl) carry the medicine case (or bag) for Ellen.

Suggest that negroes at the barbecue, or elsewhere, who are standing by when the gentleman rides up on his horse, be provided with cloth to wipe the dust from the gentleman's boots.

January 11, 1939

Apartment 305
Georgian Hotel Apartments
1415 Ocean Boulevard
Santa Monica, California

Tuesday night

Dearest Peggy and John,

Gosh! But I wish you were here so I could talk for about seventeen hours! There aint strength enough in my fingers to write all I'd like to say. And to your ears alone can I say the following. I have not written it to a soul and the studio is so secretive about it all I'm almost afraid to write it to yall. But I have seen the gal who is to do Scarlett. I am even yet afraid to say her name aloud. Will Price (who used to be with Federal Theatre in Atlanta) and I speak of her in hushed tones as "That Woman" or as "Miss X" and we have spent several mornings with her, talking Southern just for her stage-taught ears. She is charming, very beautiful, black hair and magnolia petal skin and in the movie tests I have seen, she moved me greatly. They did the paddock scene, for a test, and it is marvelous business the way she makes you cry when she is "making Ashley." I understand she is not signed but far as I can tell from George and all, she is the gal. Never been in movies before.

Also, have worked with William Farnum who is, I think, to be Gerald. I liked his work very much. Saw him rehearse with George. Today talked Southern for Alan Baxter who may do a bit. Saw Leslie Howard, who seems to be scheduled for Ashley and hope I shall get to coach his accent!

O. H. P. Garrett progresses slowly on the script but the English sparrows say it is David's fault. David changes everything every few minutes. Story told me by chap here is a honey. Says producers and what they do with scripts is like a Chef making soup. The Chef gets an idea from a soup he ate. He spends days making a stock that is just right. He tastes, adds seasonings, tastes again, adds again, tastes, throws away something, tastes again, and finally gets it perfect. Then he does more things to it until he has the finest soup in the universe. Whereupon, he calls in the other chefs and they all stand around and pee in it. And this, the reasonable ones of us seem to agree, is what has happened to GWTW.

But one thing sure, George Cukor is the smartest, the most delightful and the kindest man I ever saw. He told someone to put me in the office next to his own, called the Melanie Room, because it is not decorative, but severe. Someone phoned him that the office belonged to Fitzgerald who is collaborating with Garrett and Garrett is next to the Melanie Room. George shrugged his shoulders, stuck out his lower lip a foot and said, "Move Fitzgerald. I want Sue near me." So Fitz doesn't care for me, I guess. I haven't yet had the pleasure of meeting him.

Twice when I've argued over minor matters George has

agreed with me and I believe he is a square shooter, though I always watch the guy who is so damned diplomatic.

As a sample of a hard day's work, listen to what I've done today. Wandered over to the office at nine-thirty. Nobody there but me and some stenogs! Called "Stenographic" and got a girl to type some objections I wanted to make to the script. Then Price wandered in and said his engagements with Miss X were off and he would take me to Santa Monica to look for living quarters.

You see, Mrs. Kurtz and Wilbur brought me here to Hotel Washington and I am grateful but the place is dreary. And there is not a place where you can get even the first bite of decent food and you know I am a nut about my eating. So, while I am very sorry to leave them I can't stand it here any more and tomorrow I am moving to Santa Monica, to an apartment with maid service and telephone, roll-away bed, bath and enormous closet. It is about a block from the Pacific and is very nice and is reasonable, too. Winter season at Santa Monica, it appears, is time for low rates. If I should stay on into summer, rate will not go up for me, permanent or semi-permanent guest.

But back to the day. I told Price I'd rather not go without seeing George first so we gabbed until George came in about eleven. He said, "Sue, go on and Price you be sure to get Sue a nice place to live."

And he offered a studio car.

We looked at many places and decided on the Georgian (NOT because it is named that!) and got back on the lot in time for lunch. Then I talked to Plunkett of costume designs and argued like all hell about Poke's clothes (I fear not so effectually) and George phoned he wanted me to see a picture—*In Old Kentucky*—to see what I thought of the Negroes and accent and so on and could I come now. So I did. And for an hour and a half, I sat all alone in plush seats that let me sink up to my eyebrows (I mean in one of the 20 plush seats) and saw a movie, showed just for me. Then I talked Southern for half an hour with Baxter and so home to bed.

What a hard day's work! My Gawd!

George laughed about it with me and said he'd be dam sure to work me hard enough to make up for it later.

Already, inter-office communications are tickling me to death. When I have time some day I'll write you about some of them in detail. I'm keeping a diary and I will not forget 'em. But I can't even put in a diary half of the things I want to remember. There isn't time to write them nor finger pressure in me to push the keys!

Must go packing now so can move tomorrow. Much love and write when you have time.

As ever, Sue

* * *

Undated letter sent to Mr. W. T., from Georgian Hotel Apts, Santa Monica:

A funny thing happened on the set that I can't write for the paper but it can circulate around the office. For rehearsals the prop men had made up a dummy to look somewhat like Olivia de Havilland so Clark would not have to tote her so much in rehearsal scenes in the episode where the group is escaping from Atlanta to Tara right after Melanie's baby is born.

The dummy did look like Olivia in the face which was wax and the hair was arranged just as hers was. But the figure was a crude one of cloth, looked like a sawdust stuffed doll. When Clark brought it down the steps and out onto the porch in the first rehearsal, he deliberately picked it up so the quilt wrapped about it would fly open and reveal the nude sawdust stuffed figure. Everybody howled with laughter and Cukor looked stern and we all thought he was angry at the delay in rehearsal. But he wasn't. He said:

"Olivia, I do think it was rude of the prop men to make this dummy's figure exactly like yours." And all day he would say at rehearsals, "Not the funny looking dummy with Olivia's figure this time, Clark. Take the real dummy, this rehearsal, Olivia de Havilland, last of Warner Brothers."

January 12, 1939, Memo to Eric Stacy

Page 1. First Sequence:

Under essential props you list "lean possum hounds."

...nothing is more typical of Georgia than the hound. ...Suggest either Mr. Kurtz or I should check on appearance of the hound dogs.

Page 2. Second Sequence:

Scene 4 indicates Essential Props as tools for chopping cotton.

My understanding is that there will be a change in this plantation activity and either show planting cotton or plowing, because dogwood blossoms seem essential and cotton is not chopped while dogwoods are blooming. If cotton planting is to be shown, Mr. Kurtz can tell you about the negro who would be dropping the cotton seed behind the plow.

Page 4. Scene 9 shows chickens and geese as Essential Props.

Suggest guineas as typical fowl for Georgia plantation...Very picturesque fowl...lend a very nice atmosphere and pictorial effect...True for scenes 14 and 16.

January 12, 1939, Memo to Menzies and Yoch

I feel that it is essential to show cedars somewhere. The red cedar is so typical of middle and north Georgia and people who have read the book remember Scarlett going down the avenue of cedars. Of course, Miss Yoch knows there is a vast difference in the appearance of a Georgia cedar and those which people around here tell me are cedars.

Also suggest that "mullen" is a fine typical weed which would be seen along the road where Gerald rides...picturesque and pretty wild plant found all over Georgia...might also grow in front of the negro cabins, as a weed that has just sprung up...I have excellent pictures.

A handwritten note at the bottom also suggested jimson weed.

January 12, 1939, Thursday

Last night I was too tired to write. I moved to Santa Monica, the Georgian Hotel Apts., where I have a kitchenette, bath, living room with roll-a-way bed and a grand closet. Will Price's flowers made the room look fine and bright when I arrived. For a moment, I was lonesome as the devil and almost wept but I got so busy unpacking I forgot it. I had a cocktail, a good dinner and walked ten blocks, hunting a grocery store so I could make my breakfast coffee. Ocean right in front of me. Town about three blocks from me. Quiet sleeping quarters, good service and all seems fine so far.

Yesterday was the most exciting day of all I guess. At ten, George took me over to Stage 11. He said, "Now, Sue, if you don't mind getting your block knocked off, just tell me when you think I do anything wrong over there." We were making tests of William Farnum, Thomas Mitchell, Gertrude Michael (Talladega), Peggy Shannon (gorgeous creature with loveliest eyes and shoulders in the world) and Marla Shelton.

The men for Gerald and the gals for Belle Watling. Tommy Mitchell was marvelous. Talked long with Farnum who remembered playing in Macon long ago in *Julius Caesar*. The tests were fun. Shall clip copy from *Telegraph* about that part. Best of all was seeing how Cukor works with people. He is MARVELOUS. No wonder he makes such grand pix. He is patient, gentle, courteous, encouraging. He gets out of an actor all there is in him. And he is so cute and so good natured.

And a diplomat of the finest flavor. Ought to be at the Court of St. James's. Example is conversation he had with Miss Vivien Leigh over phone, when somebody told him she couldn't work today:

"Look, Vivien, how are you darling? --- Oh Vivien, look dear, what are you doing today? --- Oh, yes, dear, but don't you know we have to get that work done with Price? --- Oh, of course darling. Look, Vivien, what do you think of Miss Smith as a possible companion for you? --- You don't. Well, I don't think she is so good. But look, my darling, you must have someone. You can't be wearing yourself out over incidental things. I must have you to work with me. --- Yes, dear. Well, dear, I'll expect you this afternoon at four. --- I know, darling, but I'll expect you. Goodbye, my dear. I look forward to seeing you."

Tomorrow, by the way, my day's work consists of spending the day with Vivien who is British and trying to teach her to say "no" and "don't" and "store" and things so they don't sound British! Gad! What a hard day's work. Studio car to take me to a swank home to spend the day with a beautiful girl who is charming and wealthy and interesting. Lawsy me, to think of being paid just to talk!

Today, "talked" for Maurice Murphy who is to do Charles Hamilton. Also to a wild man named Jim Craig who aspired to be a Tarleton twin. A delightful heart-breaking fool from Tennessee who's been out here for some spell. Also talked to Leatrice Gilbert, daughter of John and Leatrice Joy Gilbert. Looks like her dad, worse luck for her, but hasn't so many teeth.

Yesterday met Laura Hope Crews who is Aunt Pitty Pat. She is adorable and made friends with me quickly. Says she intends to haunt me to learn my accent. I'd love to be haunted. We quickly found we both adored Julie Hayden and that gave us common ground.

Either Walter dislikes me or he is timid or something so I have started to win him over (Miss Fannie). I phoned today that George had some pix he wanted Walter so see and kidded the boy along and he sounded more friendly. Told him "How you come on" should be answered "Poly, thank God," or "Just tolerable, thank you, ma'm." He liked it. Begin to think he is timid of new people.

Oh, yes, wanted to record yesterday AM. George said, "Eric, I want to see tests of James Bell."

Eric said, "Good God, you've seen those, George, weeks ago."

George said, "You are a liar, Mr. Stacy." And the cute Mr. (Oh, no, not Stacy, it was Arnould, talent scout) said, "Mr. Cukor, I challenge you to a duel."

That's the way these fools carry on all the time. They are grand.

Will told me a good one on interoffice communications today. Seems David writes them all the time and when David was in Bermuda Mr. O'Shea took up the habit. George would come to work and find a stack that high on his desk. He'd look at them, flutter them over, and pitch them into trash. Repeated day after day, the pile grew higher and higher. Finally George pitched the mess into the trash and yelled! Then he phoned Mr. O'Shea. He'd be goddamned if he'd read any more notes and they jolly well just as soon quit writing them. O'Shea said this and that and things were important, and so on, but George laughed at him. After a while George started rehearsing a talent find. He kept it up a few minutes then began to dictate.

"From George Cukor to Mr. O'Shea, subject Notes and so on. It is now 11:08. I am engaged in rehearsing Miss So and So (and very good she is, too). I assure you it is a pleasure to make this report to you, my dear sir, etc." Then he dictated in rapid succession about two dozen of them. "Now 11:19, I have just finished rehearsing So and So."

Then one said, "Now 11:23 and I am going to begin rehearsing Mr. So and So in a few moments (and I may add I look forward to this with pleasure). But first, I am going to the Little Boy's Room."

"Now 11:30 and I have just returned from the Little Boy's Room." And after a dozen of the notes, finished with "It is now 6 p.m. and I am leaving for my home after a very pleasant but tiring day at the studios of Selznick International Pictures, Inc."

Mr. O'Shea hasn't written the boy since.

And that reminds me. Mr. O'Shea just phoned me to say David thought that was a good idea about Dolly's flying out to present honorary membership in the UDC to Vivien. And would I phone her to fly on out tonight!

Boy, what fools. You "know how we are in the motion picture industry." I told him she should be talked to about it first and arrange with her board of directors and such like. He said would I phone her right now, but I said after all it was one AM in Macon and that would hardly make

Dolly in a good humor. So I am to phone in the morning.

Well, must to bed. I am lonesome some. And I'd give a million to have Harry or Fred or Burt to tell things to. They are such good listeners.

I wish some of those fools back home would write me.

January 13, 1939, Memo to Eddie Boyle

I should like to suggest, please, that the bedrooms at Tara should look as if the mattresses were "feather ticks." The featherbed was high and smooth in the Georgia houses in the Sixties. In fact, the housemaids were instructed to make the beds so no wrinkles showed and all edges had to be very carefully straightened. No member of the household was even permitted to put a hat on the bed for fear ever so slight a dent might show in the feather mattress.

May I suggest also that standing beside a high, four-posted (or four-poster) bed there was always a hassock to make it easy for a person to climb into bed.

Sue well knew about the four-poster bed. Her parents slept in one, and they had three hassocks made from the canopy frame because the "top" of the bed was too high to fit into the Dovedale home. One of the hassocks stood beside her parents' bed.

Friday Jan 13, 1939

But no bad luck so far! A marvelous day, really.

Up early because I wanted to get letters written at the studio before work time. Nobody goes to work before ten! I got to studio at nine fifteen or so and asked for stenographic and got a girl down and wrote a letter to David saying I enclosed copy of publicity.

Last Tuesday I sent some innocuous stuff to Birdwell, as per instruction from David. The dog (Birdwell, not David) kept it until I phoned him Wednesday morning. Nothing happened. Thursday I phoned him again and a Mr. Ray, very condescending, told me they had cut of all things, my saying, "Only God could make a tree." I was furious and told him Selznick said he was not to cut copy except if I gave out info that wasn't to go out. He was ugly and I was sweet as pie. I should have told him to go to hell.

Later, George asked me what about the stuff I was writing. So I said Publicity was holding it and he asked more questions so I told him the story. He was mad as fire and said, "Goddamnit, they have no right to do that and I'll talk to David." He did, and later told me to call David, who asked what about it all, and I told him briefly that Publicity had cut this out and kept the stuff since Tuesday and this was Thursday at five P.M. and I didn't have it back yet. So David said, "After this, just send it to me."

This P.M. about four I phoned Marcella Rabwin, David's secretary who is a lamb, and she said she had read the story and thought it was wonderful. I mean she seemed enthusiastic and sincere. And she said David had been frightfully busy with scripts and she would see that he read it first thing tomorrow.

Meanwhile back to this morning. I got the girl to do letters to half a dozen papers and hope to sell stuff to them all.

Anyway let's see. O yes, last night O'Shea wanted me to call Dolly Lamar about a scheme I had to have her confer honorary title of Daughter of Confederacy on Miss Leigh. I told him it was one AM in Macon and hadn't we better wait. This morning I phoned Dolly and she is in Florida. I was told to report to O'Shea early this morning. I phoned his office at ten and again at ten thirty and he finally showed up at eleven. Which brings me back to saying nobody gets to work until ten or eleven.

All of which means I can go early and get a lot of personal stuff done.

At eleven thirty a studio car took me to talk to Miss X, who is British and is learning Southern. We talked about everything on earth, and I felt like a fool correcting her every time she said "no" or "show" or "where" or anything else that sounded British. I left her at twelve-thirty, returned to studio, had lunch in a projection room—a sandwich and milk while I saw *Green Pastures* for Eddie Anderson (Uncle

Peter), and for Negro who is Pork. Eddie is wonderful for Uncle Peter but I am a little dubious about Pork.

Saw Ina Claire and the Grand Duchess Marie of Russia in George's office. Talked to Murphy again and to Jim Craig who is handsomer than Apollo himself. A good egg and a fool if there ever was one. Maybe Stuart and Brent Tarleton.

Met Ben Smith tonight, candidate for Frank Kennedy and nice man.

Talked with Eddie Boyle who gave me a new slant on technical advisors! He said when Platt came to do sets, he (Eddie) was scared to death and soon found to his delight Platt was human and fine. Then I said everybody is so fine and he said, "Christ! We like human beings. You just don't know. The technical experts who have come out here and told us how to run our business have been terrible."

Then I realized they expected me to be a butt and they are pleased that I am not. S'funny. I was scared of them and they were scared of me!

Gosh! What a goofy place! A little man, whose name I keep forgetting, rushed into the Melanie Room today and said, "Why wouldn't that Negress with the soprano voice, somebody Anderson, why wouldn't she be a good Mammy?"

I meekly murmured that Marian Anderson got a lot of dough for one concert, and he exclaimed, "Jeeze. Selznick's got plenty of dough. I think it would be a knock out to get Anderson, write in some songs for her and have her as Mammy."

Now that would sound like it came out of a play! Maybe I'll put it in one.

Everybody else out here is writing for the movies. Eddie Boyle, set dresser, who bought me two cocktails today, is doing one about the war. He was with Princess Pat Regiment and loves to talk about it. Will Price is writing a scenario. I bet the prop boys and the script girls are all doing them.

I am beginning to pine for the flesh pots. If Freddie were here! Or Mark or Harry Schofield! Or Boots. We could have FUN! Think I'll start a movement. Bet I could maybe get

Boots out if his Dad ever took a notion it would help him.

I want to go somewhere and dance or to a show or even to get some drinks and talk. I want to hear Fred wisecrack and to look at familiar faces and to listen to Harry talk with that wise cracking sarcastic manner and that luscious voice.

O well, you can't have everything, honey.

That reminds me. Better call up Honey Chile!

January 15, 1939

Dear Peggy:

There are so few persons to whom I can tell things! Gawd! Would I like to talk to you and John for a couple of hours!

For instance I can confide to your shell-like ear that I am mighty sick at heart at the idea of three Britishers—Leigh, Howard and de Havilland—in the parts of Scarlett, Ashley and Melanie. De Havapuss, especially, gives me a pain at the middle. From private sources, I learn that she is from California, was poor as the devil, is from a family that is nothing at all and now she has gone pseudo British! Will Price says her accent is thicker with British than the London fogs are thick and he thinks she is the hardest nut to crack in the outfit. And I think Vivien is the toughest nut to crack. I think Leslie will get it all right. He had more sense than anybody I've seen around here—except Cukor, who is a grand person.

I have had a fine encounter with Pappy Selznick and though he is a nut he is pretty decent. I wrote you the requirements that I send Publicity to Birdwell. Well, Birdwell is the revolving bastard if there ever was one. He kept my copy four days and edited the hell out of it. Pappy, because George brought it up with him, asked me about it and I told him the whole story, being as gentle about it as I could be and taking care not to sound uppity and accusatory. David went up in the air, told me to send the copy to his office in the future. I did and he okayed it, noted that he found it very interesting and did not edit out a single word. Left in all the Birdwell gang had taken out! So, I am for Pappy even if he didn't invite me to go to Bermuda.

I am sending you the note from Birdwell. Please return it to me when you have showed it to John. No hurry—just send it back when you write.

My apartment grows on me. I like it. The maid is colored and very pleasant. The light is good, the place is quiet and looks very homey and sweet.

Talked to Annie Laurie and Wilbur yesterday about feather beds at Tara and they agreed and I insisted that they must be. Eddie Boyle, head of set dressing, is a good egg and we get along fine. I really think the exterior of Tara is lovely and I am sure the credit belongs to Wilbur who insisted on square columns and a rambling look. I have insisted on the magnolia tree out Scarlett's window and oh yes, a funny thing.

They wanted cotton chopped while dogwoods were blooming and Wilbur and I had a time stopping it. They will plough instead. I nearly died when they asked me if they couldn't show cotton right at the front yard! Miss Yoch who is landscaper is a fine old sister, hard featured and looks like Calvin CooliPacedge but she is smart as hell. In fact, everybody out here is smart. I have found out there is no place for lack of efficiency at the movie making business and I am scared to death I'll not do something I should do. Up to now have not found much they haven't thought of. Did succeed in making them take livery off Pork and they have promised to make Gerald's clothes look like he had worn them a year or two and I made them take riding britches of English design off Gerald and put his plain pants in his boot tops.

Am aiming to stand by my guns, too, to make Prissy and other little Negroes NOT wear ten or twenty pink bows on their hair! But I can see a fight coming. They think plain "wrapped hair" is not pictorial. If I hear that word "pictorial" again, I'm likely to scream.

I reckon your clipping bureau will send you the things I write to *The Telegraph* about the production. I hope so, for

I want you to see them so you'll feel like you hear from me often.

Laura Hope Crews who is Aunt Pitty Pat is a darling. She is so thrilled over doing the part and has read the book nine times. I am not sure whether Tommie Mitchell or William Farnum is to be Gerald. Both are good and I think George inclines to Mitchell but he is not yet signed.

Eddie Anderson, who was Noah in *Green Pastures*, is to be Uncle Peter, you may know, and I think he is excellent so far as accent goes and his looks are pretty near right, too. I could like him to be a mite thinner and less well-fed looking, but he's not bad. I aint quite so happy about Pork who is to be done by a man named Polk who played Gabriel in *Green Pastures*. His accent is rotten but maybe I can teach him.

George agrees with me that Hattie McDaniel (who is signed but not announced I understand) is not the right Mammy and he is still looking. He agrees with me she lacks dignity, age, nobility and so on and that she just hasn't the right face for it. God knows where they'll find a good actress who looks right and talks right.

Am going riding this afternoon with Will Price and to see *Run Little Chillun* with him tonight. George is paying for the tickets so I can see the Negroes for possible roles. It is Fed Theatre, all-Negro-cast show.

Thanks for sending me the clips from Atlanta papers.

My love to you and John and write when you have time. And how are things by now? People out here ask me about you all the time, wanting to know how you look, etc. You ought to hear the song and dance I give them.

Love, Sue

The column that was eventually published in *The Telegraph* on January 26, 1939, is the one that Birdwell slashed. The material he deleted followed her description of Tara and its grounds on Forty Acres as she first saw it on arrival and is given here:

But only the front and one corner of the house exists. The back is wide open, except one end where there will be some back-yard shots made. That is where the well stands and where fig trees grow and a clean-swept yard looks like any Georgia country yard.

And, yes, there is the shelf with the bucket of water, the gourd and the wash pan, not far from the well.

That Tara is only for exterior shots. The other Tara is inside a huge building. And even here I got a surprise. I walked into the wide hall with its simple stairway, exclaimed over the parlor with its green velvet curtains from which Scarlett makes her dress when she goes to call on Rhett, and then looked at the little room which Ellen used as an office.

Across from the parlor is the other parlor but only a small part of it is made—just enough to look like a room when shots are made that would show through an open door a portion of the adjoining room. But even that didn't prepare me.

Down the long hall, which has a back door with a small fan light, I noticed a door leading to a room back of the office.

"I must see that room," I told myself, walked on down the hall, peeped in, and found only space.

It made me a little unhappy to see such a beautiful door with its well-executed panels, leading nowhere at all.

But you can't stay unhappy long around this place.

January 16, 1939, Memo to Walter Plunkett

I am sending over a picture of a costume you might like to see. It was a favorite "get-up" for girls in Georgia at costume affairs in the 1860s, and I thought you might like something of the sort on someone in the crowd at the Bazaar.

Attached to the picture is an explanation of colors. The costume is one which the girls liked to wear to show that they gave allegiance to the Georgia Hussars.

January 17, 1939, Memo to Selznick, floor Plan of Melanie's house in Atlanta

Dear Mr. Selznick:

In the novel GONE WITH THE WIND, Miss Mitchell repeatedly refers to Melanie's house as a "little house."

On page 730: "The little brick house that Ashley took for his family..."

Page 732: "The little house was always full of company."

Page 737: "In the nights of late summer, her small, feebly lighted house always full of guests."

Page 738: "It crowded the little, flat-topped house, forced India to sleep on a pallet in the cubbyhole that was Beau's nursery."

Page 791: Melanie's small parlor looked serene."

Despite the continual references to a small house, there are definite indications that Melanie's house was not really small.

Page 730: "The house had originally been two stories high, but the upper floor had been destroyed by shells.—The house was high from the ground, built over a large cellar, and the long, sweeping flight of stairs which reached it made it look slightly ridiculous—two fine old oaks which shaded it, and a dusty-leaved magnolia—The lawn was wide and green—pink and white crepe myrtle bloom."

Page 731: "the six rooms—were soon scantily furnished."

Page 747: "There were three rooms in the basement of Melanie's house which formerly had been servants' quarters and a wine cellar."

I have drawn up a probable floor plan with the quoted paragraphs in mind, and I have been mindful also of these facts:

Almost every Southern household in the Sixties had a hall extending the full length of the house, with a parlor on each side of the front hall. Often the parlor doors were folding doors which were large and tall, and when opened gave a free view of the hall and the room across the way.

Since the action on Pages 795 and 799 in Miss Mitchell's novel indicate that the ladies can see what is happening at the front door, I think Ashley's house must have had the folding doors. Certainly these are permissible if they would further the action of the photo drama in any way.

Originally, the house probably had a parlor on each side of the hall; to the left of the entrance the dining room was back of the parlor, and behind that a butler's pantry (pantry about half the size of the dining room—the place to which servants would bring the hot covered dishes from the kitchen in the yard).

When the house was converted for Melanie's house, the parlor would have remained in the same place, and the former dining room might have been Melanie's bedroom, with the old butler's pantry used as a nursery. Then the open doors between the nursery and Melanie's room and between the parlor and Melanie's room would have enabled the anxious mothers in the parlor to her any noises from the children in the nursery. (Page 791: "The quiet breathing of Wade, Ella and Beau came through the open door of the nursery.")

On the opposite side of the house, the dining room would be the front room opening off the hall with a bedroom back of that. (Perhaps formerly the library.) And still another bedroom can be back of that.

For the purpose of the action of the photo drama, the plan of the house might be reversed as to left or right without doing any violence to the Southern feeling.

The plan of the house may be elastic except that it should, to my mind, have a hall down the center with the rooms opening off it on both sides.

The fireplace may be placed wherever the pictorial effect is best, but the usual house in Georgia in that period would have chimneys at each side, and the fireplaces in the front rooms would be as I have suggested in the drawings.

I attach two sketches. No. 1 with the parlor, Melanie's room and nursery (converted from butler's pantry) on the left as you enter the house. On the right are dining room, and two bedrooms (or the back bedroom could be the kitchen). Since there were no bathrooms in those unhappy days, and there was no plumbing for the kitchen, the exchange is possible.

No. 2 is for a smaller house. On the left as you enter the hall is the dining room with a bedroom back of this and the old butler's pantry converted into another bedroom.

On the right is the parlor at the front, with Melanie's bedroom back of this. The "cubbyhole" in which Beau slept might be an end to the back porch, partitioned off and boarded up.

Tuesday Jan 17, 1939 (Ghost walks tomorrow)

Hard to realize I have not written in this thing since Friday. All I remember about Saturday is that George Cukor didn't come to work, Will Price and I went to Miss Leigh's house to meet Leslie, and Leslie Howard excused himself for a minute and stayed away nearly an hour. So, Will and I asked the English maid if there was a drink in the house, and there was, it seemed, Scotch and soda. We had a drink, then Leslie came back, apologized and the lesson went on. Will left me there with a Scotch under my belt, I had no lunch and spent a very chilly afternoon riding with Miss Leigh who was looking for houses—or a house. We saw a number, among them the loveliest thing with a pool and calla lilies and marvelous furnishings in which once stayed Mary Pickford and Buddy Rogers. And we drove up the hill to the place where Kay Francis lives and it is divine.

To the studio, very late, then home, shopped for a coat and shoes and could not find shoes I liked. Bought a lovely tweed top of blues and greens with a fleck of scarlet in it.

Wrote letters to lots of people and went early to bed—somehow tired though I don't know why, exactly. Maybe I was trying to forget it was Saturday night and what the gang at home were doing.

Sunday I was amazed when the telephone waked me to realize it was ten o'clock. Will Price was calling, asking me to go to ride at two and to have dinner and then the show. He brought me a marvelous handful of poinsettias and then we rode all over the country—no the city—for it was so foggy there was no use trying to do scenic effects off mountain tops. We stopt at the Brown Derby in Hollywood and had a rum punch which was very iffy-looking, all packed in ice an inch thin but didn't have the kick of a butterfly kiss.

Rode on. Stopt next at an outdoor bar and had Bacardi. On to Pasadena Playhouse, then to old familiar bar (to Will, not me) for two Cuba Libres. Thence to the home of Yoch, a darling person who is costume something or other at the Pasadena Little Theatre School, had written a book about costumes and is utterly friendly and swell. We had a rum Collins and then cooked supper, coffee, sausage, grits, sweet potatoes and hot biscuit and had fun! Then to *Run Little Chillun*, all Negro cast, directed by Negroes, music by Hall Johnson. Federal Theatre project. First of show dull and slow, but last scene in Negro church, superb, with Hall Johnson songs that were perfection itself. Looked just like the church Scofield and I went to.

But phooey on the past! Today I met Clark Gable.

He would not have been worth a whole paragraph by himself before today because I have never liked him. But I did like him when I met him. He is dynamic, quiet, polite, human and fairly bursting open with IT. I mean what Elinor Glyn and I call IT, as exemplified by Lady Daisy Somebody who was Elinor's friend and always came into the room with a piping bullfinch.

How'm I doing? Falling for the movie idol of a billion femmes. George's secretary, a darling gal named Dorothy Dawson, called me and said would I come in please. Mr. Gable was in Mr. Cukor's office. I powdered my face, fixed my lipstick and went in. There sat the God on the sofa beside Cukor and before him stood Lambert, of wardrobe, Plunkett of costume design, and two other men with notebooks.

Clark had a dozen sketches before him. He rose as I came into the room. So did George, and George said, "Miss Myrick, this is Mr. Gable.

I murmur "how do you do," but he stepped forward, offered his hand, turning on the full force of smile and dimple and said, "I am so glad to meet you, Miss Myrick."

His palm was moist and he had the look of a man with so much red blood, so hot as it were, he couldn't help a little perspiration. His hair is too long and his eyes are very blue and his lashes beautiful. He wore a tan coat over a creamy yellow silk sports shirt, a tie of raspberry and yellow stripes (very yellow) and gray trousers and looked fresh-washed. His shoes were tan and had very thick soles.

George said, "Sit down here and let's see the pictures you have of neck wear."

I sat between Clark and George and showed a picture of a man in a collar with wing ends and with a tie, soft and rather large, and with a frill on his shirt, and Clark was enthusiastic.

"That's the tie I meant, George," he said, taking the photo from me, and he demonstrated on his neck how that was a becoming tie.

George laughed. And then George asked how is it tied and both Gable and I said in concert, "wrapped around from front then brought around again and tied in a bow." And he gave me a look of "aren't you wonderful?" He is not upstage and he is friendly.

They showed him materials for suits and many sketches and he liked this one and not that one and they made changes and in all we talked about half an hour.

Well, now that's over, let's see. Early this morning we experimented with Mammy's headrag. Then went to see Tara and to discuss with George and Wheeler where the grave yard should be. Then to the office and then with Price to see Vivien Leigh at make up where an army of men and women were fixing faces and hair and eyebrows and mustaches and things.

Met Margaret Tallechet, who is very lovely to look at and talked to Leatrice Joy Gilbert again and got a call from the office to come talk to Leslie Howard again. He is darling and the friendliest person alive. We chatted and he read his lines and he'd say, "love" and then to me "How do you say it once more?" and I'd say it and he'd say it just as I do. And we talked of Mr. Chamberlin and of Henry Ford and he laughed heartily at my telling of Yankee Baiting and "a foe-doe Fo'd." He is a darling, positively. I know he would always be good natured and nice and never impatient nor haughty.

O Lawd, what a day was yesterday. Feeling none too good because I had been up till two Sunday night, I got to work trying to be cute and chipper. Read mail and dictated some stuff and hung around in Cukor's outer office. Found out production date is set for Monday, the 23rd. Everybody looked dark. Men began coming in by twos and threes and finally the inner office of George was full of people. By eleven they shut the doors. But meanwhile George, Mr. Ginsberg (honest his name is Ginsberg and he is a vice president, in charge, I think, of holding down expenses – you know, "we made only a million bucks last month so everybody stop using so many pencils") and others had asked poor Dawson to phone Selznick's office three times each, but no David. And it seems nobody dared call his house. So they went into a huddle. I don't know what happened up to about 11:30, but George sent for me then to talk about whether the curtains at Tara could be of two shades of green in order that Scarlett's dress might be more becoming. I pursed my lips and looked very wise and said "Let me think a moment" and while I thought a second, six men sprang into the breach to say why it would be all right and I could tell by George's face he thought so, so I said gravely it would be (thinking it could be all along but not wanting to answer too quickly). Then George asked me to stay for the conference and I stayed and was torn between bug-eyed astonishment at the quickness of George's mind and his familiarity with every detail and a desire to burst out laughing at the pitiful effort everybody made to postpone the start of production. Nobody is ready and even the cast is not finished but David wrote FADE OUT so he thinks they should start shooting.

During the day the whole place was a madhouse and everybody looked what he was scared to say. Stacy (ass't director) told me and Dawson at lunch confidentially he had told George to go on and start but David was a damn fool and there would be a lay-off after two days because not enough stuff was ready to go on after the first sequence. Stacy says THIS time everybody will be ready to cut everybody's throat after the first week instead of after the fifth as usual! And he looked at me and said, "You're going to have plenty of headaches, young lady." I have an uneasy feeling he is right.

Well, at six-thirty last night as I was about to depart the phone rang and Miss Keon said in dulcet tones like the lark singing "Tis Morn," "Mr. Selznick wants you to draw a sketch of the plan of the house Melanie lived in."

I nearly fainted, and she explained it was just a floor plan. So I said I would, in a weak voice, and she went on to say they were having trouble about some of the action, etc. So I asked what pages showed the action they wanted and she said she'd look, just a minute. I held the phone and being scared and worried I muttered under my breath a rather cussing word. There was a fine laugh and she said, "I heard that!"

She is a good egg, for when I phoned this morning she laughed with me about it and said she knew she'd like me.

Anyway, I stayed up until midnight studying and making a plan and then couldn't sleep because I was nervous. Up at 7:30 to meet Kurtzes at breakfast and talk over house plan with Wilbur and all day today I've been busy as a bee reading the new script to make notes on suggestions and errors which I'll dictate tomorrow morning early.

Now to do some copy to send home. And I should do three letters.

January 18, 1939, Memo to Eric Stacy

Subject: Food on the table at Twelve Oaks Barbecue

Page 23 of the script describes table groaning with food. I am suggesting some of the things that might be on the table:

Peach pickles
Peach preserves

Scuppernong preserves
Fig preserves
Cucumber pickles
Watermelon rind pickles and preserves
Spiced pears
Pear preserves
Beaten biscuits
Fried chicken
Chicken pie (in covered dish in silver holder, probably the old-fashioned equivalent of a modern casserole)
Cakes—coconut and pound cake, no elaborate icings or frostings
Early garden leaf lettuce with hard boiled egg or garnish
Casters holding vinegar, salt and pepper
Glasses for lemonade, and silver pitcher for lemonade or water
Silver coffeepot, sugar and creamer
The best china and flat silver for serving
Linen napkins

The decorations for the table might be a few garden flowers. Blooming at that time would be daffodils—but the chief decorations would be tall stemmed china cake plates.

Page 25: "boys bring plates to Scarlett..."

Suggest that on those plates might be barbecue, pickles, beaten biscuit, fried chicken, and cake.

January 18, 1939, Memo to Selznick

Subject: GONE WITH THE WIND
Script Suggestions Pages 1 through 44

Here are suggestions I have to offer on the GONE WITH THE WIND script through Page 44. I hope to get more of these to you during the day.

Copies of my report are going to various departments so that those concerned with production will be aware of these suggestions.

Page 5, sc. 7: "Gerald gallops into a pasture of blooded cattle."

These cattle should be Jerseys or Guernseys. No Holsteins or Black Angus were known in the South in the Sixties.

Page 5, sc.6: "Follow Gerald as his horse jumps across a narrow stream to a glade."

Native Azalea would be in bloom at this time, and would add color about the stream. Also Red Bud is flowering at this time and might be near a stream.

Page 5, sc.9: "-'snake fence' made of split logs."

The "snake fence" might have Wild Honeysuckle climbing on it, as Wild Honeysuckle is very prolific in Georgia. It is not in bloom at this time, however.

The fence should look aged, and an occasional small weed or China Berry bush might show alongside since the Georgia roadside fence would not be neatly kept.

Page 6, sc. 12: "About them are dogwood trees full of blossom."

Suggest Red Bud effective as shrub with Dogwood Trees. It would be blooming at the same time as Dogwood.

Page 10, sc. 19: Pork addressing Ellen: "He tuk on terrible at you runnin' out ter hulp dem w'ite trash..."

The word "hulp" should be "hope" or "holp."

Page 10, sc. 19: Jonas Wilkerson speaks of plowing the "back 40 acres."

The phrase "bottom land" is a typical Southern phrase and could be substituted for "back 40 acres."

Page 14, sc.35: "The O'Hara carriage ... waiting in the drive."

Carriage cogs might be added to this scene.

Page 16, sc. 36: Scarlett, leaving the room, takes a dish of olives with her.

I never saw an olive until I was about fourteen years old.

On a Georgia plantation of the Sixties,

everything to eat that could be grown on the place was plentiful, but strange or imported foods were unusual. I, therefore, suggest that Scarlett take with her as more typical of Georgia two or three beaten biscuits. This is a very small, thin biscuit about an inch and a half in diameter, and probably a quarter of an inch thick.

Page 17, sc. 38: Change olives to 'beaten biscuit.'

Page 18, sc. 41: "The Wilkes' butler – offering tall frosted glasses."

A small sprig of mint should show in the tops of these glasses to prove to Southerners that this is mint julep.

Page 23, sc. 54: "—white-capped negro house servants are carrying..."

The negro man servant would not wear a white cap. Those who are carving the meat and working about the pits might be bare-headed or they might wear dilapidated hats (Mr. Kurtz has described these in detail in his report).

The man servants who are waiting at tables would be bare-headed. The negresses who served would wear "head rags." Since these negro women would be house servants, they would possibly wear white head rags.

I am suggesting to Mr. Stacey a list of food which might be shown on the table at the barbecue.

Page 23, sc. 54: Three or four negro boys to fan the flies about the barbecue and three or four others to fan the flies while the men are cutting the meat and serving would be appropriate.

Page 26, sc. 60: "—young ladies who are resting for the evening gaiety..."

A nice touch here might be one or two small negro girls with palmetto fans keeping the young ladies cool while they nap.

Page 27, sc. 65: "—men grouped around punch bowl..."

I should suggest it might be well to show in addition to a punch bowl, several decanters and glasses for drinking whiskey neat.

In a group of Southern men, there would be many who would prefer straight whisky to the finest punch known to man.

Page 28, sc. 66: "Stuart Tarleton savagely helps himself to another drink from punch bowl."

It seems to me that Stuart Tarleton, recently fired out of the University and a rather wild young man, would be more likely to take a straight drink.

Page 34, sc. 75: "Negro boys bring saddled horses; men mount and ride away."

There would probably be four or five negro "body servants" who would ride away with their masters.

Page 38, sc. 85: The wedding reception

Somewhere in the group at the reception Mammy should be seen. No wedding, birth, or death in the South would be complete without Mammy's presence.

Page 40, sc. 87: Mammy speaks: "Aint you any sentiment a-tall?"

The word "any" should be changed to "no."

Page 42, sc. 90: Uncle Peter's second speech: "She's too young..."

Drop the "s" and have Uncle Peter say: "She too young."

Page 42, sc. 92: Uncle Peter's speech..."you is as bad as Miss Mellie..."

Should read: "You's bad as Miss Mellie."

Page 44, sc. 97: Decorations for Bazaar:

There would be little ivy used for decorations at the Bazaar because Southern Smilax is very prolific and makes a very beautiful decoration. Mr. Kurtz has submitted a full report for decorations at the Bazaar, I believe.

Wednesday, January 18, 1939

Got my first pay check today. Feels mighty fine to get paid for talking to Vivien Leigh and Leslie Howard and tomorrow to talk to Clark Gable.

At quarter to six, tonight, went for a cocktail with Boyle then to look at furniture and lamps and stuff for sets. Not home until almost eight. Wrote Ken and Burt and the bank and check mailed to Dannenberg's (department store in Macon) and Fran (letter, not check) and thanked Horance

Mitchell for nice letter. Must write Fullie and Malora soon.

Metro Goldwyn Mayer's new offices are hermetically sealed and can't open windows. It has only artificial ventilation. One control button on Mayer's desk. If he is cold, let the rest of 'em burn up and vice versa.

Wrote notation to David today on first 44 pages of script and read another sixty pages. Wrote notes to Stacy on items in script like "beaten biscuit" and "fried chicken" and things for the table at the barbecue. Sent column to Birdwell and dictated three letters to screwballs who are asking me for jobs.

Had date with Yoch but George busted it and sent me to Vivien's for two hours. Spent an hour with George and David trying to decide who is good Tarleton Twin. Jim Craig is so beautiful but not good. Calls me Aunt Sue and says I am just like every aunt he has. Can't remember other boys' names. Must remember to get them.

Today met Scott Fitzgerald and made an ass of myself! George and David and I in the projection room waiting for a picture to start. In comes mousy-looking inconspicuous man with tow head and gentle look on is face. George said, "Miss Myrick, Mr. Fitzgerald."

We murmur "howdys" and I think the guy must be one of the hired help— maybe the man who operates the booth. George turns to the man and says, "Scott." The man sits down. I laugh gaily and say "Do you just call him Scott to be funny or is his name really that?" And they all shout at the way my face looks when George said, "This IS Scott Fitzgerald."

Was my face red? But David made me feel better when he told of somebody who said, "Who is Scott Fitzgerald?" and David said, "Don't you know who Scott Fitzgerald is?" and the person, embarrassed, said, "O, you mean the actor!"

Nice little girl named Evelyn Kaufman is good secretary for me and very friendly.

Met Bobby Keon today—the gal who overheard my mutter in the telephone when I was shocked at David's wanting me to draw a floor plan of Melanie's house. She is a good egg, very fat and gay and good natured.

Good lunch on the lot today. Mushrooms and lettuce and ice cream. So brought home two rolls and had them with coffee for supper. Anyway home late because Eddie Boyle took me for a cocktail at six and then we worked an hour on furniture and stuff.

Hope to get off to go on three-hour drive with Eddie to look for knick knacks. Must ask George tomorrow.

Almost midnight. Must to bed.

January 19, 1939, Memo to Selznick from Sue and Will Price

...the Garrett script of January 16, 1939, included innumerable attempts at written Southern accent for the white characters.

...this is extremely dangerous as it prompts the actors immediately to attempt a phoney Southern accent comprised merely of dropping final "ings" and consonants. A phoney Southern accent is harder to eradicate than a British or western accent.

...the script should be retyped with all attempts at written Southern accents taken out so that we may teach the accent from Standard English. This, of course, excepts characters like Belle Watling who are written in dialect in the novel and all negro characters as well.

January 20, 1939, Memo to Selznick, Garrett, Keon

I have the following recommendations to make on the Garrett script.

P. 79, sc. 200: Big Sam and negroes speak. One says "Goodbye, Ma'm"

Change "Ma'm" to "Mistis."

P. 82, sc. 210: Scarlett tells Rhett Mellie is going to have a baby.

I have thought a great deal about this frank statement of Scarlett O'Hara's to Rhett Butler. The Southern woman of the Sixties was extremely reticent about discussing biological matters. Even though Scarlett is a hellion, it is doubtful in my mind that she would have so far forgotten the proprieties instilled in her by Ellen and Mammy as to blurt out frankly to a gentleman the fact that a baby was in the offing.

P. 91, sc. 237: In the Dispatch Rider's speech the word "hull" appears twice.

The word is not good Southern dialect. The Dispatch Rider would say "whole army" not "hull army."

P. 124, sc. 359: Mammy says "Your mudder."

Mammy would more likely say "Your ma."

P. 134, sc. 398: "Only scattered blooms still cling to the plants, many having already fallen to the ground, for this is late November."

There would be no blooms falling in late November. Perhaps this is a typographical error for scattered "bolls." In late November there would be a few bolls of cotton with scattered locks of cotton on the ground, perhaps, and a few partially open bolls clinging to the stocks.

P. 135, sc. 402: Pork's phrase "bahnyahd valet."

This phrase seems inconsistent to me. The Southern negro of Pork's type would scarcely know the word "valet" and I sincerely doubt if the phrase "bahnyahd valet" would ever occur to him.

The phrase seems Harlem to my Georgia ear.

P. 135, sc. 403: Mammy says "Mist' Gerald, de pail."

I note that in several phrases in the script you changed the phraseology of the negroes, according to a former suggestion of mine, to make the characters say "Marse Gerald." I suggest that this phrase be used throughout.

The Georgia negro scarcely knows the word "pail." Mammy would say "bucket."

P. 148, sc. 455: Scarlett says, "She's out back."

This is not Southern phraseology. Scarlett might say "She is in the back," or "She is at the back of the house," or "She is on the back porch."

P. 151, sc. 466: Pork's fourth speech. "But Ah gotta

know how much money haf' you got lef'? In gol'?"

The phrase would be more typical if Pork says "But I hastah know. How much money is you got lef'? In gol'?"

P. 162, sc. 485: Mammy's second speech. "From who?"

Mammy would say "Who from?"

P. 178, sc. 517: Scarlett's second speech. "tuckin' them to sleep under eiderdown quilts."

It seems to me it would be more typically Southern to have Scarlett say "Tuckin' them to sleep in feather beds."

P. 183, sc. 527: Big Sam's last speech. "Hawse, mak tracks!"

This phrase has a Harlem sound to my Georgia ear. Suggest Big Sam would cluck to the horse, crack the whip and say, "Giddup, hawse."

P. 201, sc. 570: Show window of Savannah gown shop "Madame Napier Imported Gowns."

It is extremely doubtful that anybody in Georgia ever toured to Savannah to buy handsome gowns. There was no French influence whatsoever in Savannah and I think people in Georgia would fall in the aisles laughing at the idea of buying gowns from a French modiste in Savannah. Though aristocrats lived in Savannah, in those days it would not have been considered a seat of culture and, though it was the earliest of Georgia's settlements, the town had never been noted as a shopping district. In the early days imported materials and clothes came there from England and the English influence was paramount in Savannah.

I suggest it would be more consistent for Scarlett to do her shopping in New Orleans.

P. 203, sc. 575: Mammy's second speech. "Don' you dare drap it!"

I suggest the phrase would be more Southern if Mammy merely said "Don' you drap it."

Mammy's third speech: "Dat's whut Ah is."

Mammy would say "Dat's who Ah is."

Mammy's fourth speech: "You kin polish his feet and so on."

I suggest the phrasing be changed to have Mammy say "You kin wash his foots and shine 'im wid de curry-comb an put 'im in brass harness, etc."

P. 206, sc. 583: Mammy's first speech: "dis maks 'tree gin'rations, and so on."

I suggest this be changed to read "Ah done diapered dis chile's Ma and Gran'ma an now Ah done diapered her. An dis sho is a happy day fer me."

P. 209, sc. 588: Mammy says "You shouldn't be doin' dat."

I suggest change the phrase to "You oughtn't ter be doin' dat."

Mammy's second speech: She used the word "troubln'."

I suggest that the word "troublin' " be changed to "worryin'."

Mammy's third speech: "She's in one o' dem moods."

I doubt that Mammy would know the word "mood."

"She got one o' dem spells."

P. 211, sc. 595: Bonnie says "I don't either suck my thumb."

This phraseology is foreign to a Southern child. Bonnie might say "I don't, either!" Or she might say, "I don't suck my thumb."

I well remember being shocked at the use of the phrasing, as you have put it for Bonnie, the first time I heard a little Yankee child use it.

P. 215, sc. 600: In this scene it is indicated that India is the person who has spilled the beans.

The matter of India's tattle-telling to Rhett on Scarlett is one on which I have strong personal convictions.

I believe the author of GONE WITH THE WIND deliberately introduced the character of Archie, an ex-convict and a fearless, low-class man, in order that he might be the person who would dare tell Rhett and the women of the group about Scarlett's "unfaithfulness."

Probably I am straining a point. But I feel that India has been built up as a character who would never dare tell a man that his wife was unfaithful to him.

I fully realize that in your effort to shorten the script you felt it necessary to omit Archie. None the less, I still feel that Archie is the only person in the book who would have dared tell of Scarlett's misbehavior.

P. 220, sc. 616: Mammy second speech: "All ready? It's near eleben o'clock."

I suggest change Mammy's phraseology to read "It's nigh 'leben o'clock."

P. 221, continuation of sc.616: Mammy says "jes tuck you in comfy."

I suggest change to "Mammy'll fix her chile."

P. 221, sc. 617: Mammy's second speech: "Dat's whut he done tole me to say. He's lef' town, and so on."

I think it would be a little better to have Mammy say "dat's whut he tole me to say. He done lef' town."

P. 222, sc. 620: Mammy's second speech: "One ob dese days, and ... ."

Suggest change to "Some o' dese days."

P. 230, sc. 645: Bonnie's second speech. "They're 'normously high."

The sentence might be made to sound more Southern if changed to read "Why I jumped Aunt Mellie's rose bushes and they're a heap higher'n that."

P. 232, sc. 657: Mammy's second speech: "De fun'l am set for"

The most common error made in writing dialect for negroes is the substitution of the word "am" for "is." The phrase should read "De fun'l is set."

Mammy's third speech: "He jet' set starin' "

I suggest change the word "starin' " to "lookin'."

P. 233, sc. 657: Mammy's first speech: I suggest change the word "'fraid" to "skeered."

P. 235, sc. 665, and P. 236, sc. 673: My interpretation of the description of these two scenes is that you mean "Coming up the stairs" to mean inside stairway.

The description of Melanie's house given in the novel clearly says there is no second floor to Melanie's house.

Perhaps you intended the word stair to mean the steps leading up to the porch. If so, I have no quarrel.

Personal letter to her brother and his family

Georgian Hotel Apts.
1415 Ocean Ave.
Santa Monica, California
Friday night, Jan 20th, 1939

Dearest Chan and Fullie and the Girls:

You'll have to send this on to Betsy to read because my time is so limited I just can't get much writing done. During the day I am bust every minute—though it is exciting and fascinating work—and I have to ride the trolley for twenty-five minutes to get back to Santa Monica where I live and then by the time I get some dinner and read the paper and do an article once in a while for the paper, I am ready for bed. I haven't been to a movie since I came two weeks ago tomorrow. But last Sunday afternoon I went for a long ride and then to see an all-Negro cast production at the Federal Theatre, called *Run Little Chillun*. It was delightful with Hall Johnson music and very "niggery" if you know what I mean. I am sure Fullie does. The Studio paid my way so I could see some of the Negroes considered for the GWTW production.

We have about cast the Negro parts now. Eddie Anderson, who was Noah in *Green Pastures*, is to be Uncle Peter. Mammy is to be played by a big Negress and a good actress, Hattie McDaniel. Prissy is a girl named Butterfly McQueen (of all things) and Pork is to be done by Oscar Polk who was Gabriel in *Green Pastures*. I have nothing to teach Hattie McD, but the others need some coaching on accent. This is not for publication, I mean it must not get in the papers but you may tell it to any friends if you like.

Personally, I am very happy over the choice of Vivien Leigh. She is lovely to look at, a swell actress and the way she is dropping her British accent is wonderful. I have spent many hours with her and she sounds fine. I am thankful that George Cukor, director, is determined to have no phoney Southern accents with "I" pronounced "Ah" and consonants dropped all over the place. We are merely trying to get Southern idioms in the play and to have people speak in good English with no accent of any sort—as any good actor does. We will eliminate western "R's" rolled all over the tongue and British staccato and New Jersey sound and so on. Of course, we'll have Belle Watling talk like a Georgia cracker and the Negroes talk like Negroes.

I am going tomorrow to the home of Leslie Howard in Beverly Hills to coach him on accents for two hours. He is completely charming. The funniest thing happened to him this morning. He was in the make-up department having his hair made more blonde for the role of Ashley. The man finished blonding Leslie and the actor looked at himself, stared again, drew back, then leaned to the mirror once more.

Then he muttered: "Er- Bah Jove," and he pressed his hair down where it stood up from recent washing and drying, and said, "It looks so strange. Cawn't I have some oil to make it lie down a little?"

The make-up man said, "Sorry, Mr. Howard. It'll just have to fly. If you put oil on it you'll have green hair tomorrow."

And Leslie looked helpless and said:

"Isn't that extrawdinary!"

The make-up department is marvelous. They can turn a brown-haired man into a red head in ten minutes. And the way they make mustaches look natural and glue on beards and false hair has my eyes popping.

I hope Tip or Lil or somebody is getting to you all the things I write back for *The Telegraph*. I think Tip said she is sending them. I want to have you know all the things that are so fascinating here but I can't get much writing done outside that for the paper.

Chan, I enjoyed your grand letter all about Christmas! And I enjoyed the notes from Virginia and Betsy, too. All of you write when there is any news and write anyway, now and then, even if there is no news.

Your letter went to Macon and then came to me here so it was well travelled before it reached me. I think it must have got to Macon just after I left.

Please remember me to the Whites when you see them again. I remember what a marvelous time I used to have with Joe. He was the finest goof I ever knew.

If I can get another Dec 16th article, I'll have it sent to you. I'll ask next time I write to anybody at *The Telegraph.*

I better sign this "dictated but not read" for I am too sleepy to read it to see what typing errors I've made. I hope you can make it out.

Much love to all of you.

As ever,

Sue

If you forget the address of my house, write care Selznick International Pictures, Culver City

P.S. I almost forgot! I have met Clark Gable!

Friday night, January 20th (1939)

Peggy, my love:

There is only time for a brief note but I thought you'd get a bit of amusement from knowing the ending of the script – as she now stands – God knows how many more times I shall be obliged to read a "final script."

Scarlett has clung to Rhett and practically flung herself on him begging him not to leave her and vowing she has always loved him, but he takes her clinging hands from his manly neck and strides out of the scene. From now on I quote (as Mr. Jordan Masse says "ad verbatim, ad illiteratrum, ad punctuatium:"

Scarlett gazes helplessly after Rhett. Now Mammy appears behind Scarlett.

"'Honey chile—"

Scarlett turns and flings herself into Mammy's arms. Scarlett sobs like a little girl:

"O Mammy, he's gone again! How'll I ever get 'im back?"

"He'll come back. Didn't I say de las time? He'll do it again. Ah knows. Ah always knows."

FADE OUT

I knew they'd manage some way to make it seem like a happy ending. Lord knows they need to, after the way they have telescoped the story to make everybody die within half an hour. Honestly! What Garrett has done is leave the first half of the script just as long as ever (though he has re-written it—and not to its improvement, if I do say so) and shortened the last part to make it look as if somebody dies every few minutes.

What the hell, of course. Just thought you'd get a laugh out of it and I imagine you need one after the hounding you're getting

I am cooking up a scheme to take you out of the lime light and throw the spot on Dolly Lamar—who'll love it. If it works, you'll see it in the papers and I'll be ace high with the publicity department and David. If not—some day I'll tell you about it. Anyway, it is a swell idea.

Got to finish some stuff and get myself to bed so I can get up at 7:30 to be at the office before nine for a publicity conference. I'm always sticking my neck out, it seems. If I hadn't been so smart thinking up the scheme I could have slept until 8:30; for I usually get to the office at ten.

Please thank John or ask him to thank someone in his office who sent me clippings which came a day or two ago. I was so busy answering dam fools who want jobs in the picture that I can't write my friends—Now laugh, dam you!

Love and stuff and things,

Sue

Note: Sue's scheme apparently did not work out. The UDC Chapters objected to the idea, and no record could be found that Vivien Leigh was made an honorary UDC member. Mrs. Lamar, President-General of the UDC, however, publicly approved of Vivien Leigh as Scarlett.

January 21, 1939 Memo to Lyle Wheeler re

Dilapidation after "De Wah"

I am suggesting a list of things that will perhaps be of value to you when you begin to show the devastation that followed Sherman's march through Georgia. I am quoting from THE WOMEN OF THE CONFEDERACY, a work which is entirely dependable.

"Bottles, gourds, and old tumblers served as lamp bowls. Small rolls of cotton as wicks.

"When the supply of candles and oils was exhausted, a last resort was found in torches made from the wood of the resinous pine. (Note: light-ard or lite-erd is the country-Georgia term.)

"Old paper had a variety of uses. It served to cover broken blinds and window panes; to cover walls and fill quilts and comforters.

"Broken chairs, stools, and tables were replaced by homemade articles, while improvised wooden boxes draped with muslin took the place of commodes.

"The growing scarcity of chinaware—women made practical use of pots without tops or handles and of chipped cups, saucers and plates—a more energetic group resorted to the manufacture of pottery. The products of their labors were rough, course, and rudely enameled, but the cups, saucers, plates, pitchers and wash bowls were exceedingly useful."

Defacing of lovely woodwork or beds, desks and so forth, as though scratched by bayonets or hit by rifle butts, is a good way to show the army had passed through. I also suggest a caster cut out from one corner of the bed, or one side of the davenport as effective.

Remove support so that springs in sofas will sag.

Beading or carving on pieces of furniture might be knocked off.

Occasional slight tears in wall paper.

A broken bit of plastering on the parlor wall that might show a malicious soldier had deliberately beaten on the wall with his gun butt.

Decorative bits of plastering for cornices might

show occasional breaks.
Ornamental picture frames might show broken places.
A mirror might show cracks and small pieces of the glass broken out.
A blind might sag on its hinges.
Several of the slats in the shutters might be broken out.

January 21, 1939, Memo to Lambert

When you begin making clothes for the women in the Reconstruction Era, you might find of some value a chapter in a book I have—THE WOMEN OF THE CONFEDERACY. There are three or four pages which describe the ingenuity of the Southern women in evolving garments when the blockade was imposed and Confederate money was of no value.

In another memo to Lambert that day, she forwarded two photographs of men typical of the "country town" lawyer, as aides in helping him to plan the costumes for Mrs. Merriweather and Mr. Randolph. (In the Garrett script, January 18, page 16, scene 152.)

Saturday, Jan 21, 1939

Rained like the devil today. Sunny California, phooey! But studio car took me to Leslie Howard's at 906 Beverly Drive—Telephone is Crest 15860. Yah. How many gals would give an eye tooth for his phone number! His house is masculine and English looking. In perfect taste and no Hollywood look. He is utterly charming. He likes the legit stage, makes movies just for the money, and will not stay in Hollywood longer than for one picture because he thinks this place is "murderous for an actor." His house has stairs near the front door and two steps lead down into the living room that has high beamed ceiling of wood (natural, looks like walnut) and plaster ivory walls. There are many etchings, a cream faille sofa, a light green rug, a dark green chair and other chairs in walnut with one easy chair in taupe with rose and henna and black design (subdued) and the draperies are taupe with henna and black design. On the baby grand piano were snap dragons that are positively indecent in their lushness and huge size. They are as big as chrysanthemums worn by sponsors at football games. In the book case are mostly biographies, Bolitho's Henry Eight, several Henry Eights, Queen Victoria, Disraeli, Gladstone, and so on with complete Galsworthy and with many poets—Byron, Shelly and so on. And the books look as if they've been read!

I waited for him and the maid brought coffee and I smoked Leslie's cigarettes. Presently he came down. I heard a voice somewhere saying, "Miss Myrick, dear, I am so sorry," but I couldn't see Mr. Howard. Then he repeated it and I looked up to see him peering through a tiny window on the stair—a window with no glass but with a copper vase (pitcher shape) and little doo-dads in it.

He apologized for being late, saying he had London on the phone. He wore faded looking blue pajamas and an old dressing gown and slippers that looked as if he had them two years. He filled a pipe, asked permission to smoke it, and we began on the script. After we worked a while, we talked and he is utterly charming.

I feel very popular about the studio, for every few hours Price sends in some young men to practice Southern talk on me and they are all candidates for Charles Hamilton. They say over and over: "I love you. You are the most beautiful girl in the world. I love you. May I—dare I hope?"

Yesterday morn saw test for Conrad Nagel as Frank Kennedy. He was nice. Also saw tests for two screwballs who want to be Tarleton twins. One is George Bessolo from Kentucky and California and the other is Fred Crane from New Orleans. They were so funny pretending to fight duels with their canes. Both had hair dyed a bright red for Tarletons.

Coached Peggy Shannon on Belle Watling. She is the prettiest thing I ever saw—but not lush nor lusty enough for Belle as I see it.

Maurice Murphy is a beautiful Charles Hamilton. Saw tests for Jo Ann Sayers, Evelyn Keyes, also. Keyes is beautiful blonde.

Note: In *White Columns in Hollywood* (Susan Myrick, edited by Richard Harwell) Harwell reports on page 67, footnote 1: *By the time* Gone With The Wind *was finished, George Bessolo had changed his name to George Reeves. His and (Fred) Cranes' names were reversed in the credits. Actually Crane played Brent Tarleton and Reeves played Stuart Tarleton.*

Sunday, January 22, 1939

THE PRODUCTION MEETING OF LAST MONDAY (JAN 16)

Assembled in Cukor's office: Costume department, wardrobe, art department, assistant director, assistants to the assistants, dialog man, me, George, and—Mr. Ginsberg! He is vice-president in charge of holding down expenses.

The bomb thrown into camp is the announcement from DOS that production will start next Monday—one week hence. Nobody is ready and there are from all sides growls of "He thinks as soon as he writes FADE OUT it is time to shoot!"

CUKOR: Where is Platt? He should be here.

WHEELER AND MENZIES in chorus: Platt okayed everything before he left and we have proceeded on his outlines.

CUKOR: But he should be here. You can't dress a set for a picture by long distance from New York nor by a sketch. Platt should be here. You have to look at things and change them around. What's the use of calling in an expert from New York and having him leave town just as you get ready to shoot. When did he plan to come back?

WHEELER: Whenever we call him.

GINSBERG: Does he fly?

WHELLER: Yes

GINSBERG: Well, call him to come on back. No use paying a man if he can't be on the ground when he's needed.

CUKOR: He should be here. Can't you call him and tell him to get that cabbage green for the curtains along with the darker green we want to use for the dress?

PLUNKETT: I can order the stuff out from the east.

CUKOR: Well, tell him to come.

WHEELER AND MENZIES: We'll call him. Shall we say Friday?

GINSBERG: Look, don't four or five of you call him. Get together on this thing and just make one call.

Telephone for Ginsberg:

GINSBERG (on phone, talking to Gable's agent. Nobody's been able to find Gable.) Where is he? Tell him to get him. Get in touch with us right away. Maybe after next week we can let him have a few days off. — Well, don't say anything about the days off. Just tell him we have to see him.

CUKOR: Blankety blank! I can't lead an actor to the costume department or take his measurements by long distance. All I do is direct a picture. Now Mr. Wardrobe, what have you to say? Who have you seen?

LAMBERT: (Mournfully) Nobody.

MITCHELL: (Hopefully) I have the dimensions of Butterfly McQueen if that will help.

LAMBERT: I can't make clothes by height and weight. I have to take measurement for shoes, dresses and god knows what all.

MAKE-UP: It's important that I see them, too, just as quick as I can. I can't design eight hair styles and a score of beards in one day. I have to see them right away.

CUKOR: Has Gable been in at all, Wardrobe?

LAMBERT: (Still mournfully) Nobody.

CUKOR: Well, all I do is direct a picture. I can't lead an actor around like a child. Somebody get Mr. Gable.

Ginsberg goes into the other room to phone Gable's agent again.

CUKOR: All right, what else, Mr. Make-up?

MAKE-UP: I have a lot to say. If I can't get Miss Leigh I can't design hair dressings for her. It takes time—

LAMBERT interrupts: If I can't get measurements, I can't make clothes. The costumes are designed and I've been ready to make clothes for more than a week. Dresses have to be fitted and re-fitted. I can't make dresses in one night. They have to be fitted and when they are finished you have to see them and Selznick has to see them, and Miss Myrick has to pass on them. You have to see them on the actors on the set. They ought to be tested for color photography.

CUKOR: Well, we'll get them in today. Somebody get Gable. Price, is Leigh coming in today? Where is Howard?

PRICE: Miss Leigh is coming at twelve and Howard at three.

CUKOR: Somebody get them on the phone and get them out to wardrobe and make-up. All I can do is direct a picture. I can't.....etc.

WARDROBE: Are all the characters set?

CUKOR: I think so (knowing damn well that nobody is set but Scarlett, Melanie, and Ashley).

WARDROBE: How about Hattie McDaniel?

CUKOR: I'm not certain.

SOMEBODY: How about Gerald?

CUKOR: I'm not certain.

MITCHELL: I have the measurements of Hattie McDaniel.

WARDROBE: I can't make clothes by height and weight.

GINSBERG: The Negro costumes won't take long; they are simple.

LAMBERT: (resignedly) It takes time to make anything. When is Prissy coming?

MITCHELL: Wednesday.

GINSBERG: Somebody meet her and bring her straight to wardrobe from the train.

MAKEUP: I've got to see her!

GINSBERG: Where's Pork?

MITCHELL: He's here.

GINSBERG: Where?

MITCHELL AND ARNOULD TOGETHER: We don't know.

GINSBERG: For Christ sake, isn't he here?

MITCHELL: Yes, he's in town but we can't find him.

He came in Saturday, registered at a hotel, and next day left and didn't leave any address.

GINSBERG: Why in hell don't you find him?

MITCHELL: (In a deadly voice) I'm no damn detective.

REPEATED AD INFINITUM ABOUT HATTIE, POLK, ETC.

GINSBERG: How about the Tartletons and Suellen and Belle Watling?

MAKEUP INTERRUPS again and again to say he has to see them.

STACY: (speaks for the first time. Has been sulking meanwhile.) They are not selected.

GINSBERG: Well, get it done.

STACY: When Mitchell sends them to me for a test, I'll make it. If we get the tests made tomorrow we can see them—with luck—Thursday. Then we can pick the cast, get measurements (deadly sarcasm), plan makeup and get costumes made.

GINSBERG: We will start shooting Monday.

STACY: All right. We start Monday. But don't blame me if there is nothing to shoot Tuesday, Wednesday and Friday.

GINSBERG: All right. We start Monday. Arnould, get the people lined up. Test today at four.

Later, four Belle Watlings pull each other's hair in Arnould's office, at four.

January 23, 1939, Memo to Selznick

It is difficult for me to make a decision on the matter of your letter to Margaret Mitchell about writing a scene for the GONE WITH THE WIND script.

Because I have been a long time friend of Miss Mitchell's and because I have seen what difficulties have beset her since the book made her famous, I feel a great sympathy for her, and I know how truly she has been disturbed over the complete disruption of her private life.

I had a short personal letter from Miss Mitchell today in which she spoke of the troubles which have been hers since the announcement was made that Miss Leigh would play Scarlett O'Hara. She says among other things:

As you can gather, life has been a hell since the Leigh story—remarkably enough, however, I have personally heard few protests about her. But the phone has not let up one minute and the papers have been on my neck constantly. From now on I am giving no statements, because everything gets twisted, and I get into trouble."

I know that you have been faithful to Miss Mitchell's dialogue on the script, and that your sincere effort has been to get the feeling of the book into the picture, so I realize that you would find Miss Mitchell's aid invaluable for additional dialogue. Therefore, I dislike to say what I honestly think. But, to be honest, I must say that I think Miss Mitchell would be unable to comply with your request.

January 24, 1939, Memo to Lou Forbes

Sue forwarded information from Miss Dorothy Blackmar of New Orleans to Margaret Mitchell, who returned it to Sue:

"If I can be of any assistance in connection with the Confederate music needed for the filming of GONE WITH THE WIND, do not hesitate to call on me. I have a burning desire to see this picture carried out historically correct in every detail…"

Sue wrote: I am passing this information on to you for whatever it may be worth. From previous conversations with Miss Mitchell, I know that she has great faith in Miss Blackmar's authoritative information.

Sunday morning, January 29, 1939

The past week has been hectic. The worst of it began Wednesday with final rush for the start of GWTW on **Thursday** at eight a.m., shooting a long shot of Tara and then close up of Scarlett and the Twins on the porch.

Newspaper clips will give much of what happened so I do not record here.

Friday morning when we started to shoot the scene with Gerald and Scarlett, right after he has jumped the high fence and she caught him, it was cold as the North Pole and we worked with chattering teeth. After rehearsing over and over (George walking up and down and me right after him and trailing also, two script girls) until about nine, George said he was ready for a full rehearsal. They said "Ready," blew whistle, shrilled a siren and yelled "Speech, quiet!" then an air plane came over.

We relaxed. All got set again. Started again, yelled "Cut." Fog began rolling in. George took Vivien and Tommy Mitchell and me up to Vivien's dressing room and he rehearsed the scene. He is amazing. He is vital, compelling, patient, and knows how to get perfection from the actor. He talked and talked to the two principals, explaining what the scene meant and analyzing every emotion and every movement. Something like this:

Look, Vivien, you see you are saying "blub so and so and so and so." What you mean to say is "Think you're so goddam smart, Pa, don't you. Proud of yourself, huh."

Then to Mitchell, *See, Tommy, right here you are prophetic. The love of the land will come to her. Right now she is young and stubborn, like you. You know it. You feel sorry for her.* (And he repeats.) *She is too young to realize what it all means. She is stubborn and obsessed with the idea of Ashley. You know she can't be happy with a goddamn fellow who reads books and looks at paintings. You know he isn't her kind. You say to her "blub blub blub so and so and so." See, Tommie, "now look here daughter, do you understand what all this goddam foolishness is about. This reading books and stuff when they ought to be acting like men. Jesus Christ, they aint men. They read books. They don't play poker. See here now, daughter, do you really understand their ways?"*

Once in a scene he said:

You realize what the land is. You are older and wiser and you have had experience. It's like, you know—it's a lovely thing. Rolly Lee's mother is so understanding. Rolly's wife was having a baby and Rolly's mother was there. Rolly was walking up and down and worried to death over everything, and the girl's sister was there and she was so unhappy about the pain and trouble and everything. But Rolly's mother said, "Ah but wait until she hears that baby's first cry. It's worth everything. She'll forget she ever had a pain."

See, she understood. She took it all philosophically. That's the way you are, Gerald. You know she is just young and that the suffering now is not really anything. The land is all.

Right here, Tommie. It must be beautiful. Romantic. Sentiment. Get a little of the fey in it. Irish, Tommie."

And so on and on, all the time making gestures and grimaces! But inspiring, just the same. No wonder he is the highest paid of all directors. He jollies people and he's patient and kind.

But like the rest of the folks I've seen here, he likes to do the talking. I never before saw people who never paid the least attention to what others said. They are all so full of their own business they have no time to listen.

Went down the other evening at six to see costumes for Vivien and there occurred the typical rude act. Selznick was drinking a Scotch and soda when I arrived. We sat down on the sofa in the living room of the bungalow that serves as dressing room for the star. She paraded and showed frocks. A pretty secretary asked Cukor if he'd have a drink. David said, "George never drinks." The young lady fixed a new drink for DOS, one for herself and not a damn word did anybody say about "Miss Myrick, would you care for a drink?"

It burned me up!

The talk was typical Hollywood. I mean, it sounded like all the talk in books and plays making fun of this place.

Selznick said Vivien's bust was too small and grumbled that she had to have SEX if she attracted Rhett and obviously meant that SEX had to have a big bosom. He asked Vivien if she had put sponges under her bust and told her she was still flat chested. After she went out he said if Jean Harlow could look like she did why couldn't wardrobe fix Vivien up. There was general laughter, everybody showing that they knew Jean needed no sponges.

I blushed like a fool. Not that I was actually

embarrassed. I don't know why I did. And felt like a perfect fool.

Yesterday at rehearsal, George asked me if the group could sing after the family prayer and I said "No," quite definitely. Then I said I never heard of singing at family prayers though I was not brought up in a very religious family.

"Obviously," said George and went on with his work.

So far, have found only one person who makes me sick. He is music department head, Lou Forbes. He is so damned important and officious. He wants a white military band at the bazaar. I objected. He said it was historically all wrong for the Negroes to play for the dance and that a Negro orchestra could NOT play a waltz or a polka! Made me mad a-plenty. I argued him down, too!

We went over and picked out the Negroes.

He told me he insisted upon a certain Negro, Bailey, as he was head of the Union and would keep the others out of any trouble and would also save them money. "I'd have to pay them $5.00 a piece for coming out here today if I didn't have Bailey. As it is he'll fix it up so the boys get their fares to and from the studio and save us all that money."

I can't keep down a notion that the money saved is split between Forbes and Bailey. Maybe I'm a suspicious skunk.

I fear I am actually becoming convinced that I am good. I never believed folks back home who said I'd be so popular I'd never come back. And now I am all proud that people do seem to like me. Marcella Rabwin said I was so tactful and enthusiastic. David kidded me about my enthusiasm. Seeing a test run and George asked me how I liked a certain hair do. I said, "I'm CRAZY about it." DOS grinned: "Does look like you'd show some enthusiasm."

Walter stopt me and said, "Everybody on the set is saying that nice Miss Myrick. You won't have any trouble with her. She likes everything."

Hazel Somebody, the hairdresser, came up, opened her arms and said, "I'm just going to kiss you," because I had insisted that hair of the Sixties must look smoothly done.

She had threatened to resign the day before it seems because David insisted on a wild hair do for Scarlett.

The arguing that goes on! It took two hours to decide about Scarlett's hair and the girls did six do's for Suellen.

January 31, 1939

Sue attended the trade and press screening of *Made for Each Other*, staring Carole Lombard and James Stewart, by special invitation of David Selznick. She made no record of the event in her diary.

February 1, wire received from W. S. Kirkpatrick, editor, *Atlanta Georgian*

Miss Susan Myrick

All Atlanta behind little Katheryn Nimmo Howard, of Atlanta, for part of Bonnie. Her family, my close personal friends, members of pioneer Atlanta families. Will appreciate any help you can give her. Please wire when and if she gets part. Her selection valuable publicity. Regards. W. S. Kirkpatrick

February 6, 1939, Memo from Cukor

Another reminder that when we reach the scene between Gerald and Scarlett we should give particular attention to Miss Leigh's accent, and probably have her go one step further—because I still feel that if Miss Leigh can win the audiences on the accent problem in the Twin Scene and in the scene with Gerald, all remaining dangers of her casting will be obviated. Since there is a possibility of the Twin Scene being eliminated, the scene with Gerald becomes doubly important on this question. I therefore would like Miss Myrick and Mr. Price to work with Miss Leigh on this scene even in advance of our reaching it.

February 12, 1939

Moved to Stonehaven Apartments, Hollywood. Bruce Lane brought me over in his car; we went to grocery store and bought groceries, then he took me out to dinner and to movie and back home. Seems nice to be in an apartment where I have a stove and kitchen and dinette. Place is pretty drab after my own apartment and books and vases and flowers and things. But it'll do. Fold away bed, bath, dressing room, ironing board, stove with oven, maid service every day and clean linens. Forty-five a month without daily service—six bucks more for daily service. I am taking service so I don't have to make up bed or do dishes.

Sunday, February 12, 1939

Dear Peggy:

A fine feeling it is to sleep until ten on Sunday morning, I can tell you.

Progress on the movie goes forward with dull moments followed by great fun as when George threatens to use a Simon Lagree whip on Prissy or tells her we had a Prissy before her and he killed the last one. She is really good in the role though not so young nor pine-stem-legged as I could wish. But when George tells her three things to do she can't remember them. I sit off and laugh to myself and know that I could manage her by telling her one thing, letting her do that, and then telling her another.

I got a great kick out of meeting Ina Claire who visited on the set the other day. I wish you could have heard her talk about the movie industry. It was marvelous the way she made fun of the whole caboodle. She says GWTW is the finest book since Tolstoy wrote and that when she had finished the part where Beauregard is born and the group escapes to Tara she thought there could NOT be anything else to read—but found plenty more just as thrilling. Says it is the most marvelous book for sustained interest she ever read.

We all nearly died laughing when we were shooting the birthing scene. While the camera men were fixing the million things they have to fix, Olivia lay in bed and read GWTW once more. George saw her and ordered the "still man" to make a picture of it for you. He is sending it along, herewith. He asked me to write you since he is, he says, a poor letter writer. He talks so often of you and admires you greatly and he is a keen man all right, for he said John is the perfect husband for you and he knows John is a wonderful help to you.

When John phoned George the other day, George called me to come with him to the phone, that Marsh was calling.

Then he told me the whole conversation, though of course I kept my mouth shut about it. I think you and John were damned swell to do what you did.

I am moving to Hollywood. I am not sure it is the wisest place but it seems convenient—it is less expensive than here and is close to shows and shopping while this place is miles from anything at all. Will Price brought me here to live and I didn't know any better. I think he was something of a butt to put me here! I have lots to tell you about him and other things that are not to be written.

From early morning to late at night we work. Much of the time I am honestly doing nothing at all but am I always on hand! There at 8:45 and until about 7:30 most evenings then half an hour to get a car and get home. I bet when I get back to that white collar job in Macon I'll not know what to do with my spare time!

It is all much fun. Cukor is full of cracks that keep everybody in a good humor. I like Vivien greatly. I'm really quite crazy about Vivien and Clark is all right. The really swell people are the hair dressers and Lambert the wardrobe man and the script girls—much as Hobe Erwin allowed so long ago.

John's (Marsh) sister is so nice. She said she wanted me to come to dinner but for me to call her when I had more time as she understood how difficult it is to play and work at the same time. She is much like John in her manner though she doesn't look a mite like him.

Finally managed to persuade Publicity to let Kirkpatrick have some pictures. He had nearly driven me nuts. Had my picture made with Leslie the other day so don't be surprised when it comes out in *The Georgian*, as they promise to let me send to *The Telegraph* and *The Georgian*.

Must get some lunch now as I have only had two cups of coffee so far as breakfast is concerned.

Write me care of Selznick Culver City for I am not quite sure of the Hollywood address as I write this.

Much love to you and John,

Sue

Tuesday night, February 14 (and Happy Valentine's to you!)

From Los Angles

Dear Peggy:

Somewhere in Gilbert and Sullivan is a line that goes "with a sense of deep emotion I approach this painful case." Well, them's my feelings tonight.

When the morning *Hollywood Reporter* said Cukor would quit I refused to believe it. But on the set, I knew there must be truth in the report for all faces were wreathed in gloom and crew gathered in knots of threes or two to talk in muted tones. George came in a moment later, cheery as usual with a "Good morning" for everybody and no hint of anything unusual on his face.

Morning wore on and everybody asked everybody else about it. Finally I got up nerve enough to ask Eric Stacy and he gloomily said he thought there was no hope of patching it all up and his only reaction was that George had been damned patient not to have resigned before.

It is really and actually true; George finally told me all about it. When there was a lull and I had a chance I said to him that I was upset over what I'd heard and he said come and talk to him. So we sat down and he talked—not for publication he said, but because he liked me, felt responsible for getting me into a mess and wanted me to know the truth. He hated it very much he said but he could not do otherwise. In effect he said he is an honest craftsman and he cannot do a job unless he knows it is a good job and he feels the present job is not right. For days, he told me, he has looked at the rushes and felt he was failing. He knew he was a good director and knew the actors were good ones; yet the thing did not click as it should.

Gradually he became more and more convinced that the script was the trouble. My dear Peggy, I notice you said in your letter that Garrett is just cutting the script—telescoping it, in other words. But you are wrong, my duck. David, himself, thinks HE is writing the script and he tells poor Bobby Keon and Stinko Garrett what to write. And they do the best they can with it, in their limited way. Garrett is just a professional scenario writer while Howard knows dramatic values and—O hell, you know what Howard is.

And George has continuously taken script from day to day, compared the Garrett-Selznick version with the Howard, groaned and tried to change some parts back to the Howard. But he seldom could do much with the scene.

(Before I forget, Scott Fitzgerald is gone, I learned today. He left two weeks ago the girl told me! Maybe he walked out on David's writing of the script. God only knows!)

And Peggy, I swear on my word of honor that we often get a scene (say about 2 ½ pages script) at five in the afternoon that we are to shoot tomorrow morning. How in hell can I teach Vivien how to pronounce words or Leslie how to say "store" and "love" and such words when he gets the lines at quitting time in the afternoon and starts acting them at 8:45 next morning! And how can George study scenes and plan out action when he doesn't know what he is to shoot some days until he comes on the set at 8:00 o'clock!

So George just told David he would not work any longer if the script was not better and he wanted the Howard script back. David told George he was a director—not an author and he (David) was the producer and the judge of what is a good script (or words to that effect) and George said he was a director and a dam good one and he would not let his name go out over a lousy picture and if they did not go back to the Howard script (he was willing to have them cut it down shorter) he, George, was through.

And bull-headed David said, "Okay, get out!"

All this is written for brevity and therefore is not exact wording but the sense is right.

I am sick, right down sick over it all. I am afraid with nobody—I mean George—to back me I'm going to have a worse time than ever getting anywhere. That Twelve Oaks set has about got my goat, already, and George had promised to make them cut down in size at least, even though they do have two stair cases. With George gone, God knows what they will do to that house.

Of course you're going to tell the reporters the truth when (or IF) the picture is ever shown. Wilbur and I have already planned to go to the South Seas when the picture is shown for we know what a raspberry we will get about things. We fight just so far and then compromise. Swap this for that like when you swapped a colon, two exclamation points and a semicolon with Macmillan for removal of the hyphen in cape-jessamine!

I just re-read your sentence "I have an idea they are using the Sidney Howard script for the first part of the movie—I imagine they are following the book to the end of the war with few changes." Well, dearie, you got another thought. The Howard script is beautiful. If I wasn't scared of my life, I'd mail you one. It is just the book in spirit every inch. The Garrett opus does follow the book in a fashion but it does such queer things. For instance there are numerous sentences that are pure exposition and not disguised at all and no actress on earth can say them so they don't sound like they are exposition – many are in parenthesis or in Italics!

I understand the Kurtz situation perfectly. That is one reason I expect to stick here if they appoint Harpo Marx director. Unless they fire me—and don't tell anybody, they may and I will not care a damn if they do since George is leaving. Eric told me he would not be surprised if they threw all of us out and took the picture over to Metro to make it with a whole new crew

God pity you tonight! I bet your phone has not stopped ringing since the announcement reached the papers that George was quitting! I am afraid this is the barrage following the Vivien Leigh storm center that you spoke of. I don't know why you don't just tell the whole bunch to go to hell!

Walter told me today he hoped I would some day tell you he tried his damnest to have costumes as you wished when you so kindly talked to him about them and he had read the book a score of times and that even if you did not believe it when you saw the picture, he TRIED. I saw his book of layouts and he had two hundred pages and quotes from the book every time to prove his costumed design. But Selznick wants the picture to be a sex affair between Rhett and Scarlett and by God he is going to have her look pretty no matter what! Did I tell you Hazel Rogers, hair dresser, threatened to resign because David wanted Scarlett's hair to hang down like what Hazel called a Hollywood floozy? She would have gone, too, if I had not told George I thought the hair-do was terrible and not of the period and that Mammy and Ellen would have killed Scarlett before they'd have let her go out like that. So George made David change the hair dress and Hazel withdrew her resignation. Hazel is a darling!

Well, I gotter go to bed. I am worn out with the day's excitement. I hope this letter does not put you back into a fever. I reckon the papers already have done so since the announcement of George's resignation!

With love and hoping you are the same,
Hashimuro Togo,
Sue

Friday, February 17, 1939

Strangely enough last entry involves Fairfax, Edna Naud and Price and tonight all of them are involved in my thoughts.

NOTE: She must have destroyed that entry.

Fairfax phoned to invite me to dinner tomorrow night and said Price might bring me only he isn't sure he is coming. But I am going early on bus and someone will bring me home. And that Sunday Edna was expected, she arrived, but late, as was her wont in our school days together. Only I had forgotten how often she was late. I had a partial date to go to her house tomorrow but broke it to go to Fairfax's. And last, but not least in the chain, Price got the axe today. I am sorry for two reasons. I hate to see him fired and I also hate to do the extra work which will be mine since he is out.

Since word of George's resignation came to us all Tuesday, life has been a mixture of riotous giggling and gloomy outlook. Many others besides Price have been swept out with a broom. And meanwhile, those of us left with nothing to do have sat about and made cracks and told stories. I spent several hours in Walter's office yesterday, listening to his stories of how goofy Hollywood is. This one is especially incredible:

In New York he received a wire: "Come at once. Pix to start right now. Offer you so much to do costumes. Must arrive as soon as possible." Walter flew to California with no time lost. The producer's secretary told him to go read the book as there was no script ready and to report to producer tomorrow a.m. Sitting up all night, Walter finished the book, making notes on possibilities for costumes. Next morning, he reported to the producers' office to be told to wait a bit. He sat in the outer office and read New Deal literature for hours. Finally was told sorry but the producer could not see him today—too many other production problems. But Walter should come to producer's house tomorrow at 8:30. Accordingly, Walter grabbed a taxi the next morning and showed up at the house at 8:30. Butler was veddy veddy soddy but couldn't wake Mr. Producer. Walter waited. Finally butler told him producer apologized and please wait for him at office, be in about 11. Walter waited, reading more stuff in the outer office. Waited all day.

About dark, producer's secretary told Walter to go to "Treasurer Department." There, embarrassed, the treasurer told Walter the producer had found to his amazement that he had forgot he had already got someone else to do the costumes. They were already sketched, approved and made up. Would Mr. Plunkett not tell it to the press and here was a handsome check!

Sounds impossible but I believe anything after the story of the script.

Rumor saith we shall not start production again for two weeks, but DOS, Mahin (writer), Victor Fleming and Menzies with others are going to Palm Springs for this weekend to write a new script! Fleming will not work without enough script to shoot a week ahead at least.

Reggie Callow and Eric Stacy are good eggs. They tell me not to worry and Fleming is good man and they swear pictures are not made in other studios as they are here!

Monty Westmore, head make-up man, tells a good story, too. He was cabled to report at once in London. Charles Laughton was to do Cyrano and Monty was to do heads and beards, etc. Monty dropped everything and grabbed the first and fastest boat. Arrived in London, called the office and was told to report in the morning. He did, but secretary told him to come back the next day or call the office. He called and was told to call the next day. He got mad and the next day when the secretary told him to call tomorrow, he swore a few times and demanded to see the Boss. Boss, on phone, was soothing and said he'd come to Monty 's hotel at once to talk to him. Arrived there, he told Monty not to get so excited—there was no script yet. Monty nearly had a fit and asked where was Charles Laughton. "In Switzerland, learning to ski," said Boss.

When Monty recovered from a faint, he said well, if Laughton could be got home at least Monty would work on plans for Cyrano's nose, etc. Boss sent wire for Laughton to come on home and he arrived at 2:30 that night, phoned Monty and insisted Monty come on over to the flat. Monty dressed and went and they drank a few. Laughton was wearing hair down to shoulders and walrus mustache and Monty was relieved. The next day they toured shops and got all information needed about make-up, gadgets and appearance for Cyrano. Monty made plaster cast of Charlie's face and head and worked up Cyrano nose. Then made a rubber nose, fixed to Charlie's face, and they had a test shot made.

Monty said when he saw the rush he almost died laughing at the short, fat, big-nosed Cyrano and he told Charlie he didn't see how he had the nerve to play it. Charlie replied he was on his way to the producer's office to tell him where he could put that script. (Since none had been written yet, it appears producer was saved the trouble.) But the next day, Charlie had short hair cut and clean shave and thus was a Cyrano production lost to the world. But Monty loafed in London for two months, drawing salary and expenses and having a fine time.

Bill Menzies says John Frederics is going to create a new color and call it Tara—and as he says it Bill M. twists his hips and talks in a high, girlish voice. Then he adds, "probably it will be brindle." Lambert says Frederics (hat man from New York) had a marvelous idea—he wanted to put his own name on the hat box in which Rhett brings the hat to Scarlett from Paris. Lambert played it straight and agreed it was a marvelous idea and phoned O'Shea (lawyer) to see about legal complications. O'Shea not in, of course. Later Lambert sees O'Shea and O'Shea asks what did Lambert want to see him about, and Lambert tells the story—again with a straight face. O'Shea looks him over and calls him a name one should smile when he says.

Met Frank Morgan and Nancy Carroll in dressing room. Nancy trying out for Belle and being made up. Frank trying out for Frank Kennedy. Bill Menzies says Frank is practically paralyzed with drink. Bill is the funniest thing about this place.

Went over to Publicity today—ostensibly to take clips Peggy sent—but really because I was bored and wanted something to do. Sat with Ferguson and Frank Frederickson upstairs and had pleasant visit. They are good eggs like all newspaper guys. Frank Frederickson said he was coming by to see me this evening. Am only half-way believing him.

Keep thinking of odd things so this sounds jumbled. But fear I'll forget if I don't write them down as I think of them.

Olivia came on set one morning with a package in hand. George said, "Present for me, Olivia?" She said, "Sorry, no." George said, "Well, better bring me presents. It's a good way to get closeups, dear, bringing gifts to the director." He is a darling and I am so sorry he is gone.

Last day George shot: Leslie having trouble with sword; suggest hooking in holder, not tying with that leather thing. George said OK and then, turning to me, asked if that would make Lee turn over in his grave. I said probably not as Ashley wasn't a military man, anyway, just a man who read books and played music! George said they would have to send me on tour with the picture, to explain things, like the man who used to point with a stick in the old lecture days with a magic lantern.

I fear there is more truth than poetry there!

Howard, coming to work at 8:30, an hour late at that, says to chauffeur, "Look at all these people. What are so many of them doing up in the middle of the night like this?" (He loves sleeping late.)

George laught about me teaching accent to Hattie, Polk and Butterfly. Says it reminds him of the time when he was complaining of having to work so hard directing *Dinner At Eight*. Friend replied, "Yes it must be difficult, directing John Barrymore in the role of a worn-out actor, Marie Dressler in the role of an old lady who had a mind of her own, Jean Harlow as a hussy, and so on." And says George, my hard time is just about the same, teaching Negro talk to Hattie McDaniel.

This morning in Eric's office, Gibson (man in production office) was walking around with axe on his shoulder, ready to get somebody's head.

At twelve today, arrived at Leslie's house to teach accent. Waited until 12:25 when he appeared, smoking pipe, looking very blond and handsome, wearing gray pants, sandals with no socks, a shirt unbuttoned and not tucked in his trousers. We sat in the sun on the patio and he took off shirt and wiggled his toes in the sun as he talked. He is utterly charming and completely disarming. The secretary is not pretty but quite charming. Only she can't hide her feelings very well! Mrs. Howard is in England.

Beginning to think Vivien is something of a stinker. She is getting temperamental. Leslie says the poor little girl ought to change her tactics—do one of two things: Give up the role and take the consequences or work at it and stop being disagreeable. Trouble with Vivien is she is in love with Laurence Olivier and he is going to New York soon and back to England and she wants to go. Poor thing. Can't blame her for being unhappy.

Ina Claire on set looking divine in brown suit, shoes and brown fur hat. Talking of the movie industry and laughing at the notion of no script for GWTW after all these years. Said the business is terrible, anyway. Reminds her of some great monster-like things you might see at Coney Island, hairy, enormous, with huge mouth stretched open and paws reaching for whatever it can get. It devours everything in its path and goes out of the path to get everything. It stands there chewing, red mouth partly opened, spilling people out of its mouth, chewing, slobbering, perhaps swallowing one or two finally, and then it belches them back up! "You and I and thousands more, doing well, doing things that, if not important in the sight of the world are at least important to us, sucked into the maw of this giant monster, to be slobbered upon, dropped to the ground and never again to be happy."

Hazel Rogers, hair dresser of 18 years experience, is so nice to me and is a darling. She asked where does a ghost keep its clothes?

Mrs. Freeman, formerly of Atlanta and now married to a producer here, visiting on set, talking of Peggy to Ann (stand-in for Olivia). Said Peggy never went out, was almost blind, never cared for society and had few opportunities for fun, and Scarlett really represented Peggy's repressed desires!!!

Butterfly McQueen, christened Thelma, acquired her name because she danced so well in Federal Art Project *Mid Summer Night's Dream.* She reads *Esquire*, says she likes the pictures and George Jean Nathan.

Vivien doesn't like Garbo. Said she was on set with Garbo for several days and Garbo withdrew from all, sat alone. Only remark Vivien heard was "Life is a bane."

February 1939, Memos to Eric Stacy

Sue reported her daily work with the cast members on their speech and accents, and several are condensed here to show the frustrations that she must have felt with attempting to schedule time with the lead characters.

Feb 18 (Sat): Met Leslie Howard for one hour. Talked to Miss de Havilland who is going out of town for the week-end but I have an engagement with her for 2:30 Monday.

Feb. 20: Worked with Miss de Havilland from 2:30 until 4:00. Worked with Mr. Howard from 4:30 to 5:00. I understand Miss Vivian Leigh has gone away for a rest and that so far no one has been able to get in touch with Mr. Gable.

Feb. 21: Worked with Mr. Howard for an hour. Miss de Havilland was having a session with the dentist and was unable to see me.

Feb. 23: Worked for an hour with Miss de Havilland today. Tried to make an engagement with Mr. Howard but he was having still photographs made and then had an engagement with the dentist.

Feb. 24: Both Miss de Havilland and Mr. Howard had engagements with their dentists, and I was unable to have a lesson with either of them.

Feb. 25: Worked with Mr. Howard this morning for an hour. Called Miss de Havilland three times and each time was told by the maid that Miss de Havilland was out and she did not know when she would return.

Feb. 27: Miss de Havilland was out of the city today. I called Mr. Howard's house several times and was not able to get in touch with him.

Sunday, February 19, 1939

Had a fine visit with Bruce Lane whose real name is James Yancey Brame the Sixth. He is handsome, attractive boy who is doing bits in movies. Used to be Western star but since singing cowboys came in has only got bits. Trying to get in stock to go to San Francisco and on to Broadway. Also, trying to get in GWTW. Met him when he was doing bit part in bazaar scene. We had drink or two, had supper here at my apt, went to see Yoch in Pasadena, where we met some interesting folks, none of whose names I ever learned.

But pleasant evening.

Lane is boy who helped me move from Santa Monica here. All is convenient and I enjoy being able to cook for myself and not have to eat out all the time.

Lane has been very nice to me. Is going with me tomorrow to see what can be done about second-hand car for me.

Yesterday had lunch with Leslie Howard, Vivien Leigh, Laurence Olivier, Leslie's secretary and some man whose name sounded like Forbes—turned out to be John Balderston. He is with some movie company. Ate in garden at Leslie's. Martini, then soup, baked ham, green salad, Roquefort cheese with Sherry in it, Sherry to drink and a dessert of gelatin something, then coffee. No TEA.

The other day, when at Leslie's for accent lesson, we sat in sun in patio. Leslie took off shirt. Hairy chest but wore locket around his neck on a fine gold chain! No socks, and sandals.

Lots of fun sitting in Eric Stacy's office listening to gossip. Monty, Reggie, Litson, et al. wise cracking about everything. Reggie says "S I P" (Selznick International Pictures) means "Seldom in Production" or maybe "Semper Intra Pictorium." Sings song:

Cheer, work for ole S I P
So Ginsberg can earn his sal-la-ree.

Bill Menzies sings: "She was only a parson's daughter, pure and stainless was her name," in marvelous cockney.

Liston says why make GWTW? Didn't Selznick just make *Trade Winds*? Reggie says time to change the name of the picture now, he's changed everything else.

February 23, 1939
Dear Peggy,

For yours and John's private consumption – Ben Hecht and John van Druten are writing on the new script. Publicity refuses to permit the info to be given forth to the waiting public but it is true, none the less. I met both van Druten and Hecht at lunch with David, Fleming and Wilbur the other day. Van Druten told me he had just finished GWTW in fourteen hours straight sitting and he was punch drunk but prepared to go to battle with the script. And the Fleming, David, Hecht and van Druten combination were preparing to go into conference right after lunch. I'd give my right ear to have heard the conference! Fleming seems a bright chap though he is a sour puss if I ever met one. He is keen as a whip, though, and the ideas he has about proceeding with the film seem good to me. He is all for filming some stuff in Georgia and don't be surprised if you hear we are going to be down there any time. I told him I'd love to go help look for a location!

His honor DOS has the idea now (or had day before yesterday) that the picture would open with the firing on Fort Sumter. Honestly, I never dreamed there could be a place in the world like a movie lot. They change their minds every time they take a breath. I'd be wetting my pants if I had four principals hired at seven, four-fifty and such thousands apiece a week. Clark gets $4,500 and Leslie $7,000, so Stacey says, and Stacey doesn't talk gossip. He knows. And the four principals are just sitting around loafing and drawing their pay. Of course they don't count my little stipend but I aint earning it right now, I can tell you—though I would never admit it to anybody else.

The gang around here is marvelous. I have gotten to know them well enough now to kid with them and they tell me all the cracks made and know I'll keep my mouth shut and it is fun to loaf in Eric Stacey's office and gossip at what we please to call a production meeting.

Monty Westmore who is head make-up man is the funniest guy in the U. S., including Canada. He was born in England but he talks like a roughhouse guy in a comedy, and as if he were born in Joisey. He swears with every breath and knows all the stars and tells their worst points. Like all the other folks out here, he hates the guts of actors and actresses and adores talking about their private lives and washing their very dirty linen for us while we roll on the floor with laughter. He told the other day about going to

Mae West's apartment to take measurements to make some wigs for her when he worked at Paramount. Mae's bed, he told us, is wide enough for six men to sleep in—then without a change of countenance he added "no doubt six men had slept in it" and continued the tale. Mae, he swears, finally sent for him to come on into the bedroom (he'd been waiting in the living room for her to get dressed) and when he went in, she came to greet him with the usual swish of hips, wearing a negligee which "you could spit through." He added later that her "shame hair and her hair on her head weren't the same color."

Gawd, that guy is funny. I'll tell you more that he told if I ever get back to Georgia. Speaking of return date, I asked Eric when they figured I'd be through. He said, "Well, if you have a date for Thanksgiving dinner, you will probably make it."

Living now at the Stonehaven Apartments I find life more pleasing. Hollywood is more centrally located and shops and things are nearer than they were in Santa Monica. I have a good kitchen, too, where I can fry my own side meat and that is very fine, for restaurants as a steady diet make me ill.

There is a young Jewish kid at Publicity who definitely disliked Birdwell and when I showed him the review you sent from *Time* of Birdwell's book he almost kissed me. The folks in Publicity are pretty good eggs.

Cukor came in the other day (Monday, I think) for a moment and told me to tell you he is sorry not to finish this production because he likes you and the book so much but he just couldn't go on with the thing when he felt it wasn't as good as it should be. I had told him you had writ me you were sorry for him to leave the picture. I miss him a lot for he was so fey and full of pep. But I think Fleming is going to be a good director though I'll never like him personally as much as I did George.

I started this at the studio but Eddie Boyle, set dressing fellow in the art department, came to ask me to let's go get a drink and I did. It is now 7:30 and I'm home. Eddie is getting a divorce tomorrow and he was nervous and wanted consolation so Aunt Fannie (Squeers) did her best—and incidentally downed two Scotch and Sodas in acceptable fashion. Did y'all go to Press Convention? Who was there? Was it fun? I bet not so much as when I went with you and John to Savannah and Swainsboro last time.

Love and kisses,

Sue

By this time, Birdwell had been replaced by Victor Shapiro.

February 28, 1939, Memo to Selznick, cc. Bobby Keon

Suggestions for lines for Mammy in Scene 36, page 18, where Suellen and Scarlett slap each other in carriage enroute to Twelve Oaks:

Mammy:

Miss Scarlett! (in scandalized tone). Miss Suellen, behave yo'se'ves! Actin' lak po' white trash chillun. Wheah yo' manners? Me and Miss Ellen ain't raise you up to do no sich! Ef you caint behave an' ack lak ladies, Pork kin tu'n dis car'idge 'roun' rat now an' carry yall back home.

OR

Mammy:

Behave yo'se'ves! Miss Scarlett! Miss Suellen! Actin' lak po'white trash! Ef yall got ter ack lak chillum you kin tu'n 'roun' and go rat back home. Ole enough ter to go parties, you ole enough ter ack lak ladies.

OR

Mammy:

Stop dat! Wheah yo' manners? Yall ain't chillum no mo'. Ain't me an' Miss Ellen done tried ter teach you know ter behave yo'se'f?

February 28, 1939, Memo to Bobby Keon

Subject: Shooting script, Feb. 27, pages 1 to 38 incl.

I find very few things in this script to which I can object in any way. I am sure that will be a great delight to you! However, according to your request, I am making a few suggestions.

Page 4, sc. 4: Mammy's speech: Instead of saying, "Miss Ellen and me," have Mammy say, "Me and Miss Ellen."

Page 5, sc. 5: Scarlett passes tree where pickaninny is ringing bell: I cannot tell from the script where the quitting bell is located on the grounds at Tara. It seems to me that the script indicates the bell would be near the front of the house. If this is true, the location of the bell is not correct. The plantation bell must be located toward the rear of the house, preferably well to the rear. I am sure that any person who had lived on a Southern plantation would have serious objection to the quitting bell being placed at the front of the house.

Page 5, sc. 7: In Big Sam's speech, the word "yesterday" should be "yistiddy."

Page 11, scs. 18-19: Pork's speech (last speech on page): The word "no-accounts" should be "no-'counts."

Page 18, sc. 38: This scene where Scarlett and Suellen slap each other is open to criticism, I believe. Mr. and Mrs. Kurtz and I agree that this scene would be subject to criticism because well-reared girls of fifteen and sixteen would scarcely be quite so childish. Particularly since Mammy is sitting on the front seat of the carriage does it seem strange for the girls to be indulging in slapping. Mammy is a stern disciplinarian, and if the girls should slap each other in her presence she probably would turn the carriage around, take them back home, and wash out their mouths with soap.

Page 38, sc. 85: The wedding reception of Charles and Scarlett: I feel very definitely that the presence of Mammy at the wedding reception would lend authentic atmosphere to this scene. May I suggest that Mammy stand a little apart from the end of the receiving line? She should stand far enough from them that she does not actually appear a part of the receiving line; but she would be in the room where the reception is being held, and many of the guests would feel that they should speak to her just as they would speak to Ellen, for Scarlett is Mammy's "chile" as much as she is

Ellen's.

Possibly this suggestion will help: Two guests might precede Ashley and Melanie in the receiving line, and those two guests might move on to Mammy, saying something like this:

Guests: "Good evening, Mammy. Miss Scarlett certainly is a beautiful bride, isn't she?"

Mammy: "Evenin', Mistis. Evenin', Marster. Yas'm, Miss Scarlett sho is beautiful, but she ain' no whear beautiful as Miss Ellen was when she was a bride."

As you see, I am no script writer but am merely giving this dialogue as suggestive.

March 3, Friday

Started shooting with Vic Fleming yesterday—re-doing opening scene with Tarleton Twins and Scarlett. Nothing new much. Vic is the handsomest guy imaginable—about fifty, I would judge. Tall, broad shouldered, dour-faced Scotchman—but good looking as can be if he smiles, which he seldom does. Think maybe I'll get along okay with him but he is not so cute as George.

Nev Reay kidding me at lunch about dinner with the Pansy crowd, i.e., Adrian, Mercedes, George, et al. But had fine time. "Some of my best friends ..." (are gay or lesbian).

Like young Frank Frederickson very much. The Jews have a way about them when they are nice of being the nicest men imaginable. Frank is a love. Took me down to get driver's license. Bought a 34 model coupe Plymouth for $348, including insurance et al. Seems pretty good.

Back to Frank, he is a darling. Buys me dopes (Coca-Colas) and real drinks and is coming for date next Monday night.

Like so much Barbara O'Neil, who plays Ellen. Find Olivia charming and friendly, but she says, "Really," too much. Vivien is a bawdy little thing and hot as a fire cracker and lovely to look at. Can't understand WHY Larrie Olivier when she could have anybody.

Leslie is a darling—a gentleman in every manner. That French secretary of his is the trouble. Remember what

Lambert said about her. Ned Lambert is good egg, head of wardrobe and got more sense! Find Plunkett is a grand guy, drew me some marvelous sketches. I like Monty Westmore more than anybody. I mean he is funniest guy I ever saw.

Lordy, how they waste money at the movie lot. Bought fifteen dozen roses for a shot that won't last ten seconds. Handsome gowns that will not be seen more than a flash to the waist. Skirts that have 12 yards satin in them pinned up so won't step on them, never see the skirt in picture! Lambert says costs $10,000 cleaning bill for picture. Other night worked till eight. At 7:45 Clune served sandwiches and coffee, etc. Stopt fifteen minutes after served supper. Why in hell couldn't somebody have told him we'd be through then? Probably make the shot over, too. Were shooting arrival of Ellen and her talk with Gerald and with Jonas Wilkerson. Robert Gleckler, who was Jonas, died. New man is Vic Jory, handsome and Spanish villain looking.

Was greatly thrilled today when Hattie McDaniel (Mammy) and the colored girl, Louise, who works in wardrobe, told me I was the nicest person on the set!

Last Sunday went with Bruce Lane (James Brame) to Bear Mountain and Arrowhead and Snow Valley to ski and slide on toboggan. Much fun. Big Bear is 8,000 feet up and snow was five feet deep. Picked oranges in valley at San Bernardino on way up; in two hours, playing in snow.

Goofy sign in Beverly Hills on restaurant: "Chez Godam." (Seen from bus at Renoff and Renova.)

Wrote story about Barbara O'Neil today to send to *Stylus Post-Dispatch*. Hope for better luck than with the story of Anne, stand-in for Olivia, I sent to Memphis paper. Never heard from them at all.

If I weren't so lazy I'd do a story to submit to *Colliers* on this picture, me as technical advisor and what I have to do, et. al. Especially accent story. Maybe I'll get at it sooner or later.

Note: Sue did write the article for *Colliers*; see Appendix XI for listing of her articles.

I miss Dorothy Dawson, secretary to George, and miss George terribly but Vic is right nice, after all.

Shot scenes in hall of Twelve Oaks Thursday for the first time, and I almost died at the magnificence of the place. Looks like the Grand Central Station or the Palace at Potsdam. I almost expect train callers to come bawling out the schedule! Hall is big enough to put Westover in (see Appendix XII). Stairway comes from TWO directions and landing is about the size of an ordinary hallway. Looks about fifty feet from floor of hall to next floor! Lordy! What movie makers do think about the intelligence of the public. I tried to tell David it was too grand but couldn't. Vic knows it is too grand. He laughs at it. Also Gable laughs at it.

Vivien is pouting about lines and is showing much temperament. Lambert opines we have a nervous breakdown coming if something doesn't happen. Wish it would come and they'd postpone the picture long enough for me to have a vacation in Macon!

Frank (Frederickson) swears he is going back to Macon when I go. He would be a great fit with Burt and some of the eggs there. Shock some of my friends, I expect, though!

Most of the men here are married or too young to notice me. And what chance have I in this mess of young and beautiful gals who have been Queen of the May and Miss America!

One gal, extra who is Miss America, was standing around the other day and somebody asked Price something about her. There was much talk and finally Price said something about getting the Tart before the horse!

Note: Price's firing was undone, but Sue made no record.

In scene with Gerald and Scarlett, Gerald says, "No woman ever changed a husband yet." Cameraman muttered, "Yes they have, too. In California, the women change husbands every few weeks. Just rush off to Reno and change them."

Work goes on with me up at seven every morn and not home until about eight. Vic sees rushes after work and that means pretty late to leave and 30 minutes to drive home.

I'm getting pretty sick of it, I can tell the world, and I reckon I'll die before it is all over.

Bruce Lane coming over in a few minutes. We're going to grocery store and then cook supper. He is not so much fun but I am lonesome and he's company—sooo!

March 8, 1939, Memo to Selznick

On page 21 sc. 45: Ashley speaking to Melanie, says:

"Nobody can accuse Melanie of being insincere, can they, my darling?"

The people of the Sixties were very stilted in conversation and they avoided anything which might give the most remote suggestion of sex in it. Therefore, I feel that Ashley should not call Melanie, "my darling."

I realize that the term "my darling" was probably written in to show the relationship between Melanie and Ashley. Nevertheless, I still think the words should be eliminated from his conversation.

On Page 31, sc. 66: Ashley's speech,

"Now, please—don't go tweaking his nose any more—you will be needed for more important fighting, Charles. And after all, Mr. Butler is our guest. If you'll excuse me, I'll show him around."

I feel that this speech would have a little bit more Southern Period sound if we eliminate the phrase "after all."

March 9, 1939, Memo from Menzies to Price, cc Klune and Myrick

Requirements for terrain opposite Tara: Rolling country in spring, green with plowed red fields, minimum amount of fences, and if possible some large oak trees, dogwood in bloom and pines in the distance. The action entails a ride of a horseman more or less across country, negroes working in fields plowing and of course no indication of telegraph poles, paved roads, signs or houses, except buildings that might be outlying farm buildings.

This will be shot showing the horseman riding so it will entail considerable area, possibly a 360° panorama.

Also required are shots of slave quarters, fruit orchards

in bloom, shots of hill roads possible to use for Confederate troops coming home from war, also dramatic type of scenery among pines showing no plowed fields and apparently a good distance from any habitation. The principal requirement is very lush, rolling, peaceful countryside.

March 10, 1939, Memo to Selznick and Keon

May I suggest additional changes in dialogue.

Page 26, sc. 57: Scarlett says, "Now isn't this better than sitting at an old table? A girl hasn't only two sides to her at a table"

Note: "A girl hasn't only two sides to her" isn't Southern in sound and it is not good English, so I think it might be changed to read:

"A girl hasn't got but two sides..."

which is not particularly good English, I admit, but does have a Southern flavor.

Page 26, sc. 59: Stuart Tarleton says, "There's a lot more to it than hunting, Scarlett. You've got to know more about sabers and strategy, don't you, Brent?"

The Southerner usually says "You've got to know more....haven't you?"

Page 51, sc. 150: Rhett Butler says: "I'll tell you, Scarlett O'Hara, if you'll take that Southern belle simper off your face."

I'm afraid that this line from Rhett will offend your "Southern belle." If he would just say, "...take that simper off your face," I think it would be less dangerous. I know that even I, who have not the usual Southern belle attitude, felt a slight qualm when I read the sentence. So, I feel it would be better to omit it. The use of that phrase would bring the wrath of the UDC upon our heads.

Sunday night, March 12th, 1939

Dear Peggy:

So much happens and every night I say "Dear God, help me to remember this till I get to Peggy where I can tell it," but I doubt if my feeble brain can contain it all.

Indeed I did read *I Lost My Girlish Laughter* and right now I think I wrote it! You know, don't you, that the gal who wrote it was David's secretary for a year or so? Honest, Peggy, I think David is a screw ball pure and simple—at least if he isn't pure he is simple. May God have mercy on the soul of Jock Whitney and his money for I swear these fools are spending enough to make ten movies. The castle they have built for Twelve Oaks! And the extras they are paying to decorate the lawn and the hall and the piazza for the set! There were 250 extras at the outdoor shots we made in Busch Gardens in Pasadena (incidentally the barbecue setting looked like the palace at Versailles) not including the twenty colored waiters and cooks, the ten maid servants and five Mammys and ten little Negro chillun and fifteen white chillun! And that ten acre field of the Anheuser Busch gardens was stinking with people and horses and tables and benches. And I bet Queen Mary hasn't as much royal silver as the Wilkes had at that barbecue. You'd have died laughing if you could have seen my face when I went to inspect a plate they brought to show in a close up for Scarlett. I must have looked some of my disgust. On the plate was a bone about the size you'd feed a mastiff or a St. Bernard with a bit of meat clinging, a serving of potatoes that would have been enough for the Knights of the Round Table and a huge slice of cake—about what you'd serve five guests. I persuaded the prop man to remove the bone, put on a slice of meat, take off half the other stuff and then walked off the set and frowned up. I can't decide whether to bust into a sort of wild insane laugh about it all or to walk off the lot and tell them where they can put the picture.

But of course I'm sticking. In the first place, I know that I AM stopping lots of mistakes and gross errors, so the few score I can't stop I'll just try not to think about. And naturally I am having some fun and I am curious to know just how many strange things they will do before it is all over.

I enclose a note from Walter that I know you'll enjoy. Before I had Walter's note I had written David a note (having observed the stupid notation in the script). I had also written a second note to David when the next script came out with the same thing; I had been in conference with Bobby Keon, assistant script writer on the subject and had written a third note to David at the behest of Lambert, wardrobe head. And so far as I know the damned thing is still in the script!

Not for any ear but yours and John's, the company is sending a second unit to Mississippi to try for landscapes to shoot. They are also sending a unit to Georgia to see what they can find, later. I am suggesting to them to try in the neighborhood of Milledgeville for shots of ploughed red fields—the old prison farm site is rolling and pretty well cultivated. I also advised to try near Athens and get stills and moving shots and then show them to Wilbur and me for approval. If the dam fools don't sell the audience on terrain that looks like North Georgia, I think they are sunk. Anybody can tell from the brief shots of Twelve Oaks exterior that the place is in California. It just doesn't look like Georgia.

Ben Hecht is now gone. He was in the hospital while he was working the last few days on the script. I don't blame him! Van Druten and John Balderston are now working. We have 60 pages marked "completed script" but every few days we get some pink pages marked "substitute script" and we tear out some yellow pages and set in the new pink ones. We expect blue or orange pages any day now. Even Vic Fleming laughs at the script situation and told me the other day to write him some ad lib lines, that God knows they'd have fifteen writers, I'd just as well try my hand at it, and probably couldn't be any worse than the others! Vic is not a fool. He grinned back of his ears the other day when he asked me if we ever had anything like this Twelve Oaks in the South. I shook my head, grinning wryly and he said, "Maybe the po white trash would like it because they could say it was just like Grandpa's that Sherman burned down."

I returned Col. Telamon Cuyler's letter—he had written me much the same thing. He also says our flag is not right and, dammit, that is one thing I know. Wilbur and I found out from the last authority—Battle Abbey at Richmond and Mamie Chestney at Macon. And if poor Col. Cuyler thinks the bazaar scene is too elaborate and looks like Versailles, as he said, God help him when he sees Twelve Oaks! I hope I shall not be there to witness his running fit!

Yep, we are re-shooting the bazaar, and Walter Plunkett and I are plotting to get the bonnet off but we are doubtful. You see, the fools paid John Frederics of New York a hundred bucks for that bonnet and they are bound she'll wear it. If we get it off the fair Scarlett I'll buy you a dope when I come home! I am getting cynical now and sort of getting like Mr. W. T. and Mr. P. T. that time they drank the "don't keer likker." When the picture is shown I can go to Pago Pago with you to keep away from it all!

But by God I am enjoying it and some of these days I'll find complete happiness telling you and John the whole story.

Best of love.

Sue

April 3, 1939, Memo to Selznick

May I presume to offer a suggestion about the music that will accompany GONE WITH THE WIND?

I have thought a lot about it and I think it might be extremely effective to have Hall Johnson's choir do a musical background that is a sort of songs-without-words chant, somewhat after the manner of the music that accompanied *Green Pastures* in its stage appearance. In that show the music was more closely related to the text of the play, I am aware, but even so, I believe it would prove effective for GWTW.

There is a feeling of sadness in the voice of the Negro that would prove tremendously effective, I believe, in scenes that show the depressing conditions that come with the war and with its aftermath of Reconstruction days. And Hall Johnson knows the Negro voice and the conditions of the South better than almost anyone. You know, probably,

Johnson was reared in Georgia, born of a woman who was a slave and that he lived in the "white fokes' back yard" when he was a boy.

I do not mean that I think a Negro chorus should appear visibly in the picture, but I suggest that an unseen choir of Negro voices make a part of the background for the picture and that songs which have no words might be particularly effective.

If you don't like my suggestion, just throw this in the waste basket. But I am so sincerely interested in making GWTW the best picture ever made that I can't help offering suggestions.

April 7, 1939, Memo to Selznick

Thank you for your note about the Hall Johnson choir music for GONE WITH THE WIND.

Your question about Margaret Mitchell's ideas on Negro songs for the picture:

Miss Mitchell expressed herself to me many times concerning Negro singing and her objection was not to the songs of the Negroes but the manner in which they have been handled in some of the movies she has seen. She expressed the hope that at no time in GONE WITH THE WIND would the field hands come up and sing on the lawn at Tara or Twelve Oaks and that the cooks and house servants would not gather on the front steps to sing, because the Southern mistress of a house would not have it so. The Negroes sang at their field work and Mammy or Cookie might hum or even sing softly as she went about her work but never would she sing so loudly that the mistress could hear her and certainly she did not entertain guests by bursting into song.

I feel that I know Miss Mitchell's ideas on the song business well enough to be sure she would have no objection to having the Hall Johnson songs as background for the picture. Her objection was to having the Negro choir appear as part of the visible picture, and she hoped that there would be no modern Negro-song treatment of the stylized sort.

Easter Sunday
April 9, 1939
Dearest Peggy,

It is something like months and months since I wrote you and there are so many things I want to tell that I am fair to bursting. To begin with – SIDNEY HOWARD IS BACK ON THE SCRIPT! Came back last week. I haven't the faintest idea how many folks that makes in all who have done script. I lost count after the first ten and all I know is Howard is somewhere about the sixteenth, though he may be the twentieth.

Well, about the hoop skirts standing in rows like so many headless bodies—I finally got that out. But the scene they shot of gals taking their afternoon naps at the barbecue is going to put you in bed when (or IF) you see it. I told David the gals would have their hair loosened, their corset strings unlaced and there would be two to a bed or maybe three if he wanted them lying cross wise. He wanted their hair to look pretty and vowed that loosening corsets would let the busts sag and I tried to argue him into my way of doing but he had his way. That was the day before we shot the scene. The day we did shoot it, AFTER it was finished, in walked DOS, known as Pappy, and said to me, "Sue, was it all right for those girls to be lying down with their hair all done up and with their corsets on?" I was so dam mad I almost busted. I think maybe the scene is to be shot over again. I don't know.

But the stuff they've shot in the Atlanta streets is very thrilling. The daily rushes are perfectly beautiful. The red earth looks just right and the people fleeing the city are very exciting. You know, or at least maybe you don't—they've telescoped the story so much that the flight from Atlanta and the Atlanta fire are just the same as the night Rhett and Scarlett leave for Tara with Melanie and the babe. So the flight is not just a few folks leaving beforehand. There are shells bursting right outside the city and folks are beating it for other places.

I think the funniest thing of all that has happened is the note Pappy Selznick wrote me about the accents. He wrote: "It is probably superfluous for me to remind you that the Yankee officer in the jail scene is not to be coached on Southern accent."

Harry Davenport, who is Dr. Meade, is divine. He makes all manner of fun of the movie in general and Pappy's tactics in particular and he keeps his mouth shut so I can giggle with him about things. He is the cutest old man in the world. He is about 75 and is a marvelous Dr. Meade. Sounds just like a Confederate Decoration Day orator when he talks.

And I adore Laura Hope Crews. She is cute as hell and more fun than any body except you and John. She thinks Annie Laurie Kurtz is the most marvelous thing she ever encountered and doesn't believe she is real. Says nobody could really be that sweet and gentle and naive and innocent and Southern. While she makes fun of Annie Laurie in the same breath she thinks she is adorable—if you see what I mean and I THINK you do.

Had lunch with George Cukor last Sunday and am going out today to Easter egg rolling on his lawn and a swim in his pool. He is certainly a delightful person.

Last Sunday, Mrs. Bowden (Note: This is not Allie Bowden, Sue's sister, but John Marsh's sister) came in to see me for a few minutes. She and Anne had been to church in Hollywood and dropped by to say hello and I was sorry to have to leave but had to get to George's. I plan to have them to eat dinner with me soon if there ever comes a night I get off from work at a decent hour. Katherine (Bowden) is a honey.

I am invited to a party for young Bill Kirkpatrick next Satdy and as all *Herald Express* crowd will be there, I expect to have much fun. He is very bright and is swell company and his wife is charming. She is one of those damned efficient Yankees who make me feel so noaccount! Their young son (about two) is the cutest thing I ever laid eyes on.

O yes, I aimed to write you long ago about the result of

our efforts to get the widow's bonnet and veil off Scarlett at the re-shooting of the bazaar scenes. I tried to be smart about it and took it up first with Walter (who is a love even if he is a Pansy) and with Ned Lambert, who is also a love (even if he aint no Pansy). They agreed with me (as they had done the first time) that the thing is ghoulish and we went in a body to Pappy. But nothing doing. Pappy wanted the effect like that and like that it continues to be. The bazaar scenes, re-shot, are much better I admit but Scarlett still wears the veil and bonnet.

One day I think this picture is going to be a grand mess. Next day I am thrilled over it and think it is going to be marvelous. The street scenes are so fine I think the thing is a *Birth of A Nation*. And the new script we have for the scene with Scarlett and Dr. Meade in the hospital for the wounded men is thrilling as can be. Many changes in the book are made, necessarily, and some of the script in the past has been stinking but this scene is thrilling as can be. And the scene where Scarlett meets Big Sam is a tender and beautiful one. I had a time, though, convincing Vic Fleming that Scarlett wouldn't fairly hang on Big Sam's sweaty neck. The Negro who plays Big Sam is enormous, black, shiny-eyes and very white of teeth. He is very good at dialect too.

I had an hour's talk with Hall Johnson the other evening and he is intelligent and delightful. He telephoned to ask me for an appointment and I was delighted at this idea about the music as a background for GWTW. I wrote a note to Pappy and told him about Johnson and what his ideas were and said I thought them good and would be glad if Pappy would talk to Hall and see what might be done.

Of course, I didn't tell Pappy but I don't like Lou Forbes, who is in charge of the music, and I am scared of what he may do. So, I am both surprised and happy to have Pappy write me back that he has been considering Hall Johnson. But he adds: "I understand Miss Mitchell objected very strenuously to having Negro singing as a background for his picture. Will you check that for me?"

I wrote back that your objections were to having the field

hands suddenly burst into song on the front lawn at Tara, etc., and that I felt sure you'd have no objections to Johnson's choir as a background, an unseen background. Hall's idea is that his choir will sing—perhaps without words—and never be seen—that they furnish overtones for the picture much as they did in *Green Pastures*, though in that play (the stage version, not the movie) they were more closely related to the movement of the play. If you saw the stage version of *Green Pastures*, you remember the choir was never seen.

I do hope Pappy will see Johnson and listen to him, for Johnson, raised in Athens, Georgia, has a marvelous understanding of the relations between black and white and his music ideas are fine. He thinks GWTW is the finest book ever written and told me how unhappy it makes him that some of his race failed so miserably to understand it and criticized the black and white angle of the thing. He referred to various criticisms and decried them greatly. His grandmother and his mother were slaves and he spent his youth in the white folks' back yard at Athens.

I got to stop and take a bath to go to George's, so must stop. Much love to you and John.

Sue

Sunday – Happy Easter!

April 14

I have met Sidney Howard and he is delightful. We had a long talk and he told me the story of his script writing of GWTW. Two years ago last fall, DOS asked Howard to come out here and write the script. Howard arrived, phoned DOS office and was told David would see him tomorrow. Well, Howard waited five weeks (drawing about $1200 a week) and DOS never did see him, so Howard got sore and went back to New York.

In three weeks, David missed him and phoned what the hell and come on back at once. Howard was, by that time, in Massachusetts at his farm and he said he was sorry but he was just sitting down to dinner and he would not think of coming right back. Hung up.

David called back a half hour later, persuaded at great length and finally Howard said he was sorry but he not could come for several weeks because he had just bought three heifers and he would not leave them. They would be calving in three weeks.

David didn't know what a heifer was but he finally got a promise that Howard would come in three weeks. He did come, stayed five weeks and wrote the first draft. Then he went home, promising to return shortly and do finished work (polished or final draft) when David would tell him just how long, etc.

Months later, DOS phoned he was coming to New York and they would cut the script. Howard said he was then engaged in rehearsals of a play in New York and couldn't work, but DOS insisted and finally Howard agreed to work from 9 to 12 each day on the script.

As he had expected the Selznick outfit took six suites at the Algonquin and phoned Howard. Howard went up. They made definite engagement for the next morning at nine. Howard appeared and David was asleep and had left word NOT to be disturbed. Three more days Howard went and the same thing happened so he didn't go anymore.

Then came fall of '39, and DOS, in a frenzy, phoned he'd go to Bermuda and cut the script. Howard said NO, his wife was about to have a baby and he wouldn't go. There was a quarrel and Howard told David to go to hell and take the script with him.

This time, Howard had come out for some work at MGM, David got hold of him and promised him $1500 a week for two weeks. David was to work with Howard every day. Howard had been here ten days when he told me this and so far had seen David twice—both times on the set, writing fresh lines for scenes that were so bad even Vic refused to play them!

Wedding scene now demands all Tara crowd. Madly we question what'll they wear and where in hell would they get any clothes in the 1866-67 period and how would they get to Atlanta etc. But the scene must be, it seems. Ned Lambert scared me to death asking what order of nuns Careen would join. But I found out: Charleston—Ursalines.

Monty Westmore again (priceless man!) made me give estimate of cost of the picture. I made it high as I could and said $35,000 ought to cover cost of wigs, makeup, etc. It'll surely run $45,000. They just throw money away.

Monty, also, laughing about changes—particularly this working for three years on picture and on Friday have to decide about clothes for wedding scene that has just been written in. Monty says:

When I first came over here last December Bill Menzies took me on stage ten where it looked like a museum. Pictures covered every wall—all sketched how the entire picture would be made. There were miniature sets for every scene and even miniatures of costumes and sketches of costumes all over the place.

I am a little near sighted and I needed binoculars to look at the sketches but I pretended it was fine because I knew there was no use looking at the things; they wouldn't be like that when it was ready to shoot.

Monty knew his pictures.

He prophesies Vic won't last. I think he is right. Vic told me today he was tired to death and he was getting the jitters and he thought he would just have to quit. He and I are getting very friendly. He told me today I did nothing but make trouble, I was no good and why didn't I go on home. Then he put his arm around me and kissed me on the forehead and said, "You're all right, Susan, and my God! You do smell good!"

April 15, 1939, Memo to Selznick, cc Bobby Keon

Since re-reading the chapter in GWTW book beginning page 790, I find that there is no necessity to establish the fact that Scarlett and Frank live across the street from Melanie. The book indicates that Frank had taken her over and if any question arises we can presume that Mammy had gone with them for her own protection as well as for

Scarlett's.

Concerning those speeches of Archie's that might be given to Mammy:

Page 792: Speech where India is angry that Archie spits in the fire obviously would not be appropriate for Mammy's character.

Page 795: Archie's speech "guinea hens…." This speech may be given to Mammy and I suggest following dialect: "Yawl soun' lak guinea hens cacklin'. Better hush an' see who dat comin' up de walk. Hit don' soun' lak Mistuh Ashley."

Page 795: Second speech of Archie's is all right for Mammy. I suggest that Mammy say, "Who dat?"

Page 796: Archie's speech beginning "shet yore mouth." This speech may be given to Mammy by changing the tenor of the remark and having her address Melanie in a muttering tone. I suggest: "Don't tell him nuthin', Miss Mellie. He jes' er plain scalawag."

Page 797: Archie's speech beginning "Set down, pick up yore sewin'." Also Archie's speech p. 798, "Set. I'll tell you…." These two speeches would not be suitable for Mammy because they indicate that she has been taken into the confidence of the Ku Klux. While Mammy could, of course, be trusted with any secret it is unlikely that important plans would be communicated to her unless there was some very good reason for so doing. Therefore, I believe that if these speeches are necessary for the advancement of the drama of the scene it would be wiser to give them to one of the white women of the group rather than to Mammy.

Page 799: Archie's speech beginning: "Hark, set m'am." This speech, of course, may be given to Mammy and I suggest this change in dialect: "Shhhh—hosses is comin'."

Page 799: Speech where Archie is asked to open door. It is quite all right for Mammy to open the door of course. (Book indicates here that Archie has knife and pistol. Of course, Mammy would not have these. If anyone is to handle a pistol in this scene it seems to me that Melanie is the logical one.)

Page 800: Archie's speech, "Don't you question Miz Wilkes' word." This speech would be entirely too impertinent for Mammy.

Page 800: Archie commands the women "Sew." Mammy might say this speech if you wish and I suggest that she say "Yawl better sew."

Page 803: Melanie orders Archie to take Ashley to his room. If you wish to use this in the scene it is permissible for Mammy to endeavor to assist Ashley to his feet and help him from the room.

Page 807: Rhett says he needs Archie to run errands. Speech beginning: "Brace up, he won't die." It is scarcely necessary for me to say that Mammy would not go on this errand.

April 16

To dinner last night with Vivien Leigh. Present: Mercedes, in silver gown very high collar, strange belt of metal, dress like mom's gown belted in, reaching to feet clad in slippers like Turkish ruler's; Isabel Jeans, who wore at Cukor's last Sunday the hat with Easter egg in it, this time wearing heavenly evening frock of wine and black with fur cape very expensive looking; Rolly Leigh and Larry Winter whom I had met at George's; Stephanie somebody who is in the movies and doing a thing called *The Dove* with Leo Carillo; Rex Evans, huge and very funny, Sidney Howard; George; Sonny the secretary of Vivien, and Will Price.

Leaving with Second Unit for Chico tomorrow night.

April 18, 1939, Memo to Sue from Marcella Rabwin

Dear Sue:

What do you think we should do in this situation?

Attached to the memo was a letter addressed to Mr. Selznick:

May the two daughters of General John B. Gordon, of Georgia, who appears in Margaret Mitchell's book, have the very great pleasure of watching some of the filming of our Georgia story?

When I thanked Margaret Mitchell for her tributes to my father, she said, "If you could only know the long paragraphs about General Gordon I had to cut out, because my publishers insisted that I shorten my book by eliminating much about those who were not a part of the story action!"

My sister and I have taken an apartment at this address, and shall be here several weeks; but we hope to have the privilege of seeing the filming of some scenes where the principal characters—Clark Gable, Vivien Leigh and Leslie Howard—appear. For this reason I am writing you now, so that your convenience and our wishes may be made to accord. Of course, we can hardly get too far out on any location scenes, as we have left our car in the East, and being thrifty souls we wish to avoid too great expense for transportation to your scene of activity.

I have read with interest Miss Myrick's letters sent to a Macon, Georgia, paper and have a letter-acquaintance with her. Her articles have made us all the more eager to see "Gone With The Wind" *in the making.*

We shall be most grateful for a welcome to your studio and a suggestion from you as to the best time to go when the three stars mentioned are performing.

Very sincerely yours,
(signed) Mrs. Frances Gordon Smith

Note: We have no copy of Sue's response, but this letter illustrates just one of the many pressures Sue had to deal with while in California. Georgians—in fact many Southerners—who had money and gall apparently wanted the "inside tract" on GWTW. Sue mentioned to family members that she had many requests from strangers—some wanted to visit the set, and some wanted her to get Selznick to let them (or family members or friends) screen test for roles.

April 20, 1939, Memo from Shapiro to Myrick at Chico

I am returning herewith your original yarn from location. We have taken care of sending it as you requested to Kirkpatrick, Burt and Tounsley.

Listen, honey child, you're too good a reporter for me to tell you what to look for and write on location—facts, human interest, impressions, expressions, climax and smilax.

Your day to day story will give us a good idea of what is happening. If, of course, you want to send us a chatty letter, not covered by your yarn, or if you have any ideas for stories that you think spring out of the location, we would appreciate your good offices.

Attached herewith is a carbon copy of a wire I sent to Mace Litson which is self explanatory.

We all cher wish you all there the bestes and let you all know that we miss you all. In other words, love and kisses from the publicity department.

April 20, telegram to Mace Liston from Victor M. Shapiro

Suggest handling press gracefully as possible. Advising them you prefer rather not be interviewed or quoted telling them only atmosphere shot being taken, making no reference to doubles or comparison with Southern locale. Suggest permitting them watch shooting, however, so they can report what they see. Know you and Myrick will handle situation with tact and diplomacy and if forced give interviews. Suggest Myrick speak with them mentioning your activities as she is completely conversant with our policy angle, and talks press language. Regards. Victor M. Shapiro.

May 3, 1939, Memo to Selznick

Subject: Suggestions and possible shots to indicate Siesta hour at Twelve Oaks.

A portly gentleman under an arbor leaning back in a chair, feet on another chair. In one hand he holds palm leaf fan, in the other a glass from which he has drained the last drop of mint julep. His Panama hat is pulled down to shade his eyes and his heavy breathing indicates a pleasant sleep following a full meal.

One barefooted small negro boy is fast asleep in the sun. Beside him sits a second barefooted negro boy who is sleepily whittling on a stick using an old knife. Almost asleep himself, the whittler uses a small shaving which he has whittled from his stick to tickle the bare foot of the sleeping boy who slightly twitches his foot but otherwise does not stir.

A long-eared mule wearing a bridle but no saddle or harness is standing in a pose of indolence. On his back is a negro youth who has turned around to lie in a sleeping position with his head resting on the mule's rump.

A snake fence (this must be a split-rail fence) marks the edge of a field. Weeds and grasses grow in the fence corner. A small tree shades this area at the end of a plowed row. Standing with his head in the shade is a sleepy, drooping mule hitched to a plow stock. The negro, who has reached the end of the row, attracted by the shade, has lain down near his plow with his head in the tree shadow and is fast asleep. In the picture also should be crockery jug with a corn-cob stopper removed.

A pair of mules standing in droopy, sleepy posture hitched to a wagon either in field or on road or in wagon yard.

Tortoise-shell mama cat and six or eight kittens sleeping in the sun. (This may be Maltese cat if preferred.)

Colored mammy asleep in a rocker under a tree. A palm leaf fan hangs from one hand. On her shoulder a cat is sleeping, and on her lap is another.

A negro girl about sixteen years old is churning the milk in an old-fashioned crockery or wooden churn with dasher. She makes one or two last lazy moves of the dasher, then puts her head on her hands on top of the dasher and goes to sleep. A cat may reach up with its paws on the churn in an effort to get up to the cream as the girl sleeps.

A negro boy about ten or twelve years old, obviously dressed up for the barbecue at Twelve Oaks, is wearing a suit very much too small; coat sleeves and trouser legs are too tight, and his collar fits very closely. The youngster, in an effort to get relief from tight clothing, has lain down beside a small stream of water. He is fast asleep with his bare feet in the water and in each hand he holds one of his boots.

A negro man sits on the ground beside a scare-crow in a plowed field. Across the negro's lap is his shot-gun. His head is nodding and he is about to go to sleep as crows peck at the ground near him unmolested.

A pair of goats hitched to a ramshackle little wagon graze in leisurely fashion while little negro boy sleeps calmly in the goat wagon.

A hound dog turns around three times as though chasing his own tail and lies down to pleasant dreams.

As a colored mammy nods in a rude chair in the back yard she is disturbed by the "pot-rack" of several guinea hens. She reaches down, slips off her over-large shoes, throws one at the guineas, and settles back to sleep.

May 5, 1939, Memo to Selznick, cc Ned Lambert

Mr. Lambert says that you want an expression from me on the subject of Bonnie's riding habit, and whether she would ride astride. On page 988 of the novel, Miss Mitchell says:

When Bonnie was four years old, Mammy began to grumble about the impropriety of a girl child riding "a-straddle in front of her Pa wid her dress flyin' up..." the result was a small brown and white Shetland pony...and a tiny sidesaddle with silver trimmings.... The only flaw in Bonnie's possessive joy was that she could not still ride astride like her father, but after he explained how much more difficult it was to ride on a sidesaddle, she was content and learned rapidly.

The description of Bonnie's riding habit on pages 988-989 indicates again that she rode sidesaddle.

So Bonnie had her blue velvet habit with a skirt that trailed down the pony's side and a black hat with a red plume...."

Saturday night, May 27

On Wednesday, the 17th had my fortune told by Lola. She told me a lot of stuff about dirty blonds and breaking with a blonde and dark man in my past and that I should be rich and happiest in 1940 and also would always have lots of money.

Thursday night, the dirty blonde called me. Hope the

rest of the fortune works out as well!

* * *

Things I want to keep in mind. Friday, 26th, afternoon off to go shopping. Santa Barbara Sunday 21st. Straight week all very nice. Broke date with Bill Mueller for dinner, Bill sick and it seemed the right thing to do. Call about 9:30 Wednesday. Phil Harris Thursday 25th. Pretty stinking. Friday 19th met Bob Kearney. Tuesday, supper at Beachcombers; saw "Ellen O'Hara O'Neil." Nice gal.

* * *

Looked back over diary and found reference to wedding scene. Well, we never made it! I wrote notes to DOS about why not in the courthouse or city hall, etc. Much talk, decided must be church wedding. Stuff about clothes, who there, etc. While I am at Chico, get called how would Scarlett sign name. All at sea. They don't take my advice. But when I get home, find substituted check for $300 to pay taxes on Tara in lieu of wedding scene. Signature: Scarlett O'Hara Kennedy.

* * *

Almost pulled a big boner! Got scared to death today when I found it out. Realized as I read scene to be shot today that Bonnie called Rhett "Daddy." All wrong. Got it changed but had to check back for hours to see if "Daddy" had been used before and I had missed it. Boy, would I have been in a mess. Okay, though.

Sunday about ten and I've just had two cups of coffee and feel pretty fine.

May 28, 1939

Dearest Peggy:

Much amusing water has passed under the bridge and many troublesome droplets have gone, too, since last I managed to get a letter to you. (My Gawd, that almost rhymes. Undoubtedly due to my training in helping David write script.)

One of the recent amusements I must tell quickly before I forget it. Vivien and Clark were reading the new script—delivered hot off the press at three for rehearsal at three-fifteen and it was the morning-after-the rape scene. Rhett comes into the room where Scarlett is lying in bed and the script says she is humming a song of the period—obviously very happy. Clark grinned at her and said what was she going to sing and she said I would have to suggest some Southern song of the period. Whereupon I, with my usual quick-wittedness and my fine acquaintance with the South and the period, suggested

"It aint what you do, it's the way that you do it."

They yelled so loud that people came in from the next stage where *Intermezzo* is being shot to see what was the matter!

I hope you—you radioless person—are familiar with that song which is now raging on all the ether.

Sidney Howard has long gone and I miss him. He was so delightful and so understanding of the true situation. When he left he came to say good bye to me and I asked if the script were finished, he said yes, it was, but no doubt David would re-write it and it would not surprise Howard if DOS called him back from New York in a month or so to rewrite it once more. You know, I think, that the script is now about fifty pages more than when Howard first wrote it and is twenty more than Howard wrote it the second time after fifteen more writers had re-written it. I saw all the cut stuff the other night—all we have made since the 24th of January. It took from nine to eleven-thirty to run it and God knows how much more there is to make.

Our production schedule that came to us yesterday is meant to show us through to the finish and with two directors working the first unit we are scheduled to be through on June 22. Sam Wood is going to shoot on one stage while Vic shoots on the other and I am to dash madly between here and there. And besides those, Bill Menzies has a third unit working at things where doubles are used and making Montages and so on. I can't find out from anybody at all what is going to be my situation when the production is closed for this, it seems, is the way they do things! On the 22nd if we are really closed by that time, Vivien is to have a five-week holiday and the stuff we have made is to be re-cut and reviewed and then previewed and cut some more and plans made for re-takes and new script will be done for some scenes and so on. Then she—Vivien—returns and we make re-takes. Eric says they will surely want me for re-takes. But what the hell they expect me to do during the five weeks interlude I don't know. If they want to pay me and let me just sit, I can do it. But if they want me to go home and come back, I don't know. How in hell can I go back to the paper for five weeks and then come back here for five more!

I am trying to get up nerve to ask David flat out what will be the situation. I am hoping to make him keep me on the pay roll and have no work to do so I can go about California and see things I want to see.

I haven't written you in such ages I think I have never told you about the Chico trip where I went with a second unit to take exteriors and we loafed for two weeks and got only four shots because we wanted clouds and there were no clouds! I had a divine time. I wore a play suit and loafed in the sun and rested to beat the band. If I hadn't I would have been throwing things by this time and picking at the covers. The whole company is so dam tired of the picture they are ready to cut each other's throats at any moment.

Things that used to amuse the hell out of me make me a little sick now! For instance, this is really funny but it made me tired because it meant more delay. The other morning we came as usual at nine to work. Vic was worrying about the way Vivien's hair was done—it didn't match for some other stuff he had shot that was the next scene after what we were to do that morning. He called the hair dresser, bawled her out and she said she was sorry but Mr. Selznick had okayed that hair do three weeks ago and she had the signature to prove it. Vic said it didn't matter, that was not right. There were arguments. He called me. I agreed with the hair dresser that Vivien would look like a fool lying down for a nap with her hair done in curls and puffs and so on. Vic argued she didn't have time to change her clothes and do her hair, as the script indicated she went hurriedly to Mellie's. So it raged. At ten, Vic phoned David. He wasn't up, of course. We stalled around until eleven when David called back and he listened to the talk, then said he insisted the hair be done as he had previously said it should be done. We got the first shot in the can that day at one-thirty! Eric Stacey never ties his shoes until the first shot is made and he laughed that day and said his feet were getting sore from the way his shoes slipped on and off.

Note: In her copy of Flamini's *Scarlett, Rhett, and a Cast of Thousands*, Sue wrote in 1975, on page 214 beneath the printed copy: "Stacy wore laced-up shoes. He never tied them until one scene was shot (each day). Sometimes, he never got them tied."

I forgot to say that up at Chico I met a camera man who was lots of fun. He was back here for ten days and I had a marvelous time dancing with him and doing (going to) attractive bars. Now he is away on assignment and I don't know when he will be back. Meanwhile I am enjoying the prospect of Lee Hutchins, former Fort Valley-ite and good friend of Aaron and me, who is coming here to work next week. He does something for the government about plant diseases and is to fix up the cherry trees of this part of the world. Seems they are wasting with some mysterious malady.

I spent the day with John's sister the Sunday before I went to Chico and haven't seen them since. Ashamed of not calling for they are such grand people. Dr. Bowden (John Marsh's brother-in-law) is utterly charming. The day I Sunday-dinnered with them they had guests from the University, also, who were lots of fun and told good stories and made my day most delightful. The Bowdens live about as far from us as—well, it is about like your going down to Milner for Sunday dinner. The limits of Los Angles, you know, are just outside Shanghai, China.

I am Sunday-dinnering today with some Britishers, yclept Pearsons, who are pretty nice. So I must stop this and gird up my loins in the pretty new frock I bought myself the other night. (I have to shop after dark at little cheap stores that stay open late because I never have time off in the daylight.)

Best love to you and Johnnie,

Sue

P S Almost forgot. The stuff about the Yankee soldier was most amusing. Thanks. Paul Hurst played the Yankee and did it right well. I did NOT have a note on his accent, either.

Sue

Tuesday, May 30, 1939

Memorial Day but no holiday! I worked from nine to seven, and then to ten. Shot over and over Mammy's walk up stairs with Mellie, crying about Mr. Rhett and Bonnie's death. We began the shot after lunch yesterday, worked on camera set up all afternoon, started to shoot the scene about six, took out for dinner at 7:30, worked till quarter to ten—then they told us to go home, seeing that Mammy would never get the dialogue. She had been given the two pages of script, all of it her lines, only a few hours before. She just naturally needs more time. So back this morning and got first take about twelve-thirty but kept on till two. We finished that shot before we had lunch. I ate with Ernie Haller, head cameraman who is very nice person and Tilly Thompson, script gal. Enjoyed a Martini before lunch for had stayed up very late evening before playing Pitch, had lost about a quarter and then slept late and had not had breakfast. Did not mind working today as had nobody to play with anyway. The available gentleman who is interesting had gone to Long Beach for the day and I was not invited. Home about eight tonight, read *Telegraphs* of two days and ate supper and now waiting, sort of hoping phone will ring. But shan't be surprised if it does not.

Funny thing about the funeral design for movie. Mrs. Deighton came to Forty where we shot in morning and told me she had put through the order for rosebuds and crepe streamer. Now they had wide moiré ribbon and wreath. I said stick to the first design as I had talked it over with Bobby. Got to set after lunch (we moved in from the Forty) and flower man and Arden (prop man) were fussing about. The roses were ENOURMOUS—a funny wreath of greenish white flowers—wrong, no crepe yet, bunch of carnations available, spray of valley lilies looking like bridal bouquet ready. Of available stuff, I used spray of carnations, got sewing woman to fix crepe streamers and sent Arden to get Vic to okay. Spray pinned on door. Shot inside all afternoon. Today got ready to shoot Mellie's entrance, Vic said wreath wrong. Made Arden call best florist in town and get small buds and we used them.

Today all were supposed to get double pay for the holiday. DOS walked on set, unshaven, rumpled, etc., about eleven. Arden said: "Look. He can't fool me. Just came to get double pay today!"

Noise on set drives Fleming wild at time. Other day he called to Eric, "I wish you'd give this crew about a teaspoonful of hysterical powders."

Today Viv said, "David wants me to be aged, wants circles under my eyes down to my navel. I am 26, Scarlett was 28. I don't want to look so goddamn old!" DOS sent note to Monty saying Beau at eleven months must look three months older than Beau at eight months, and Monty must be sure about make-up. Aging a baby three months for a shot is funny but funnier yet is they shoot the eleven-month old Beau when the child is really fourteen months and wait four months and shoot Beau at eight months—using the same child.

Wednesday, June 7, 1939

Pay day and an extra day's check today because we got double time for working on Memorial Day.

Ernie Haller took me to lunch and told a story about a

man stopping on the eighth floor at a hotel, staying in a room that looked down over a wing and the occupants of the lower room had left the shades up. The gentleman stood and watched proceedings in the room below and finally figured out the room number and telephoned the room. The man answered. "This is God calling," said the watcher. "Aren't you ashamed of yourself?"

* * *

Stories about Republic—the quickies all the time. One is "Never mind the actors, go ahead and shoot."

* * *

Monty Westmore tells of being in the make-up racket many years ago. "Had a sort of pulpit on a raised platform so the guys and dames at the other end of the long room would see one over one another's heads and I'd stand up there and give them the dope about make up." Then he had a dramatic school, used to take pictures of them emoting with a movie camera but no film in it! Monty once worked with Buster Keaton on movies. Tells of scene where Keaton was looking at himself in the mirror and Monty doing make-up on him, sticking crepe hair on, and there were three mirrors and they used spirit gum and Buster couldn't find his own face nor could Monty—they stuck crepe hair all over each other and made the funniest movie ever made—by mistake.

Monty tells of Phil Goldstone, a director in old days, who said, "A rock is a rock and a tree is a tree. Make it in Griffith Park. The park is free."

Victor Jory tells of producers meeting he was called into. *Midsummer Night's Dream* was just finished and these birds thought if it made a hit they'd produce a Shakespearian drama. Asked Victor (who had played in many Shakespeare plays) what suited best—*Macbeth*, *Hamlet* or *Othello*. Vic said *Macbeth* appealed most but some producer held out for *Othello*. Another said, "No, that wouldn't do in the South because Othello was a Negro."

"He wasn't," protested Victor.

"But he looks like one and that would be all the same," protested the producer.

Another producer said, well they could change it and make Othello a white man and Vic protested. "You can't do that. You can't change Shakespeare."

"Who's producing this picture?" demanded the producer. "Me or Shakespeare?"

* * *

On June 3 complete shambles on the set. We went to make wild tracks because nothing to shoot, for Sam Wood was still working on the shot he had been on for the third day and should have finished the day before. We had done all Gable's wild track—about an hour's work—when David came in and made them do it all over because he thought maybe it wasn't right yet. It took us until two forty-five and I thought I'd die. Then we loafed until 5:30 in the afternoon and worked until eleven.

Note: Wild tracks are recordings of the tone (sounds) of the area where the movie is being shot when it is quiet and when it is naturally noisy, usually when the camera is not rolling. Background sounds shift when the camera moves, and without these "wild tracks" for the sound mixer, the shift in ambient sounds will be noticeable. Even lights give off recordable sounds.

Cline said he had worked an hour to get set up and then Wood said, "Can't we do this better with a boom?" Haller said if you wish sir and Wood said let's get a boom. Haller said it would take about an hour and a half so Wood said okay let's shoot it. Cline says he and Ernie knew all the time Sam wouldn't use a boom in that little place.

Shambles last night too. Went for rehearsal at 7:30 and supposed to finish by eleven. Well, at 9:30, nothing done and Vivien furious. Turned out the set had been built too close to black background and it was impossible to light it. Vivien told Ray Cline it was inexcusable inefficiency and he said, "Yes, but so what. It would take another hour to get it ready," and she said, "Well, so what?" She could go home and we could shoot it tonight. So they are shooting it but I didn't have to stay.

Home at seven. Called Gladstone 6461 but no answer so am doing my column, this stuff and some letters. Have to do a column as guest columnist for a United Press fellow. Seems rather nice chance to get name in many papers so must get at it.

* * *

Later—about eight:

Have written four letters and the Sunday story. Back to clean up desk and found notes I must write down. Out at Agoura, location Hearst ranch—green man picked up bushes fixed in a box and grumbled "These bushes have wormed in every shot today."

Bill Menzies telling how he flew to Paris to prove physical courage, scared to death of plane. Betty said she had to have a brandy or she couldn't board the plane and he thanked god and took four or five. Soon as he got aboard he asked for a brandy. The steward said, "Beg pawdon, suh, but cawn't seerve until we are off the ground."

Soon as they were off the ground, Bill had more. Says he doesn't yet know what Paris looked like for he was too drunk and when he got sober it was time to get drunk again so he could bear to fly back.

Bill also tells of being on stage with Doug Fairbanks, Sr. Doug loved practical jokes—sees all these guys are merry andrews! One day forty men on set. Doug hired forty to goose 'em. Took off hat as signal and everybody goosed. Men hanging on rafters, climbing up walls, doing back flips and though nobody goosed Bill he climbed a parallel ten feet high just out of being scared. Can't bear to be scared, he vows. Jumped ten feet when anybody pointed a stick at him after we killed a snake. After the day's work (20 hours started at one a.m.) Bill, Sam, Harve, and Will got stinking.

Will wanted to bring me home from Studio. Thank heaven Tilly Thompson the script gal asked me to ride with her and I went on and left word for Will I'd gone. He phoned me about ten.

Bill says he likes roughing it in a pent house at the Waldorf. Did think of Biltmore at Santa Barbara but was scared he might look out the window and see a mountain.

Somebody asked Jack Cosgrove "to what do you attribute your ceaseless energy, Jack?" Jack was about asleep and had drunk ten beers. Jack never opened his eyes and replied, "Fornication."

Somebody remarked about memo from DOS and Jack said, "I think that guy is a disappointed title writer he sends so many g-d memos."

June 16, 1939, continued

We do not have the first pages for June 16.

Bill Herbert, chief of publicity, called me in office, showed me a letter from McBride Publishers, asking my address. Wonder what they want.

Eliza Wilson, writer for *Screenland* and something else, asked me today if I would like to do article on Vivien Leigh for one of the magazines, promised to write editor tonight. Should like to do it.

Viv says Scarlett had no sense of humor but she was funny. Viv discovered it when she read book after she took the role. Says she came here for a vacation (really to see Larry of course) and they begged her to take the role and she never wanted it. She hates pictures and intends to return to the legitimate stage. Never to do nightclubs. Has not seen California. She hates it and if she can say "Don't know it," she won't be embarrassed. Says she hopes to see the rest of America but wants no part of California. She is great at pantomime, loves it, admires it, says she is not good but Larry is wonderful. Today she is gay, enthusiastic, volatile—down to the depths yesterday and the day before, cried all day, cross and mean to the girls. Today exuberant, giggling, gay, got present and three wires from Larry in one day. Mobile face, changes with moods. Not the same twice say all her friends of her pictures. Not two-faced, but a thousand of them!

Like Sherwood Anderson, Clark Gable was a "sweet"

man, generous with his time and kindliness; everybody on the GWTW sets adores him—hairdressers, makeup men and women, electricians, grips, cameramen—everybody. He could do no wrong.

When we were shooting the scene where Rhett and Mammy were making up past differences just after the birth of Bonnie, there chanced to be a 10-minute break while electricians adjusted some lights to suit the camera's angle. Clark slipped me the key to his dressing room, asked me to fetch him the bottle of Scotch. I fetched it and he got one of the crew to empty the bottle of make-believe bourbon which he and Mammy had been sharing in their scene and then replace it with real Scotch whisky, all done furtively and unseen by the director or the cast.

Shooting resumed, Mammy took a big swig of what she thought was tea and her discovery of the Scotch brought coughs and whoops of laughter, breaking up the scene entirely. Had anybody else pulled such a stunt, the director would have hit the ceiling. As it was, he and the cast and crew had a 10-minute laugh and shooting was begun again.

Olivia, too, was "sweet." Vivien Leigh was not. She was bright, beautiful, intelligent and a magnificent actress, but she didn't bother to be friendly. Only when strangers came on the set and she wanted to impress them with her "Southern-ness" did she make an effort. "Are the visitors from the South?" she asked me. "If they are, I want to make my eyes look as green as possible."

One evening at Vivien's home, Laurence Olivier was one of the guests, and following dinner, he and Vivien played a "game" which they called "way to kill babies." Each would act out a fashion for destruction of a child while everybody else guessed what was going on. Vivien, for example, acted as if she were driving a car, talking the while to some little thing sitting beside her. Then she lifted the imaginary child to her lap, affectionately murmuring little love messages into its ears. With a sudden move, she jerked the phantom child from her lap, threw it out the window and drove rapidly off, smiling and humming as she went.

June 29, 1939

Lew Smith's report of a story that is Walter Pigeon's favorite: Englishman calls a friend over the phone, takes hours to get central. Gives the number Ealing 1234. Central asked him to repeat the name designation: Britisher replied, "Ealing—E as in 'Erbert, A what the 'orses eats, L where I 'opes you goes, I for me, N 'negg what 'ens lays and G for Gesus Christ, give me the number."

* * *

Tommy Mitchell, riding wooden horse; "Hate snakes and I'm scared of rats too and if I had my ways I'd never get near a damn horse." Talks of dialogue, says "Moronic bastards..."

* * *

Vic shooting scene with Pitty and Rhett, "Shoot one without the lamp."

Clark: "Why not shoot one without the actors?"

Vic: "Hell, we shot the whole thing without a book."

We wait and wait to get a shot. Vic: "Jock Whitney's father is spinning in his grave."

Vic peeling orange for me at Forty on June 26.

We shot scenes with Mrs. Merriweather and Phyllis Callow and Rhett. Vic: (as Laura says she doesn't have cue at right time) "Clark, if you'll just turn your back, I'll get her in."

Clark: "Turn my back to the camera? You'll never get her in if you wait for that." Then Clark demonstrates how he walks up and down, restless pacing, and he walks backwards so he faces camera and mugs it up.

End of diary.

Leslie Howard (Ashley Wilkes) with Sue

Victor Fleming and sue

Sue and Olivia de Havilland

The following pictures Sue took in California, or others took of her, probably with her camera. All were in her GWTW scrapbook.

Sue at the "wrap" party

Alicia Rhett in Charleston, SC

Preparing for Christmas scene at Aunt Pittypat's house

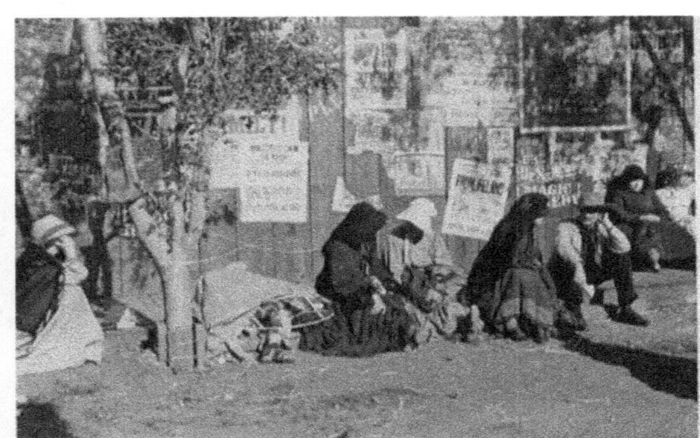

Extras dressed as refugees from war

Sue at rest

Sue at the "wrap" party

The City of Atlanta
requests the honor of your presence
at a special showing of
"The Battle of Atlanta"
Cyclorama, Grant Park

honoring
Mr. David O. Selznick
Mr. Clark Gable   Miss Vivien Leigh
and other distinguished guests
Friday afternoon, December fifteenth
nineteen hundred and thirty-nine
at half after twelve o'clock

Buffet Lunch

Please present
card at door

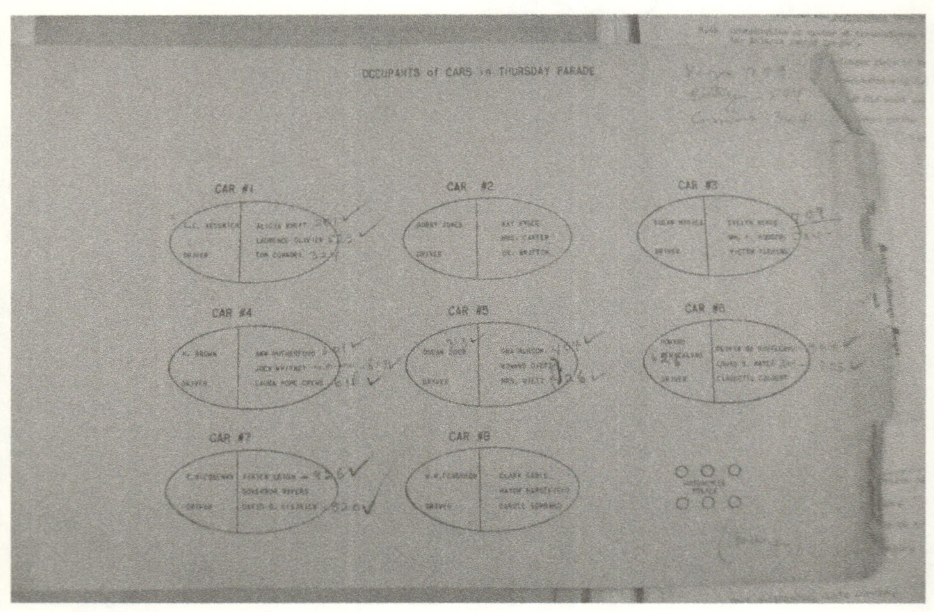
OCCUPANTS of CARS in THURSDAY PARADE
CAR #1
DRIVER
CAR #2
DRIVER
CAR #3
DRIVER
CAR #4
DRIVER
CAR #5
DRIVER
CAR #6
DRIVER
CAR #7
DRIVER
CAR #8
DRIVER

Reserved For
SUSAN MYRICK
TECHNICAL ADVISOR

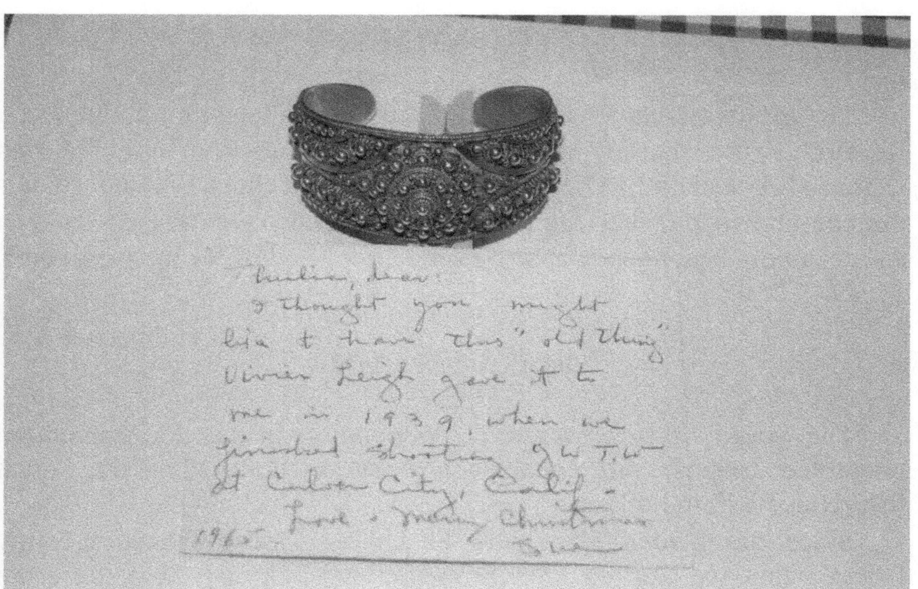

dear:
I thought you might
like to have this "old thing"
Vivien Leigh gave it to
me in 1939, when we
finished shooting G.W.T.W.
at Culver City, Calif. –
Love & Merry Christmas
1965
Sue

THE SMMA

The group of Sue's friends who sent her the telegram about social life dying when she left Macon called themselves The Susan Myrick Memorial Association. They gathered together at times to lament Sue's absence and to plot her return. The SMMA also established its own somewhat off-beat agenda at some time after Sue left for the west coast. It read:

Agenda for the SMMA

The Susan Myrick Memorial Association in solemn convention assembled proposes to consider a problem that is causing great disturbance within our body.

Since the United Daughters of Union Veterans have recently declared that we Confederates burned down our own homes we are therefore resolved:

1. That the Yankee members of the SMMA may do us great harm. Under the guise of friendship, they may come to our homes, set fire to the building and then swear that the fire was started by us.

2. That the Yankee members might leave our homes with their pockets lined with our best table silver and our jewels. Then, naturally, they would swear we stole our own treasures.

The SMMA is further resolved that:

The Yankee members will not be thrown out of the association provided they accede to certain demands. We feel that they should be removed from the membership but we like them and we would hate to give up associating with them, drinking their Yankee cocktails and breaking their Yankee light-bread with them. Therefore if they will accede to the following demands we shall keep them as members.

Item 1. Each Yankee shall take the Oath of Allegiance to the Confederate States of America. He shall further be required to swear he will uphold the honor of Southern Womanhood and set no fire to anybody whatsoever.

Item 2. Each Yankee must further swear to shudder three times when the name of William T. Sherman is mentioned. He must swear to carry at all times a Stars and Bars on his person and to never read another copy of *Uncle Tom's Cabin*. He must not, further, even listen if the words

"Uncle Tom" are spoken and he must never, never cross the ice.

Item 3. The Yankees must further swear that they will genuflect at the mention of the name of Robert E. Lee, also at the sound of the word Traveller. They must swear to bow three times when the following names are mentioned:

A. Dorothy E. Blount Lamar
B. Joel Chandler Harris
C. Jefferson Davis
D. Margaret Mitchell
E. Rhett Butler

Item 4. Said Yankees must further swear that they will sign the Oath and swear they were not subject to duress. Each one will seal the signature with his thumb print.

(If any member's thumb print is found to bear a tattooed profile of the head of Abraham Lincoln, he is automatically expelled from this organization.)

* * *

The organization members were eager for Sue's return, but when the final scenes of the movie were shot and the movie "wrapped," they learned that Sue would not be returning to Macon but going on a lengthy vacation. The SMMA went into an uproar, eager to celebrate her return, afraid they would not be first to greet her. They immediately fired off a letter:

SUSAN MYRICK MEMORIAL ASSOCIATON

HONORARY PRESIDENT
Mr. W. T. Anderson

President: Robert Quinlan

Vice Presidents:

Perry Mahone	*Frances Kenyon*
Edwina Nims	*George Burt*
Betty New	*Margaret Powell*
Adelbert Kenyon	*Arthur Nims*
Malora Rozar	*Mayberry Rozar*
Habenicht Casson	*Blythe McKay*
Fred New	*Doris Jelks*
Albert Jelks	*Louise Blount*

Vice Presidents in Absentia:
Frances Shelburne
James Shelburne

Secretary: Kenneth Cameron

June twenty-eight, 1939

Dear Miss Myrick:

The Association in a recent secret meeting (you may gain some idea of the secretiveness of this organization when I tell you that even the members themselves didn't know it was meeting) resolved that the secretary write you enquiring just when it (the society) might reasonably expect your return. There will be of necessity a large amount of work preparing the details of reception and the committee in charge (composed of the association as a whole) would like to get to work on these details as soon as possible. If you could therefore let us know approximately or the real date as to when to expect you and by which means of transportation, the society would greatly appreciate such a courtesy.

Thanking you in advance for this information, I am
Very cordially yours
(signed)
Kenneth Cameron
Secretary

Miss Susan Myrick
Selznick International Pictures
Culver City, California

Sue wrote back:

Hollywood, Calif. July 6, 1939

Mr. John K. Cameron, Sec, S M M A
Macon, Georgia

My Dear Mr. Cameron:

Your communication, dated June 28, 1939, reached me only today (how come yall didn't buy air mail stamps?) on account of I've been visiting at the Samarkand, indeed a delightful spot (adv) and only a few minutes ago returned to the Stonehaven.

Needless to say, I feel highly honored that your organization has seen fit to plan for my welcoming and also needless to say, I am pleased like a child at Christmas because of the whole thing. You know me, of old, John, and you know that I love attention like nobody else in the world, I reckon.

Honestly, Ken, the dam letter almost made me burst into tears. I nearly (but not quite) tore up the string of tickets I have, that takes me home the long way around, so I could hurry back and be welcomed by yall.

At the present moment I am unable to tell the exact date of my arrival. It is contingent upon the way my money lasts, the time my relatives will let me visit them and the length of time Lake Louise lures me. For I am coming home by

Lake Louise, Banff, the Sooo and soo-on (that's nearly as good as Eddie Nims could do). However if you all want to plan on my reaching home about the middle of August that is pretty sure to be a good guess and I'll let you know the manner of my return, the day and hours at least a week before hand.

Meanwhile, I have a note from Caroline McCord, saying she is going home for the rest of the summer; so be sure to add her to the list of honorary vice presidents or something.

By the way, vice must have reared its ugly head since I left Macon—if I may judge by the long list of vice presidents you have accumulated.

My best love to all the members, presidents, honorary vice presidents, honorary presidents, secretaries and worthy grand matrons and worthy past masters of the S M M A and especial love to you, Mr. Secretary.

Yours all a tremble

(signed) Sue

SUE'S RETURN TO MACON

All did not go as planned when Sue returned. Blyth McKay, one of Sue's colleagues on *The Telegraph*, described the return in detail; even the honorary president of the SMMA drove from Macon to Athens to Winder and started back to Macon in search of Sue.

All the weeks Sue was gadding about Canada and the East there was much talk of getting up a barbecue for her and stirring up things when she came back and many questions about the moment of arrival.

Last Sunday, a wire came saying she would reach Athens at 2:55 Tuesday afternoon. With all the talk that had gone on for weeks, things should have been in a fine state of preparedness, but nothing definite in the way of a celebration had been arranged, so a meeting was called Sunday night and ideas were discussed. It was a wonderful babble about pigs and music, pennants and food, but out of it emerged a barbecue and plans for some to go to Athens to meet the train and others to meet Sue and that entourage at a fork on the Clinton road.

Most of Monday, Malora Rozar and Fran Kenyon skipped about town seeing about a hog and the rest of the food, and badges were printed for the members to wear and a Negro orchestra was hired and Perry Mahone, Bob Quinlan, Caroline McCord, Ken Cameron, Louise Blount, Margaret Powell, Hebe Casson and Ellamae Ellis League and other members of the association phoned back and froth discussing this and that.

Tuesday morning three cars set out for Athens, Caroline McCord taking her sister Marian Ellis, who is here from New York, as well as Ken, Bob and Doris Jelks to meet Sue. Ellamae League and Margaret Powell set out in another car and W. T. Anderson left a little later. He was the first one to get to Athens, though, and pulled into the station just as the Seaboard train pulled out.

Not seeing any more members of the welcoming committee and not seeing Sue, Mr. W. T. asked people about the station who told him no woman had gotten off there. Could he beat the train to its next stop, he asked. They said maybe he could, so he did. He dashed to Winder and looked there for Sue, thinking that she'd gone on to Atlanta when she saw no one in the Athens station, but no Sue was on the train.

In the meantime, just after Mr. W. T. had dashed away from the station, Caroline's car-full had rolled up. They saw no Sue, but when they asked at the station they were told a woman had gotten off and gone away in a car with a man. That made the would-be welcomers furious, for they thought Mr. W. T. had whisked Sue from the station so they began looking around Athens for them, but all they could find was Margaret Powell and Ellamae driving around Athens looking for the station. They all held a consultation and decided that since they'd been a little late, probably Mr. W. T. and Sue had started on and were awaiting them on the edge of town, so they headed back toward Macon. But still no Sue in sight.

By the time the two cars reached Madison they were all feeling flat and discouraged and disappointed. Finally in Madison they stopped at a drug store, and all of a sudden the town of Madison was startled by shouts and shrieks—there came Sue riding along with her sister, Lillas (Mrs. L. C.) and Dr. Lindsley of Milledgeville, her three little Lindsley nieces and their chocolate ice cream cones all over her.

Such commotion as there was for a while, with all the welcomes in Madison all the more excited because they had been postponed from Athens. And then in the midst of the excitement up rode Mr. W. T., catching up with the rest of the welcoming committee after his jaunt to Winder.

In all the hub-bub it took a while to get the story straight, but it seems Sue did get off the train in Athens, and felt a little flat when she saw no one there to meet her after the SMMA had been talking about welcoming her for so many weeks. Then the day was saved by the Lindsleys, for she saw them coming. Dr. and Mrs. and the Three Little Girls. They tucked her baggage into their car, and then went to a garage to have a tire fixed. They were waiting at the garage while the Macon groups were ambling all over Athens looking for Sue and while Mr. W. T. was dashing along the road to Winder. They had to continue to sit there until the Maconites left Athens and were headed back this way, and then caught up with them in Madison. The Lindsleys consented to part with Sue there, and from Madison to Macon she rode in first one and then another of the three Macon cars, arriving at the Clinton road greeting spot in the last of the three.

Waiting there impatiently were Fred New, who had the top down on his roadster so he could drive Sue into town in it, Albert Jelks, Mrs. Piercy Chestney, Hebe Casson, Louise Anderson, Eddie and Arthur Nims, Malora and Berry Rozar, Perry Mahone, Jane Wilkes (who had come down from Atlanta for the celebration), Fran Kenyon, George Burt and Sue's devoted friend and cook Mary Brown.

A huge horseshoe of cardboard, ornamented with red and pink zinnias and yellow and orange marigolds, most of which dropped off before Sue got there, was hung around her neck, she was presented with a great gold key to the city, pictures were taken, there was much flag-waving and shouting, and then the triumphant procession, ten cars led by two motorcycle policemen, paraded into town and back to Shirley Hills where Mr. and Mrs. W. T. Anderson let the SMMA give the barbecue in their garden. At the foot of the Anderson's driveway the orchestra played and then it came on up in the garden and played Southern airs through supper. It didn't know Marching Through Georgia which Perry Mahone suggested and George Burt whistled for the orchestra leader.

From then on there was chatter, much chatter, interrupted for a few minutes when Sue dashed off with Fred New to the hospital to see his wife Betty, and their new little daughter, and then resumed when they returned—all about Gone With The Wind *and Hollywood and movie starts and glamorous names.*

Holding flags, Louise Anderson and Fred New
Holding Key to the city, Albert Jelks
Holding Sue's hand, Bob Quinlan
On Sue's right, Maggie Powell

The Memorial

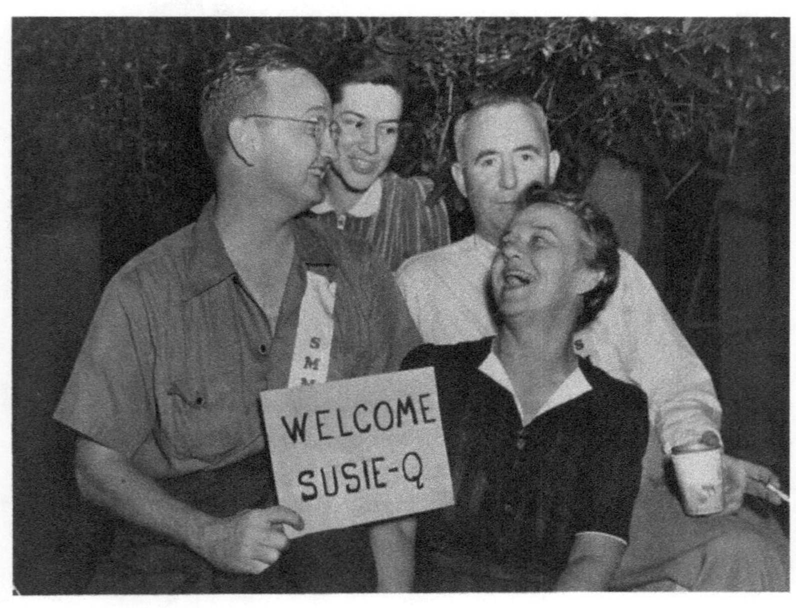

Welcome Home
Left to Right: Fred New, Blythe McKay, P. Mahone, Sue

In a GWTW spoof in Macon, Sue stands by her impersonator, Hamilton Holt, on the stage at the Walter Little Room of the Hotel Dempsey.

Left to Right: Marian F. Ellis, Hebe Casson, Marg Powell, Blyth McKay, Sue, Jane Howell Wilkes, Perry Mahone, Ken Cameron, Berry Rozar, Louise Anderson

"The Susan Myrick Memorial Association"
requests the pleasure
of your company
on
Tuesday, January twenty-third
at nine o'clock
to meet
Miss Susan Myrick

Please reply
215 Georgia Casualty
Building

Present this card

Hotel Dempsey
Corkage charge

Front: W. T. Anderson (in car), Mamie Chestney, Malora Rozar, Berry Rozar, Blythe McKay, Doris Jelks (Mrs. Albert). Back krow: Mary Powell, Perry Mahone, Jane Wilkes, Louise Anderson, Ken Cameron, Bob Quinlan, Sue, Heebe Casson, Mary Brown, Ella Mae League, Albert Jelks, Caroline McCord

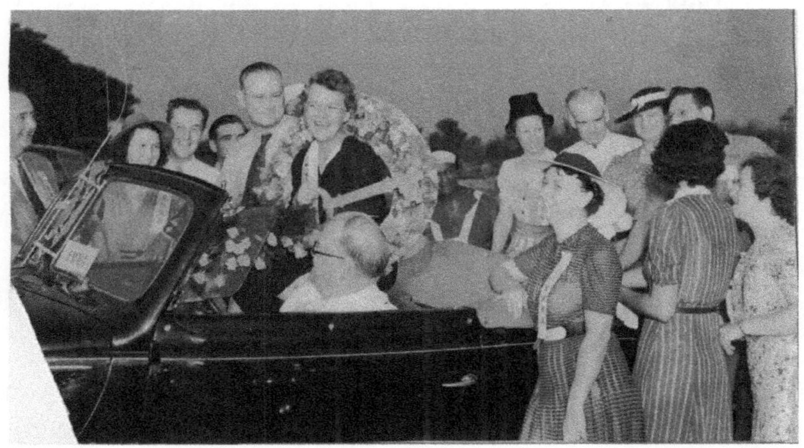

In car, W. T. Anderson; standing in front of car, Malora Rozar, Blythe McKay, Edwina Nims. Back row: Perry Mahone, Louise Anderson, Kenneth Cameron, George Burt, Bob Quinlan, Mary Brown, Ella Mae League, Albert Jelks, Caroline McCord, Hebe Casson. In horsewhoe, Sue.

Sue was a prolific and popular speaker and much in demand before her time with Selznick in Hollywood. Soon after her contract with Selznick ended, she entered a contract with MGM Studios to work in their publicity department and took another leave of absence from *The Telegraph.* For that work, she had to relocate to Atlanta. One of the conditions of this contract was that her work with MGM would not interfere with her already scheduled appearances or with future appearances to speak on her time in Hollywood. Her going "on tour" to speak was, of course, of benefit to MGM, as she thereby promoted the movie.

Thus she could not stay home, but was soon travelling around the country promoting the movie for MGM. Sue's speaking schedule for MGM to promote GWTW, from September 1 through December 12, 1939, included 48 talks in 30 towns to more than 4,000 people. Audience sizes varied from as few as thirty to as many as 1,000 at her Alma Mata (GN&IC), by then renamed Georgia State College for Women.

In an unusual radio broadcast, Alicia Rhett, the Charleston, South Carolina, actress who played India Wilkes in the movie, interviewed Sue about the movie. The show was broadcast by WTMA in Charleston.

In November, 1939, *The Telegraph* gave this list of seven days of Sue's GWTW speaking engagements:

Nov 29—Waycross Pilot Club's Bosses night
Dec 1 & 2—Mount Berry Schools
Dec 4—Jaycee's of Griffin
Dec 5—Combined meeting of Rotary and Kiwanis clubs and Women's League in Athens
Dec 6—University of Georgia. She became an honorary member of a national journalism sorority after the address.
Dec 7—Combined meeting of the Civitan, Rotary and Kiwanis clubs at noon, and a woman's group in the afternoon (in Macon)
Dec. 8—Officers' Wives Club at Fort Benning

She drove a lot of miles on what would today be considered "back-country" roads, at a time when the average miles per hour was 40-50.

In her weeks of travelling for MGM, Sue received telegraphs, letters, and phone calls from people who missed her while she was on the road. She kept in her diary the second letter from Anna Ingraham of

Sparta, written November 28, 1939.

Dear Miss Myrick:

I have just returned home and to my sorrow, I found that you are going to leave once more. I can assure you that we all are sorry.

You are a good friend, not only to your race, but to the colored race as well. You are numbered among my good friends. Feeling as I do that you are a friend of the old South as well as the new South. My husband came out of slavery, educated by Mr. Alexander Stephens, so I feel that I have a claim on the old South as well as the new South. I do feel that you are one of my good friends, and I appreciate your coming and seeing the school and the children, and also thank you for the beautiful article that came in the newspaper. I was in Boston, at that time, was the cause of my delay in writing and thanking you.

Since you have seen our plant, would appreciate if you would start a movement to get a dormitory for the old slaves and daughters and helpers that have been in the families, when you get all straight. I have more children than room. Have a feeling that you are going to help me.

A lonely colored woman working to help the race.

Sincerely,

Anna S. Ingraham

We do not have a copy of Sue's response to this letter.

* * *

PREMIERES: ATLANTA AND MACON

Sue had spent weeks dashing over the state to promote the movie, and when she was in her Atlanta office where she worked for MGM, she helped plan many of the events for the world premiere to be held in Atlanta on December 15. She was in charge of the seating in cars for the great parade down Peachtree Street. She also had the task of arranging who would sit by whom for the premiere itself.

But these mundane duties did not—and could not—dampen Sue's excitement over the upcoming events. Her enthusiasm over the premiere was boundless. Like the thousands of fans who stood outside the Grand on that December 15, while spotlights beamed into the sky, Sue became another fan who thrilled to see the movie beginning to end, not just the daily rushes. And that night, her mind was not on technical matters but on the joy of the final production and the unbounded delight that she had contributed to Peggy's enjoyment of the movie.

Sue's report on the premiere appeared in the Sunday *Telegraph*, page 1. The headline read: **Myrick Seeks Rest After Gayest Week**. The subtitle: **Sue Is Tired But Happy After Gone With The Wind Gets Big Launching**. Under her by-line Sue wrote:

Margaret Mitchell Marsh, looking about as big as a minute and as big-eyed and scared as Br'er Rabbit, spoke in her usual gracious and friendly fashion to put into words what everybody in Atlanta was thinking about the movie made from her own novel:

"Of this picture I feel that the only expression adequate for use is that one made trite by usage many times. We have just come together through a great emotional experience.

"I know it was to me. And I know I'm not the only one whose eyes have been wet tonight."

The ovation given the stars had been tremendous, but it was insignificant beside that thunderous clapping of hands that came when Peggy Mitchell walked down front at Loew's Grand Theater Friday night in answer to the demand of the public and Mayor Hartsfield.

By now, all of you who read this must know that Atlanta took the picture to its heart even as it had taken the novel and that all the critics have exhausted all their superlatives in an effort to say how really good the picture is. And naturally I am happy over it all, feeling that, like Prissy, "I had hope a little," with the making. I'm happiest of all that a few kindly souls expressed their approval of the Southern accent.

It has been the gayest, maddest, hard-workingest week of my life and certainly the happiest, this past seven days. So, it is difficult to put down coherently something of what went on.

What pleased the visiting celebrities most is the thing that all Georgia will be delighted over. David O. Selznick, Vivien Leigh, Clark Gable, Olivia de Havilland and all the rest of the guests said over and over that the spirit of

Atlanta was the finest thing they ever encountered. The vast throngs who greeted the stars at every possible opportunity, the wild cheering for the guests whenever they appeared, the acclaim the city offered the picture–all these delighted the hearts of the visitors and most of all they liked the good nature and the good behavior of the hordes of people who crowded the city streets.

"Nobody has tried to snatch a button off Miss Leigh's coat and nobody has grabbed at the arms of any one in the party," said Mr. Selznick. "Here we have seen what you mean when you speak of Southern hospitality and Southern politeness."

What pleased me most of all was having a police escort! You see, I had to make a speech at Decatur on Wednesday and that was the day Miss Leigh, Mr. Selznick and Laurence Oliver were arriving and I had to go to the airport to greet them, so I had to get to Decatur and back in a hurry. Bill Coleman, who is my boss, said he would arrange it and when I came downstairs to get into the waiting car two policemen jumped astride their motor steeds, let 'em have the spur and away we went. John Gilpin never had half so much fun on a ride as I had on that one.

Sirens wide open, the cops hit it up to 45. Past the wrong side of street cars, through red lights, breaking all the traffic laws, we went. My driver thought I had been taken with a case of hysterics, for I laughed until the tears flowed at the idea of all that putting-on-the-dog. But don't think I didn't love it.

Back from Decatur the same way we came, then along with a score of other Selznick and MGM workers, I scooted in fast time to the airport. But the real thrill came, of course, the following afternoon when we went again to the airport, this time to meet Clark Gable and Carole Lombard and to parade back through the streets where Confederate flags and bunting and smilax vied with Christmas lights and thousands of people to say welcome to the guests.

Clark Gable made the perfect speech when he was

introduced to the people from the balcony at the Georgian Terrace. "The mayor told me you had 300,000 people in Atlanta," he told the cheering crowd. "I know there are three million of you on the streets tonight. And it warms the hearts of all of us to have your welcome."

That night was the Junior League ball, the beauty and splendor of which you have already read about. But I must tell you the fun it was to judge costumes along with Wilbur Kurtz, who had just got home from Hollywood, and with John Hay Whitney who is an adopted Georgian and a witty and charming gentleman. The clothes were so lovely that judging was a most difficult task, but the crowd seemed pleased with the decision. Mr. Whitney avowed it was a shame not to have everybody see the clothes in close-ups as we judges had done so that the beauty of the fabrics and details of design might be shown.

The ball was additional fun for me, too, because of a visit to the press room in the auditorium and greeting old friends of the press, all of whom asked about George Burt, who seems to be a great favorite with the gentlemen of the press of Georgia.

Of course, nothing compared with the thrill of the premiere and to this moment, I haven't the slightest idea what I said over the microphone when I stood outside the Grand, scared pop-eyed under the blaze of the five searchlights that gave out eight million candlepower each.

Cars and people had been so jammed that our progress to the theater had been slow and two blocks away all movement stopped. A gracious policeman offered to get us through the crowd if we wanted to walk. We did and I was so excited at having a policeman holding me by each arm (and not being arrested) that I could scarcely think of anything else. Besides, my head was whirling with the exultation that filled the city and captured the hearts of everybody. So, when a gentleman greeted me and asked if I would say a word over the air I was weaker than any new-born colt you ever heard of.

Next morning some friends told me I had said the right

thing. I hope so. I have no idea what it was.

At intermission I struggled into the lobby of the theater, along with a thousand other idiots, but I was rewarded when I had an opportunity to greet "Miss Dolly" and Mr. Walter Lamar. "Miss Dolly" was her usual handsome self, gracious and radiant, as she received compliments from dozens who came over to talk. I also chatted with Edward Shorter, who was a lucky holder of a ticket to the premier, and I had a brief glimpse of R. A. McCord, Sr.

Later, however, I saw a few other South Georgians when I went to the after-premiere breakfast party given by Chip Robert and Mrs. Robert. Mrs. Will Vereen of Moultrie was looking so young and pretty in a white lace evening gown that people were asking which movie star she was. And with her was Mr. Vereen, looking very proud of her. He spoke of his regret as missing the appreciation dinner for Mr. W. T. Anderson in Macon and vowed that Macon is the nicest place in the world except Moultrie.

At the party, too, were Senator and Mrs. Walter George and there was a charming Mrs. Marshall of North Carolina who told me she is sister of Mrs. Pliny Hall and there was a Mr. Draper, who is a great friend of Louise and Lamar Trotti's, so I felt a fine glow of admiration for Maconites once more.

Oh, yes, at the party were Senator McAdoo, Mrs. Louis B. Mayer, Alicia Rhett, Ann Rutherford, Laura Hope Crews, Evelyn Keyes, Ona Munson and many other celebrities. But of course you've already read about those.

Well, Vivien Leigh has gone from Atlanta, but the Scarlett O'Hara she put upon the screen will long remain in Georgia. And Clark Gable and Olivia de Havilland are on their way home, but Melanie and Rhett will be here a long time to come.

Atlanta has quieted down to business as usual and the flags and the bunting will be folded and put aside. But the fun and the thrills and the excitement of *Gone With The Wind* will linger for many a moon in the minds of everybody.

As for me, if anybody cares to know, I expect to sleep

for 48 hours.

The stars and her friend Peggy took the spotlight that night, as they had the preceding two days in Atlanta. But Sue's time on center stage was coming, and in January, to her delight, Sue took the spotlight in Macon.

On January 27, 1940, the night before the Macon premiere, the SMMA hosted a ball in honor of Sue at Macon's Dempsey Hotel. Johnny Hamp's orchestra, from the Ansley Hotel, provided music; the Dempsey's Walter Little room was decorated with swags of cherry laurel that formed garlands about the ceiling and pillars, and with banks of palms as a background.

Macon turned out for Sue as Atlanta had turned out for Peggy, Gable, Leigh and the others. Earlier in the week, *The Telegraph* stated that ticket prices for reserved seats would be $1.00 for the opening night in Macon.

The morning after SMMA ball, *The Telegraph* reported:

Miss Myrick received the guests with the bachelor members of the association, Robert Quinlan, Perry Mahone, Kenneth Cameron, Jr., Habenicht Casson, Delmar Warren and George Burt.

She wore for the happy occasion, a handsome gown of white satin back crepe, the very full skirt sweeping into a train and the untrimmed bodice supported by narrow straps. The matching bolero with long sleeves which were wide at the shoulder and fitted below the elbow, was trimmed with a design done in glittering paillettes in blue and coral held with gold threads. She wore orchids at the shoulder, an orchid in her hair and carried a colonial bouquet of sweetpeas, valley lilies, roses and other pastel shaded flowers.

The next evening, January 28, GWTW premiered in Macon, and some 1,000 people turned out for the event at Macon's Grand Theatre in Sue's honor.

The Telegraph labeled the event *the most colorful inaugural for a motion picture in Macon history. Hundreds of people who had not been able to get tickets to the first showing crowded the sidewalk and street in front of the Grand to catch a glimpse of Miss Myrick and other evening-dressed first nighters. Others who attended lingered in the lobby until after she had entered. She stopped many times on the way to her seat to respond to words from friends.*

She was dressed in a long lavender gown and a gray squirrel coat.

Her flowers were orchids. A band played as she arrived and while she made her way slowly through the lobby.

David O. Selznick's message to the Mayor was flashed onto the screen before the movie began:

I wish I could be with you to pay tribute to Susan Myrick for her splendid contributions to Gone With The Wind. *I feel that the apparent satisfaction of the South in our efforts is due in no small measure to Miss Myrick's advice. In addition to her talents and conscientiousness, her personality and charm won a high place in the hearts of Hollywood.*

Applause came spontaneously then, and again when Sue's name appeared as technical advisor.

Margaret Mitchell also wired the Mayor:

It is a great disappointment to me that my illness prevents me attending the Susan Myrick premiere of Gone With The Wind. *The film itself shows what an excellent job she did in helping to make the general atmosphere of the play and the speech of the characters pleasing to Southerners. I would have been happy to have been there to join in honoring her.*

Sue received many telegrams of congratulations, but the most notable came from David O. Selznick and from some of the cast.

Selznick wired Sue:

Macon folks have a right to be proud of a real credit to a Southern gentlewoman. Congratulations to you on your night, and thanks again for your help on Gone With The Wind.

From Clark Gable came this message:

Dear Sue, about the time you get this congratulations your friends in Macon will know how grateful we must be for your great help in the making of Gone With The Wind. *Kindest personal regards.*

A second wire from Gable:

Dear Sue, I learned a lot about Dixie from you, so put me at the head of the congratulatory parade tonight.

From Vivien Leigh:

My very best wishes to you, Sue, and allow me to add my voice to the acclaim that is yours. The voice, incidentally, remains a bit on the Dixie side.

From Olivia de Havilland:

I wish I could be there to offer my most sincere good wishes to you. This is next best, but all the same straight from the heart.

* * *

Sue's work with GWTW did not end with the Macon premier in January 1940, but extended well into 1940. In November that year, she took another leave of absence to work with MGM in planning the first anniversary party for GWTW.

After her work was finally finished for MGM in 1940, Sue received not only the agreed upon salary, but a bonus.

Her tax forms for 1939 show her income::

The Macon Telegraph 1089.00
Selznick Studios 3059.25 (for movie work)
MGM 1042.00 (for speaking tour)
Stories sold 680.00
Miscellaneous income 12.50
Total 5990.75.

The stories sold included a feature article for *Colliers*, for $500.00— always talked about the fur coat that *Colliers* paid for.

Income for Calendar Year 1940
Salary: 1338.19
MGM 1858 (including a 250.00 bonus)
Speeches 500.00
Miscellaneous income 440.05
Total to 4136.24

The 1939 income was a big jump from that of the year before her GWTW adventures, which, together with some investment income, came to a total 2069.00—quite a good income during the depression.

GWTW IN LATER YEARS

The aura of *Gone With The Wind* followed Sue throughout her career and into her retirement, with people writing her, calling her, and visiting. One of the first compelling events for her came shortly after the Macon premiere. A group of Maconites performed a burlesque of GWTW—in poetry format—and Sue was one of the characters. The show was presented at the Kiwanis Club 1940 meeting at the Walter Little Room of the Hotel Dempsey. She was photographed after the show beside her counterpart, played by Hamilton Holt.

Twenty-two years after the movie's release, MGM invited her to the second premiere, held again in Atlanta. Sue wrote:

The so-called "second premiere" of *Gone With The Wind* in Atlanta, last Friday night, was a true time for "remembering when" for the majority of the people who were at the opening performance. It was for me a mixture of sadness and great joy.

A reunion with David O. Selznick, producer of the movie, and with Vivien Leigh and Olivia De Havilland, was a delight; but remembering the real premiere of December, 1939, I was saddened by the absence of Clark Gable, Leslie Howard, and others of the cast whom death has claimed. Especially was I sad that Margaret Mitchell could not be there, as she was for the first showing.

So tiny, she was, and so gracious and happy at the fine movie version of her book, that she warmed the hearts of all who knew her, and all those who met her for the first time. Slightly under five feet tall, Peggy Mitchell had a heart twice as big as her body, and her charm flowed out to all who came in contact with her.

Clark Gable, at that premiere, avowed he was scared to death at the thought of meeting her, but when he did meet her, he fell hard: "She is the most fascinating woman I ever met," he said.

It was a delight for me, as I watched the movie (for the umpteenth time) to realize what a magnificent job David O. Selznick had done with that production. Today, nearly 22 years after the movie was made, the show will stand up with the best picture ever made. For color, for photography, for a fine adaptation of the book, for the excellent acting, for the technical details, the picture is as good as if it were made yesterday instead of in 1939.

The house was filled with people who had seen the first show back in 1939; it was apparent as they applauded for the first words on the screen, and as they applauded to the echoes of the appearance of the names of the stars. Particularly warm and enthusiastic was the applause when

Clark Gable's name appeared; the rafters shook.

Olivia De Havilland is as beautiful as she was 22 years ago. Changed only by reason of a pleasing maturity, she is young looking, big-eyes, smiling, gracious, a lovely-to-look-at woman.

Vivien Leigh, though still a beautiful woman in anybody's group of Miss Americas, has changed, somehow. She doesn't look older, she just looks different. She was asked whether she would do anything different if she had to do the role of Scarlett today. She said yes, that as she watched the performance she had seen a dozen places in which she felt she could have done a better job. But she added when one has matured sufficiently to understand a complex personality, one is too old to look like an 18-year old girl.

I doubt that anybody would agree with Miss Leigh. Everybody is certain that no better Scarlett O'Hara could be put on stage or screen than the one Miss Leigh gave the world.

At Sea Island Kiwanis Club, October 10, 1939.

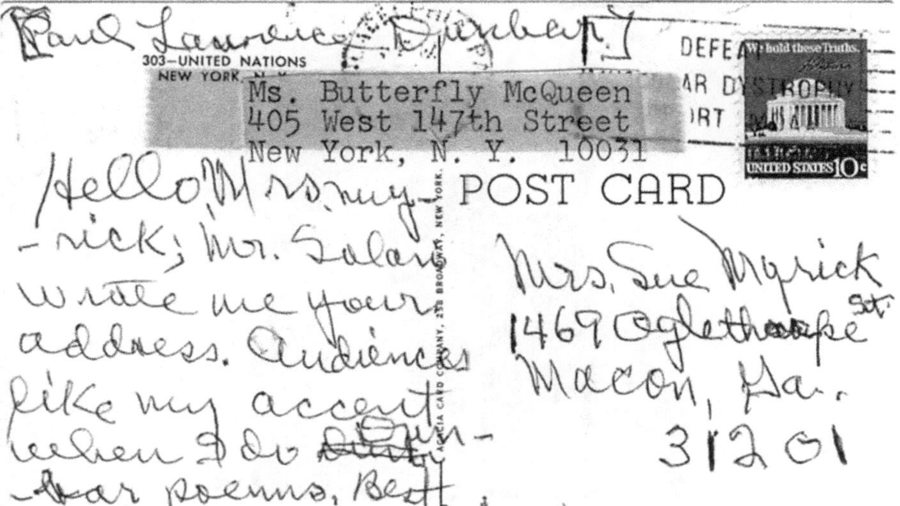
Paul Laurence Dunbar

303—UNITED NATIONS
NEW YORK

Ms. Butterfly McQueen
405 West 147th Street
New York, N. Y. 10031

POST CARD

Hello, Mrs. My-rick; Mr. Solan wrote me your address. Audiences like my accent when I do Dun-bar poems. Best

Mrs. Sue Myrick
1469 Oglethorpe St.
Macon, Ga.
31201

Sue's beads were gift from Peggy in early 1930s.

At the 1967 premiere in Atlanta, (the sixth world premiere) Left to right: Evelyn Keyes (Suellen O'Hara), Olivia de Havilland (Melanie Wilkes) Victor Jory (Jonas Wilkerson) Ann Rutherford (Carreen O'Hara) and Sue.

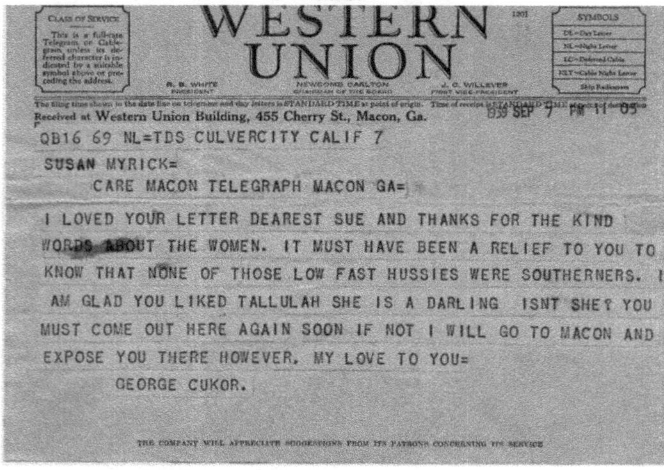

WESTERN UNION

CLASS OF SERVICE

This is a full-rate Telegram or Cablegram unless its deferred character is indicated by a suitable symbol above or preceding the address.

R. B. WHITE, PRESIDENT — NEWCOMB CARLTON, CHAIRMAN OF THE BOARD — J. C. WILLEVER, FIRST VICE-PRESIDENT

SYMBOLS
DL = Day Letter
NL = Night Letter
LC = Deferred Cable
NLT = Cable Night Letter
Ship Radiogram

Received at Western Union Building, 455 Cherry St., Macon, Ga. 1939 SEP 7 PM 11 05

QB16 69 NL=TDS CULVERCITY CALIF 7

SUSAN MYRICK=

CARE MACON TELEGRAPH MACON GA=

I LOVED YOUR LETTER DEAREST SUE AND THANKS FOR THE KIND WORDS ABOUT THE WOMEN. IT MUST HAVE BEEN A RELIEF TO YOU TO KNOW THAT NONE OF THOSE LOW FAST HUSSIES WERE SOUTHERNERS. I AM GLAD YOU LIKED TALLULAH SHE IS A DARLING ISNT SHE? YOU MUST COME OUT HERE AGAIN SOON IF NOT I WILL GO TO MACON AND EXPOSE YOU THERE HOWEVER. MY LOVE TO YOU=

GEORGE CUKOR.

THE COMPANY WILL APPRECIATE SUGGESTIONS FROM ITS PATRONS CONCERNING ITS SERVICE

I'm sorry to hear you have been ill, Miss Myrick. I hope you are well rested and better, now. "Prissy".

Sue at a GWTW/MGM publicity event, Charlotte, NC, 1940

GEORGE CUKOR

April 16, 1965

Dearest Sue

It was mighty fine to catch up with that elusive Oscar - at long last. I was delighted. But it was the affection, the excitement with which my friends greeted this happy event that touched my heart.

Grateful thanks for your sweet note, dearest Sue, and all loving regards.

Always George

- - Don't you think it's high time that you came out to California again? I do.

Miss Sue Myrick
1469 Oglethorpe St.
Macon, Georgia

At the 1967 premiere in Atlanta

Sue in parade, with Victor Jory, 1967, Atlanta.

GWTW FRIENDSHIPS

The companionships that developed on the set continued—Sue would write about various cast members in her columns over the years, and cast members stayed in touch. Cammie King invited Sue to her wedding. Prissy sent her notes, including one of encouragement when Sue had a heart attack. And Sue kept up with the news of those she had met—she wrote columns about various cast members over the years.

She wrote with fondness of Clark Gable when he died.

Clark Gable's death adds one more to the list of those fine actors who are now gone, who made up the cast of *Gone With The Wind*—Leslie Howard, Laura Hope Crews, Hattie McDaniel, Ona Munson, all of them loveable people who were kind to me when I worked with them as technical advisor on the movie, way back in 1939.

Like a few million other women, I found Gable (everybody on the set called him "Gable") a most loveable man. He was kind to and considerate of all of us, he never once gave any indication of feeling himself as important, he was as friendly to me and to the electricians and hairdressers and make-up men on the set as he was to the producer or the director or Vivien Leigh.

I recall with a deep sense of appreciation one unusually friendly thing he did for me. I was writing columns back for *The Telegraph* about progress on making the movie, and what I wrote had to be submitted to the director of public relations before I could mail it back to Macon. One day the PR man decided he didn't want the public to know some of the things I had put in the column, and I was sitting at one side of the set, feeling rather woebegone and wondering what I'd write to replace the couple of pages the PR man had taken from me. Gable walked over and sat down beside me and wanted to know why I looked upset. I told him.

"Well, no, don't fret about what that old scoundrel did to you," he said. "Would it help to fill up the column if I told you about my estate?"

Would it!

So, he sat for half an hour, chatting about his "14-acre estate," telling me about his ranch house, giving me little intimate stories of his life at home, stories which of course made the best column I ever wrote.

His unfailing, easy going humorous outlook made life on the GWTW set a happy place.

Bless his heart. Clark Gable was a wonderful, loveable man. His death brings me a sadness that goes deep. I doubt that we shall ever see his like again.

* * *

The friendship with Peggy and John Marsh did not die with the author's death. Sue's friendship with John continued, and she went to Atlanta on occasions to attend concerts with him. In his letter to her about the first concert and her staying overnight, he wrote that "to avoid contretemps," she was invited to stay at the home of their mutual friend, Mary Singleton, who was an employee at the Georgia Power Company.

She remained faithful to her friendship with Peggy Mitchell for life. When she saw or heard any untruths about her friend, Sue raised her weapon—her pen.

She called out David Niven, the actor; she stated in her columns that he wrote untruths about Peggy in his book. She said his work was about as inaccurate as one could possibly get. Niven said Peggy was a school mistress. She was not. He called the payment from Selznick ($50,000) for movie rights "measly." Not in the middle of the depression, Sue said; and that amount was the highest price ever paid for a "first novel."

Sue said Niven wrote that Peggy and her husband were on the "knife edge of starvation" while she wrote the book. Not so; they lived in comfort. Niven said that shortly after the GWTW premiere Mitchell was knocked down and killed by a car in Atlanta and died penniless.

Sue often told her siblings and other relatives of the vast amounts that Mitchell contributed to a local black college—money that came from GWTW—as scholarship funds that ensured an education for financially strapped black youths. Many black students' medical school education was financed totally by Mitchell.

Niven said that Marsh was "first a clerk and then a minor executive in the gas company," when in fact he was director of public relations with the Georgia Power Company.

Many stories floated around about Peggy soon after the book's release, and as the rumors continued, Sue would counter them. Peggy herself had a wry laugh at many of the stories. She said, "I could stand it when people said my husband or my father really wrote the book. I didn't mind much when I heard I had gone blind—I almost did from reading proof—but I was slightly upset when I heard I had a peg leg."

Sue contradicted Cleveland Amory; she wrote that in *The Saturday Review* he claimed that Peggy kept a loaded pistol beside her bed every night of her life until the news of her first husband's death came to her. Sue stated firmly, "I spent a good many weekends as a guest at the Mitchell-Marsh apartment and since there was only one bedroom, John Marsh slept in the day bed in the living room while Peggy and I had the bed in the bedroom. If she had a pistol anywhere near that bed, I never saw it. And my eye sight was pretty good, back then."

Another author whose book contained errors about Peggy is Adela Rogers St. Johns, who said that "Within weeks Peggy Marsh's book had been rushed into millions of copies." Not true, says Sue. "I was on a visit to Peggy in early 1937 (the book was released to the public in June, 1936) and she showed me the leather-bound copy of GWTW which the publishing company had sent to her at Christmas 1936, with an autograph which said this, the millionth copy, was a gift to her from MacMillan." Six months, not six weeks, said Sue.

Sue said that Ms. St. Johns also claimed that Stephens Mitchell, Peggy's brother, had given the manuscript to a girl from Atlanta who had gone to work for a New York publisher and she took it to New York. Not true, said Sue, again.

Sue was sure that Stephens had not seen the manuscript. Sue herself had asked Peggy once if she could read the book she'd heard Peggy was writing. Peggy's response was that she'd never shown it to anybody but her husband and anyway it was not nearly a complete book. Besides, she would just as soon walk in her bare feet down Peachtree as show the manuscript to anyone.

Just as Sue used her column at *The Telegraph* to counter such tales about Peggy, she used it to extend praise to the writers who were faithful to Peggy's memory and her desire for privacy. She praised Richard Harwell for this work on *Margaret Mitchell's GWTW Letters* and Roland Flamini for *Scarlett, Rhett and a Cast of Thousands*, his book about the production of the movie.

Sue said that Finis Farr's book *Margaret Mitchell of Atlanta* is "perhaps the best story about her that has been printed, but I regret the publication of letters and stories about Miss Mitchell which she regarded as strictly personal." Sue said Peggy would cringe to see them in print.

She herself had destroyed such personal letters from Mitchell.

Just as rumors abounded about Peggy, so they ran amuck across the country about the movie. Some claimed it was filmed in Georgia. A home in South Carolina was the subject of a news article as the site of the filming of the opening scene of Scarlett and the Tarleton twins.

Sue said over and again that none of the movie was filmed outside of California.

She reported that she constantly received letters from people asking about the filming and about the "sequel." More than one aspiring author wanted Sue to read their manuscripts of their version of the sequel. Some people asked Sue to get Mitchell herself to write a sequel. Others wanted Sue's version of what really happened.

In 1954, while still recovering from illness, Sue helped prepare a brochure on Peggy for the Atlanta Public Library, for its dedication of the Margaret Mitchell Room (on December 15). In a letter to Sue, Peggy's nephew called the brochure "a splendid piece of work. I know of nothing which would have pleased Margaret more than to have read your article."

THE 1967 PREMIERE

Sue's Stories

Returning from a trip, your usual traveler to Vienna, Paris, Rome, or even to Atlanta or Perry, Georgia, will tell you about what and where he ate: Pastas in Rome, truffles in Paris, whipped cream in Vienna (everything is served "mit shlag" there), steaks in Atlanta, beaten biscuits in Perry.

So, I reckon I'll be forgiven if I tell you about eating at the Premiere doings in Atlanta when GWTW stars caused a rash of cocktail parties, luncheons and dinners.

Mayor Ivan Allen and Mrs. Allen entertained at a luncheon where he presented all the ladies with corsages, each made of a fragrant gardenia. When I thanked him for the cape jessamine, he was pleased that somebody knew what cape jessamine was. He knew all right.

The meat at the Allen's luncheon was something to talk about; tender flavorful pieces of beef, about an inch thick and two inches in diameter, cooked up with a sauce whose

French name I can't spell, and served with fresh broiled mushrooms, the meat downright fit for the gods, much less the stars of GWTW and a group of press representatives.

The cocktails served by the Stephens Mitchells at their small and "private" buffet, the evening of the Tara ball, were accompanied by caviar, combined with shredded raw onion, causing me to think I need some of Scarlett's "Florida water" to gargle lest a dancing partner faint at the smell of me.

For the buffet dinner in the Sixties—shrimp and salads and exotic dishes I didn't even taste (there wasn't room on my plate, much less in my innards) and great lovely slices of prime roast beef, and lobster Newberg.

I refuse to speak of what we had at the champagne party which followed the showing of the GWTW film.

I'd rather speak of a couple of persons who were Maconites, of a sort. Mrs. Pamela Johnson Patterson, with her husband, was at the Mitchell party; she came over and introduced herself to me, avowing she was a Macon native and asking about old friends, here, particularly about Perry Mahone and Mr. North Winship.

And Mr. Tom Baldridge, a promotion man with Metro Goldwyn Mayer which owns rights to GWTW now, went to Mercer University and later was with the movie house here. He asked about Mrs. Piercy Chestney, whom he remembered as a "charming, vivacious lady," who was president of the Better Films Committee.

To hear Olivia de Havilland speak of her 33-year old son was a shock for everybody within the sound of her voice, for Miss de Havilland looks as young and beautiful today as she did when she was playing Melanie.

In Atlanta for the "World Premiere," as Hollywood insists upon calling the sixth showing of the film, Miss De Havilland avowed she was Southern in all her affiliations, that her 33-year old son was half-Southern because his father was Southern, and that her second husband came from "the South of France." She told me her second son has just been drafted into the Army of the United States, although he and she have been long living in France.

Some there be who thought Mellie's beauty was possibly due to those smart Parisian outfits she wore, and they were gorgeous, I'll admit, but that woman's beauty is mostly due to the marvelous lovely bone structure of her face and the beauty of her complexion. Her skin is fair and as dewy and fresh as that of a six-months-old baby, and her hair is golden and her large lovely eyes are a rich brown. She wears little make up. As for the hair color, only her hair dresser knows. It looks to me as it did in 1939.

Olivia, by the way, was about the only woman at the festivities who wore a hat. At the luncheon which Mayor and Mrs. Ivan Allen gave for the movie stars and the visiting press at the Marriott Hotel, Olivia's suit was of a soft orangey-tan. About as close as I can describe its color is to say it was like the inside of a ripe pumpkin. The hat matched the suit in color and was of a material which looked to my unfashion-wise eye like sheared beaver.

At the Tara ball, she wore a rose colored gown of flowing chiffon with ten million tiny beads on the bodice. For the Premiere, she chose a satin gown whose color she called "orange ice."

"I showed the two gowns to a couple of bachelors in New York and asked them, which one to wear to the ball and which to the Premiere," she told. "They chose the rose colored one for the ball—said it LOOKED like a ball; the other looked like an 'occasion.' "

At the luncheon given by the Atlanta Historical Society at the Swan House, she looked about fourteen; she wore a beige woolen skirt (almost mini—but not quite) with a blouse of a soft green. "I call it deep lime" she told me.

"It's such fun to have a dress made in Paris," Olivia said. "At Dior's they bring out such lovely fabrics and they stand around and talk about whether this or that is more becoming to your style and everybody is so gracious."

As if EVERYBODY wouldn't be gracious to so modest and gracious a lady as Melanie!

THE TARA BALL:

As Written by Susan Lindsley at the time

Sue telephoned me from Macon and asked "Do you want to go to the Tara Ball for the re-release of *Gone With The Wind*? It's being put on by MGM at the new hotel in Atlanta."

Who could think of saying no to such an invitation? She reminded me I couldn't wear my jeans or pedal pushers—the event was "veddy" formal. So I set about to gather up a pair of long white gloves, an appropriate evening gown, and heels. Unable to find a matching pair of heels, I had a pair dyed to match the dress.

I left work early that day to get my hair fancied up before I met her friends—the ritzy and the famous from thirty years ago. I journeyed the four or so miles down to the Regency Hyatt House, a new, much-talked-about, and most fabulous hotel in Atlanta, with a circling restaurant that gave changing views of Atlanta and surrounds.

I had not expected to run into anyone I knew, except Sue of course, but met up with Reg Murphy, a reporter I knew from my days with *The Macon News*. Although on different papers, with different "hours," Reg and Sue had become friends when he was in Macon. Reg had given the Regency its reputation—he worked for a public relations firm in Atlanta and handled its account with the Regency. The Tara Ball was the grandest event for the hotel.

The glass elevator gave me a view over the lobby and other floors as it rose upward. As I looked down onto the lobby it seemed to stretch for a city block. A cocktail lounge hangs suspended in space a couple of feet above the floor. A country girl, reared only eight miles from Sue's home place, Dovedale, I was awed by the building itself even before I reached Sue's room.

When I arrived at her room, I received my instructions for the evening from Sue. Most important was to look out for Betty (I don't remember her last name), a Washington, D. C., reporter. When I met Betty, I must be sure to let her know that Sue liked her and was impressed by her.

A dignitary of MGM came to escort Sue off to go to the Mitchell home for supper. My escort—a local cop who filled in for the MGM representative who had not arrived—guided me to the cocktail lounge where the press was lapping up the free alcohol and chatting rapidly away in accents Sue would easily have labeled as mid-western, "downeastern" or even one of the variety of Southern accents. The topics ranged from GWTW and Sue to new movies and Hollywood scandal.

I met too many people at the cocktail party to remember names, but I did find Sue's friend Betty. When we met I said, "Oh, you're the lady Sue told me is such a good reporter," or some such words. A male reporter from Ft. Lauderdale said that Betty and Sue had a mutual admiration society going. Before the evening was over, I saw why. The gal had an abundance, but not an overabundance, of self-confidence.

The Ft. Lauderdale reporter regaled the two of us with his woes of the day. He had been selected only two hours before to replace the producer of *Batman* (William Dozier)—husband of Ann Rutherford—who had decided that he did not want to escort his wife in the Grand March into the ballroom.

He had a suit, of course, but not one with tails, so he had gone out to rent a tux. Another reporter grabbed up his formal suit. But when he dressed, the reporter discovered he had no clip to fasten the tie behind his neck. He said he almost crawled over the floor looking for any kind of a pin, but the maid had ensured nothing was left on the floor. Finally, he said, someone provided a safety pin, and he was able to get to the cocktail party. "After the past couple of hours, I need this." He lifted his drink, and we all laughed.

When supper was announced, we all adjourned to the banquet room. Half a dozen tables had been set, with many more glasses and silverware pieces than I was accustomed to. I decided to watch Betty so I wouldn't do anything to embarrass Sue, even though she wasn't there, and with Betty as my unofficial social guide, I had no problems.

MGM fed about forty of us that night. Our meal was simple, filling and substantial: A huge filet, baked potato with sour cream, broccoli, and salad. I don't know what was in the salad beside tomatoes and cucumbers and lettuce—it contained a few items that I'd never seen before, being a country girl and unused to the city's fancy foods. The waiters were college kids who lacked the skills of the people who waited tables in the only other hotel restaurant I had eaten in—in Lagos, Nigeria, last year before the violence broke out. The youngsters seemed as out of place as I felt in the swanky Regency.

I learned that the hotel also had more than a dozen other dining rooms and banquet rooms that could be reserved for parties.

After supper, I was going upstairs with Betty, on my way to join Sue, when we bumped, almost literally, into Ann Rutherford and husband. Betty knew everybody and introduced us. When Ann learned that Sue was my aunt, she raved about how wonderful Sue had been with everybody in California, lo those many years ago. As we chatted on, Betty told Ann about the problems with her escort's "uniform" and encouraged her to tease him about it. Ann laughed, but said if she did, he might tease her back—and suggest she go upstairs, take off her nightgown, and put on something suitable for the evening.

Her green evening dress, which did not look like a nightgown, consisted of a flowing net with flowers over a sheet of deep green. (Don't ask me what it was; I don't know the material and that's one of the reasons I no longer write for the society page of the paper.)

When I reached her room, Sue had returned from the Mitchell's and had changed from dressy go-to-supper clothes to her gown. She looked fabulous. I'd never seen her that dressed up—I'd seen her in her work clothes at the paper and in her casual slacks at our home, and in costume at the Macon Little Theatre, but she looked spiffy, dignified and royal in her long gown and white gloves.

We were ready for the Grand Event early, so we had a few minutes to talk. I told Sue about my friend Carol watching yesterday's parade down Peachtree Street. Oh, how I envied Carol, who was able to get away from her job to watch it. She had waved and clapped and whooped as the cars drove by her; and then had run down the street to get ahead of the cars so she could see them all again—for six blocks.

Carol said that Victor Jory and his "wife" had been real troopers, waving and smiling at everyone. Only it wasn't Jory's wife—it was Sue in the car with him.

Sue's roar of laughter filled the room..

I commented that the money MGM was spending on the shindig had to be horrendous, and Sue replied that they'd blow $50,000 or more—nothing against the $5 million profit they'd earn. Stephens Mitchell nets about $30,000 a year in royalties from the book, and when the movie-rights contract with MGM ran out recently, MGM paid Mitchell $5 million to re-purchase the rights.

Not bad for just being born the brother of someone.

Time for the big event was getting close, and the two of us went down to the "waiting room," where the people who were to be in the Grand March were gathering.

Sue introduced me to Victor Jory and teased him about being thought of as her husband from the parade. She also razzed him about being such a villain. I told him that he had done such a good job as the bad guy I had really disliked him. Before I could say more, one of the MGM men led him away to meet some other dame who was as awed by him as I was.

Next thing I knew, Sue was surrounded by local personalities who apparently rule the social world of Atlanta. They chattered and threw questions to her like a flock of mockingbirds throwing notes into the morning.

"Oh, Miss Myrick, how hard was it to teach Mammy?"

"What was Clark Gable really like?"

"Miss Myrick, was Butterfly McQueen like Prissy?"

"Miss Myrick, how long did you work for MGM after you left Hollywood?"

"Miss Myrick, did you get to ride any of the horses in the movie?"

It was "Miss Myrick, this" and "Miss Myrick that." Before the night was over I became used to everyone calling her "Miss Myrick," although I'd never heard her called anything other than "Sue" or "Susan."

Answering their questions, she told them about her 6-week contract running seven months; that Vivien Leigh was easiest to teach to talk "Southern," and yes, it was true that she did not have to coach Mammy. When Sue spotted Olivia De Havilland she broke away from the crowd and went to meet her.

As soon as Olivia learned I was Sue's niece, she told me how much she had enjoyed hearing Sue speak in all the Southern dialects as she told stories to the cast and crew when they took a break. Everyone, she said, appreciated Sue's ability to help them differentiate sounds people put to some letters and how some letters were just dropped in our Southern language, and she said that Sue's knowledge of the Old South was endless. She laughed and said that only Sue could get by with telling Selznick what to do.

It was time for the GWTW celebs to prepare for their grand entrance, and, since my MGM escort was still at the airport, my police escort led me into the ballroom and to the table reserved for Sue—on a platform above the ballroom floor. At least the cops escorted me in and not out.

I tried to soak up everything that was going on—a group of MGM execs hovering around a table; mobs of paying guests (mostly young people dancing to the un-South music of the Beatles), and the almost frantic scurrying of some of the MGM people.

Then Tara's Theme filled the ballroom and the Grand March began. Mayor Hartsfield and Olivia de Havilland came in, under the raised swords of Confederate soldiers. Sixteen pairs entered beneath the arch of swords—with a time lag between entrances while the people applauded. Sue and Olivia de Havilland got the loudest applause.

The couples marched across the ballroom to the bandstand, where they turned and formed up as two couples together and re-crossed the room; they then formed up as two rows of eight couples and returned to the bandstand, where, with giggles and smiles, they broke into pairs again and danced.

Ann Rutherford said later that evening

The Grand March was a mess. They had us backed up some stairs so we had to come down into the lobby to enter the ballroom. They didn't give us any directions except to march back and forth, joining up to make a line across the ballroom. A line of thirty-two couldn't get through that crowd.

Everybody must have thought we were nuts because we got tickled on that last loop and started giggling. That's when we decided to heck with it all and broke up the march.

Not knowing what else to do, they danced instead of just walking off the floor.

After their "grand march dance," the GWTW group came to the raised platform to their reserved tables. A drunken MGM executive sat on my left, and Evelyn Keyes sat beside him; she was sandwiched between *two* drunken MGM execs. She seemed to be absolutely bored with the proceedings, but who wouldn't with nobody sober to talk to? Victor Jory sat a couple of chairs beyond her left. Sue sat on my right. Olivia de Havilland and Ann Rutherford sat at other tables.

The celebrities did not dance again. Although Tara's Theme was played, the dance music was mostly for the young people—the jitterbug, twist and rock and roll. The evening gowns were more suited to a Strauss waltz than to the gyrations that swung the skirts high—I thought of the bobby sox and cotton skirts of ten or so years ago that were common for these lively dances. Those who had paid for tickets to attend the ball, however, danced merrily, with no concern for their skirt tails.

Sue suggested that I have the GWTW-ers autograph my program for a souvenir, which of course I did. Again "Atlanta's Finest" came to my rescue, for I had no pen, knew none of the celebrities had one, and so borrowed one from "my" cop. Then I flitted from table to table.

When I approached Olivia de Havilland, she started talking about Sue again and had me laughing as she tried to tell me about Brer Rabbit and the Tar Baby in dialect. She still looked about 30 instead of nearly 60. Mayor Hartsfield had said she had "certainly preserved herself well." She had. She still looked like Melanie, except much healthier, and a little heavier, though certainly not plump.

Speaking of look-alikes, Ann Rutherford now looks a little like Bette Davis, and Evelyn Keyes somehow reminded me not of an O'Hara but of Belle Watling with her feathered boa (I asked someone what you call the thing) of several shades of several colors.

People moved constantly about on the platform, and a half-dozen cops patrolled back and forth along the edge, trying to keep people away. One, not my escort, asked me if I had a seat there. "Yes. Why?"

"I was going to tell you to leave the platform if you didn't. My job is to keep the public off of here."

But it was impossible to keep people away from the edge—away from Sue. All of Atlanta crowded the side of the platform at her table, some just to speak to her, some to be able to tell their grandchildren they had been there and seen her and heard her tell some of her stories. She thrived on the attention. Who wouldn't? She had certainly earned it.

Everybody had the idea of getting autographs, too, for the cops got the assignment of carrying programs and pens from table to table as people came to the edge of the platform to ask for autographs.

I got everybody's signature, and of course, the most important one for me, Sue's, on the program cover.

GWTW ON TV—1976

Sue's next big celebration of GWTW came in 1976, when family members, the SMMA and other friends gathered to party when the movie was released on TV on November 7. Her niece and niece's husband, Lil and John James, threw a party at the Idle Hour Country Club in Macon the night that GWTW opened on TV. They called it a "Memorial Party," in honor of Sue and the SMMA. Surviving members of the SMMA attended, as well as the "important personages" of Macon and Bibb County.

Sue wrote to her friend Dee Shelburne, member of the SMMA:

"We had drinks and such goodies as chicken livers wrapped in bacon, and then later, everybody fixed his own sandwich and got coffee or other drinks and sat down and watched the program. It was a grand party. I haven't had so much fun since the Junior Prom."

An hour-long "preshow" of Sue, Stephens Mitchell, Olivia de Havilland, and Victor Jory discussing GWTW, produced by WSB-TV (Atlanta), ran first. "It was mostly ME," Sue wrote. The first half of the movie was then shown, and the second half ran the next night.

John James and Delmar Warren fixed up SMMA ribbons for the original members who attended. Sue described her ribbon as "about half a mile long, stamped in gold 'The Memorial.'"

In her letter to Dee Shelburne, Sue brought her up to date on each of the SMMA members. Sue wrote:

Lawdy, we are all falling to pieces, but last Sunday night you wouldn't have known it.

Ellamae League has had a stroke and still looks sick.

Bob Quinlan has arthritis in his ankles and can scarcely walk, and is also facing another operation for hernia.

Blythe McKay, retired for about five years, looks smart, as always.

Fran and Del Kenyon (up from Savannah): Fran looks lovely and Del looks like a movie star.

Margaret Powell Lewis (down from Asheville) is SO handsome and her husband is RICH. She looks great. She brought pictures of the original barbecue of 1939.

Caroline and Fletcher McCord: Caroline has cancer but looks mighty well and gets along pretty well. Fletcher, with diabetes, does fine and is so funny and bright and witty.

Delmar Warren, on the wagon for two years, is fine.

We all wished for you and Jimmie. I bet a score of people said "Wouldn't it be great to have the Shelburnes and Ken with us."

DID RHETT RETURN?

Before Peggy's death, Sue was asked to encourage Peggy to write a sequel. Afterwards, Sue received letters asking her: Did Rhett come back? Why don't you write a sequel?

In October 1970, Sue received a letter urging her to write a series of columns about Scarlett and Rhett—and whether or not they re-united—since Margaret Mitchell had not written a sequel and Sue was more familiar with the characters than anyone else.

Sue's response was a column on October 29, 1970, which read in part:

If I were smart enough to write a sequel to GWTW, I'd begin right away and try my best to sell a million copies in the first year of publication—as Margaret Mitchell did.

I'm sorry to be unable to comply with your request, and I hasten to console you with the knowledge that you are not alone in your wish to know whatever happened to the lives of Rhett and Scarlett.

I don't know what happened to the two Southerners. I could argue either side—Rhett did or didn't ever go back to her. One might believe that Rhett was the sort of man who was finished forever with a woman whom he considered not worth loving. Or, one might argue that Scarlett always got what she wanted, SO she got him back.

After all, you can scarcely blame Miss Mitchell for not going on and on with the story. She had written a book 1,036 pages long.

Of course, today's never-ending story of the Forsyte Family goes on and on. But I doubt that Miss Mitchell would have written a sequel to GWTW even if she had lived to be an old woman.

SUE'S SEQUEL TO GWTW

In 1976 (June 17) Sue finally broke down and wrote her version of what really happened to Scarlett and Rhett. If you remember that period of our history, our country was still in the shadow of the hippie movement, slightly akin to the Roaring Twenties, but less genteel.

You've heard the news that MGM and Universal Studios will produce a sequel to GWTW. It had to happen. If one Deep South picture can gross millions, two should gross at least twice as much.

Besides, talk of a sequel to Miss Mitchell's epic has been going on for 40 years. Back in the 1936-37-38 period Margaret Mitchell got thousands of letters and many phone calls from all over the United States; everybody wanted to know if Rhett went back to Scarlett. And many wanted Miss Mitchell to write a sequel of her book.

Peggy Mitchell Marsh, who had her secretary file thousands of letters, once showed me a letter that suggested a plot for the sequel: Rhett should go back to Scarlett and they should move to Tara, restoring it to its former beauty, and they should rear a large family on the plantation.

I remember that during my stay in Hollywood when the movie was being made, there were five or six "final scripts," each showing a different ending for the movie. One of them depicted Scarlett throwing herself at Rhett, clinging tightly to his manly neck and begging him not to leave her; she had "always loved him." But he took her arms from his neck and strode off into the yonder, while Scarlett gazed tearfully after him.

Enter Mammy: "Honey child," she says, and Scarlett flings herself into Mammy's arms, sobbing like a child.

"Oh Mammy, he's gone. How will I ever get him back?"

And Mammy pats her and says "He'll come back. Ah know. Ah always knows." FADE OUT.

Maybe MGM and Universal producers will follow the example of Mr. Selznick and put on a campaign of publicity that will bring results as did the one when Selznick looked all over the country for an "unknown" lovely to play the role of Scarlett. This time, the campaign will be to find a script worthy to make into a sequel for GWTW.

I suggest something like this: Rhett and Scarlett have restored Tara and Mammy and Prissy are on hand, along with Prissy's descendents. There are loving scenes of Scarlett the Second and Rhett Jr. sleeping in Mammy's lap. And the Hall-Johnson descendents sing as they gather peanuts. Letting peanuts take over in North Georgia is a bit out of line as to historical facts, but after all, President Jimmy Carter raised himself to the White House by way of peanut fields.

Down the Big Road a piece will live Beauregard Wilkes, and flashbacks will show the GWTW scene of Beauregard in his father's arms at the time of Mellie's death. The Wilkes scion will marry Scarlett the Second and there can be tender loving shots of the grandchildren being fondled by a white-haired Rhett and a silver-haired Scarlett.

We can manage some way (nothing is beyond Hollywood) to have the marriage of Scarlett the Second and Beauregard at Westminster Abbey. And what fine discussions of the rise of the South can come about among the wedding guests, which will surely include Robert Toombs and Alexander Stephens.

For a scene, late in the movie, we can have the engagement of Rhett III announced to a descendent of Jonas Wilkerson and Emmy Slattery. Imagine what a wonderful scene when Scarlett learns that her great-grandchild is about to marry a Slattery-Wilkerson chile.

Gee! Maybe Hollywood will hire me as a script writer.

PART V
AFTER GWTW

EXPANDING DUTIES

When her work ended with MGM, Sue returned to *The Telegraph*, and her duties quickly expanded. In February 1941, she was named editor of the *Georgia Magazine*, the Sunday supplement to the joint *Telegraph and News*. She wrote many of the feature articles for the magazine as well as laid out each issue, which, for most people would have been a full-time job.

But she continued with her speaking engagements, which took her over central Georgia; she never stopped her free lance writings, and she remained dedicated to the Macon Little Theatre, as an actress and member of the board of directors.

The War Years

On December 8, 1941, the day after Pearl Harbor, and within an hour of President Roosevelt's signing the declaration of war on Japan, Governor Eugene Talmadge created the Citizens Defense Committee to coordinate the internal war efforts in Georgia. Sue was appointed a member of the committee.

Sue was assigned to the task of "War Editor" when the United States joined the Allies in World War II. The assignment was a natural extension of her work as a feature writer. As far back as 1931, she had written extensively about Ft. Benning, military training and costs, the politics of war preparedness, profiles of officers, and military recreation. Another war duty she began in 1941 was to write about activities at the newly established Camp Wheeler and at the Army Air Force Base, Warner Robins.

I didn't know a bomber from a half-track but I covered the local military installations during World War II: Infantry at Camp Wheeler, Air Force at Warner Robins and basic flight training for British cadets at Cochran Field.

The first consignment of trainees at Camp Wheeler came from New England and the accent and idiom of the Deep South fell on uncomprehending ears: "You all say 'hey' when you mean 'good morning.' Where I live, when somebody says 'hey,' they mean look out you are about to step in a hole or get hit by a falling log." "What *do* these Georgians mean when they said 'Y'all come back, heah?' "

"She asked me would I carry her to the show Saturday night? Do I carry her in my arms?"

When a contingent of trainees came in from Charleston, S.C., nobody understood anybody else's speech, but the British accent soon became familiar to Maconites. Girls began to stop saying, "Y'all come back, heah"; they said, "Toodle-oo, ole thing."

General A. Robert Emery, commander of Camp Wheeler, avowed his major difficulty with trainees was the mess hall: "The Southern men won't touch broccoli and the Yankees refuse to eat turnip greens."

World War II brought celebrities to Macon. Among them was columnist Henry McLemore, who became famous at Wheeler as the only private who ever filled his canteen with Scotch whiskey instead of water when he went on a 20-mile hike. Henry continued to write his column on a borrowed typewriter at the paper while he trained at Camp Wheeler. He made friends with everybody on the staff.

Because we both were ardent knitters, Henry's wife and I became good friends and the two came often to my apartment, a third floor walk-up. One evening when I answered his knock at my door, Henry offered me, with a deep bow, the fire extinguisher he had taken off the wall on the second floor. I never found out how he managed to get it off; I only know that he left it on the third floor stair landing and the apartment supervisor never did figure out how it got there.

* * *

A somewhat humorous story came from Cochran Field and was illustrated with a picture of a pig holding an empty plate out to a farmer, who was jumping with frustration. Seems that local pig farmers had used the "slop" (leftover food) from Cochran to feed their pigs, and with the shortage of food in 1943, the army cooks didn't let leftovers go to waste. Soldiers did clean their plates into the "slop bucket," but un-served food found itself served again the next day—e.g., corn went into the soup pot, leftover potatoes became hash browns the next day.

Sue used this story to caution housewives that they, like her, should look for more ways to save and use leftovers.

Sue's articles were not limited to *The Macon Telegraph*. One of her feature stories about going on maneuvers with the Sixth Army Corps in August 1942 also ran in *The Macon News*. She was escorted by two officers of the Second Quartermaster Regiment—one her brother-in-law, Edwin Bowden, a colonel. When she finished a cigarette and sought somewhere to discard the butt, he showed her how to field strip it. She geared this story to the cleanliness of the army—a campsite left spotless after five days of military encampment, and a mess so neat the colonel's inspection led to only one fault: A can of soup was turned upside down.

Sue also had empathy for the families of the enemy, as shown in this article, written in 1968 about WWII.

Lightning

Reading a brief dispatch that told of two soldiers who were killed by lightning at Elgin Air Force Base, Florida, the other day, I was reminded of a similar tragedy at Camp Wheeler, during World War II.

During the latter days of the war, as the Allies were beginning to win and many prisoners had been taken, the Government began a prisoner of war camp at Wheeler. Prisoners from Germany and from Italy were sent here and Maconites talked easily of "POWs," looked at the men who rode through town on their way to various jobs, and remarked on the good treatment the USA gave prisoners of war.

The prisoners were "farmed out" in various ways, especially hired by the day to work on farms which were providing food for our Allies. The men were paid by the farm owner at a rate set by the Government, and most of the men preferred working in the fields to sitting around camp with nothing to do.

One day, a group of Italian prisoners working on a farm near Macon encountered a thunderstorm; they left the field to take shelter beneath a large tree, and lightning struck and killed three of the men.

The Telegraph sent me to cover the story of the funeral, which was held at St. Joseph's Catholic Church in Macon, with the local priest holding the service, which was conducted in accordance with the Catholic religion of the dead Italians. All the POWs at Wheeler were permitted to attend the funeral, and they were sitting together, all wearing the uniforms in which they had been captured; uniforms frayed and tattered from hard wear, but brushed and clean and as neat as circumstances would permit.

The POW friends had gathered field flowers from the grounds around the camp and each man brought a few blossoms in his hand, flowers that he took up and laid reverently on the caskets of his friends.

It was a touching, moving performance, and most of the congregation wept, thinking of the parents, the wives, the families of the dead men, families so far away, families who had perhaps been relieved to know their men were captured and would thus escape death on the battlefield.

My own thoughts wandered, to wonder if I were an Italian mother and my son were a POW and I got word he had been killed by lightning would I believe it? I was afraid not. It would be hard to believe in the kindness of the enemy, especially in that day when German cruelty was so infamous.

* * *

Her war-time subjects included the two most important subjects for a soldier—food and himself—as well as any subject assigned or suggested. She wrote about military maneuvers and travelled with soldiers to their training fields. She rode in the military jeeps and wrote about the vehicles.

When she attended a training battle between the Red and Blue armies "over what seems to be half the state of North Carolina, taking bumps and eating dust and learning something of what armies must do under actual conditions of warfare," Sue earned a sort of Purple Heart. She came home eaten up with red bugs and sunburned, which of course she worked into her article for the paper.

One of her strong human interest feature articles told of a World War I veteran who had wanted to join up immediately after Pearl Harbor, but could not pass the physical. As a mail carrier, he decided that he could do his part by selling war stamps—before the government asked letter carriers to add that duty to their regular ones.

Sue also actively helped the locally assigned military men to assimilate into local activities. As a member of the Macon Little Theatre, she was active in seeking military men who would be interested in participating in the theatre's productions. With local men being drafted, sometimes in mid-rehearsal, the men at Camp Wheeler and Robins Army Air Force Base were a welcome addition to the Theatre.

Her duties as War Editor, however, were more than just writing about the local soldiers and military activities. She chaired the campaigns for war salvage and for the Red Cross, as well as other programs that the Government asked newspapers to sponsor. She served on the Bibb County Price and Rationing Board as information officer and kept readers informed of rationing regulations and price controls.

Extra duties also included charity work—in 1943, she began conducting the Goodfellows' drive to feed the Macon needy at Christmas.

Sue in fur coat that Collier's paid for, interviewing James Farley (Postmaster General), while Macon's postmaster, Mr. "Pat" Patillo, looks on. (January 1940)

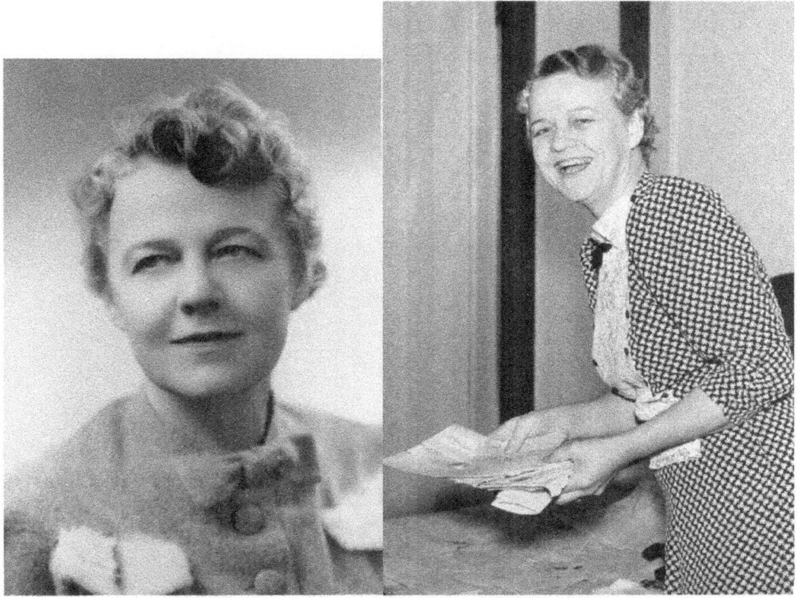

About 1939 **Checking the mail**

1944

Sue in passenger seat, Col. Edwin T. Bowden in rear seat

Mr. & Mrs. Peyton Anderson, W. R. Smith, Sue, at Press Institute

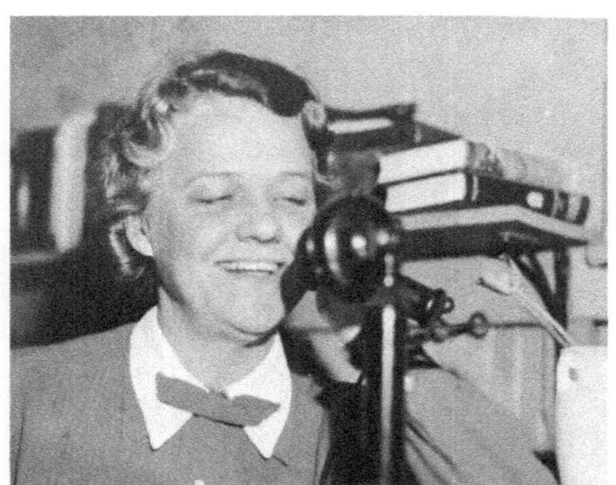

9-8-74

POLITICS

Sue did not take an active role in political races, but she let a few people know her position. When she met Marvin Griffin, then governor of Georgia, at a Georgia Press Association meeting, she told him that he was perhaps the most charming man she had met in a long time, but "I can't vote for you because you're such a crook."

One can only wonder if he remembered her remark years later, at the 50th Georgia Press Institute in 1978, when he and Sue were both speakers during the Nostalgia Session.

Griffin, Sue often said, earned fame as the governor who bought boats for state parks, but, unfortunately, the boats wouldn't float. In the long run, what did that matter? The parks he bought them for didn't have any lakes.

She received a letter from a friend who lived in Boston during the 1940s, who wrote that Sue should be ashamed of Georgia, with its three governors. Sue wrote back that it was better to have three governors than to have a mayor elected while in jail.

Shortly before her death, she asked the mayor of Macon not to cut down the trees along her street to widen the road. His response was that Sue would be dead before that happened. After her death, the mayor proclaimed a Susan Myrick Day and invited the family to attend the celebrations. No one in the family did.

FARM EDITOR

The year 1948 became a pivotal time for Sue. On her vacation, she travelled to Europe with her sister Allie, who was researching a family history, and the sisters visited the family ancestral home.

After her look into the family's past, Sue came home to broader responsibilities and a return to her farming roots. She was appointed farm editor of the Sunday *Telegraph and News*.

That same year, she was elected president of the Macon Little Theatre, which demanded her time in evenings when shows were underway and often on weekends and evenings when shows were in the planning stages.

She later said:

I staggered up the ladder of success to the position of farm editor by way of covering many 4-H Club doings and recounting the successes of Future Farmers of America as well as reporting on fat cattle shows and prizes awarded in agricultural matters at county fairs. When the top award went to a "shorthorn milking bull," my managing editor almost fired me. It took the dean of the College of Agriculture at Athens (University of Georgia) to convince him such a creature existed.

In fact, the appointment came after a conference of publisher and staff about the direction of the paper in the future. They decided to emphasize agriculture since middle Georgia was basically dependent on agriculture. Sue was the logical choice for the position since she already covered many agricultural activities and had an agricultural background.

Her new responsibilities required her to travel to farms and agricultural events within a radius of up to 50 miles from Macon. She interviewed farmers and discussed soil conservation and erosion with landowners and tenants alike. She promoted use of cover crops to enrich the soil over the winter months. But she also gave equal attention to the young people on the farms—she attended their livestock shows and contests at county fairs, wrote of their meetings and individual efforts and saw the young men and women of rural Georgia as the future caretakers of the soil.

As if she didn't have enough to do, she began a weekly radio talk show to discuss agricultural matters with her guests—farmers and conservationists.

In less than a year as farm editor, Sue had come to realize that the farmer's lot had not changed since her childhood. She wrote an article—not a column, in July 1949:

The Farmer's Lot

Dagwood's expression that "Husbands are a sorry lot" might be paraphrased to "Famers' lots are sorry ones." Particularly now that rain is so badly needed in many sections of Georgia.

Talking to James V. Hobbs, instructor for Bibb County Veterans on-Farm-Training class, the other day, I found out some of the complaints of Bibb County farmers about weather, proving the farmer's lot to be sorry.

One man, according to Hobbs, said he kept waiting and kept waiting for a rain so he could set out some late sweet potato slips. Finally he got plumb discouraged about the rain and decided to set out the slips anyway. He got three giant sized drums and filled them with water, with some considerable effort, one might add, and then set them at the sides of the field, ready to plant and water the slips. He had no more than got his potato planter rigged up and hitched to the tractor and started across the field, when a thunder storm came up and the rain fell in such torrents his tractor bogged down and he could not get it out of the field.

Another farmer declared he selected the wrong field for his cotton and corn, this year. "The rain has fallen continuously on the cotton," he said; "the boll weevils are flourishing. Not a drop of rain has fallen on the corn fields, and the corn is wilting and drying up from the drought."

Still another farmer declared he "must be holding his mouth wrong." The rain fell on his neighbor's lands, he said, but not on his.

"I was sitting on the front porch, Sunday, watching the corn wilt, and a big cloud came up. I was so sure it was about to rain that I went out and put my dogs under shelter so they would not maybe get distemper," he said.

"Well, we could see the rain pouring on the land across the road and the wind blew all around us and the thunder rolled. But we didn't get a drop of the rainfall."

He shook his head in mock misery: "I just had to cuss."

Reminds me of a story Corra Harris once told me. The author of *A Circuit Rider's Wife*, Mrs. Harris lived in later life in North Georgia and ran a farm. She said on Sunday she watched her corn drying upon the stalk, the broad green leaves withered and sick, and decided she'd pray for rain.

The she took another look and she said: "Lord, I have planted this corn and fertilized it and worked it. If you want to wither it up with the heat and drought and have my mules starve, you must know more about it than I do."

One Bibb county farmer had a good stand of watermelons, in the early summer; then, dry weather came and the vines stood still for weeks. Came a rain and the vines started to grow, but the farmer found so many of the vines dead that he just plowed up the field and planted cow peas.

Somehow it seems sad to swap cow peas for watermelons.

The farmer's lot can certainly be a sorry one.

* * *

On March 6, 1949, the farm page of *The Telegraph* carried stories from at least nine counties, and several about 4-H Clubs; it also carried the report on livestock auctions in Georgia. Beginning the next day, her first column as associate editor appeared, and she wrote two columns for the editorial pages each week. She also continued her daily Fannie Squeers columns, as well as serving as editor of the weekly farm page for *The Telegraph-News* Sunday edition, and also covering all farm and agricultural events and news, including organizations such as the Farm Bureau, FFA, 4-H, and the REA.

She adored the young men—girls were not considered farmers but future homemakers—of the Future Farmers of America, an organization founded the year she joined *The Telegraph.* After attending one of their annual conventions, she wrote:

The boys are serious about their work; they attend meetings regularly, listen to speeches, discuss their future plans, sing, hear contestants who are vying for state honors in various ways. They are in dead earnest about the business of being leaders in their communities, about being good farmers of tomorrow.

No person could sit in a meeting of those young farmers of tomorrow without a renewal of faith in the future, without a warm and moving emotional experience; no person would fail to choke a little as he listened to the words they spoke.

* * *

A few years later Sue revisited the days of King Cotton and considered the changes in farming since her childhood. Excerpts from her three-quarter-newspaper-page article are given here:

Seventy-five years ago, Georgia was a one-crop state, and all farmers were loyal subjects of King Cotton.

The era of the big plantation with its slave labor was

gone; the freed Negroes had become tenants or share croppers; most Georgia planters had lost the major portion of their lands because of the War Between the States, hardly two decades ended; and the State, devastated by Sherman's troops and the rigors of the Reconstruction Era, was straining to lift itself by its bootstraps.

The farm population, 72 per cent of Georgia's total in 1884, was struggling to adapt itself to the changes brought by *The War*. There were nearly three million acres planted to cotton, the only cash crop. Cultivated with mule and plow, and minus fertilizer, the acreage produced 807,000 bales of cotton, about one-fourth of a bale per acre. Corn, grown on two and a half million acres, produced 10.5 bushels per acre.

Corn was by no means a cash crop; it was grown for feeding the mules which worked the crops, and, in a small measure, for hog feed. The hogs of that era were largely of the razorback type, sometimes known as piney-woods rooters, long, lean animals that foraged for themselves in field and swamp. There was no market for hogs; they were grown for home consumption and for feeding the share croppers.

On most farms there was a milch cow but often she was of the breed which some wag has called the "Poland China" variety—"she was so po' you propped her up with a pole and milked her in a china cup."

But those days are gone forever.

Television antennae have replaced the martin gourds which used to stand in country house yards; the old well from which the farm family laboriously drew water is gone and in its stead is the electric pump and the deep well that supplies water for the modern bathroom found in most farmhouses today; the kerosene lamp has been replaced by the electric light; the unpainted farmhouse on stilts is gone and in its place is the modern, comfortable painted home, with its landscaped yard and shade trees; the electric stove has replaced the old range that was heated with wood, cut and hauled in laborious fashion.

The mule barn is gone. So is the mule, replaced by tractors and the latest in farm machinery sheltered from the weather in a well-constructed shed. Many an old mule barn has been converted to a poultry house or a hog parlor. And paved roads lead to good farm markets where the farmer can find a buyer for his produce.

Sue recounts how these changes came about, and one of the vignettes reflects her love of both farming and laughter.

Seems a farmer tried to diversify and decided to plant tobacco. When he had harvested his crop, he had nowhere to sell it so he took it to the local cotton warehouse for sale. The warehouseman explained that he had no use for the tobacco; the farmer said he had nowhere to sell it, and finally the warehouseman said he would ship it to market with his next load of cotton and report its sale to the farmer the next Saturday.

Came Saturday and the farmer was on hand. The warehouseman sadly reported that the tobacco did not bring enough to cover the cost of shipping and the farmer owed him $2.00.

"But I don't have two dollars," the farmer said.

"Well, then you come to town next Saturday, bring me a rooster, and I'll call it square."

The next Saturday the farmer returned, with a rooster under each arm.

"You didn't need to bring me two roosters. I'd have settled for one," the warehouseman said.

"Shucks! I've got another load of that durned tobacco out here."

In the article, Sue also pointed out that by the late 1950s many cotton fields had become pine forests. Dovedale, too, had lost most of it tenants, and its cotton and crop fields had been planted in pines.

* * *

One of her duties as farm editor was to travel and speak to groups, and she soon became as much in demand to speak to farming organizations about conservation of soil and water as she was to speak to social groups about GWTW.

Sue recalled words of her father—don't let the land lie idle in winter—feed it. And the best food for starving land is a cover crop. Blue lupine became a favorite topic.

I wrote so many stories about the soil-building, water-holding forage crop blue lupine that Wright Bryan, then editor of *The Atlanta Journal*, introduced me to an audience as "The Bloomin' Loopin' Queen." Said he:

All South Georgia was sad and droopin'
'Til Soil Conservation discovered Blue Lupine,
And now the world is fresh and green
And Sue's the Bloomin' Loopin' Queen.

BLUE LUPINE VS. KUDZU

When *Time* ran an article about the *Atlanta Constitution*'s columnist Channing Cope, who bore the nickname of Kudzu Kid, Peyton Anderson responded with a letter to the editor of *Time*:

TIME July 29, 1949
KUDZU KID & LUPINE QUEEN
Sir:

In Georgia, we are very proud of Channing Cope and the work that he is doing for the farmer. You have beautifully described his activities and the admiration all Georgians hold for him [TIME, July 4].

[But] Miss Susan Myrick, Associate Editor and Farm Editor of *The Macon Telegraph,* probably the only woman in the nation to serve in this capacity, swings more influence with Middle Georgia farms on soil conservation than anyone [and] is regarded as the informed and most helpful person in the area on agricultural problems.

Known as the "Blue Lupine Queen," Miss Myrick can challenge the "Kudzu Kid" any time. Blue Lupine, incidentally, is a nitrogen-bearing plant used extensively for winter cover crops in the South. It stops erosion, and adds millions to the income of Georgia farmers.

PEYTON ANDERSON
Publisher

TIME responded:
Macon Telegraph
Macon, Ga.

If *The Macon Telegraph* (circ. 34,000) had as many readers as the Kudzu Kid's *Atlanta Constitution* (circ. 187,000), Publisher Anderson's case for his farm editor would carry more weight. It is nevertheless true that Sue Myrick, born & raised on an oldtime cotton plantation, knows the answers to many Southern questions.* Her pet promotion is soil conservation, and she has done much to popularize the Blue Lupine, as Cope has the Kudzu.—Ed.

*She was hired by David Selznick to teach Clark Gable, Vivien Leigh, *et al.,* how to "talk Southern" in *Gone With The Wind.*

OTHER DUTIES

Sue became a member of the Board of Control of the Farmers Club of the Macon Chamber of Commerce in 1947, a position she held for ten years. She was elected president of the Club in 1952. Sue was the only woman to serve as president or even to serve on the board. Joe Parham, editor of *The Macon News*, wrote:

By golly, she stood up there as pretty and sassy as a young peach tree in bloom.

And the men of the Macon Chamber of Commerce's Farmers Club stood up to give her an ovation on her election.

In 1962 she helped the Association of Soil and Water Conservation District Supervisors build up interest in an annual essay contest on soil and water conservation, which had 12,000 entries in 1962; prizes totaled $7,400, and included an $800 college scholarship.

ANOTHER PROMOTION

In September 1948, with less than a year's time as farm editor, Sue was given the added responsibilities of associate editor. When Peyton Anderson, publisher, announced that promotion, he said her appointment was in recognition of her work on the newspapers and in keeping with the duties now assigned her.

"Miss Myrick has worked untiringly toward better farming practices and toward the general improvement of our agricultural economy in Middle Georgia," he said, "and it is the desire of the Macon newspapers to recognize her work and to affirm their continuous support of this program in this manner."

When Sue's promotion was announced, she received this telegram:

We have just read about you being made Associate Editor. We think it is wonderful news and hope it means that you will have to come to Atlanta and associate more with us up-country people who love and admire you so much.

Peggy and John Marsh

Her appointment as associate editor of *The Telegraph* brought many letters of commendation from individuals and the press who were familiar with her work. These include a letter from Walter C. Johnson, secretary-manager of the Southern Newspaper Publishers Association (their publication carried her three-part series on W. T. Anderson), in which he said he was wondering if Georgia had not started something in the naming of women to the position of associate editors.

The Milledgeville *Union-Recorder* said: "Baldwin County has many sons and daughters who have risen to positions of prominence, but none bring more pleasure and satisfaction than that of the promotion of Susan Myrick."

The first column Sue wrote as associate editor reflected her farm page, her now-permanent home town, and her interest in and knowledge of history. It began:

"The terracing of a 1,200 acre field on the farm of Dr. A. T. Coleman near Dublin, recently, brought to light the fact that the farm was one of the plantations formerly owned by George Michael Troup, who was governor of Georgia in 1823, the year that Macon was founded."

And it ended with a look to the future, as all farmers must:

"It is good to know that at least some part of the land which Governor Troup owned in Georgia, more than a century ago, is in good hands, and that soil conservation practices will make the land fertile for many more centuries."

OUR DAILY BREAD

As if she did not have enough to do, in 1950 Sue decided to write a text book for the third grade—on the importance of soil conservation. She wanted it to be entertaining, not just educational.

She planned this book after discussions about the soil conservation essay contests *The Telegraph* sponsored with the president of the National Association of Soil Conservation District Supervisors. He told her the lack of material available to students made it difficult to have an educational program. He also said education on the subject should start in the primary grades.

So Sue began her book.

Her newspaper duties and her speaking engagements did not interfere with work on the book, nor did work on the book slow down her performance of her newspaper duties. Within the year, the book was finished.

"This book presents in simple form the rudiments of soil and water conservation, to teach children that everything we eat and everything we wear comes from the soil, and to give them an understanding of protecting and replenishing the soil's fertility," Sue said.

It was written in the form of a story that children enjoyed, and illustrated with photographs from the Soil Conservation Services Regional Office at Spartanburg, S.C.

Dr. James Burdette, head of the education department of the Conservation Service, reviewed the book for technical accuracy and commented to Sue that this type of material was greatly needed across the nation.

Sue said the book was written in a regional manner suitable for Southern readers. As examples, the children in her story go "barefooted" and play in "creeks." She said it could be easily adapted for children in other regions of the States.

To slant it to the age group she wanted, the third grade, she consulted with her cousin, Nan Whitehurst Ingram, who had served as director of the nursery school affiliated with the Georgia State College for Women and also directed the Head Start Program in Milledgeville.

She also got advice from Mrs. Fielder Goodman, primary grades supervisor of Bibb County Schools, and from Dr. M. D. Mobley, state director of vocational agriculture instruction.

The book was used in several Southern states as a routine text book for third graders for a number of years. It is now considered a "rare book."

The Georgia Press Association issues a monthly publication, *The Editor's Forum,* to editors and publishers of Georgia newspapers. The forum carries articles and ads for their intended audience, as well as articles about these men—no mention of "associate editors." One column is headed "Lady Fingers" and usually features the wives of the publishers and editors. In the April 1950 edition, however, neither wife of an editor nor an editor, Sue made the "Lady Fingers" column for having been "in the headlines" three times in 1950—for her book, for being elected to the presidency of the Farmers Club of the Macon Chamber of Commerce, and for being honored by the Women's National Press Club.

She became a special news item in the *Forum* when she was named Woman of the Year by *Progressive Farmer.*

DAR

As her newspaper duties increased, Sue began to give up some of her commitments to social and civic organizations, including the Daughters of the American Revolution. She had joined years earlier, on the James Dowdell line (her Virginia-based ancestor)—membership number 233706. She was active in the Nancy Hart Chapter in Milledgeville. As a staff member of the paper, she was ideal to serve as publicity chairman.

With her educational background in elocution—from the Friday poetry recitals in the Dovedale School to her classes at GN&IC—she was a perfect choice to present programs; we found, however, records of only one presentation, on George Washington, the Patriot, which she presented in June 1931. By then, her job on *The Telegraph* demanded much of her time, and she lived some thirty miles from Milledgeville.

In 1950, she resigned membership in the publicity committee and in the DAR because of her increased responsibilities with the paper and the distance to travel to meetings.

Other Resignations

Her writing was extensive. Besides what she produced for the newspapers, she frequently wrote freelance articles, many about her time in Hollywood, but many about other subjects. Her early freelance work, written while she was a teacher, centered around physical education. Over time, she published in many general publications—e.g., *Colliers*, *The Detroit News*, *The New York World*, and *Southern Living*.

Her duties constantly expanded at the paper. One, which seems to be "simple" was, however, demanding: Prepare the history column titled "20 years ago today." That project meant search the morgue for the correct issue and then read the paper to determine which stories would be of greatest interest to the Macon readers.

Years later, she was the lead item in *The Telegraph*'s "50 years ago today" on December 13, 1988, the anniversary of her being picked by Selznick for work on GWTW.

As her duties grew more demanding, Sue found it necessary to surrender some of her "outside" memberships. Besides giving up her DAR activities, she relinquished her presidency of the Macon Farmers Club in 1951. Later, although a Life Member and member of the board, she also became less active in the Macon Little Theatre.

EQUALITY FOR WOMEN

As a woman whose job was usually done only by men, Sue decried those who wanted to keep women "barefooted, pregnant and in the kitchen." She felt that any job a man could do, a woman could do as well (if not better).

The men who covered sporting events objected to women "encroaching" on their territory and often would express negative opinions about what women knew about sports. She was knowledgeable about a variety of male sports. Together with Mark and Willie Snow Etheridge, she attended the Sharkey-Stribling fight in Miami in 1930. She attended the minor league baseball games held in Macon; and of course, she had majored in physical education and coached teams. So Sue responded with the article below, which, when published, probably made the rounds of the sports writers of both *The Telegraph* and *The News*.

From the Southern *Newspaper Publishers Association,* November 20, 1954:

LET THE LADY IN!

Susan Myrick—Macon (Ga.) Telegraph

"Go back to your knittin', kitten," is the advice Wally Reid, sportswriter of *The Macon News*, gives the femme who moaned when she was denied admission to the Yale Press Box. Wallace seems to think that because women do not play football they have no right to write stories about football. He uses a strange sort of thinking, I think. He might as well argue that a newshawk who has never been in jail has no right to do a piece about a guy who was in the clink without bail.

He might as well claim that because a fellow had never been indicted for murder he had no right to type out a story on an electrocution. Or, that a fellow who was not a doctor could not cover a hospital story about the triplets born to Mrs. Peppercorn.

The sports writer on our esteemed contemporary (that is a phrase which seems to be the accepted way to speak of the chap with whom you disagree on the other newspaper) indicated that women may write sonnets and cook meals and wash dishes but they just plain can't keep a baseball score. He insinuates that we, the poor women, don't know a base hit from a foul ball and that we think the reason the umpire wears that little pillow on his front and the mask on his face is for fear the batter will go mad and try to bat the ump.

Reid admits that women occasionally let mere man peek into the woman's world and permit him to see a fashion show or walk inside a beauty parlor. Well, for crying out loud! Hasn't he heard that men get permanent waves and facial massages and hair cuts in women's beauty parlors? No wonder he doesn't recognize the fact that I can keep a baseball score as well as he can, that I know what the old business meant that said "Tinkers to Evers to Chance," that I know what a triple play is and that I (and many women like me) know even what a Texas Leaguer is.

I don't want to cover a football game, goodness knows. It is a heap more fun to watch the game and enjoy it without having to make any notes or write down who ran with the ball or who tackled whom, and such. But I come to the defense of the women. If we want to cover a football game or a baseball game or a field hockey game or whatever, and if the Boss thinks we can make the grade, we don't want any male sportswriter saying women ain't got no business in the Press Box.

Sue was as knowledgeable about "male" sports as she was about fashion and women's sports. She attended football games at Georgia Military College in Milledgeville when in her teens—in fact, her mother complained that everybody hurried through their meal and ran off to the football game on Thanksgiving Day and she would no longer prepare a fancy meal.

Sue attended (and often wrote about) the professional baseball games in Macon in the 1930s, often with Charles Herty. He is not remembered by many today—in the early half of the twentieth century, he gained fame for being the first football coach at the University of Georgia; for designing the football to its present configuration, and for his chemical research, which made it possible to produce paper from pine trees. He and Sue were friends for many years.

In the 1960s, she recalled:

I counted it a great honor to know Dr. Herty, and though we were not actually kin to each other, I called him "Cousin Charlie' and he called me "Cousin Susan"; it was all because his family was kin to a family which was related to me by marriage.

Cousin Charley loved baseball and so did I. He was in Macon often during the thirties when Macon had a baseball team that was popular, and Dr. Herty and I went to many games together, down at Luther Williams Park. He could almost always call a play before it happened.

He took great delight in an episode that occurred in Milledgeville, his birthplace, at the dedication of the tablet in his honor. Everybody who was anybody assembled on the campus at the college. A colleague sent a telegram of congratulations from New York City, addressed to "Dr. Charles Holmes Herty, Milledgeville, Ga."

It was returned to the senders with the notation: "Herty unknown here."

In March 1930, Herty began a letter to Sue's sister Lillas, "I was just about to say 'Cousin Lillas.' " Much of the letter was scientific. He ended with "It has been a great joy to me to know Susan and I hope some day I am going to have the pleasure of knowing you personally too." They did meet and became fast friends—Lillas's husband and Herty worked together on pine pulp research.

Sue loved the Okefenokee Swamp and had visited it several times to fish; Herty gave her a book on the history of the swamp and signed it

To "Cousin Susan"
a good sport
With the best wishes of
Chas. H. Herty
4/22/30

SMOKING CHALLENGE 1964

When Sue had a problem with her throat, her doctor told her she had to quit smoking. She gritted her teeth over the matter—and on the way home she stopped at the drug store. She wanted a carton of cigarettes.

Not the way most people would stop smoking. At home, she opened up every pack, put each one beside an ashtray and a filled lighter. Asked why, she said if she could stop with the temptation in front of her all the time, she would be able to stop permanently. She never lit another cigarette.

But she wrote about cigarettes and smoking on more than one occasion. In a column about the price per pack going up to sixty cents in the vending machines, she says: "Looks as if we'll have to grow our own. I recall that during Depression Days when cigs were 12 cents a pack, I thought seriously of growing my own. Trouble was I feared I'd try to raise the brand I liked and end up with some other kind that I would not walk a mile for."

In a 1968 column, she wrote of the National Society of Non-Smokers naming a "non-smoking winner." Her words: "Somebody please call this award to the attention of the American Cancer Society. Maybe, next year, I'll be the best something of the year—the woman who stopped smoking and stayed off the fag for nearly four years, now."

AWARDS

Sue won her first award, for physical prowess—diving—while a student at Battle Creek, and then gained national attention as the nation's first Superwoman. In Macon, she won a blue ribbon at the local horse show. Her other awards were for her skill with language, her ability to adjust to any situation and to any people, and her dedication as a newspaperwoman.

She won her first honors for the farm page less than a year after her appointment to the position of farm editor and only a few months after her appointment as associate editor. It came from the state-wide organization of supervisors and technicians of the Georgia Soil Conservation Districts in November 1948, when they presented her with a certificate at their annual meeting in Atlanta.

State Representative Stephen Pace said, "I believe that every farmer in Georgia will approve of this action and will always be grateful to you for the keen interest you have taken in them and their lands."

In an unsigned editorial, *The Telegraph* stated:

The soil conservation program in Middle Georgia with which Miss Myrick has been identified so effectively for a long period of years has a double objective. The first, of course, is to prevent the top soil of our farms from being washed into the ocean or the gulf. But this program ties in very happily with the program of increasing Georgia's livestock, both as to beef and dairy cattle as well as hogs.

The idea is that where a given area has been practically exhausted by years of planting to row crops, such as cotton, with the result that its fertility has been destroyed, it should be planted to pasture on which livestock might graze through the greater part of the year. Perhaps it would be advisable simply to plant this acreage in a cover crop, such as blue lupine, or Austrian peas, which would be turned back into the soil at the proper time and thus restore the nitrogen content.

This is the work which has been going on steadily in the districts which practically constitute Middle Georgia, and Miss Myrick, in her capacity as a member of The Telegraph *staff, has been in the forefront in persuading Georgia farmers to co-operate in this soil conservation program and its corollary, the increase of our livestock industry.*

The recognition given Miss Myrick is deserved in a most eminent degree.

Later in November, the soil conservation technicians and

supervisors from three Middle Georgia soil conservation districts paid special tribute to Sue with a plaque in recognition of her work on conservation projects.

Participating in the surprise banquet were more than 50 representatives from the Central Georgia Soil Conservation District, the Middle Western Ocmulgee River SCD, and the Piedmont SCD. T. H. McGibbony, supervisor from Greensboro, was master of ceremonies.

Sam Nunn of Perry (father of the senator from Georgia) presented the plaque, which read:

"Presented to Miss Susan Myrick for her outstanding services and leadership in promoting soil conversation in Middle Georgia, by the supervisors of the soil conservation districts in Middle Georgia."

O. D. Hall, Athens, assistant state conservationist, praised Sue's work and declared that her *Sunday Telegraph and News* agriculture page is "one of the finest I have ever seen. It has carried the story of better farming and soil conservation to the farmers of this section more than anything I have read," explained Hall.

J. C. Lidell, assistant regional conservationist from Spartanburg, S. C., also commended the work and asserted that "the South is well on its way to becoming the Nation's No. 1 economic asset."

Nunn praised the Macon newspapers for their leadership in conservation work and explained that the honor was "particularly befitting Miss Myrick, who has been in charge of that phase of the newspaper's program for several years."

Arrangements for the banquet were made by Carl Huggins of Perry; T.H. Brown of Wrightsville, and G. E. McWhorter of Milledgeville. John Monroe, Vienna, presented a special gift to Sue from conservationists in the Middle Western Ocmulgee River district which is comprised of nine counties.

A telegram from T. L. Ashbury, state conservationist, who was unable to attend, said in part: "With her supersonic jet propelled lilac and old lace personality and attitude, she is a modernized spirit of the old South, doing a great job for the land and the people she loves so well."

WOMEN'S NATIONAL PRESS CLUB
1367 National Press Building
Washington 4, D. C.

Telephone EXecutive 3418

April 2, 1950

My dear Miss Myrick:

Here are a few last-minute notes about the WNPC dinner to be given on Saturday night, April 15.

Mrs. Mary James Cottrell, member of the Board of Governors, will call you at the Statler Hotel some time Saturday.

Please be on hand for a reception in the Federal room of the Statler at six o'clock, before the dinner. There you will meet President and Mrs. Truman and other special guests, pictures will be taken, you will receive a corsage, and preliminary details will be taken care of.

Hold Sunday afternoon open for a tea with Mrs. Truman at Blair House.

We are all delighted that you are coming, and looking forward to meeting you.

Most sincerely,
Josephine Hemphill
Josephine Hemphill
Member of the Board

Miss Susan Myrick
Associate Editor
The Macon Telegraph
Macon, Georgia

Sue receives award for best farm page in nation; award presented by A. A. Caruse on behalf of the National Editorial Association's Better Newspaper Contests for 1956.

Sue receiving award in 1962 from National Association of Soil and Water Conservation districts from Association president Marion S. Monk, Jr.

IN APPRECIATION

for 42 years of

Faithful and Devoted Service

we honor

SUSAN MYRICK

As much as any other single person, Sue Myrick is an institution within an institution. Her name and the name of The Telegraph and News are almost synonymous as symbols of conscientious newspapering and of youthful spirit wedded to mature judgement.

Her first column appeared in The Telegraph in 1928; her first story saw the light of print in 1929. Since then she has held a great variety of responsibilities with the Macon papers and has done them all well. Her efforts in behalf of soil and water conservation have been particularly effective and have gained her national recognition.

Her fame as a writer is equalled only by her renown as a speaker and she has gained for us many thousands of friends, speaking on every subject from A to Z.

Many a reporter and editor found Sue Myrick a real friend on first coming to the Macon papers. The cubs called her "Miss Myrick", and appreciated her helpfulness. The veterans called her "Sue" and valued her advice.

Now, on this occasion, as we wish for her many more years of happiness, good health and a rich life, we say to Fanny Squeers, to one of the best of reporters, and to one of the most capable of editors--- not goodbye, for the newsroom will always be your home---but good luck, fair winds, and God bless you!

MACON TELEGRAPH PUBLISHING COMPANY

CORPORATE SEAL — MACON TELEGRAPH PUBLISHING CO.

President

Dated: January 1, 1967

Daughters of the American Revolution memorial to Sue and other outstanding Milledgeville women

Invitation from The White House

November 1948, Sam Nunn (left; father of Senator Nunn) presents award to Sue from the soil conservation technicians and supervisors from three Middle Georgia soil conservation districts.

GREATEST HONORS

Special Citation

In February 1963, at its annual conference in Denver, the National Association of Soil and Water Conservation Districts presented Sue with a special citation "for presenting a continuing, dynamic and convincing appeal to farm and nonfarm Americans in behalf of the protection, development and wise use of land, water and other natural resources" and "for years of devoted and understanding interest in the day-to-day affairs of people engaged in agriculture."

Of all of her awards over the years, this one meant the most to her—it's the only one she asked *The Telegraph* to list in her obituary.

Best Farm Page

She was extremely proud of the one she accepted on behalf of the paper for her farm page being named the best in the nation. The National Editorial Association sponsored a Better Newspaper contest, and in June, 1956, Sue received the award at the Association's 71st annual convention in Louisville, Kentucky.

Sue's farm page won on the basis of an entry showing that during one year, the paper published 51,758 square inches (about 1,203 newspaper columns) consisting of 7, 229 articles and pictures of farm news and features in the daily *Telegraph* and the Sunday *Telegraph & News*.

Articles included state and local farm items, national farm news, market reports, editorials and forest fire and river stage information.

Judges said: "the entry of *The Macon Telegraph* was outstanding with the best, most consistent service to agriculture. This is an outstanding farm editor doing an excellent all-around job."

The farm news published by the *Telegraph* in 1954, if printed on a continuous sheet of newsprint, would extend 281 feet.

Fun Awards

November 4, 1974, Bert Struby, then editor of *The Telegraph*, received a "letter to the editor" in the form of a poem, written by Jordan Massee, Maconite who then lived in New York City.

To The Editor of *The Macon Telegraph*
(A few lines by your Guest Sports Writer of November 4, 1974)

If I were the Grand Mogul of you-all
Who watch or play the game of baseball,
The Dean boys I'd surely swap you,
Along with DiMaggio—and Marilyn too.
I'd even trade Mickey Mantle, and give you
Ty Cobb, Lou Gehrig, Babe Ruth—all;
And just to be fair, I'd dare to
Move Yankee Stadium to your Tattnall Square
And call it the Beauregard-Lupin'-Lee,

If you'll swap one Susan Myrick—
Just for me!

Sue's hand-written note at the bottom of the page reads "it went round and round to *The Telegraph*."

The Good/Rotten Egg

Among the scores of columns I wrote for *The Telegraph* over the years was one making fun of the ubiquitous "Miss Something-or-other" whose picture was always appearing in the newspapers: Miss Florida Grapefruit, Miss Spirits of Southern Georgia Turpentine, Miss South Georgia Peanut, Miss North Georgia Chick, et cetera, et cetera.

A week later I wrote about the beginning of the effort to persuade people to slow down on eating food that contained high portions of cholesterol since eggs contained it and I could not face a day without an egg for breakfast. A few days later, three men representing the Georgia Poultry Association presented me with a plaque that named me "Miss Georgia Good Egg."

My fellow reporters began calling me "Miss Rotten Egg."

Other awards Sue received for her work, including posthumous awards, are listed in the Appendix XIII.

WOMEN'S NATIONAL PRESS CLUB

The Women's National Press Club invited special guests in the newspaper field to attend their annual festivities in Washington, D. C. as they honored women of special achievement. Sue was one of the guests, invited by Jane Stafford, president of the organization.

Sue wrote:

In 1950 the Women's National Press Club in Washington, D. C., invited me to be one of its honored guests at the festivities of its spring meet: A cocktail party, a banquet with President Truman addressing the club, and a tea for the honored guests at the Blair House, where the President and his family were living while repairs were being made on the White House.

Diked out in my new evening gown and a pair of long white gloves I could ill afford, I was on hand for the cocktail party where I met my old friend Olivia de Havilland, the Melanie of *Gone With The Wind*, as well as other celebrities. Who wore white gloves to the cocktail party? Me. Not another soul.

The thrill I had when Truman entered the banquet hall, with the Marine Band's Ruffles and Flourishes, was such that I forgot the ill-gotten gloves. I remember nothing the President said in his speech; I do remember how pretty Margaret Truman was, much lovelier than the press photographs I'd seen, and how Mrs. Truman looked no more glamorous than the usual small town housewife in her Sunday dress.

The next afternoon when the tea at Blair House was about half finished, Mr. Truman came in by a side door, radiating hospitality and friendliness. His handclasp was firm and he made me feel as if I were a longtime friend who had voted for him many times.

* * *

Gertrude Smith, a colleague at *The Telegraph*, gave more details about the event.

"Dripping with celebrities" is the terse way Miss Susan Myrick describes last week-end in Washington, D.C., where she was one of six

newspaperwomen honored by the Womens' National Press Club.

But she is not terse for long. She talks on lyrically about the annual dinner and stunt part of the Press Club, having tea at the Blair House with President and Mrs. Truman and meeting the Veep and his charming bride.

She was one of six newspaperwomen over the country who were special guests at the dinner Saturday night "in recognition of their contributions to the journalistic profession."

The week-end got off to a gay start at a cocktail party Friday at the home of Doris Fleeson who writes a syndicated political column. Our Miss Myrick soon felt right at home chatting about Macon friends with several guests. When she was introduced to Mrs. Truman, the First Lady asked about a former Maconite, Mrs. Margaret McKenney Cavendish. Another guest, Mrs. Ann Williams Wheaton who is public relations director of the Republican National Committee, said she was related to the Lamar family here.

Many national figures were present, including Chief Justice Vinson and Mrs. Morris Cafritz, party giver extraordinary.

A reception at the Statler Hotel Saturday evening was a "small affair with only about 100 present," reports Miss Myrick. It was there she met Vice President and Mrs. Alban Barkley, the latter wearing a green satin strapless evening gown.

She talked to Gordon Gray, who rose from a private at Camp Wheeler to be secretary of the U. S. Army in seven years and is the next president of the University of North Carolina.

The Maconite and Miss Olivia de Havilland had a time reminiscing about the filming of Gone With The Wind. *"Olivia had become a proud mother since GWTW days," said Sue, " so she took snapshots of her son out to show me."*

"Every person at the dinner was famous," said Sue. "The Truman family, ambassadors, cabinet members, court justices and Perle Mesta were among those present."

Mrs. Truman entertained at a small tea (just about 30) on Sunday afternoon with daughter Margaret assisting.

While chatting with guests, Mrs. Truman turned to Sue and said, "You think you're in the Blair House, don't you?"

Bewildered, Sue replied, "Why, yes."

"Well, you entered Blair House, but this room is really in the Lee House which adjoins the Blair House. In order to enlarge the Blair

House, the walls between them were torn down."

Sue did not tell the reporter about her entrance to the tea. The story has been told by her sister Allie M. Bowden. Sue stayed with Allie and Edwin Bowden in Washington when she was there for the event. They drove her to the tea, and had to cross the river—on a draw bridge. Never, Allie said, had the bridge been up when she wanted to cross it, until that day. Just as they approached, the bridge began to rise, and they knew they could not have Sue to the tea on time.

She was the last to arrive, "dressed to the nines," and as she entered, Olivia de Havilland cried out, "Sue!" Conversation stopped as the actress ran across the room and embraced Sue.

SPEECHES

It would be impossible to give details of her speeches across the South. At agricultural meetings, she was often introduced as the "bloomin' loopin' Queen." Sue always discussed the importance of conservation—"Look at China today," she said. "It was once wealthy, but her people neglected the soil." She also stated that "The greatest product of the soil is man."

Her topic was "Human Resources from a Woman's Viewpoint," at the Land and People Conference in New Orleans in 1962. Chairman of the conference was Secretary of Agriculture Orville Freeman; some 1,000 people from nine Southeastern states attended, and seventeen Southerners were on the program as speakers.

At women's clubs and writer's clubs, she told about her role in production of GWTW. At her alma mater in Milledgeville, she spoke to the Progressive Farmers Club about an essay contest she was directing for the Macon papers. At times, she expressed strong opinions about social needs.

For example, she told members of the Macon Exchange that "Apartment houses, not nursing homes, are needed for the elderly." She said such a project would enable persons living on social security to have their own homes without burdening their sons and daughters. She suggested that federal funds could be used to finance such a project—one had been in use in Columbus for five years at the time.

This letter typifies Sue's response to information about planning for one of her speeches:

Mrs. Kenneth Dawson
402 Eastwood Drive
Dublin, Ga.

Dear Mrs. Dawson:

I hope you have not given me up as a writer of something you can use as a hand-out for a newspaper. I herewith submit a page that your editors may cut as they wish. I am sure you will provide for me the information about time and place of the dinner, etc.

I also enclose two photographs as you requested. I flinch when I look at the pictures—I really don't believe I look like them, but I hear tell cameras do not lie, so I have to accept the pictures.

I shall expect you to write me any further details that I need to know. I am guessing you want my talk to last about 40 minutes. Maybe I can keep an audience listening that long. If you see any guests yawning you can signal me to cut my speech short.

Please let me know what motel I have a reservation in, and let me know the hour you expect me to be all dressed up and ready to eat dinner. I hope you do not want me to stand in a receiving line. My feet always hurt when I stand in a line.

I do not need any props for my talk. I don't have slides. I just stand up there and talk and hope the crowd gets a laugh now and then.

Looking forward with pleasure to meeting you and your friends, I am

Sincerely yours,

Susan Myrick

She enclosed a one-page "autobiography."

After she spoke at Dublin, a member of her audience said "Susan Myrick can make a talk on turnip greens interesting."

In 1954, she spoke in Greenville, South Carolina, during a two-day conference on soil and water conservation. In his column titled "Women Take Soil Conservation Spotlight" in the *Greenville Piedmont* (January 21, 1954), David A. Tillinghast stated:

There have been several high points in the program, prepared and offered by President George Davis of the district supervisors and his committee but none surpassed the experience that came my way yesterday afternoon as I heard a lady arise before that audience of 95 percent men and talk agriculture as two-fistedly as any hard-handed male who ever jerked a No. 13 Oliver plow around at the end of a furrow.

No. 13 Olivers are probably as obsolete as rubber-tired buggies but there once were such things to burden stock and try the endurance of men.

This lady speaker, who had only to utter the fewest words to qualify for her role was Miss Susan Myrick, farm editor of The Macon Telegraph, *way down in central Georgia.*

She had the agricultural background, she had the present day information, she had the inspiration and she had the stories to do as fine a job of spell-binding as I have seen a woman accomplish in many a day.

Straight from the shoulder as any man would have done (and I apologize for even making the comparison) she presented an understanding and interpretative line of thinking that was organized as dynamically to emphasize in proper perspective the basic role soil conservation must play in American economic security as I have ever heard it done.

As Miss Myrick poured out her heart-and-soul grasp of the meaning of soil and water conservation, its significance to every level of society and the fact that getting this significance over to the public is a must, I couldn't help but feel that if in the few years that she has turned her talents to the movement she had developed such a fervor, surely the necessary education of the public could be done by the rest.

* * *

"When I first got hold of him, all of Clark Gable's "R's" were triplets. This is the way he said, "I can't afford a four door Ford'".

In imitation of Prissy, "Miss Scarlett, I don't know nothin' about bringing babies".

Here you are telling the Montgomery Rotarians than soap must be made on the increase of th moon, or it will "swink" up to nothin'.

Someone described one of Sue's speeches as "like going to Brer Rabbit's laughing place." She certainly earned lots of laughter at her speech to the Macon Writers' Club, which had previously made her an honorary member.

Sue's talk:

Can't tell you how proud I am to be honored by the Writers' Club. And Betty's introduction has made me feel more than proud. I feel like that cow that was grazing in a pasture alongside I-75. She looked up and saw a trailer truck, bearing in huge letters: Milk, Pasteurized, Homogenized and Vitamin D added. She chewed her cud a couple of chews and said "Makes me feel very inadequate."

I've had the pleasure of being the introducer at the annual breakfast—Margaret Long, Celestine Sibley and Willie Snow Ethridge—this is my first time as the introducee—and it's more fun.

I was introduced one time at a meeting in Twiggs County—a farmers meet where I was to talk on Conservation. I was Farm Editor at that point. The tall, tanned, farmer who introduced me was obviously making his first public appearance. He wasted no time in introducing me. He said: "Ladies and Gentlemen, everybody knows Miss Sue. Here she is."

I had thought to call this talk "Remembrance of things past," but you know how modern titles are half mile long—"And poor Dad, they hung him in the closet and I'm so glad"—"Dealing on the Boston to Berkley Forty-Brick Lost Bag Blues"—"Who was the lady I seen you with on the way home from the Forum the other night"... So, I decided to go mod and call this the "Banes and Blessings, the joys and sorrows, the virtues and vicissitudes and the glooms and glories of a newspaper job."

I assure you the speech will not be as long as the title!

There were vicissitudes, all right. There was Mark Ethridge, my editor. When I first started as a reporter, I'd turn in a piece of copy I thought was just great and he'd tear it to pieces and make me write it all over again, advising as did the editor on Front Page that nobody ever read the second paragraph—get it in the lead.

Working on *The Telegraph* was a blessing to me, who hated getting up early. As a teacher I had been obliged to be at the school by 8:30. At *The Telegraph*, it was half past nine.

It was a joy to be invited to the good parties that businesses gave for the Press. Chicken livers wrapped in bacon and rare roast beef. But a bane every December when I had the job of raising $12,000 for Salvation Army Christmas giving.

You've heard a thousand times, I expect, the old line about meeting such interesting people when you work for the paper. Well, that is truly one of the joys—as well as a sorrow. I'll never forget the lady whom I met once at the paper. She came to ask me to do her a personal favor—to write the obit for her husband who was ill and she feared would not live long. I took notes and promised to do the obit. She insisted I write it and let her read it. I did. She initialized it as correct. Then she opened her purse, offered me a twenty. Man, that was about a week's salary for me at that time! But I explained we were not permitted to accept tips for writing obits and refused the money. She continued to press it on me—embarrassing me greatly, and I continued to refuse. Then, she leaned across my desk and pushed the bill down the front of my low necked shirt waist. Incidentally, he lived ten years longer.

But all unpleasant episodes are forgotten when I remember the blessings of interesting people. I'd never have met Margaret Mitchell if I had not worked on the paper. I first saw the little four-foot-eleven-inch, auburn-haired, pretty girl at Carrollton at a Press conference. She came into the auditorium and asked if she might sit beside me. She introduced herself and we chatted, before the speaking began. There were a heap of introductions—Georgia Press presents dozens of more or less important people. Then, a couple of long winded speakers took over. When the break came, she asked if I'd like to go to the little girls' room with her and I accepted. Once there she said hesitantly—remember this was in the Twenties—"Do you smoke?" I said I did and we lighted up. It was the beginning of a long friendship.

Another "interesting person" was Frank Daniels, then on *The Journal*, now with State Archives. Frank, along with Peggy Mitchell, always avowed my story of going to school with a girl named Lulu Bobo from TyTy was a beautiful lie. One day I had a note from him. He enclosed a clip from *The Journal*, the obituary of Lulu Bobo from TyTy.

He wrote: "I'm wondering if your friend was killed by a dumdum bullet or the bite of a tsetse fly. Chances are fifty-fifty. Bye-bye, Mrs. Bobo."

He had sent a copy to Margaret Mitchell who wrote by the same post, "Always considered you the world's biggest liar. I herewith apologize. Was death caused by beri-beri?"

I wired the two of them: "No, not dumdum bullet or tsetse fly. It was beri-beri. She is as extinct as the dodo. Beri-berial neath a jujube tree in Pago Pago."

Peggy replied "How about a pawpaw tree or the titi bush."

Frank wired: "A box of bonbons or a rumbaba for your wire. It was a lulu. Oui. Oui. Too too divine. Did the bulbul sing at the funeral?"

As for interesting people, there was in *The Telegraph* building the funniest and MOST interesting person in the world—John Duncan Spencer, who wrote a daily column for the paper, "More Otherwise Than Wise," signed JDS.

Note: In two of his columns written during World War I, which Sue saved in her files, JDS wrote:

Personal. TO S. M. Milledgeville. Seems I can't get it right in the column. Drop over sometime and I'll tell you about it.

Personal. TO S. M. Milledgeville: Beg your pardon. Why didn't you say so?

My little cubby hole at *The Telegraph* office on Cherry Street was next door to Johnnie Spencer's and we became good friends and I spent many a delightful hour listening to stories of JDS's. He stuttered and he liked nothing better than to tell stories about how he got ccccccured of his stuttering and scarcely sssstammered at all, now.

When he first came to *The Telegraph* he was a reporter. The time was when a big Confederate reunion was scheduled for Macon. Somebody called in and wanted to give a list of celebrities who were to attend, and the editor told Johnnie to take the names. He laboriously wrote down the names as they were given—some twenty odd names. Then, the caller said: "Would you please read the list back to me, now," Spencer said: "H-h-h-h-hell no s-s-s-sir."

First story I ever sold was about Spencer. I sold it to the *Literary Digest*, a magazine that most of you are too young to remember, but perhaps you'll recall the magazine went out of business shortly after their political poll said Alf Landon would beat FDR? I always claimed that I folded up the magazine.

As a columnist Spencer was widely quoted throughout the nation. He pointed out pungent stuff with shrewd, jocular and droll observations. One of his paragraphs reminds you of today. He said of Mrs. Herrick, of the National Labor Relations Board, strongly criticized for her remark about Hitler: "A lady official of the US should at all times try to keep her mouth on such a high plane as to make it next to impossible for her to put her foot in it without spraining her knee. Truth is, a lady official's mouth is in the home." The words might have been written today about Mrs. Martha Mitchell, wife of the Cabinet officer.

Spencer wrote about everything. He said of Mr. Ford, "He is making paint out of soybeans but the report is it is not fit to drink."

He hated bread pudding, spinach, carrots, strawberry shortcake, old jokes, chain letters and parsnips. Of the last, he wrote: "The New York State Department of Agriculture declares the parsnip to be a delectable and toothsome food especially when served in flaming rum. We might risk one eye on a dipperful of flaming rum, but we wouldn't want to take on enough to put us in the mood to eat a parsnip."

He used to say he went for one year to a Baptist University but at the end of one year they swapped him for a good case of yellow fever in the interest of the institution.

Spencer loved pets, especially his pet crow. He had found the young bird, taken it home, fed it with an eye dropper and brought it to maturity. He taught it to talk and Spencer's Talking Crow was the most famous pet in the country. He bitterly resented the accusation that he had split the crow's tongue in order that it might learn to talk, said the old tradition that you have to split the bird's tongue is bunk.

He wrote of his crow, name of Jim, that he was black as the record of the Ohio gang, cuter than Clara Bow, funnier than Ben Turpin, and will talk except when you want him to show off.

He delighted in a story of Jim's encounter with a young girl who was Nuss for three youngsters in Shirley Hills. The children and the Nuss were wading in a creek in the woods which back in the twenties were thick in the area of Shirley Hills where Spencer lived. The Crow flew down from a tree limb, lighted on the shoulder of the nurse maid and said "Go to Hell." It took a week to find the girl, he always vowed.

That admonition about where to go was the bird's favorite remark, next on the list was "Starvation." He went to school during the depression.

There was a black and white cat once, Mr. Pat. When he died on Thanksgiving Day in 1931, Spencer wrote an obit for the cat that had half of Macon choking back tears.

When Mr. Pat shoved off for the Great Unknown it left us with a sickly, helpless, heart achy feeling and a Thanksgiving Day that wouldn't jell. Thursday morning when we were burying him in one of his favorite spots in the yard, a thrasher stopped on a blackberry vine, nearby, and commenced singing. The lady of the house, who is even sobbier than me, stopped crying long enough to ask if we thought he was singing a prayer for Mr. Pat. Of course, we didn't but we said we did and somehow the lie seemed to help us both. It's funny how a little thing like that affects one. Anyway, Mr. Pat was a loving and lovable cat. We miss him and we'll go missing him more than we know how to say."

Now the story I'm about to tell you belongs to both the joys and the troubles of newspapering. Among my duties as time went on there came a day when *The Telegraph* was always sending me somewhere to make a speech. Maybe it was because nobody else on the paper wanted to make a speech as I did. Anyway, I talked on everything you can think of—conservation, farming, etiquette, good cooking, how to hold your sweetheart, what to do about divorce and God knows what all. I even got invited to speak at a convention of morticians in Greenville, S. C. Since they offered to pay my expenses and give me an honorarium, I accepted the invitation. I could get a plane from Macon in the early morning, arrive Greenville in time for an afternoon rest, get dressed up, make a talk at the banquet and catch a plane back to Macon at 10 p.m., and arrive home in plenty of time to get to the office the next morning.

I went, I ate the banquet food, I made the talk. The rest of the evening the morticians and their ladies were to dance. I was to catch the plane. But about eight p.m. word came of thunder storms, fog, rain, mist—no planes were flying. So, I went to the dance. About 11 o'clock I said to Charlie Peace, editor of the Greenville paper, who was on hand for the do, that I must go get a wire off to Peyton to say I would be late returning to the desk, tomorrow. Charlie, a good friend of Peyton's said let him send the wire and I said that would be kind of him, and I went gaily dancing with some handsome undertaker.

Next day, I arrived in Macon at early afternoon, went to office, to encounter Peyton on the steps to *The Telegraph*. "Where on earth have you been?" I mumbled that I had been delayed because of weather troubles. He pulled out of his pocket a telegram. "Look what the Western Union waked me up to hear, last night," he said.

The wire Peace had sent him said: "We liked Susan so well we decided to keep the body overnight."

I said why didn't you write Charlie, "It's summer and I hope you're not running out of ice."

Taylor Smith, then managing editor sent me to Atlanta for the whoopdedoo in honor of General Courtney Hodges on his return from World War II. That was my only scoop of the war, and a perky hat was largely responsible. Back then—1946, women wore hats. Maj. Gen Hodges was a native of Perry, Commander First Army in ETO and first of the generals to come home after VE Day.

I wore my best suit and a silly hat made of starched white lace that looked as if I wore a bunch of paper lace doilies on my head. I was nervous as a cat. I milled about the Georgian Terrace with newspaper men, camera men, and a hundred or so military police. Everybody wanted an interview with Mrs. Hodges, who had come to Atlanta to meet the general, but she refused to see any reporters. She vanished. Nobody knew where to look for her. Planes droned overhead, mikes stood in place on the balcony of the hotel, policemen held back the crowds, a woman fainted, babies cried—all the usual things that happen when a famous general comes home and crowds waited to view the parade.

An MP came up to me and whispered "Pardon me, Maam, but aren't you Mrs. Whoosis. No. Well, she's got a hat just like that one you got on. I can't find her. Will you give her a message if you see her. Tell her the general has just reached Five Points and she can come down stairs anytime now."

I found a lady with my hat on, beckoned her aside and said she'd better call Mrs. Hodges, the general is at Five Points. My attitude showed plainly that I was a member of the secret police, or maybe the FBI and furthermore I was a great favorite with the general.

I followed the lady to the phone booth, listened while she told Mrs. Hodges to come down by the freight elevator. I took my stand at the freight elevator, got my interview, scooped all the reporters and the wire service on how long the general would be in Atlanta, whether his wife would go to Washington with him and when he would go to Perry to accept the plaudits of his townsmen.

Not my prowess; just a silly hat.

The old *Telegraph* building stood as some of you remember on Cherry Street, about where J N Neel Co. is now. Creaky stairs which we must have gone up and down 20 times a day, largely to get down to the little eating spot next door which was the called the Wisteria. Mr. Smith ran it. We all called him Smitty and adored him. He was good to us about letting us eat off the cuff. When the banks closed that Depression year, and most of us had only a dime or so in cash, Smitty let us charge meal tickets—a $2 one lasted a couple of weeks—coffee a nickel, a sandwich for a dime.

The ribald men of the staff called the Wisteria the

Ulcerteria, and some even spoke of it as Our Roachery, but we loved it. There was at one time working as a waitress in the Wisteria a lovely looking girl whom all the reporters whistled at, who later went to New York and become the wife of Sugar Daddy Browning.

There was also, later on, a good looking blonde at the cash register who attracted whistles. Of this blonde a lovely story. We had a tall dark and handsome reporter on our staff who incidentally was much smitten with Gertrude Smith, now Mrs. Trawick. But he didn't get very far there. He went to fill a date with her one evening a little worse for drink, and that ended that.

One afternoon about four, when at least half the staff was in the Wisteria having a cup or a coke, Tall-Dark-and-Handsome was in a booth up near the front door. In came the ex-husband of the blonde cashier waving a pistol and inviting his wife to come with him or else. He shot into the air and all of us clients dived for the floor hiding behind the furniture as best we could. All, that is, except Tall-Dark-and-Handsome. He leaped for the gunman, brought him down with a flying tackle Joe Namath might have envied, and when we looked out cautiously from our hiding spots, Tall-Dark-and-Handsome was sitting astride the gunman who lay on the floor on his back. The reporter had his pencil and a piece of copy paper and was asking the gunman—name, address and how come you're shooting at the lady.

You probably heard you don't have to be crazy to work on a newspaper but it helps. I'd say most of our staffing in the old days of *The Telegraph* were screwballs. I use the word advisedly. The dictionary says a screwball is a term used in billiards when the cue ball hits the object ball in such a way as to cause it to spin crazily. That was our staff—always spinning crazily.

But we had some greats on our newspaper. Besides Mr. W. T. and JDS, and Mark Ethridge, we had Jimmy Jones, sports editor; Perry Morgan, now editor of the *Charlotte Times Observer*; Frank Hawkins, now editor of the Pittsburgh paper; George Burt, now editor of the *Louisville*

Times; Edwin Tribble, now editor of the *Washington Star*, Jack Tarver, now big shot with *Journal-Constitution*; Gene Patterson—He said he learned newspapering at my knee and his mother told him to stay away from those joints.

An example of a thoroughbred was George Dixon, another celebrity I should never have known if I hadn't been a newspaper woman. *The Telegraph* invited George to speak at the Press Institute at the University of Georgia and I introduced him. I was always introducing somebody. You know seven times a bridesmaid never a bride. That's one reason I'm so thrilled to be the introducee today. Well, George Dixon and I sat on the stage at the University chapel building along with others of *The Telegraph* news staff, and when I finished the introduction and started back to my chair, George met me half way. He put both arms around me, leered at the audience, which consisted of dignified editors and publishers as well as a few score university students, and said, "Most of you didn't know that Susan Myrick and I are having an affair."

When the laughter subsided and I sat down, covered with blushes, he walked to the front of the stage and began his speech: "Students, editors, publishers and fellow rum pots."

Among "interesting persons" in Macon was one called the Water Marvel. He made his living selling kindling wood—lightard knots, that is, but he yearned for higher things. He could float for hours in the water without moving, and he wanted to teach all the sailors in the US Navy how to swim. Naturally, he came to *The Telegraph* for publicity about his marvelous ability to float and he wanted Mark and Mr. W T to persuade the Congress to appoint him as Swim Teacher to the Navy. He got small cooperation and he kept coming back to ask for publicity. One morning he told Mark in rather vituperative language that the paper would not give him publicity because he was not a rich man. Mark, out of patience, exclaimed: "GO DO something and we'll give your publicity." "Do what?" "Oh, go jump in the river."

So the Water Marvel arranged to jump into the Ocmulgee on a certain afternoon at 3 o'clock and Mark, true to his word, put a piece in the paper announcing the hour of the jump. I was the Patsy who had to cover the jump story. It was a cold, nasty afternoon, drizzling rain. A crowd of about 16 curious ones assembled at the Spring St. Bridge and Mr. Marvel with teeth chattering, clad in a bathing suit, covered over with a raincoat, passed the hat to take up a collection before the jump. He got a contribution of one thin dime. He refused to jump. But I had a story!

Because I wrote a column of advice for the lovelorn, that attempted to advise any who wrote a letter on such things as how to get him back when love had cooled, whether it as good manners to keep calling the boy friend when his mother had told your mother to stop you from calling, how to order a meal at a swanky restaurant, and how to introduce the boy friend to Mama, I was the one who got all the phone calls the switch board didn't know who else to give them to.

The most asked question for years and years was when was the Brown House Fire. Most of you never heard of the Brown House, a hotel across the street from the old railroad station on Broadway, then known as Fourth Street. That was before the present Terminal now on Fifth Street. The Brown House was the town's best hotel and was a popular stopover for rummers. Right now I can't remember the date of the fire—somewhere along about 1910, but I do know the fire caused the biggest excitement ever known in Middle Georgia until the time Miss Dolly praised Abraham Lincoln when she meant to toast Jeff Davis.

The late Mrs. Dorothy Blount Lamar was president general of the UDC and was always in demand to make a talk on matters of the Confederacy and the times and persons of *The War.* Along in the early thirties, somewhere, she was the major speaker at a banquet held in Macon in honor of the most important officials of the UDC who had come here for a convention.

Miss Dolly, a handsome woman who knew how to do a

marvelous job as a speaker, talked at length about the late Confederacy president. Then, picking up a glass of water, she offered a toast: "To this great man, this stainless Christian, the dauntless soldier, the first and only president of the Confederacy, Abraham Lincoln."

A year ago *The New York Telegram* wrote to see if they could get a piece of mine that I did on the idea of ridding the world of the neonism, more dangerous than Nazism—You-Can-Do-It-Yourself-ism. I wrote an essay on how you can remove your own appendix and one on how you can make your own likker. The New York paper wanted that one and I said sure why not. They sent me $25 which was gravy. I didn't airmail it, just regular postage.

A publishing firm in New York saw the piece and wrote why not do a book. So for several months I sat before the TV set writing a book during commercials. When I finished I counted the pages, all 8 by 11, good bond, double spaced one side of the paper—there were 600 and something. A real Thomas Wolfe thing. It cost me more than $3 to send it off. A month later a letter came "Be patient," it said. And to this day I have not heard a word.

I hope you enjoyed my piece when I became angry at Dr. Kinsey and conducted my own "Sexual Behavior of the Richwood Female." A doctor's wife submitted the piece to the *Reader's Digest*. The magazine wrote back "We enjoyed Mr. Comstock's little satire and passed it from desk to desk and all had a laugh. However, it is not the kind of thing that would interest our readers." Why would *Digest* readers be so different from *Digest* publishers!

This letter was a great help to me. I found out that others who could write a heap better than I can had trouble with publishers.

In her kind introduction Betty referred to my childhood days on the plantation; that fact, along with my having Peggy for a friend, was responsible for my going to Hollywood to serve as technical advisor on GWTW. Riding over the field with my father I learned a lot about farming and it stood me in good stead in California. My favorite story of my stay out there for seven months is about chopping cotton.

Note: Sue told the cotton chopping story so many times she did not write it out for this speech. The story is given in Appendix XIV.

About the nicest thing that newspapering brought to me was being elected honorary member of this club. Had it not been for those years on the newspaper, I could not have been chosen to be a part of this group, I'd never have had the delight of close companionship with the late Mrs. Piercy Chestney, who was one of the finest characters anybody could ever know, and I'd have missed the pleasure of being chosen your speaker for today. I DO thank you for inviting me.

Sue was still speaking publicly as late as 1976. By then, glaucoma prevented her driving at night, and the organizations not only paid Sue and her expenses, but also covered the expenses of her chauffeur.

PART VI

RETIREMENT

HEADLINES

Sue's retirement was the primary story on January 2, 1967, top right hand column of page one, the location of announcements of wars and peace treaties and secessions.

She is shown with publisher Peyton Anderson presenting her with a silver tureen and tray. The story itself leads with: "The farm editor of *The Macon Telegraph and News*, an associate editor of *The Macon Telegraph*, a columnist for *The Telegraph* editorial page, and Fannie Squeers have retired."

Anderson said:

As much as any other single person, Sue Myrick is an institution within an institution. Her name and the name of The Telegraph and News *are almost synonymous as symbols of conscientious newspapering and of youthful spirit wedded to mature judgment.*

She has capably handled the great variety of responsibilities with the Macon papers. Her conservation efforts have been particularly effective and have gained her national recognition.

He mentioned that in her 40 years with the paper she had continued to write columns even while on leaves of absence—in Hollywood with GWTW and while on tours in Europe and on vacation in Hawaii she sent back columns on what she did and saw. (He did not mention her failure to polish the cuspidors, however.)

Many of her duties had been in service to various organizations in Macon and Central Georgia. As well as chairing the Goodfellows' Christmas drives, she served as a member of the advisory board for the Salvation Army and the Family Service Agency, as a member of the organization promoting the preservation of the Ocmulgee National Monument, and hosted a weekly radio show for farmers, and spoke to groups all over the Southeast.

* * *

Robert Ray, who became a colleague in her support for conservation, was one of many who wrote a letter to the paper. Like others, he recalled their shared history.

Ray was eleven when he met Sue—she came to his family's farm in search of a story. Young Robert and his calf "Ruby" became the subjects of her article. The boy raised the calf from age three days by feeding it with a nursing bucket. (A nursing bucket has a nipple in the side, near the bottom.)

Sue succeeded in making him feel important and encouraged him to work harder. “She visited our farm many times, and her stories were always written from her heart because she dearly loved farming and the people associated with agriculture.”

In adulthood, Robert served with Sue on the board of the Ocmulgee Soil Conversation District and also on the Board of Control of the Macon Farmers Club, “where she was highly respected by the entire membership, who, by the way, were all men.”

“Miss Sue didn’t need the ERA laws—she was a leader.”

Sue made annual visits to the Ray farm to pick peaches—“she would not allow anyone to pick them for her. I always saved one of my nectarine trees especially for her visit as she always called them her ‘slick plum’ peach.”

Retirement, however, for Sue did not mean “sitting back and relaxing.” She continued to write her twice-weekly column for the editorial page—the last one appeared on August 17, 1978, only about two weeks before her death. But Sue finally had time to pursue her hobbies—especially painting and travelling. Like her work before retirement, her painting hobby led to awards.

PAINTING

Sue began painting in the 1950s when she decided to take some lessons from a friend who was teaching at Wesleyan College. Lucille Blanche, a well-known New York artist, was conducting some night classes.

“I thought it might be fun,” Sue said. “And then I got hooked.”

She took only about a dozen lessons and vividly remembers her first painting—a watercolor of a bowl of fruit on a table. Not knowing that watercolors were transparent, she painted the table and then the bowl of fruit, and the table made a line through the apples and pineapple.

In her early painting days, she visited her sister and brother-in-law Allie and Edwin Bowden, in Casco Bay, Maine.

“I was used to the Georgia coast with acres of sand dunes and sea oats. The Maine coast is rocky and the view is of all kinds of boats. I just went crazy.”

She was enthralled by a small fish house on a dock, with steps going down to low-tide level—about 12 feet. “I had the best time, all by myself.

I did my sketch and went home to show what I had done. When Edwin looked at it, he laughed so hard I thought he was going to have hysterics. I had painted the steps backwards. Anyone trying to go down those steps would have fallen headlong."

Sue said she had never heard of perspective before, and still had a problem with it in her work. Comfort came, however, from knowing that most amateur artists have similar problems with perspective—sometimes lines that are supposed to go up seem to go down.

Her sister Katie, an art major at GN&IC, was a big help to Sue. "When I get stuck, I call Katie and do what she says, whether it really makes sense to me at all."

Although she sketched in charcoal and pen and pencil, her favorite medium was watercolor. Her favorite subject, wildflowers.

On the other hand, one of her favorite paintings is of a tall, stark old house on the highway between Macon and Milledgeville. When the highway was widened, the road cut off most of the front yard and left the house "exposed in its severity." Her painting is realistic, but she exaggerated the height and narrowness, so the painting emits a haunting atmosphere.

Sue stated that "the saddest thought about amateur artists is that theirs is calendar art, and though it may be good in its own way, it's not fine art."

Mountain Classes

In August 1972, Sue and her friend Virginia Hall, an art teacher, joined a group at "the Painting in the Mountains School" at Burnsville, N. C., near Mount Mitchell. Sue said that she never did see the top of the mountain—fog thicker than London ever saw hunkered down on that mountain all the time.

Mornings, they painted at the cemetery, they painted mountains, they painted silos and barns and falling down buildings; afternoons, they painted in the studio.

Our paintings were not masterpieces, but it was nice for me to see that only two of the students were much better at artistic work that I. Virginia Hall was the toast of the crowd. Most of us were pedestrian painters, whether at models, mountains, still life or whatever.

No work, not even pulling fodder or hoeing corn, is

harder than painting for the amateur.

I heard so much talk of color and shade and tint, all in terms of names by which colors are called in paintboxes or tubes, that I can no longer think of a flower as "purple," for instance; I think of it as "A combination of alizarin crimson and cobalt blue." Nothing is "green" anymore; "it's hooker's green with a little yellow ocher."

I couldn't look at a mountain and just enjoy its beauty; I had to think of it as—say, "a wash of yellow ocher and then a mixture of green and blue and a little burnt umber."

Painting, or trying to paint, is a frustrating thing.

One time, I got all hot and bothered about painting with pigments of native clay. I gathered clods of clay near an abandoned kaolin mine and got all set to grind that clay into dust and use it for painting. It took me days and weeks to find something in which to pound the stuff. I finally got a friend who was a bank teller to let me have two of those heavy cloth sacks money is stuffed into for transporting. And I got my hammer and began looking for something on which to place the sack of dirt for pounding. I didn't like to use my grandmother's card table or the second-hand antique dining table I owned.

I finally settled on my back steps, which are of brick, and I pounded merrily, crushing a number of fingers and ruining a dollar-and-a-half manicure. It took me about three weeks to pound that clay and put it through a sieve.

Painting Exhibit

Sue and Virginia Hall displayed some of their watercolor artwork at the Macon Little Theatre for the duration of the run of the play *Come Back, Little Sheba*. Virginia Hall had been art director for the Bibb County Schools and at the time of the exhibit was art consultant for the Instructional Materials Center of Bibb County.

Sue and Virginia had both been on the board of the Macon Little Theatre, were long-term friends, sometimes travelled together, and also painted together.

Although Sue's favorite subject was wildflowers, she painted a variety of subjects—fishing boats and lobster pots in New England;

houses, farm equipment and sea oats in Georgia, and of course wildflowers wherever she was. Her paints travelled with her to New England, to New York, to Florida and to Texas when she visited family members.

The Contest

Sue entered an art show sponsored by the United Daughters of the Confederacy in October 1977 and came away with the blue ribbon for one of her wildflower watercolors. Asked if she had entered other shows, Sue said not often. Most art shows require an artist to exhibit fifteen or so pieces, and she said it's just too much trouble.

"If it's not good, I'm ashamed to show it, and if it is good, I want to keep it." When she does exhibit a painting—"something good"—it's always marked Not For Sale.

Sue's sister Katie quoted Lucille Blanche, Sue's teacher, as saying that "Sue has quite a feel for water color. Her work is very good." Katie also praised many of Sue's paintings, describing them variously as "looks like a Japanese painting," "very modern and exciting," and "unusual, good composition, interesting subject."

Sue did not paint every day, but only when she saw something that excited her—a warped tree outside her window, for example. Or, when seeking subjects with her sisters, finding unusual shapes and colors in structures and scenery. She did not care for the ordinary.

Posthumous Exhibit

The Macon Little Theatre exhibited many of Sue's paintings for the duration of the play *Relatively Speaking* (September 30-October 7, 1978) shortly after her death. The works were exhibited with permission of her niece Lil James. The pieces were chosen from Lil's collection as well as from those owned by other individuals.

Virginia Hall, secretary of the board, was responsible for selecting and hanging the artwork. She said the tribute would combine two of Sue's long-time interests—the Little Theatre and art.

TRAVELLING

From the time she completed her courses at GN&IC, Sue travelled—to Michigan, Nebraska, Boston and New York for work and further schooling. After returning to Georgia, she travelled in her work both as an educator and as a newspaperwoman. She covered the soap box derby; the launching of the dirigible Macon in Ohio. She went south to fish, and north to fish. She returned to New York multiple times for Broadway shows.

She vacationed in Europe before World War II, when she ventured to France and Spain, saw bullfights, met Papa Hemingway, and "walked her feet off" in Rome. She went to Hawaii when Allie's husband Colonel Edwin Bowden, was stationed there before the Second World War.

Shortly after the war, she and Allie and Edwin went to Wales, to visit Bodorgan, ancestral home of the Myricks, where they met Sir

George Meyrick and toured the home. The fields in front of the mansion were home to fallow deer; a special coop housed white dove; an outbuilding provided the site for the workers to dress out the game killed by family and friends on hunts.

The Myrick ancestors originated with Cadmus, King of All Wales, of Bodorgan Castle, Anglesey, where the family has lived hundreds of years. In the front hall, facing the door, hangs the family coat of arms, and below it, the two-handed sword of Llewellyn, which he carried into battle when he fought for Henry VII at the Battle of Bosworth in 1485.

The estate is entailed and passes from elder son to elder son. One Meyrick had only daughters, however, and then the elder daughter's husband-to-be agreed to change his name to Meyrick to inherit. It did not pass to the daughter.

Sue often visited friends as well as family. Art and Edwina Nims vacationed in Highlands, North Carolina, in summers to escape Macon's famous heat; Sue would join them. After Lake Sinclair was built in 1950s the Nimses purchased a site at the lake and Sue would visit them. The couple, who both were friends from Sue's early days in Macon and members of the SMMA, were killed in a boating accident on the lake when another boater ran over their boat.

In the early 1970s, Sue went to Toronto with her niece Lil and Lil's husband John James. While John attended a trial lawyers' conference, Sue and Lil visited the art museums.

After retiring, Sue took to the "family highway" between trips overseas. In winters she travelled to Florida and stayed near her eldest sister Tippie, who lived with her daughter Stella and Stella's family. There, Sue was joined by sisters Allie and Katie for one or two months, and they would share an apartment—and the cooking. Sue said they never got into a real argument over the cooking, but when it came to baking potatoes, one wanted the oven at 400, one at 375, and one at 350.

Sue would also visit her sister Katie in Rome, New York, and on her way north or south, she would stop over in Washington, D. C. to visit Allie and Edwin. The two sisters painted when weather permitted, and toured the museums as well. Her stays in D.C. gave Sue an opportunity to visit friends who had moved from Georgia to the Capital—they invited her to tea, to supper and to shows, including the National Ballet.

Summertime, when Allie and Edwin spent three months in Maine, Sue would join them for one or two weeks. She and Allie painted the Maine coast, the lobster pots, the lobster boats, and anything else that caught their eye.

After Edwin's death and Allie's move to Texas, Sue spent springtime in Austin, where she and Allie painted bluebonnets and the Texas landscape.

When she was "home" in Macon, she went to Milledgeville every Sunday to visit her youngest sister, Lillas, and her family at Westover Plantation, about 6 miles from the Dovedale homeplace. There, Sue and Lillas played scrabble and knitted beside the open fireplace in the winter months and worked together in the yard on cool spring and fall days. And they fished away many Sunday afternoons. Sue did not know how to be idle.

If she saw an announcement about an event, such as a flower show or art competition, just down the road a ways, such as in Roberta or in Perry, she would drive over to check it out. Maybe therein lay the source of a column. Or perhaps she'd glean more information about flowers or about art.

On her international trips, she often travelled with her cousin Nan Ingram or with Virginia Hall, who was an encyclopedia of art. When Sue and Virginia toured Mexico in 1970, Sue said "The crick in my neck which came from craning it to see the huge murals of Diego Rivera at the National Palace is almost as severe as the one I got looking at the Sistine Chapel."

She travelled to Europe, the Caribbean and Mexico—many of the trips were cruises or jaunts hosted by the AARP. Wherever she went, she saw the sights—historical, cultural, agricultural, scientific, literary—and the bull fights in Madrid. She visited abandoned sugar mills and the missile sites in Florida; art museums everywhere, cathedrals in Rome, London and Paris; castles in Wales and Scotland. She went to and saw whatever called to her heart, even at times retracing previous trips.

She saw the final fight of the famed Matador Antonio Bienvenido, who retired that afternoon; she noted that cotton was picked in Granada (Spain) as it had been in Georgia before the Second World War; she wrote of the erosion, the livestock, the crops, and the poverty and the wealth of the places she visited. Every city she ventured into provided one or more columns for *The Telegraph.*

In 1977, she wrote a friend of her earlier visit to Rome:

I don't blame you for taking up culinary pursuits instead of studying Latin. I, however, built the bridge with Caesar and orated with Cicero and to this day can parse his *ille*, et cetera. May I tell you about my 1954 visit to the Roman Forum. A delightful man of eighty, an ex-professor of Latin at the University of Maryland, was on the tour and at the forum he took a stand and spouted an oration in Latin and all the smart people, like me, who had a slight acquaintance with Cicero cheered him into making a second oration. Such a darling old thing he was.

In Maine, about 1950

Vacation with Allie in Hawaii

Shipboard PE on way to Harvard summer school

A visit to Westover Plantation, 1957

WRITING IN RETIREMENT

Although Fannie Squeers retired, Sue the columnist continued to write her twice weekly column. She found subjects in the news, both the written and electronic media, in family events, in her hobbies and in her travels.

She sent columns back to Macon from numerous locales in Europe and other areas—she wrote about bullfighting, the architecture of Rome, and the scenery of Italy. She often said that, in retirement, she finally had time to travel.

Sue's visits with Tippie and her sisters in Florida, and her Sunday trips to the Lindsley home near Dovedale also provided subject matter for her columns. Ofttimes, Sue or her sister Lillas would make a comment that seemed irrelevant to the conversation, and both of them would burst out laughing. Luther Lindsley, Lillas's husband, would comment, "Wasn't a bit funny, but everybody laughed." The sisters had turned their minds to childhood and their youthful mischief, and such reflections became subjects of her columns.

Just as events at Westover had provided her with subject matter when the children were young, so it continued to provide Sue with material for her columns—such as the livestock, family pets, local wildlife, and the throwaway pets.

Sue also continued to attend the Georgia Press Institute's annual meetings, and was speaker in March 1978. It would be her last. Articles about the meetings said that Sue was one of the highlights; she served on the Nostalgia Panel, which, the *Editor's Forum* reported, "held their audience spellbound with stories of the 'good old days' in Georgia newspaper history."

Among Sue's papers was an incomplete manuscript that began with page 3. She may have used it in part for some of her speeches, or perhaps was planning an article for publication other than in *The Telegraph* because it was longer than her usual columns.

Sue took a look back—again—at the past, which she stored in the treasures of her memories and seemed to always want to share with those who had not been there.

SUE'S UNPUBLISHED MANUSCRIPT—"REMEMBERING"

Scarcely one person in thousands will know that a froe is a tool which pioneer settlers used to split shingles. Webster describes it as a wedge-shaped cleaving tool (also spelled "frow"). The workman hit the froe with a heavy mallet, driving it into the wood. It had no cutting edge.

How many persons, today, in Birmingham or Atlanta, or Dallas know that a skillet is another name for a frying pan? And do you ever hear of a spider any more? I don't mean a small, eight-legged creature that spins webs; I mean a cooking utensil, like a frying pan, except it has only three legs to sit on.

Our speech as well as our attitudes and manners changed as "outsiders" came south to take advantage of climate, space, good workers and other salubrious conditions. We had to change. If you said to a newly arrived

Yankee you were "fixing to boil some goobers," he would be completely bewildered.

Speech has worn down to a uniformity, now. Few Southerners spend their lives in one locality, now-a-days, as in the past when we "put our roots down" and knew everybody in our district; knew them and who their grandparents were. Even if we Southerners live long in one place we can't avoid contact with Americans from other localities, in this late twentieth century.

So it is that today's generation does not still speak of breakfast, dinner and supper. His breakfast is a glass of something full of vitamins, not a meal of ham and eggs and hominy and hot biscuits; his dinner is lunch—a sandwich and a salad, not three vegetables, two kinds of meat, hot muffins and a custard pie for dessert; his dinner is at night, instead, and he knows naught of the vittles of your country family at suppertime in 1915, say. He knows what cottage cheese is, but tell him grandma ate clabber for supper, and he'll think you're kidding him. As for curd, made by letting clabber drip all day tied up in a cheesecloth bag, that will sound like a misspelled dirty word to him.

A scuppernong arbor? What's that? I talked to a group of students at the Honor's Program, boys and girls of top ranking scholastic standings, not one of them knew what an arbor is, much less a scuppernong, and the word "muscadine" confused them utterly, especially when I said some people called the muscadine a "bullice."

Children today eat school lunch at a cafeteria at their respective schools in cities not towns. In an occasional school in a village, the children carry lunch baskets, but no child of today "totes a dinner bucket." He doesn't even know the word "bucket," though his grandfather drew water in a bucket at the well, milked the cow into a bucket, toted the feed to the chickens in a bucket, and carried his sweet potatoes, sausage and biscuit in a tin bucket for his school "dinner"—the term "tin bucket" is a Southern term for "pail."

Seldom now is a father addressed as "Papa"; he is

usually "Dad" or "Daddy," and "Mama" is "Mother" or "Mom" or "Mommie." I remember a sister-in-law who had a Mama, a Big Mama, and a Great Big Mama—three generations. Such terms are gone forever, except in a Tennessee Williams play.

Names of Southern Belles of ye olden days were nearly always double: Sallie May, Fannie Bell, Suellen, Susie May, Sallie Fannie. Now the girls of the south are named for Hollywood stars, Sandra, Maureen, Vivien. Boys were given the names of Biblical or Greek or Latin heroes in the early twentieth century: Cincinnatus, Zachariah, Virgil. The famous Lamar Family named their sons Bonaparte (the first governor of Texas), Lucius Quintus Cincinnatus, and Zachariah.

In the South, children "went barefooted" in the early nineteen hundreds; now when Hippies, lovely looking models and almost everybody goes shoeless, the word is "barefoot" (as in *Barefoot in the Park*).

We used to go to the "Dee-po" to see the train come in, and we went on the cars when we took a trip. Of course there are no trains to come in, now, but if there were, you'd go to the "Dee-po" to watch.

Mama wore a "double gown," not a robe or dressing gown or a kimono or a negligee. It was a sort of sissified bathrobe, but it was called a "double gown."

For winter warmth, we wore balmorals. I venture to say there is scarcely a person under eighty in the Deep South, today, who ever heard of a balmoral, much less wore one. Nobody wears 'em anymore. Central heating makes woolens unnecessary.

Aiding Mama in setting the table for dinner, I would carry a waiter with tumblers on it, placing a tumbler at each place. A "waiter" for today's people is a person who takes your order at the restaurant. A "tumbler" is something in a washing machine; but in my day it was a water glass.

Few of today's younger generation would know what Grandma meant when she asked if the milk had turned. Forty years ago, milk stood in a crock beside the fireplace, waiting for the proper condition for churning—that was called "turning." The milk then was churned, and when the butter "came," it was removed from the remaining buttermilk.

In the South, we are always "fixing" to do something—we "fix dinner," we don't make it. We are "fixing" to go to town, not "getting ready." Unfortunately, "fixing" is losing out to other words.

Your grandma and her grandma spoke of the burial place for the family as a graveyard, but your parents called a graveyard a cemetery. The word "graveyard" has almost disappeared and "cemetery" is less frequently heard than in the past—God help us, the burial place is now a "memory garden."

Who today speaks of a "mess of turnip greens"? Forty years ago, a Georgia farmer might have spoken of the drought and avowed it had been so dry he had only gathered enough peas for one good mess.

How much is a "mess"? A "right smart."

What children, today, know what a scaly bark is? The trees still grow in the woods and bear the white shelled nuts that are easy to crack and provide a delicious flavor. But today's children get peanuts (not goobers), pecans and filberts at the supermarket.

LETTER FROM A YANKEE

In 1974, shortly after Sue's article "Forty Years of Such Interesting People" appeared in the *Atlanta Journal-Constitution* magazine section, Norman R. Hawley of Franklin, North Carolina, wrote to the paper:

Susan Myrick, bless her! I let my Sunday egg grow cold, while reading aloud to my wife the delightful 40-year memories of Susan, as recounted in your Mag for Sept. 8th.

I first met her years ago, while sharing the back seat of an open touring car in a parade at Eastman. We were a couple of beauty judges in a forest festival. Promptly she identified me as another dam Yankee forester from the Pacific Northwest, who had the saving grace to stay South, once he'd beheld God's blessed land. Right!

She boasted she was born in a Georgia briar-patch and proud of it. "I tell you," she bragged, "our family was so poor we propped up our cows with peanut-poles and milked them into China teacups!" On and on. I—like all others in earshot—was spellbound.

A MARGARET MITCHELL MOVIE?

In September 1977, Stephens Mitchell wrote Sue that someone wanted to make a film biography of his sister Peggy.

"The hell of it is, that people may be able to do a biography without our consent. That is a question which has not yet been determined." He wrote. "God knows what they would put in without supervision."

He asked Sue if the family allowed the biographical movie would she supervise it.

Sue wrote back:

I appreciate the trust you show in me by your suggestion that I serve as a supervisor of the film biography—in case it is allowed. For you and for Peggy and John, I should be glad to do that job; I am in full agreement with you that God knows what those Hollywoodians would do to the biography without supervision.

However, I must bring you up to date on my physical condition. I am, as you might easily realize, on the shady side of eighty and, therefore, not as full of fire and pep as of yore. I could not stand the pace I stood in Hollywood as technical advisor of GWTW when I worked ten or twelve hours a day. Perhaps we could consider my job on the film as that of a consultant with the understanding that the film maker would have to accept my decisions, which I should make after consultation with you on matters I considered borderline.

I hope such a biographical film of Peggy can be made with your consent, for sooner or later, somebody will manage to make one, and it is far better that it be made subject to your approval of what goes into the product.

Again, let me thank you for the confidence you have shown in my ability and my integrity.

With best wishes,

Cordially,
Sue

PART VII

MEMORIES OF SUE

THE THREE LINDSLEY GIRLS

The Lindsley girls were "Three Little Girls" in many of Sue's columns; they are the daughters of Sue's youngest sibling Lillas (called "Lilla" or "Lil"). Lillas married Luther Lindsley, and the family lived on a large ante-bellum plantation, Westover, outside Milledgeville. Westover lies half-way between Dovedale and Milledgeville.

SUSAN LINDSLEY'S MEMORIES

Sue was a love for each of us, and a challenge, too, in that she never hesitated to correct our grammar—she was a stickler on grammar, but mostly she gave us love and entertainment. She was always full of fun and turned even mundane events into excitement-filled adventures.

We were the focus of several Christmas farm pages—the earliest, in 1941, showed us at the fireplace in the Westover parlor, stockings hung, each in her "footie" pajamas, "waiting for Santa." Sue wrote our adventures, from battling snakes in the chicken house to our breaking and training horses.

Sue wrote a series of columns about our vacations at Lake Burton, where we stayed in the mountain retreat cabin that belonged to Dr. Sam Guy, chemistry professor at Emory University and friend of our father. Dr. Guy had met his wife-to-be on a cruise ship to Europe; as the ship pulled away from the dock, he commented that he would miss Coca-Colas the most while away; the lady next to him invited him and others at the deck rail to join her in her cabin—she had the makings for Cokes. She was a member of the Coca-Cola Candler family. Together with Sue and Allie, we spent two summer vacations in their very large cabin.

A lover of fishing, Sue talked of sharing a fishing-camping trip to Wisconsin with Allie's son Edwin Bowden, Jr., before World War II. She told us of travelling to Panama City, Florida, and to Alligator Point (near Apalachicola), with a group from *The Telegraph* to fish. On one of her favorite trips, she spent several days fishing the Okefenokee Swamp.

After the Second World War, when our family built a pond at Westover, she could be found with our mother in one of the boats, casting-rod in hand, on any given Sunday afternoon.

In that same pond, unmindful of the wildlife—turtles and water snakes—she taught us to dive jack-knifes and swan dives as well as "racing dives." She also taught us various strokes, the butterfly, the crawl, the backstroke, the sidestroke. Before this pond was built, she took us to Lake Jonesco, between Macon and Milledgeville, to picnic and for swimming lessons.

On many Sunday afternoons when the weather was too raw for fishing or other outdoor activities, Sue challenged us to games of flinch or canasta. And later, Sue challenged us over the Scrabble board—she could make a word from impossible letters. She would bring the Sunday *New York Times* with her some weekends and simply whiz through the crossword puzzle.

I don't know how old I was the evening Sue brought Margaret Mitchell to Westover, but my sisters and I had already been sent to bed. Sue brought Peggy upstairs to our bedroom and woke us up so we could meet her. In later years, Sue told me that Peggy had wanted to become a physician, a psychiatrist, but family conditions had kept her from continuing her education. I suppose that interest in personalities was one of the reasons Peggy could picture her characters three-dimensionally so well. Perhaps, too, that was one of her reasons for helping finance medical school for young black men in Georgia with her GWTW money, a secret that Sue shared with my family when I was quite young. I am so pleased that now the secret is out and the world knows how much of her book's income Sue's friend Peggy gave to the black people of Georgia. Andrew Young, former Atlanta mayor, has produced a movie called *Change in the Wind* that chronicles the relationship between Mitchell and the president of Morehouse College.

Perhaps this newly revealed information about Peggy Mitchell will help those who frown on her book and the movie to realize that she was not a bigot but was very tolerant. And although some readers say she stereotyped the black characters in her novel, she also stereotyped the white characters.

The newspaper offices were on Cherry Street in downtown Macon in those years, and Sue's window overlooked Cherry Street. The three of us would stand at Sue's window to watch the annual Christmas Parade in Macon. Sue also took us on a tour of the press room, where the linotype setter cast our names on a slug of type. I have kept mine for more than sixty years since the tour.

Sue judged horse shows, and we would sometimes join her at the show. When Gallant Bess paid a visit to Macon, Sue arranged for us girls to visit the horse and have our pictures taken with her. We each received a ring made from a horse shoe nail and inscribed with "Gallant Bess."

When I began work with *The Macon News*, I boarded with Sue, and one evening Sue held a special supper for several friends. Elvis had debuted on television and had become the talk of all ages, and Sue entertained her house full of guests with an impersonation of Elvis, from his swivel hips to his accent as she played an imaginary guitar. Everyone roared at her antics.

During the 1960s, when racial tensions were rising, I learned about Sue's long-term support of the people of color in Macon and Bibb County. I asked her if she would feel safe if a real, full-blown race war did break out. She said yes, she did feel safe, and if things were to get really bad, she could always go stay with Mary Brown, who had worked for Sue for many years.

Visiting Allie in Hawaii

Gone fishing with Allie's son, Edwin Bowden, Jr.

Cutting the fool with her dolls, probably at GN&IC

MIAMI BEACH NEWS SERVICE
MIAMI BEACH, Fla. March 00 – Mrs. Mack F. Ethridge and Miss Susan Myrick, feature writers of the Macon, Ga., Telegraph, who came to Miami Beach for the Sharkey-Stribling fight enjoy a ride on Rosie, the pet elephant of Miami Beach.

Sue (front) with Willie Snow Ethridge in Miami.

Sue's only fish on a trip to Panama City, October 4, 1946, with a group from the paper.

Sue's tolerance came from the interracial atmosphere of her childhood—she did not care about a person's race, religion, ethnic origin, or sexual orientation. But she did express impatience with anyone who failed to at least try to live up to his potential; she had no use for intellectual laziness.

When Sue disagreed, she would say "posh" before she began her argument.

Sue loved laughter and being the center of attention—and even after her death we have found new and old materials or have remembered events that brought Sue's laughter to her family, friends and readers.

She had specific rules of grammar:

(1) Don't use no double negative.
(2) Make each pronoun agree with their antecedent.
(3) When dangling, watch your participles.
(4) Verbs has to agree with their subject.
(5) Try to not split infinitives.

And you must proofread, she said, because of the man who doctored himself by advice he read—he died of a typographical error.

The farmer in her loved not only the cow's "basic list price" ($100-$200), but she had to share with me the costs of the additional add-ons:

Two-tone exterior: $50
Dispensing device: (4 spigots @ $10 each): $40.00
Extra stomach: $40.00
Product storage compartment: $60.00
Genuine cowhide upholstery: $45.00
Automatic fly swatter: $35.00
Dual horns: $20.00

Sue said that today's city children probably think the reason cream costs more than milk is because it is more difficult to make the cow sit on those little containers. "Oh, I don't know," she said. "Come to think of it, getting the cow to sit on those plastic gallon bottles that skim milk comes in can't be easy."

She liked puns, spoonerisms, and "Tom Swifties," as well as any joke or story that played on words. She wrote many of her own puns. Some dealt with flowering plants:

Your cue is “An invitation,” and your answer is “come heather.”

If a wild pink marries a Sweet William, and they get divorced, what’s the result? Bleeding Heart (Or you could let the wild pink marry a Sweet Joe Pye Weed.)

If you are not feeling well, your friend might ask, “What azalea?”

If a wife, hearing a noise in the night, wakens her husband, what might she say? “Daisy man in here.”

What is the ardent desire of girls? “Marigold.”

What might a mother skunk say to her children when a dog draws nigh with evil intent? “Lotus spray.”

And some of her puns were geographical:

Said a recalcitrant youngster to his mother, “I won’t but Danville.”

Conversation between a young fellow and his friend’s mother: “May I speak to Jim?” “He’ll call you back, he is Jessup.”

What sort of weather would you choose from Georgia counties? “Meriwether, Crisp or Green”

How do you like that girl who models for you? “Hayter”

Do you wish to come in? “Maher”

Would General Lee have carried out a scorched earth policy? “No, but Grant Wood.”

Where will I find the largest stand of deciduous trees? “In the Burchfield.”

Aunt Sue remained cheerful even in the last few days of her life. When the sun was over the yardarm, she served Bourbon to her hospital visitors. Dr. Hazlehurst was very accepting of Sue's idiosyncrasies.

She left each of us her enthusiasm for life and laughter.

MEMORIES OF DR. LIL LINDSLEY JAMES

Some of my fondest memories involve my Aunt Sue when I was growing up. Sue was a constant presence on Sundays, when she came to Sunday dinner and provided fun for us. She brought us gifts and taught us to swim and dive. We had horses, and Sue taught us the proper way to ride, to hold the reins and to post. She would go with us down to the dirt road at the end of the driveway and help us draw out hopscotch boxes on the seldom-travelled road. We went on treasure hunts.

Long before Sue became farm editor of the paper, I heard her and my father discuss soil erosion and how blue lupine and other cover crops contributed not only to soil enrichment but also to soil conservation.

Sue missed a few Sundays—mostly when she travelled, to Maine to visit Allie, where she would paint everything from lobster pots to flowers, or to Europe and elsewhere. And of course, the few times she was sick and in the hospital.

Sue was always ready to help us celebrate the holidays—Easter when she'd help Mother play Easter bunny; Christmas she brought such excitement and enthusiasm that we children could barely contain ourselves enough to sleep—she would be up with us before light to ohh and ahh over our Santa Claus.

She never tired of telling Sherman's stories of Brer Rabbit and Brer Fox or talking about Hollywood and about her many friends in Macon who did very funny and phenomenal things. Most of her stories were in dialect of one kind or another—she could switch from cockney to Brer Rabbit to Southern aristocrat in one sentence. She frequently entertained us with stories recorded in her diary and in her published articles. Sue was also a great fan of the Greek myths and could be relied upon to tell them all.

I remember very well the story of Sue's trip to Europe in the 1930s. One of the highlights of her trip was when she walked into a bar and met Ernest Hemingway. She was already a fan. My guess is that she probably knew where he was and made it a point to find him. She didn't have a copy of one of his books with her, but he signed a paper for her to put into her copy of the first edition of *Winner Take Nothing*, which she had back home.

When *The Old Man and the Sea* was released, Sue was very excited to find another Hemingway story.

Of Sue's collection of Hemingway books, eight previously belonged to Aaron Bernd and now also bear Sue's label of ownership. A copy of *In Our Time* is inscribed from Sue to Aaron: "To Aaron, hoping that Hemingway may help you while away the boredom of four weeks away from the gang and Sue."

Sue left me all of her books except her copies of *Gone With The Wind*.

Shortly after I finished medical school and came to Macon to do my internship, Sue had an appendectomy. Her doctors, Hazlehurst and Richardson, allowed me to be in the operating room during her surgery. I thought it was a great gesture from them. When I entered into the Macon medical system—only two other female doctors practiced in Macon at the time—my entry was pleasant, and I am sure that pleasantness was partially a result of my kinship with my Aunt Sue. She saw to it that *The Telegraph* carried an article about me when I came to Macon as an intern, and again when I opened my office for private practice.

She was delighted to see me come to Macon to live. It was in 1961. She'd already had a heart attack in the 1950s. It wasn't until I was older that I fully realized how grateful she was to have kinfolk in town, particularly a niece who was close to her and who was a physician married to a Mercer University Law school student.

I often travelled with Sue on her trips around Middle Georgia looking at antebellum homes, which were to be subjects of feature articles. Everywhere we went, we were greeted with open arms. People all over the state knew Sue.

She had an amazing ability to adjust herself to wherever she was. When she visited us in the country, we'd pull honeysuckle out of the boxwoods and talk country talk. Then at a formal dinner she was just as formal and nice and polite a lady as could be.

She got along with all social groups; she was full of life, an excellent conversationalist with a great command of the English language—and she always had many jokes to tell.

Sue was always generous. She gave me the painting of her as Lady

Bracknell that Lucille Blanche painted. At the time, Sue said her only requirement was for us to hang it in a "place of importance." We hung it over the mantle piece, but we don't build fires—fires dry out and crack oil paintings.

Lucille inserted information about Sue and the play into the painting, the letters almost hidden in the picture's details.

"The Importance of Being Earnest by Oscar Wilde
Macon Little Theater 1949 Susan Myrick as Lady Bracknell
Bravo
Super colossal
Sketch by Lucille Blanche"

She also took John (my husband) and me to Atlanta to pick out an oriental rug and to Athens to pick out a Lamar Dodd painting. She, of course, paid for both. She gave me the necklace Peggy Mitchell had given her early in the 1930s, before Peggy wrote *Gone With The Wind* and became famous. She wore this necklace when she was interviewed for the television show that ran on WSB-TV the night GWTW first ran on TV. And also had it on when she was photographed for the cover of *The Macon Telegraph's* TV guide for that week.

Sue's family of prewar days was "moderate." Her grandfather Stith Parham Myrick knew of the disaster that war could bring but could not stop the tide. His uncle by marriage, Benjamin Harvey Hill actively opposed secession and became a leader of the postwar period; he served as a United States Senator and distinguished himself as a peacemaker. Sue was outspoken on this issue.

Sue followed family tradition. She was distressed during the Eugene McCarthy era when her friends were being condemned because they had been members of this or that organization in the late 1930s. Her views on most of the social issues of the 1960s and 1970s were less provincial than the majority of Georgians, yet she managed to navigate successfully and productively through the times. She was very tolerant of blacks. Sue, Mr. W. T. Anderson, and *The Telegraph*'s editorial policy, together with Ed Wilson (Mayor of Macon and a professor at Mercer University) helped ease Macon through integration without the violence that erupted in other communities.

My first indication that my Aunt Sue might be seriously ill came in the spring of 1978 when she returned from a visit with my Cousin Stella in Florida. She proudly said that she had lost weight and that she had not even been trying. Her chest X-ray revealed lung cancer. She bravely received the verdict when her old friend and physician Dr. Hazlehurst told her that surgery was not indicated. She wrote Allie and Katie, her only surviving siblings, to tell them. She advised them that she was in good hands and not to worry. Sue received palliative radiation, and when metastasis in the liver showed on ultrasound, she was admitted to the Middle Georgia Hospital where she died surrounded by family and friends. She was buried in Memory Hill Cemetery in the family plot with a service as "cheap as is decent" as instructed by her will.

She was always on hand with her support when times were good or bad. She was a comfort when Westover burned. She gave us all her support and comfort when my father died in 1964 and again when my mother died in 1968.

Aunt Sue did many things for me. She taught me much. But the main thing Aunt Sue gave me was the realization that the pragmatism of Scarlett and the idealism of Melanie could be integrated into one happy and self-reliant individual.

THULIA LINDSLEY BRAMLETT'S MEMORIES OF AUNT SUE

When I was asked to write some memories of Sue I decided to begin by listing some recollections and then I intended to develop each of these further. As I developed my list I suddenly realized how good all these memories were and what a wonderfully thoughtful and generous person she was. Her gifts and the help she gave to my family were large and unselfish. We were the youngest of her nieces and nephews and we lived the closest to her in Milledgeville, about thirty miles from Macon. In fact we were the only nieces or nephews who still lived in Baldwin County, her birthplace.

Sue brought excitement to our holidays.

One of the first Christmases I can remember, when I was four or five years old, she gave us dolls and doll buggies. I so well remember us in the front gardens at Westover with them. As the years went by, she was usually at our house for Christmas Eve and Christmas Day. The presents she brought were wrapped in the most beautifully colored Christmas wrapping paper I had ever seen. Our family could only afford to give gifts of shelled pecans (picked up on the place) and dish towels made of feed sacks and hemmed with embroidery thread, and we wrapped them in plain white tissue paper. Her beautifully wrapped gifts brought great excitement and anticipation.

I remember the Easter—one when none of the three of us was yet old enough to go to school—hunting Easter eggs hidden along the boxwood plantings in the front gardens. Sue had brought them and she and mother had hidden the most beautiful candy eggs, chocolate inside and all decorated with elaborate icing. I had never seen anything so beautiful! All I had ever seen before were the boiled chicken eggs we had dyed. Again those decorated candy eggs brought such great excitement to a small child.

I remember her many Sunday visits. She always brought the Sunday paper (I think we got the local paper during the week and it was delivered by the mailman), something for lunch such as fried chicken or chicken salad, and all the news from Macon and the outside world. In fact she taught me to make chicken salad, which today is one of my favorite dishes to make. We would listen to her and Dad talk of war and politics, books they had read and football or baseball depending on the season. After lunch if the weather was bad we all stayed inside and she and mother would knit and Dad would read. If the weather was nice we went for walks in the pastures and she and Dad would discuss the pasture grasses, the clovers and the condition of the beef cows and the prices they would bring. Occasionally she would spend a night with us and I remember her outside teaching us the constellations in the sky.

When we were in high school, she loaned us her car to drive to Virginia for a week's vacation. We did not have a car that was in good enough shape to make the trip. Dad was from Virginia and wanted to show us where he was born in Dumfries, where he lived in Manassas and where he went to school and taught at William and Mary and other historical sites.

Later during my college time at Mercer University in Macon, she would come and pick me up to bring me back home to visit for the Sunday. After graduating college, I lived with her for several weeks while I took a business course in Macon. During and even after our college years, she frequently made arrangements for us to attend a show at Macon Little Theatre.

After I married, she continued to do generous things for me. For Christmas one year she knitted an afghan for me in my favorite colors. Another year she gave me her bracelet that had been given to her by Vivien Leigh at the end of the filming of GWTW.

Another Christmas she gave me a painting that she had done that had won a prize in an art show. It is a picture of a Georgia landscape done with many colors of kaolin—a landscape painting actually done with the dirt from the landscape. Another Christmas she surprised me with the deed to the land at Dovedale that she had inherited from her grandmother.

She certainly gave generously of her time and her possessions to me and my entire family. I still enjoy her many gifts and enjoy remembering all the times that we were together. I am proud of her and proud to be her niece.

EURI BELLE BOLTON

In a letter to Sue's sister Allie, she wrote:

I read in *The Dawson News* of Dawson, Georgia, that your sister, Miss Susan Myrick has passed away.

I sent a gift to the Georgia College Alumna Fund as a memorial in her honor.

When I did extension work for GSCW from 1918 to 1922, I worked with Miss Myrick in one or more Institutes for Teachers. She taught Health and Physical Education and was an inspiration to all of us who participated in the institutes—supervisors from the State Department of Education, local superintendents of schools, the leaders who taught special subjects and the teachers who attended the institutes.

I was a member of the faculty of GSCW (now Georgia College) from 1925 until 1958. During that time I heard her speak at our chapel program a number of times. She always brought a challenging message to the students and they liked her.

I appreciate very much the significant contribution she has made through her writing.

With love and sympathy from your classmate.

MRS. JAMES C. (DEE) SHELBURNE

In a letter to Allie, September 18, 1978, she wrote:

—No words on paper can help—when I saw Sue in July, I left in tears.—Somebody should be writing her story. We will all be reminded of a million stories between each and every two lines

SARA G. LANDRY

In letter to Susan Lindsley, she wrote:

Although I began reading the column "Fannie Squeers," which Sue wrote, shortly after I learned to read, I had never met her until I began dating my late husband, George Landry. George was a long-time state news editor of *The Telegraph* and the former *Macon News*. He and Sue worked closely together and shared a keen sense of humor.

Sue had the ability to communicate with the poorest farmer in middle Georgia as well as with the most erudite person in the city.

We were often guests in Sue's home and she in ours. She was an excellent story-teller and was the life of the party at gatherings of the editorial staff of the newspaper.

Frequently Sue recognized the foibles of others as well as her own and put them in proper perspective. When other staff members were criticizing the apparent rudeness of another, she once said, "He was not to the manor born."

When Sue was asked how she finally managed to quit smoking, she once said, "They told me I'd probably have throat cancer and they'd remove my voice box, and God knows I want to talk!"

One of Sue's proudest accomplishments was teaching the actors in *Gone With The Wind* to speak the Southern dialect. Sue said that after a while in California, she found herself talking just like the people out there. She would quickly go to the phone and call someone in Macon—and "get my Southern drawl back."

Sue enjoyed a drink before dinner. I once heard her say, "Heavy on the bourbon and light on the water." She explained, "I have glaucoma and too much water is not allowed."

During my husband's final illness, Sue often visited. They would sit in our den and share stories and much laughter. Her visits always brought him cheer.

After George's death, I went back to school with the goal of finishing my degree. Sue was very encouraging and assured me I could make it. I did.

As Sue's health declined, I continued to invite her and our mutual friend Clara Eschman over for dinner. Sue later paid me one of the greatest compliments I have ever received, telling Clara, "She's not only smart and pretty, but one of the kindest, dearest souls that the Good Lord ever made."

I hope Sue realized I did not invite her for dinner simply to be kind, but because I really enjoyed her company to the end of her days.

It was a rare privilege to know you, Sue.

CECILE HUMPHREY HARDY

In a letter to Allie, January 24, 1967, she wrote:

I owed Sue a debt, for she motivated me to make one of the most important decisions of my life: To enroll in the Harvard School of Physical Education. I followed in her footsteps and after receiving my diploma I was offered some work in the School with the opportunity to take a course in the Graduate School and received my masters.

I doubt if Sue were aware of my high respect and admiration; she was so clever, so stable, so self-confident and had an incomparable sense of humor.

SENATOR SAM NUNN

In a letter to Allie, September 18, 1978

Sue was indeed a great writer whose articles were enjoyed by generations of Georgians. My father knew her well, and was among those who admired her great talent. He particularly enjoyed her fine articles on agricultural subjects.

All who were privileged to know her will cherish the memory of her many outstanding contributions to the life of her community, state and nation.

MILLEDGEVILLE FRIEND

In a letter to Allie (we have only the first page) she wrote

Sue and I were at Harvard the summer of 1920. I taught with her September 1920 until March 1921. I enjoyed being with her so much. I can think of one thing that might be interesting—it amused me. She would get down on the floor and show the Harvard professors how the southern Negroes shot craps. She could mimic them so well.

ANN RUTHERFORD

At a *Gone With The Wind* event in Marietta, Georgia, on November 14, 2009, Ann Rutherford remembered Sue as “Lovely. She didn’t talk as if she had a mouth full of hot corn, and she made certain no one else did either.”

Ann autographed a picture of herself and Sue with the words: “Remembering ‘Sweet Sue’ with thanks and love.”

HERB BRIDGES

Author of *Gone With The Wind: The Definitive Illustrated History of the Book, the Movie, and the Legend*

It was a delight to correspond and later to visit with Miss Myrick at her home on Oglethorpe Avenue in Macon, Georgia. My interest was the film production of Margaret Mitchell's book, *Gone With The Wind*, on which Miss Myrick served as Technical Advisor in Hollywood in 1939.

I was preparing a picture/book, *The Filming of Gone With The Wind*, to be published by Mercer University Press in Macon. Miss Myrick shared many interesting stories concerning the day-by-day filming of this epic motion picture. Even more interesting were the photograph albums of the snapshots she herself made on the GWTW sets—the behind-the-scene photos were fascinating to me. She also showed me her GWTW working script plus the specially-bound completed script which was signed to her by Producer David Selznick.

I remember visiting with her in Atlanta during the festivities for the 70-mm movie premiere of GWTW in October 1967. It was at the GWTW Ball which was held at the Hyatt-Regency Hotel on Peachtree Street. She was seated next to Olivia de Havilland at a table in the ballroom. She was dressed in a fashionably glamorous gown and she rose to graciously greet me among the splendor of the Hollywood crowd.

It was indeed a pleasure to know Miss Myrick, if only briefly. She was somewhat brash, but a charming lady.

AUTHORS

Two authors who attended the *Gone With The Wind* event in Marietta along with Herb Bridges and Ann Rutherford commented about Sue.

MOLLIE HASKELL Author of *Frankly, My Dear: Gone With The Wind Revisited*

"Sue was Margaret Mitchell's mole in Hollywood."

MICHAEL SRAGOW Author of *Victor Fleming: An American Movie Maker*

"Sue was quite honest in her evaluations."

PART VIII

EXIT, LAUGHING

HER DEATH

Sue's headstone

Sue would have died laughing at the events surrounding her funeral. Her Lindsley nieces remember hearing Sue and Tippie discuss which of them would have the one remaining space in the Myrick lot in Memory Hill Cemetery where their parents Miss Thulia Kate and James were buried.

But there were two spots left. Anyone could easily see the two vacant places. Sue insisted that the site next to the marker was not vacant, however, and finally Tippie surrendered to Sue's insistence and said she would be happy to be buried with their grandfather, Stith Parham Myrick.

Since Sue had told John James, her executor and niece Lil's husband, that the space next to the marker was not empty, when he went to Milledgeville after her death to arrange details of the funeral, John so informed the funeral director.

But someone at the funeral home decided that Sue should be buried next to the family marker, and they began to excavate that spot for her grave—the spot Sue said was occupied.

Oops. They uncovered a very expensive burial vault.

No one in the family today knows who was buried with the Myrick family. Or when. Apparently, only Sue among the children still at home was old enough to remember that the grave site was taken. Even the plat of the cemetery did not show that anyone had been buried there.

Allie's only guess is that someone died while visiting at Dovedale. In that time, bodies were buried quickly and not shipped "home" for funerals. Allie said that her papa had probably allowed the burial in the family plot but had not marked the grave with a stone at the time.

* * *

Sue's obituary appeared in many newspapers across the South and as far north as the *Baltimore Evening Sun* and the *Daily Sentinel* of Rome, NY. Newspapers in Texas carried the story of her death, as did the *LA Times*.

Variety also recognized Sue's contribution to entertainment as well as to journalism.

In *The Telegraph*, her colleague Catherine Lee wrote that when she met Sue, she was overawed. Because a generation separated them in age, Catherine never expected the friendship to develop, but it did. When she asked Sue why she had taken a liking to her, Sue said, "Why, Darling, you were so young and cute and then I found out you were smart, too."

Catherine wrote:

Sue always had time for her friends but did not suffer fools gladly. When our son was born prematurely, my husband was appearing in a Macon Little Theatre play and the "show had to go on." The night I came home from the hospital Sue showed up at our apartment and "sat" with me until my husband returned home. Multiply that act by thousands of similar kindnesses she showed to those she loved.

None of her many friends had to ask for whom the bells tolled. We knew that they tolled for us, because we were all so diminished by her death.

Celestine Sibley of the *Atlanta Constitution* wrote: "*Sue Myrick, one of the smartest, funniest, most attractive women the state of Georgia ever produced, died this past weekend—and I can't imagine that newspapering, farming or the Georgia Press Institute will ever be the same.*"

SUE'S REFLECTIONS ON HER LIFE

What Sue Said She Never Did

I am sometimes embarrassed to think of all the things I've never done. I have never been invited to a Tupperware party, or swung from a high wire in the circus tent (the "cynosure of all eyes") or crossed the Atlantic in a row boat. I've never climbed Mt. Everest and I never rode a skateboard. I never even rode a bicycle and I can't roller-skate.

I never rode a mule down into the Grand Canyon; I never scuba-dived; I never piloted a plane, or drove a tractor, or sailed a boat.

Gosh! What have I ever done. Point—counterpoint.

While I never entered a walking race from Boston to Cambridge, I did take a group of high school girls on a hike to Gray once upon a time.

I never climbed the Eiffel Tower but I put Isoptocarpine drops in my eyes as I crossed the Alps by bus over the Furka Pass.

I never went to see Six Flags but I did make a trip (a delightful one) to the Stewart Caverns in southwest Georgia. I never dined in Buckingham Palace but I did go to tea at the Blair house, where Margaret Truman served and I shook hands with Mrs. Truman and the President.

I never fished off the coast of Cuba or caught a 200-pound marlin, but I did catch a 29-inch muskellunge in a lake in Wisconsin. The guide made me throw it back because the least size you can keep is 30 inches long.

I never rode in a Rolls-Royce but I did ride over an army camp in a jeep with a United States Army colonel during World War II.

I never piloted a plane but I did ride in a gyroscope with Amelia Earhart piloting. It was way back yonder before she tried to cross the Atlantic, and she was barnstorming and came to visit Macon. *The Telegraph* sent me to do a story on her visit and she took me riding.

I never met the Duke of Windsor, but I got to be downright friendly with Clark Gable.

I never visited the "Tallest Tower in the World" in Chicago but I did go up to the penthouse at the Georgia Power Company Building to look out across the Ocmulgee and the hills about Macon.

I never was a great athlete; I never hit a home run or

made a triple-play or pitched a no-hitter, but I could spit watermelon seeds farther than my older brother could. And if you don't think that was quite a feat you never had a brother with whom to compete.

I've never seen the Taj Mahal but I visited Jefferson's Monticello home and I spent some pleasant hours at the home of "Little Alec Stephens."

I never read Chaucer's *Canterbury Tales* except in a translation, but I did go to Canterbury and saw the worn stone steps over which thousands of Englishmen climbed on their knees. Maybe I can't count that as "counterpoint" because I did not meet the "wife of Bath" or the Doctor of Phisick.

What Sue Said She Did

I thought I have missed so many wonderful things. And then I gave myself a good shake and bethought me of the many things I have done that thousands of people have missed.

There are many things that country children do which citybred folks miss; especially, country children in the Deep South.

Did Nelson Rockefeller or Queen Elizabeth or even Betty Ford ever put a hair from the horse's tail in the chicken trough to lie overnight? Had any of those or a few million others ever been told that the hair would turn into a snake by morning?

Do you suppose Liz Taylor ever helped her big brother dam up the branch down in the pasture, making a small pond in which silver colored minnows swam, and did she ever try to catch one of those minnows with her bare hands?

Did Cher ever pull a big leaf from the yellow poplar tree, press it hard against her lips, suck in her breath hard, and pop the leaf? Or, did she tear off petals from the blossom of the poplar tree in the springtime and suck the sweet pollen from them?

Did Princess Grace or Jackie Onassis sleep on a pallet in the hall (she had to give up her bed for Cousin Mattie or Aunt Lizzie), sleeping happily with her kitten curled beside her, or lying awake to listen to the unusual sounds that she heard because the front door stood open?

Did Merle Oberon or Sylvia Sidney ever walk with Papa across the field to find a guinea nest or a quail nest? Well, I did. Holding Papa's hand and walking gingerly across the oats that stuck my bare feet, I watched eagerly for signs of a nest. When a loud noise of fluttering wings of the Mother Bob White told us the nest was near, I could scarcely breathe for the excitement, and what a delight it was to stoop down to count the eggs. Papa would not let me touch the eggs: "The bird would not come back to the nest after human hands had touched it," I thought, but I think now the idea was that I might break an egg if I got too close.

Did Roberta Peters or Marilyn Horne go hunting for chinquapins, or pick up scalybarks from the big tree down the lane? Did they ever bring home black walnuts, encased in their heavy hulls, and use a rock to break open the hulls, getting their hands all mustard-colored from the juice in the hulls?

No, I never rode on the Orient Express—but I sure had a lot of fun.

APPENDIX I

SHERMAN

Sherman, the hired man whom the children loved and who entertained them with his stories, was born to a slave mother during *The War*. When the Union Army came through Georgia and brought freedom, she honored the Yankee General by calling her son after him. Through the years of her son's youth, she told him stories she learned from her own mother.

For the Myrick children, Sherman's major duty was to entertain them every night after supper, when they would join him in the kitchen—sometimes even before he finished his supper. The youngest one would crawl into his lap and the others would scramble to be the closest in the circle at his feet.

Some nights, Miss Kate had to become firm to send the children to bed—"just one more story, Mama," they would beg, although they had heard them all more than once.

Sherman's birth name—John C. Calhoun—almost became forgotten over the years and appeared only on his property tax forms and on the newspaper he subscribed to and read faithfully. Perhaps it was Susan's parents who taught Sherman to read, for her father had built a school on Dovedale land for all the black children of the area, not just for the children of his black tenants. He also provided Dovedale land for them to have their own church, which still holds services today.

When Susan learned that Sherman's stories had been written down and published as a book, she was shocked. She had believed that Sherman made up the stories just for her and her siblings. Her love of these and other stories in rural Negro dialect led her to collect Joel Chandler Harris' books to find any of the African myths that Sherman had not told. She collected as well the stories of Harry Stillwell Edwards, a Macon man who once owned and edited *The Macon Telegraph* and also wrote in that dialect.

APPENDIX II

LAYOUT OF MYRICK HOME AT DOVEDALE

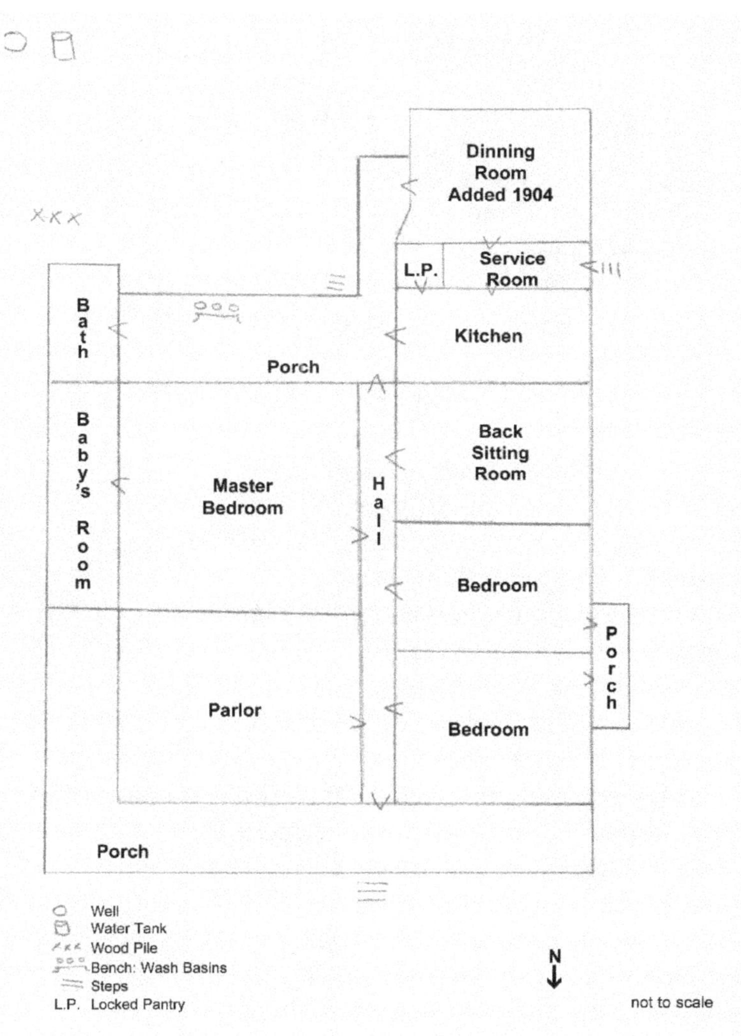

APPENDIX III

Myrick's Home-Churned Ice Cream

Beat four eggs; gradually add two cups sugar while beating until mixture gets thick.

Add one 12-ounce can Carnation milk, one 14-ounce can Eagle Brand milk, a pinch of salt and two teaspoons vanilla, mixing thoroughly. Pour into freezer churn and add enough whole milk to bring to the "fill" line. Churn, adding salt to the ice, until the mixture hardens. Keep packed in ice until served.

APPENDIX IV

A Teacher's Friday Night Dream

Listen my children, and you shall hear
Of Lady Claire deVere, deVere.
'Twas the night before Christmas in seventy-five,
Hardly a man is now alive
Who remembers who remembers the house where I was born.
And all the little sunbeams come shining in the tent.
At midnight, the Turk lay dreaming of the hour
When Greece, her knee in suppliance bent
Would tremble at his power.
As he lay dreaming the Angel song awakened our little Boy Blue.
Oh, Douglas! Oh, Douglas, tender and true!
Up rose Barbara Fritchie then,
Bowed with a four score year and ten.
Blue were her eyes as the fairy flax,
Her cheeks like the dawns of day.
And I would that my tongue could utter
The words she then to him did say.
"I'm sorry I spelled the word
I hate to go above you because, because..."
A blush of sadness, a blush of shame
Over the face of the leader came.

Of all sad words of tongue or pen
The saddest are these, it might have been.
The judge rode slowly down the lane
Stroking his horse's chestnut mane.
He drew his horse under the shade of the apple tree
To greet the maid and ask,
"Have you heard of the wonderful one-horse shay
It was built in such a logical way that it... oh but stay."
The boy stood on the burning deck whence all but him had fled;
The flames that lit the battle's wreck shone round him o'er the dead.
Then up spake the brave Horatio who stood as a guard at the gate,
"To all men on this earth, death cometh sooner or late.
And who can better die than facing fearful odds
For the ashes of his fathers and the temples of his gods,"
For I'm to be Queen of the May, Mother,
And Wynken, and Blynken and Nod.

APPENDIX V

THE WELL

In 1905, one of the hands at Dovedale died in the well. The local paper, *The Union-Recorder*, carried the story:

Tom Thomas, a Negro man, was buried in a well at the home of Mr. J. D. Myrick near Dovedale last Wednesday. The Negro went into the well to recover a pair of spectacles which had been dropped into it. In descending he struck the wall causing it to cave in. Thomas was buried beneath the debris, and when gotten out his life was extinct.

At that time, all farms had wells and all wells were hand dug, so going down into a well was a common event for farming people. In another incident at Dovedale, several years later, Sherman went into the same well, to recover J. D. Myrick's false teeth. He was half-buried with debris when the sides of the well collapsed. Other farm hands passed down the well bucket and Sherman dug out the debris and piled it into the bucket. Eventually, he managed to dig himself out. He survived, and thereafter his chores were lightened.

APPENDIX VI

LITTLE THEATRE ROLES

John Jones of the Macon Little Theatre provided this list of plays in which Sue had a role, and he said the list might not be complete.

Wedding Bells (as Hooper, the maid, 1934)
A Doll's House (as Christina Linden, February 1938)
The Vinegar Tree (as Laura Merrick, May 1938)
Through the Night (as Alicia Keefe, February 1941)
Arsenic and Old Lace (as Abby Brewster, one of her favorites, November 1942)
Good Buddies (locally written and set to music with Camp Wheeler men helping to produce it)
The Importance of Being Earnest (as Lady Bracknell, 1948)
The Glass Menagerie (as Amanda)
The Queen's Husband (as Queen Martha)
Oliver Oliver
Out of the Frying Pan
Perhaps We Are
The Torch Bearers
The Silver Whistle
My Three Angels
The Potting Shed
The Lady's Not for Burning (a concert reading in costume)
The Royal Family
The Barretts
Rebecca
Night Must Fall (one of her best)
Antique Corn (melodrama-musical)
Papa Is All (as Mama)
The Show Off
Therese
Bell, Book and Candle
Becket (as the Queen Mother)
My Fair Lady (as Mrs. Higgins)
The Drunkard

APPENDIX VII

SHOWS, BOOKS AND FROCKS

Sue reviewed books for *The Telegraph* and read voraciously; she attended shows—including stage productions, movies, and musicals—in Macon, Milledgeville, Atlanta and New York. Some of her diary entries reveal her passion for the written word and for performances. Only a few of these are given here, as illustrations.

October 20, 1937

Sunday afternoon heard Columbia chain broadcast of five compositions by modern American composers. The Roy Harris Pine Tree Symphony was nice. Two of them bored me. Louis Gruenberg (or something like that) did a non-visual opera just for radio, *Green Mansions* from the book of the same name. It was interesting and the soprano's voice was very high and child-like and lovely, but the opera left me cold. Brilliant and cold as a star on a winter night—like those in the sky in the stage version of *Ethan Frome* when Ruth Gordon and the Frome man (Massey I think) were about to slide down the hill on the sled.

But last of all was a symphony by a Negro, William Grant Still (I believe) of Harlem. He called it *Lenox Avenue* and it was delightful. Had a George Gershwin flavor. Blaring of radios in the streets, sounds of cheerful talk, lazy tap dancing, shuffling along. Then a Negro church—perfect—and then a dance that was marvelous. The piano was the best blues stuff in the world with the orchestra in the background with the feel of swing in it all. That Negro is one to be watched out for. There was a bit of Bess and Porgy feel in it too.

December 9, 1937

I saw Paul Muni in *The Life of Emile Zola*, about a month ago and which I want to record myself as thinking the best picture I ever saw in my life.

Note: She had pasted pictures of both Paul Muni as Zola, and of Zola himself, in her diary.

This week I saw *Conquest,* which is also an excellent picture, but then I am a Garbo fan of the first water and that makes me biased. She is a marvelous Countess, the only love of Napoleon's life and for the first time I like Charles Boyer. He is a fine Napoleon. A Russian actress whose name I can't remember played the mother of Count Walaska and as a senile old lady, half witted, she is superb. The best bit I ever saw in a movie, I think.

Also saw Gladys George in *Madame X* last night. It is an evidence of her ability that she made the thrice-told movie vivid and new, and with all the melodramatic mess she was convincing and moved me to tears. Young fellow named Beal did the juvenile excellently well. When he defended his mother in the court scene he was so good I wept and when she touched his hand as it lay on the banister rail along the seat where sat the prisoner, I was so choked I couldn't breathe.

* * *

Mashallah! I love the book Cat gave me to review. It is *Hajii Baba,* and I am glad I never read it before, though it is a classic for I have had so much pleasure in it. I leaped the parasangs to Persia and lived among the rogues who made life so adventurous for Hajji. I bow toward Mecca at the good fortune which is mine to own so lovely a book. Cyrus LeRoy Baldridge did illustrations that are matchless for the particular text—colorful and glamorous and with a gal who could make roast meat of anybody's heart.

December 20, 1937

Sam Harris presented *You Can't Take it with You* by Moss Hart and George S. Kaufman, and I nearly died! It is the funniest show that anybody ever presented. How on earth even Kaufman and Hart thought of so many goofy, idiotic, absurd, ridiculous, mad situations and lines I don't know. Grandpa, played by George Henry Trader, is a honey. Went to work one day and on the elevator going up to the office just decided it was time to relax so he came home and didn't go back to work for 25 years. Essie, played by Adrienne Earle, the daughter who had been taking ballet lessons for eight years ("confidentially she stinks!") was marvelous. Boris Kolenkhov, the Russian ballet teacher, played by Rene Roberti, was a WOW. The game that Penelope Sycamore starts is about the funniest thing in the show. Everybody has a pencil and paper and Penelope gives out a word. You have to write an instant reaction. Mrs. Kirby, fashionable wife of a wealthy Wall Street man, wrote:

Potatoes	Wall street
Bathroom	Mr. Kirby
Lust	Human
Honeymoon	Dull
Sex	Wall Street

January 3, 1938

Reading for review Rodocanachi's *Forever Ulysses* (may his house never fall down!). It is delightful adventure, horror and humor and much information about strange countries. Ulysses is like his ancient prototype and the epitome of the Modern Greek, too. Rodocanachi is in his fifties and this is his first novel.

January 19, 1938

Saw *You're a Sweetheart* last night with Ken at five. Music show with silly plot but nice stuff just the same. Alice Faye was pretty and her husky voice was swell and George Murray is a honey, with that homely look of his and the dance routines he puts over. Best thing in show was a burlesque on court room scene. Alice Faye was being tried for murdering Maggie (*When You and I Were Young).* Alice was Minnie Swing and she had made swing music of Maggie. Jury was chorus of girls who said "Yeah man" to everything. Marvelous tap dance rhythm for all the words—the attorney for defense, prosecutor, judge's remarks and so on. Minnie Swing was found not guilty when she pled she had brought Maggie to life—not murdered her.

January 27, 1938

Just back from seeing Mae West in *Every Day's a Holiday*, and she is a honey! The way she switches herself, talks through her teeth, rolls her eyes and makes every word she utters suggestive is simply too appealing. She wrote her own show as usual. I like her. I think maybe she is appealing to me because she is what I should like to be if I had the nerve and wasn't handicapped with a Victorian upbringing.

She is funny as FUNNY. Its wow ending is an old-fashioned melodrama, with knock-out drops and kidnapping and Doug Fairbanks fighting and street parade and all.

October 5, 1938

Yesterday had lunch party for Evelyn Hanna, author of *Blackberry Winter*, which is going into second printing. Harry Lee's new book *Fox in The Cloak* is a much finer piece of writing than *Blackberry Winter.* Just read Margaret Halsey's *With Malice Toward None.* Positively the funniest book ever done.

Have been reading a great deal of late. Just finished Margaret Fishback's witty *Safe Conduct*, in which Maggie takes fine cracks at Margery Wilson and Emily Post.

Also just read *I Lost My Girlish Laughter*, howlingly funny stuff about Hollywood by Jane Allen (pseudonym, I think).

Have two books to write reviews on: Berry Fleming's new book and Ann Morrow Lindbergh's *Listen the Wind.*

* * *

In her diary, she writes of the frocks she purchases when she goes to New York for a weekend of Broadway shows or when she purchases something for a special event. Here is one sample of a purchase, written in early 1938:

A new suit is gabardine, dark gray, very tailored, skirt 14 inches from the floor, coat wide lapels, one button, pinched in at waist line, sleeves regulation like man's suit.

New hat, felt, black, moderately conservative, crown only slightly high, tilts over right eye. Most of the hats are ridiculous. Little things like pill boxes with veils; queer messes off the face with idiotic bows. Crownless wonders, bows tied under the chin and such, but I can't take it.

APPENDIX VIII
HOLLYWOOD PEOPLE
SUE MET AND MENTIONS

This listing is simply to help identify some of the lesser known people Sue mentions in her diary and letters. It includes mostly people who tried out for roles, or were not credited for their work, or were not a part of the cast and crew of GWTW.

Anne, stand-in for Olivia
Arnould, talent scout
Balderston, John, script writer
Baxter, Alan, actor, tested for Frank Kennedy
Bell, James, actor
Bessolo, George, actor, changed name to George Reeves, played Tarleton twin
Birdwell, Russell, publicity for Selznick Studios when Sue arrived
Bowden, Dr. A. O. and Mrs. Katherine, she was sister of John Marsh
Boyle, Edward G., interior decorations
Brame, James Yancey VI, birth name of Bruce Lane
Brown, Katherine (Kay, Kate, Kath) Selznick's rep in NY, contracted with Sue; a "story editor"
Callow, Phyllis, daughter of Reggie, she played Bonnie at 2½ years
Callow, Ridgeway (Reggie), assistant to Eric Stacy
Carroll, Nancy, actress, tried out for Belle
Claire, Ina, silent film and Broadway actress
Gleckler, Robert, actor, signed as Jonas, died after shooting one scene
Cline, Wilfred M., Technicolor associate
Cosgrove, Jack, special photographic effects
Craig, Jim, actor, appeared in *Boys Ranch*, *Kismet* and other films
Cripe, Arden, on-set prop master
Dawson, Dorothy, secretary to George Cukor
Deighton, Lillian K., research
Evans, Rex, British character actor
Fairfax, known only as someone Sue met in Hollywood. Sue destroyed entry about Fairfax

Farnum, William, once the highest paid silent actor, moved into "talkies"
Floyd, Frank, dance director
Forbes, Lou, music
Frederickson, Frank, publicity at Selznick Studios
Freeman, Mrs., from Atlanta, wife of a producer
Garrett, O. H. P., script writer
Gilbert, Leatrice, actress, daughter of John and Leatrice Joy Gilbert
Ginsberg, Henry, studio manager
Goldstone, Phil, director in "old days"
Haller, Ernest, photographer
Hecht, Ben, screen writer
Herbert, Bill, head of publicity
Howard, Katheryn Nimmo, child whose parents wanted her to play Bonnie
Hurst, Paul, played the Yankee deserter
Hutchins, Lee, friend of Aaron and Sue's, visited her in Hollywood
Jeans, Isabel, actress
Kaufman, Evelyn, Sue's secretary
Kearney, Bob
Keon, Barbara (Bobby), scenario assistant (She signed notes "Bobby" not "Bobbie.")
Kern, Hal C., supervising film editor
Kirkpatrick, William S., editor, *The Atlanta Georgian*
Lambert, Edward P., wardrobe
Lane, Bruce, actor, played Hugh Isling, who went with Rhett, Ashley, and Frank on KKK raid
Lee/Leigh, Rolly, George Cukor's friend and guest at one of his parties that Sue attended
Leona, Mrs., head of research
Litson, Mason, location manager
Louise, wardrobe
Maher, Frank, recorder
Mahin, John Lee, screen writer
Martin, Marcella, actress tried out for Scarlett, cast as Kathleen Calvert
Michael, Gertrude, actress from Talladega, AL
Montgomery, Doug, actor, *The Mystery of Edwin Drood* (1935)
Morgan, Frank, actor, tried out for Frank Kennedy

Mueller, Bill
Murphy, Maurice, actor, tried out for Charles Hamilton
Nagel, Conrad, actor, tried out for Frank Kennedy
Nathan, George Jean, magazine writer
Naud, Edna, classmate of Sue's, visited Sue in Hollywood
Newcom, James E., associate film editor
Nye, Ben, associate to Monty Westmore
O'Shea, Daniel T., lawyer at Selznick Studios (listed in some indices as "Shea.")
Platt, Joseph B, interiors
Plunkett, Walter, costume designer
Price, Will, technical advisor (Sue reported he was fired in February but does not mention his being rehired.)
Prinz, Eddie, dance director
Rabwin, Marcella, executive assistant to Selznick
Ray (Mr.) in publicity department of Selznick Studios
Rennahan, Ray, Technicolor associate
Rogers, Hazel, hairdresser, associate to Monty Westmore
Sayers, Jo Ann, actress
Shannon, Peggy, actress tried out for Belle Watling
Shapiro, Victor M., chairman of publicity
Shearer, Norma, actress
Shelton, Marla, actress, tested for Belle Watling
Smith, Ben, actor, tried out for Frank Kennedy
Stacey, Eric G., assistant director
Stephanie "somebody," probably Steffi Duna
Stuart, Miss, actress
Tallechet, Margaret, actress
Thompson, Tilly, script girl
Van Druten, John, one of several script writers
Westmore, Monty, makeup and hair styling
Wheeler, Lyle, art direction
Whitney, Jock, chairman of the board of Selznick International Pictures
Winter, Larry, friend of George Cukor
Wood, Sam, replaced Fleming when Fleming collapsed and remained as another director.
Yoch, Florence, landscaped Tara
Zavitz, Lee, special effects associate, fire

APPENDIX IX

GWTW DOCUMENTS

SOME OF THE COSTS ON "GONE WITH THE WIND:"

(1) The estimated cost of Music is $99,822.00, which includes the salaries of Lou Forbes and Secretary, Max Steiner, Musicians and Copyists, also Miscellaneous License Fees and Supplies & Expenses.

(2) Salaries of Stars and Cast and Extra Talent, $466,688.00.

(3) Total cost Union Labor: $1,517,466.00

<u>Breakdown</u>:

Union employees	961,215.00
Guild members, excluding actors, writers and directors	119,433.00
Extras	108,469.00
Miscellaneous	328,349.00

(Note: Union employees are cameramen, wardrobe workers, property men, make-up artists, hairdressers, musicians, copyists, transportation drivers, carpenters, grips, painters, plasterers, laborers, electricians, projectionists, machinists, tractor drivers, prop makers, drapers, upholsterers, sound crew, special effects.

Guild members - also union labor - are film cutters, assistant directors, unit managers, artists (set designers), script clerks.

Miscellaneous are department heads, technical advisers, stenographers, watchmen, interior decorators, wardrobe mfg., office workers (clerks, messenger boys, telephone operators, etc.)

(4) Total cost of Sets, $197,877.00, as per detail attached.

(5) Total cost of Women's Wardrobe, $98,154.00; total cost of Men's Wardrobe, $55,664.00; total cost of Wardrobe, $153,818.00.

(6) Projection cost, $11,376.00.

(7) Picture Raw Stock (474,538 feet) cost $109,974.00.

(Since the Technicolor process uses three negatives this total should be multiplied by three to arrive at the total of 1,423,614 lineal feet of negative raw stock used on the picture.)

Picture Negative developed (390,792 feet) (1,172,376

(more)

To Susan Myrick

Some time ago the producers and publicity heads of all the Hollywood studios, in one of their regular meetings, decided against releasing any copy or photographs which tend to destroy the illusion of reality in motion picture. This, they had found through experience made for greater enjoyment and greater appreciation of motion picturex by audiences.

While such copy is often very interesting there is a justice in the rule which definitely helps to protect our industry.

It is for this reason I have crossed out the paragraphs making a point of the fact the exterior of Tara is only a front and the interior a confusion of doors and empty spaces.

Trusting you will appreciate this point of policy,

Best wishes

B Birdwell

Stinson

Bear Miss Susie:

Please look at scene 5760577 when you receive it mimeo'd today ---- Mammy, Pork and Prissy looking at the Butler house at end of honeymoon, for which you once wrote some lines. Now, you see, they are not looking at the bed, but merely at the new house. DOS has filled in some dummy lines; but will appreciate it if you will give us some <u>better</u> onês!

Thanks, Honey.

Love --
Bobby

CALL SHEET

DATE FRIDAY, MAR. 31, 1939

PICTURE "GONE WITH THE WIND" - Prod. #108 DIRECTOR VICTOR FLEMING

SET Ext. Examiner Office (WEATHER PERMITTING)

LOCATION 40 Acres Set #17 Scs. 166A-167-166B-166 ~~(in this order)~~

NAME	TIME CALLED ON SET	TIME CALLED MAKE-UP	CHARACTER, DESC., WARDROBE
Vivien Leigh	8:00 AM	7:00 AM	"Scarlett" #9
Olivia de Havilland	8:00 AM	6:00 AM	" Melanie" #4
Eddie Anderson	8:00 AM	6:30 AM	"Uncle Peter"
Clark Gable	9:00 AM	8:00 AM	"Rhett" #3
Harry Davenport	10:00 AM	9:00 AM	"Dr. Meade" #2
Leona Roberts	10:00 AM	9:00 AM	"Mrs. Meade" #1
Jackie Moran	10:00 AM	9:00 AM	"Phil Meade" #1
Henry Hastings	10:00 AM	9:30 AM	"Meade Coachman"
Margaret Seddon	WILL CALL		"Grandma Tarleton" #1
George H. Reed	WILL CALL		"Tarleton Coachman"
Jay Ward	8:00 AM	7:00 AM	"Printer's Devil"
Stand-ins	7:30 AM	7:00 AM	-
EXTRAS:			
112 Men	8:00 AM	6:30 AM	As instructed
196 Women	8:00 AM	6:30 AM	" "
17 Colored Men	8:00 AM	7:30 AM	" "
5 " Women	8:00 AM	7:30 AM	" "
20 Children	8:00 AM	7:30 AM	" "
350 Total			

NOTE TO MAKEUP DEPT.

Men to be made up 89
Women to be made up 66
Total- 155

WARDROBE DEPT.

Men Fitted - - - - - - - - - - 95
Men to be fitted at Call time - 34
129

Women Fitted- - - - - - - - - - 71
Women to be ft'd. at Call time - 130
201

Children to be ft'd. Call time- 20

PROPERTY DEPT.

Aunt Pitty's carriage- - 7:30AM
Grandma Tarleton " -Will notify.
Dr. Meade's Carriage- - - 9:30AM
Rhett's Horse - - - - - 8:30AM
5 Carriages, 3 Buggies,
4 Farm Wagons, 4 Army
Supply Wagons - - - - - -7:30AM
15 Civilians' horses,
5 Officers' horses- - - -7:30AM
6 ass'td. dogs - - - - - -7:30AM

CAMERAS - - - - - - - - 7:00 AM
SOUND (Ready on set)- - 8:15AM
P.A. SYSTEM- - - - - - - 7:30 AM
COSGROVE - - - - -WILL NOTIFY.

COVER SET

EXT. McDONOUGH ROAD - SET #24 - STAGE #14

Vivien Leigh	Scarlett
Clark Gable	Rhett
Olivia de Havilland	Melanie
Butterfly McQueen	Prissy
Stand-ins	-

NOTE: Lou Forbes Will pre-record quartette at night as soon as Sound is finished on set. WILL NEED PLAYBACK. Will record on Stage #10.

PROP DEPT. "Woebegone" horse and wagon.

ADVANCE SHOOTING SCHEDULE ON REVERSE SIDE OF CALL SHEET

DIRECTOR ERIC STACEY

SELZNICK INTERNATIONAL PICTURES, INC.

CALL SHEET

DATE TUES., MAY 9, 1939

PICTURE "GONE WITH THE WIND" - Prod. #108-55 DIRECTOR

SET PROCESS PLATE TESTS - GERALD & SCARLETT'S WALK

LOCATION STAGE #12 SILENT

NAME	TIME CALLED		CHARACTER, DESC., WARDROBE
	ON SET	MAKE-UP	
1 Man	10:00 AM	9:00 AM	Dble. for Gerald
1 Woman	10:00 AM	9:00 AM	" " Scarlett
CAMERAS - - - - - - -	9:30 AM		
PROCESS - - - - - - -	9:30 AM		

ASSISTANT DIRECTOR WM. McGARRY

SELZNICK INTERNATIONAL PICTURES, INC.

CALL SHEET

DATE THURS., MAY 4, 1939

PICTURE "GONE WITH THE WIND" - Prod. #100 DIRECTOR SAM WOOD

SET EXT. PEACHTREE AND DECATUR STREETS DAY SUMMER 1864

LOCATION 40 ACRES SET #17-18 SCS. 250 A-C-D-E-F-G WEATHER PERMITTING

NAME	TIME CALLED ON SET	MAKE-UP	CHARACTER, DESC., WARDROBE
Vivien Leigh	8:00 AM	7:00 AM	Scarlett #10A
Stand-in	7:30 AM	7:00 AM	For Miss Leigh
EXTRAS:-			
81 Soldiers)			
84 3 Women)	8:00 AM	7:00 AM	As fitted
22 Men)			
5 Women)	8:00 AM	7:00 AM	To be fitted on reporting
8 Colored Men)			
3 " Women)			
5 " Boys)	8:15 AM	8:00 AM	" " " " "
47 4 White Boys)			
131 Grand Total			

LATER

EXT. AUNT PITTY'S HOUSE - SET #18 - RETAKE SC. 217 - 40 ACRES

Vivien Leigh	-	-	Retake closeup

LATER

EXT. PEACHTREE STREET - SET #18 - SCS. 236-237 (DAY) SUMMER 1864.

William Bakewell	Will Call		Dispatch Rider as fitted

- -

MENZIES 2ND UNIT - 12:00M. SHOOTING

EXT. AUNT PITTY'S HOUSE - SET #18 - 40 ACRES (POINT OF VIEW SHOT).

Butterfly McQueen	12:00 M		Prissy #3

LATER

EXT. BRIDGE OVER RAVINE - ESCAPE SEQ. - SHOTS OF ARTILLERY UNIT

1ST UNIT CAMERAS- - - 7:00 AM
2ND UNIT " - - - 11:30 AM
SOUND (Ready) - - - 8:15 AM
P.A. SYSTEM (Ready)- - 7:30 A M

PROPERTY DEPT.
4 Artillery units complete
1 Ox-drawn siege gun complete
6 Army wagons and horses
6 " ambulances & horses
(24 cav. horses & Dispatch rider's roaring horse & double at 7:30AM.

IN CASE OF BAD WEATHER

EXT. & INT. TARA-STAGE #3 - SET #5 - SCS. 358 to 366 (NIGHT) SUMMER 1864

Vivien Leigh	9:00 AM	8:00 AM	Scarlett #11A
Thos. Mitchell	9:00 AM	7:45 AM	Gerald #4
Hattie McDaniel	9:00 A M	8:30 AM	Mammy #4
Oscar Polk	9:00 AM	8:30 AM	Pork #3
Standins	8:15 AM	8:00 AM	-

ERIC STACEY

ASSISTANT DIRECTOR

SELZNICK INTERNATIONAL PICTURES, INC.

CALL SHEET

DATE TUES., MAY 9, 1939

PICTURE "GONE WITH THE WIND" - Prod. #103 DIRECTOR SAM WOOD

SET Int. Tara SUMMER 1864

LOCATION Stage #3 Set #5 SCS. 367 to 378 (Dawn) (Cont.)

NAME	TIME CALLED ON SET	TIME CALLED MAKE-UP	CHARACTER, DESC., WARDROBE
Vivien Leigh	9:00 AM	8:00 AM	Scarlett #11A
Thomas Mitchell	9:00 AM	7:30 AM	Gerald #4
Hattie McDaniel	9:00 AM	8:30 AM	Mammy #4
Oscar Polk	9:00 AM	8:30 AM	Pork #3
Butterfly McQueen	9:00 AM	8:30 AM	Prissy #3
Stand-ins	8:15 AM	8:00 AM	--
LATER			
INT. TARA - STAGE #3 - SET #5 - SCS. 408,409,411 to 430,433 to 442 - DAY			
			NOVEMBER - 1864
Vivien Leigh	-	-	Scarlett #12
Olivia de Havilland	Will call		Melanie #7
Paul Hurst	Will call		Yankee Cavalryman
Stand-ins	Will call		--
CAMERAS - - - - - - - -	8:15 AM		
SOUND (Ready) - - - -	9:15 AM		

ADVANCE SHOOTING SCHEDULE
ON REVERSE SIDE OF CALL SHEET

ASSISTANT DIRECTOR ERIC STACEY

ADVANCE SHOOTING SCHEDULE

Saturday, April 1	-	Ext. Examiner Office (Cont.) Weather Perm.)	40 Acres
		COVER SET:	
		Ext. McDonough Road	Stage #14
		Int. Jail (If McDonough Rd. has been shot)	Stage #8
Monday, April 3	-	Ext. McDonough Road	Stage #14
Tuesday, April 4	-	Ext. Church & Street (Weather Permitting)	40 Acres
Wednesday, April 5	-	Ext. Church & Street (" ")	40 Acres
Thursday, April 6	-	Int. Hospital	Stage #12
Friday, April 7	-	Int. Hospital	Stage #12

NOTE:
Cosgrove 2nd Unit
Ext. L.S. Ellen's Arrival at Tara
Will be shot whenever weather and
schedule permits.

ADVANCE SHOOTING SCHEDULE

Wednesday, May 10	-	Int. Tara (Continuation) (Dawn Sequence) (Yankee Cavalryman)	Stage #3
Thursday, May 11	-	Int. Tara (Continuation) (Yankee Cavalryman Seq.)	Stage #3
Friday, May 12	-	Int. Tara (Continuation) (Yankee Cavalryman & Wilkerson Seq.)	Stage #3
		NOTE: If above sequences are completed sooner than scheduled, the Int. Melanie's House (Scarlett-Melanie Scene) will be scheduled on Friday.	
Saturday, May 13	-	Ext. Street & Square (Weather Porn.) BIG CRANE SHOT of Wounded	40 Acres
Monday, May 15	-	Int. Rhett's Room (Rhett-Melanie Sc.)	Stage #11
		Int. London Hotel Bedroom (Rhett-Bonnie Sc.)	Stage #4
		Int. Belle's Apartment (Rhett-Belle Sc.)	Stage #4
Tuesday, May 16	-	Int. Scarlett's Bedroom (Birth of Bonnie - No more babies - Dressing for party)	Stage #11
Wednesday, May 17	-	Int. Rhett's House - Dining, Rm., Hall and Bedroom + (Row & Rape sc)	Stages #11-14
Thursday, May 18	-	Int. Rhett's House (miscarriage seq.)	Stage #14
Friday, May 19	-	Int. Rhett's House (Death of Bonnie Sc.)	Stage #11
Saturday, May 20	-	Int. Rhett's House (Rhett-Melanie Sc. re-Bonnie's Burial)	Stage #14
Monday, May 22	-	Ashley's Return to Tara	
Tuesday, May 23	-	Paddock Scene	
Wednesday, May 24	-	Int. Rhett's House (Completion of set)	

ADVANCE SHOOTING SCHEDULE

Friday, May 5 -	Ext. Tara (Arrival Seq.) (Scarlett-Melanie-Gerald sc.)	Stage #3
Saturday, May 6 -	Int. Tara (Arrival Seq.) (Run thru hall and Ellen's body seq.) AT NIGHT:	Stage #3
	Int. Belle's Carriage (Belle-Melanie sc)	Stage #9
Monday, May 8 -	Int. Tara - Girl's Bedroom & Hall (Yankee Cavalryman Seq.)	Stage #3
Tuesday, May 9 -	Int. Tara - Hall (Yankee Cavalryman Seq. Cont.)	Stage #3
Wednesday, May 10-	Int. Rhett's Room (Rhett-Melanie Sc.)	Stage #12
	Int. London Hotel Bedroom (Rhett-Bonnie Sc.)	Stage #4
	Int. Belle's Apartment (Rhett-Belle Sc.)	Stage #4
Thursday, May 11 -	Int. Scarlett's Bedroom (Birth of Bonnie - No more babies - Dressing for party)	Stage #12
Friday, May 12 -	Int. Rhett's House, Dining Rm. Hall and Bedroom (Row & Rape Sc.)	Stgs.#12-14
Saturday, May 13 -	Int. Rhett's House (Miscarriage scene)	Stage #14
Monday, May 15 -	Int. Rhett's House (Death of Bonnie Sc.)	Stage #12
Tuesday, May 16 -	Int. Rhett's House (Rhett-Melanie Sc. re: Bonnie's Burial)	Stage #14
Wednesday, May 17-	Ashley's Return to Tara	
Thursday, May 18 -	Paddock Scene	
Friday, May 19 -	Int. Rhett's House (Completion of set).	

NOTE:

As soon as plates are received from Chico of Scarlett's and Gerald's walk, the balance of the walk in front of Tara at 40 Acres will be scheduled.

The BIG CRANE shot of the Wounded will be scheduled whenever Crane is available.

APPENDIX X
REFERENCE MATERIALS

Sue carried many items with her for reference, including a variety of photographs and pamphlets. One such reprint was Jessie W. Parkhurst, "The Role of the Black Mammy in the Plantation Household," *The Journal of Negro History,* Washington, D. C., Vol. XXIII, No. 3, 1938, pp. 349-369.

Other reference items she carried with her to California were *The Service of the Confederate Flags* (1926) and *The History of the Confederate Flags* (1925). by M. (Mamie) Jenison Chestney. Sue's copy of the former was a gift from Gertrude Smith (Trawick), a colleague on the paper. Two books by Marie Howard Weeden, *Bandanna Ballads* and *Songs of the Old South*, with their detailed illustrations, also served as valuable resources for Sue.

Sue carried these pictures, among others, with her to Hollywood as reference material

APPENDIX XI
BIBLIOGRAPHY

Frank Hawkins, a colleague, wrote of some of Sue's literary credits in 1938—she had published feature articles in *The Philadelphia Record*, *The Detroit News*, the old *New York World*, and various children's magazines and physical education periodicals.

Textbook

Susan Myrick, *Our Daily Bread*. The Interstate Printers & Publishers, Danville, IL, 1950, 212 pp. incl. Teachers Guide. Illustrated.

Biography

Susan Myrick, *Samuel Thomas McAfee, Man of Courage*. Southern Press, Inc., Macon, GA, 1970.

***Gone With The Wind* Articles**

Susan Myrick, Pardon my Un-Southern Accent. *Colliers,* December 1939, pp. 20,31,32.

Susan Myrick, My Friends Have Gone with the Wind. *Southern Living*, Vol. 2, No. 9, October 1967, pp. 30-33, 46.

Susan Myrick, Memoir of GWTW. *Georgia*, Vol. XVI, No. 9, April 1973, pp. 35-37, 47, 49.

Susan Myrick, Margaret Mitchell, A Portrait. *Georgia Journal*, Vol. 3, No. 2, Feb/Mar 1983, pp. 8-12. (Notes and diary excerpts assembled and edited by Susan Lindsley.)

See also *The Georgia Review*, Winter 1947.

***The Georgia Review*, University of Georgia literary magazine**

Susan Myrick, Time Must Serve, *The Georgia Review*, Vol. 1, No. 4, Winter 1947, pp. 452-459. (A GWTW article).

Susan Myrick, The Capture, the Prison Pen, and the Escape. *The Georgia Review*, Vol. VIII, No. 2, Summer 1954, pp. 184-189.

Susan Myrick, Two Old Cookbooks, *The Georgia Review*, Vol. XII, No.3, Fall 1958, pp. 273-277.

Susan Myrick, Lizzie Lynn; Or Who Started All This? *The Georgia Review*, Vol. XIV, No. 3, Fall 1960, pp. 292-295.

Susan Myrick, On Reading the Georgia *Market Bulletin* (poem). *The Georgia Review*, Vol. XVIII, No. 4, Winter 1964, p. 408.

Susan Myrick, Whatever Became of the Prom Party? *The Georgia Review*, Vol. XXII, No. 3, Fall 1968, pp. 354-359.

Georgia Historic Quarterly

Susan Myrick, Review Essay of Margaret Mitchell's *Gone With The Wind* Letters (edited by Richard Harwell). *Georgia Historical Quarterly*, Winter 1976, pp. 372-378.

Publishers Service Magazine

Susan Myrick, W. T. Anderson of Georgia (A three-part series). Part 1. *Publishers Service Magazine*, Vol. III, No. 23, Dec. 1, 1932, pp. 4-5, 20.

Susan Myrick, W. T. Anderson of Georgia, Part 2. *Publishers Service Magazine*, Vol. III, No. 24, Dec. 15, 1932, pp. 6-7, 29.

Susan Myrick, W. T. Anderson of Georgia, Part 3. *Publishers Service Magazine*, Vol. IV, No. 1, Jan. 5, 1933, pp. 8-9, 29.

APPENDIX XII

WESTOVER PLANTATION HOUSE

APPENDIX XIII

OTHER AWARDS

WOMAN OF THE YEAR: 1955

*Progressive Farmer's A*nnouncement

We recognize as our 1955 Woman of the Year in service to rural Georgia Miss Susan Myrick, associate editor of The Macon Telegraph, *and farm editor of* The Macon Telegraph *and* The Macon News.

Miss Myrick has worked for The Macon Telegraph *for 25 years, with a year-and-a-half leave of absence in 1939-40, to serve as technical advisor in making the movie* Gone With The Wind, *and later with its publicity department.*

The farm editor's friends speak of her as the blue lupine queen, because of her continued efforts to promote the growth of that fine winter cover crop. Working continuously to "Keep Georgia Green," Miss Myrick has constantly encouraged soil conversation efforts. She often writes "success" stories of farmers in her area who are doing good soil and water conservation on their farms.

With young people in mind, Miss Sue wrote a soil conversation reader for the third grade, Our Daily Bread. *The book, which has been adopted by Georgia Public Schools, is also used by several states.*

This farm editor is always ready to give a plug to farm activities by farmers, farm wives, 4-H club members, Future Farmers, and similar groups.

Miss Myrick is probably the only woman who has been president of the Macon Farmers Club. She is on the executive board of the Macon Little Theater, and has appeared in at least one play every year for the past 24 years. This editor reads widely, enjoys modern art, and even does some painting on her own.

"It is wonderful," she declares, "what lovely paintings you can make of farm machinery and farm buildings. My best one is a semi-abstract made from a sketch I did of a two-story chicken house."

Any other hobbies? Yes, she enjoys working in her own back yard building compost piles, fighting insects, pruning, trying to make a pretty yard. She used mostly shrubs and perennials. "No annuals—too much trouble," the Georgia lady declares.

Although constantly in demand as a public speaker, this "Honorary

Georgia Planter" likes to take time out for her kitchen. She enjoys cooking certain dishes especially, one of them spoon bread made by a 100-year old recipe. Look for it soon in the pages of the Progressive Farmer.

Sue's recipe:

Heat 1 pint of milk to scalding. Add 1 cup corn meal, stir and cook until smooth and slightly thickened. Add 1 stick butter, 1 teaspoon salt and 1 tablespoon sugar. Cool. Beat in 3 whole eggs. Bake in moderate oven for about 40 minutes.

GOVERNOR'S AWARD
Outstanding Forestry Conservationist

In May 1960, Sue was regional winner of the Georgia Sportsman's Federation award in the soil and water conservation division of their awards program. Her winning the Bibb County Sportsman's Federation award had made her eligible for competition for the regional award. She advanced to the state competition and in June, at the Governor's Award Banquet, she was honored as the outstanding forestry conservationist for her many articles on the subject. She was also cited for her work in soil and water conversation—her articles had served to create interest in the development of the Altamaha River Basin and other projects.

ORDER OF THE GOLDEN PINE CONE

The Georgia Forestry Association presented Sue with the Order of the Golden Pine Cone in June 1962 for "for outstanding and meritorious service to the Georgia Forestry Association."

* * *

HALL OF FAME

Myrick Articles Treasured

Editors: I was delighted to read that Miss Susan Myrick has been named to the Hall of Fame.

My mother has an August 19, 1928, magazine section of The Macon Telegraph *in which Miss Myrick wrote, among other articles, a story about my grandfather, I. M. Sheppard of Monroe County. He was the father of 30 children. (Thirty is correct!)*

The paper was found in a house in Sandersville about three years ago. It is in good condition; it was then sent to The Reporter *in Forsyth, which passed it on to my mother. We treasure it very much. It is complete with pictures of some of the younger children.*

In the same paper she also had a very interesting interview with a black man in Milledgeville, written exactly in the words the man used. It is wonderful how she wrote that story.

* * *

A three-quarter page article on page one of the Georgia Living Section of *The Telegraph and News* announced that Sue was named to the Georgia Newspaper Hall of Fame. The article gave an account of her life, from Dovedale to retirement, including her Hollywood work and many of her awards for her journalistic endeavors. It also stressed her human side.

The article by Skippy Lawson stated that "Her wit is what friends usually describe first. She loved a good joke. She was especially fond of puns and regaled friends at parties with her imitation of a Black Angus cow."

She quoted Catherine Lee of *The Telegraph*: "She wasn't the sweet mild little lady that most of her generation had to be in order to survive. She had a rather ribald sense of humor, never obscene or vulgar, but she loved a good joke and a good laugh."

Friends and family who journeyed to Athens for the celebrations included her sister Allie (only surviving sibling, who came from Austin, Texas); nieces Lil James and Susan Lindsley; cousin Conley Ingram (son of Nan Whitehurst, who lived with the family at Dovedale for a while), and colleagues from *The Telegraph*: Billy Watson (general manager), Rick Thomas (executive editor), Ed Corson (editor), Jim Chapman (managing editor) and Clara Eschmann (food editor).

* * *

GEORGIA WOMEN OF ACHIEVEMENT

The Georgia Women of Achievement inducted Sue into their rolls of outstanding Georgia women on March 13, 2008, at Wesleyan College in Macon—the site of her early lessons in painting, and only a short distance from the new location of the Macon Little Theatre and near the site of the stables where she kept her riding horse in the 1920s and 1930s.

The keynote speaker for the event was Dr. Barbara Christmas whose background is similar to Sue's: Dr. Christmas has worked as a counselor, school principal, and author.

On hand for the event were the "three little Lindsley girls" of Sue's columns: Thulia Lindsley Bramlett, Susan Lindsley, and Dr. Lil Lindsley James, as well as Valette Jordan Adkins, a cousin from Milledgeville, Conley and Silvia Ingram and numerous friends from both Milledgeville and Macon who remember Sue.

Thulia had nominated Sue for the honor; the nomination required documentation of Sue's work at *The Macon Telegraph*, her involvement in social, wartime and charitable work, her participation in the Macon Little Theatre as a founding/charter member, her work on GWTW, and her award-winning conservation work. A narrated film showed many aspects of Sue's life and work.

The proclamation presented to the family summarized Sue's achievements from the time she came to Macon in the 1920s until her death in 1978.

* * *

SUSAN MYRICK DAY

On April 15, 2008, the Macon City Council and Mayor declared the day Susan Myrick Day and issued a proclamation at the city council meeting. The daughters of her sister Lillas—Thulia, Susan and Lil—represented the family.

The proclamation listed many of Sue's accomplishments as a newswoman, but her work on GWTW was omitted, perhaps because Margaret Mitchell's donation of much of her income from GWTW to black medical students' tuition was still a secret. Also, time had passed since the African-American community in Middle Georgia described their situation with the words: "We got two friends here—Sweet Jesus and *The Macon Telegraph*," meaning W. T. Anderson and Susan Myrick.

APPENDIX XIV
COTTON CHOPPING

The debate over a cotton chopping scene began in January 1939 when Selznick asked Sue to look at a field to see if it would be appropriate to use as a cotton field. He wanted slaves to be chopping cotton when Gerald O'Hara rode over Tara on the day before the barbecue at Twelve Oaks—the day before the War Between the States began—in mid-April. Sue argued with Selznick for months—you do not chop cotton in North Georgia in April, she told him, over and over.

One of her memos read:

You may recall that I wrote you on Jan. 15 about the cotton chopping scene. The script shows plainly that O'Hara's ride is the afternoon before the barbecue; the date of the barbecue is fixed by reason of the announcement of Mr. Lincoln's call for volunteers. Since that date is approximately mid-April, I must remind you that it is not cotton chopping time; the cotton seeds have not even been planted by mid-April.

May I suggest that the scene be changed to plowing the fields?

She had to argue with Selznick, by memo and in person, for six months—until June 1939—before he finally relented and did not include the mid-April cotton chopping scene.

APPENDIX XV
DIANNE KING'S WEDDING

The invitation Sue received was for the wedding of Cammie's sister Diane, not Cammie. But Sue's imagination makes the column "Unseen Guests" a fun read.

Dr. and Mrs. Herbert Thomas Kalmus, the invitation began, and it went on to invite me to the wedding of Mary Diane King, at the church of the Blessed Sacrament in Hollywood.

I was puzzled. I knew that the name Kalmus was associated with Technicolor, and I remembered a chap who hung around the sets when we were making GWTW, who was always quarrelling with me that the dirt was too red and would not look well in Technicolor. But I knew he was only an employee of the company, not Dr. Kalmus.

Then the name, Diane King, hit a brain cell with a mighty thud, and I remembered the pretty little girl with dark hair and brown eyes, who played the role of Bonnie, daughter of Scarlet and Rhett. I remembered how we worried about the pretty child's brown eyes, because in the book GWTW the author had written that the child was named Bonnie because of her "Bonnie Blue" eyes.

I remembered, too, how hard it had been to teach the pretty little girl to "sound Southern," for she had a definite R in her speech. There was a scene where the child got frightened by a bad dream (you never saw it in the movie; it got left on the cutting room floor) and Rhett hugged her and soothed her and she kept saying something about a big bear-r-r. What a time we had teaching her to say "beah," instead of "bear-r-r."

And what a relief it was when we shot the scene that showed Bonnie riding her pony and making him take the jump that resulted in her fall and death. For we shot on that scene all day long, and since Bonnie had nothing to say, I had no accent to bother about.

I could just sit in the warm California sunshine, in the outdoor lot over at the MGM studio, and drowse and read the papers and chatter with wardrobe girls and hair dressers and Technicolor directors and costume designers and such, and not have a moment's worry lest somebody speak in a manner that would affront Southerners from Fort Sumpter to Macon.

And now little Bonnie is grown up and is about to get married.

I have a feeling that there will be a company of ghostly ones at the wedding, unseen in the midst of the happy crowd of flesh and blood folks who will wish happiness to the bride; for there must be hovering over the wedding of Bonnie Butler the spirits of Scarlett and Rhett, of Melanie and Ashley, and surely the spirit of Mammy with her red petticoat which she wore to show Mistuh Rhett she no longer bore him any ill will.

If the good wishes of such a fine company mean anything, Mary Diane King and her husband will surely have a happy life.

INDEX

A Doll's House, 119, 147, 441
A Song for Springtime, 158
A Teacher's Friday Night Dream, 14, 439
Adkins, Valette, 3, 466
Aiken, Sally, 116, 139,
Alexander the Great, 164
Alf, son of a Dovedale employee, 9
Alice in Wonderland, 22
Alice through the Looking Glass, 22
Allen, Carrie, 148
Allen, Dawson, 72
Allen, Floride, 71
Allen, Jane, 445
Allen, Mayor Ivan and/or Mrs., 325-327
Alligator Point, 413
American Cancer Society, 364
American Expeditionary Forces, 126
Amory, Cleveland, 324
Andersen's *Fairy Tales*, 113
Anderson, Eddie, 190, 193, 213
Anderson, Katherine, 153, 154, 347
Anderson, Louise, 295, 298, 299, 300, 303, 304
Anderson, Marian, 190
Anderson, Peyton, 153, 154, 156, 178, 254, 347, 356, 357, 386, 394
Anderson, R. L. , 162
Anderson, Sherwood,112, 113, 278
Anderson, W. T. , 111-113,126, 127, 131, 132, 139, 145, 153, 154, 157, 183, 254, 295, 288-300, 304, 310, 358, 389, 424, 461, 466
Anglesey, 401
Anheuser-Busch Gardens, 252
Anne, stand-in for Olivia, 248
Anything Goes, 141
Arbuckle's Coffee,71
Arden, see Cripe
As You Like It Club, 71
Ashbury, T. L., 366
Associated Press, 133
Association of Soil and Water Conservation District Supervisors, 357, 368
Atlanta Historical Society, 327
Auburn University, 7
Aunt Jennie Tough, 38
Aunt Lizzie Good, see Myrick
Aunt Minerva, 33, 41
Aunt Pitty Pat, 286
Bailey (union leader), 227
Balderston, John, 241, 253, 447
Baldridge, Cyrus LeRoy, 443
Baldridge, Tom, 326
Baldwin County, 6, 103, 358, 425
Baltimore Evening Sun, 433
Bankhead, Tallulah, 128, 129, 176
Barefoot in the Park, 408
Barkley, Mrs. Alban, 375
Baroness von Blumenthal, 167
Barrymore, John, 238
Batman (TV show), 329

Battle Creek, 75-82, 84, 94, 95, 97, 101, 128, 365
Battle Creek Sanitarium, 75
Battle Creek Toasted Corn Flakes Company, 75
Battle of Bosworth, 401
Baume, Emile,138
Baxter, Alan, 181
Beal, John, 443
Bell, Furman, 75
Bell, James, 187
Bermuda, 187, 192, 260
Bernd, Aaron, 112, 113, 126, 128, 133-138, 140, 141, 145-147, 149-151, 153, 161, 164, 271, 423, 448
Bernd, Florence, 138,164
Berne Convention, 142
Bessie, Margaret Mitchell's maid, 142, 143
Bessolo, George, 219, 220, 447
Bethel Church, 12, 42, 154
Better Film Committee, 326
Bibb Manufacturing Company, 144
Bienvenido, Antonio, matador, 402
Big Cedar Creek, 39
Big Sam, 178, 208, 210, 246, 258
Binion, Richard, 72
Birdwell, Russell, 189, 192, 194, 207, 244, 447
Birth of a Nation, 258
Blackberry Winter, 445
Blackman, Dorothy, 224
Blair House, 374, 375, 434
Blanche, Lucille, 117, 395, 398, 424
Blooming Lupine Queen, 356, 463
Blount, Louise (see Anderson, Louise Blount)
Blythe, see McKay
Bob and P., 154, 165 (possibly Quinlan and Mahone)
Bob, see Quinlan
Bobo, Lulu, 382, 383
Bodorgan Castle, 401
Bolton, Euri Belle, 427
Bone, Jesse, 72
Bone, Russell, 72
Boots, see Massee
Boudoir cap, 143, 144
Bow, Clara, 385
Bowden, Allie (see Myrick, Allie)
Bowden, Charlie (Macon mayor), 162, 169
Bowden, Dr. A. O. and Mrs. Katherine, 257, 272, 447
Bowden, Edwin Jr., 413, 417
Bowden, Edwin Sr., 341, 346, 376, 395, 400
Boyer, Charles, 443
Boyle, Edward G., 188, 190-192, 206, 207, 244
Brady, Alice, 156
Brame, James Yancey VI, see Lane, Bruce
Bramlett, Thulia Lindsley, 4, 144, 425-427, 466
Brer Fox, 2, 3, 422
Brer Rabbit, 2, 3, 72, 73, 333, 380, 422
Brickell, Herschel, 159
Bridges, Herb, 430
Broderick-Lennie, 155
Brown House fire, 390
Brown, Katherine (Kay, Kate, Kath), 131, 132, 137,145, 147, 153-155, 163, 447
Brown, Mary, 300, 304, 415

Brown, T. H., 366
Browning, Sugar Daddy, 388
Bryan, Nancy Averette, see Whitehurst
Bryan, Wright, 159, 356
Bundsman, Anton, 131
Burdette, Dr. James, 359
Burke, Billie, 156
Burt, George, 114, 141,154, 155, 158, 295, 300, 304, 309, 311, 389
Butler, Bonnie, 211, 212, 228, 267, 268, 272, 278, 322, 447, 448
Butler, Rhett, 136, 147, 194, 208, 211, 215, 227, 234, 237, 251, 256, 263, 268, 269, 272, 278-280, 294, 335-337, 448
Butterick Publishing Company, 35, 36
Cadmus, King of All Wales, 401
Caesar, 403
Cafritz, Mrs. Morris, 375
Cain, Edna, 158
Calhoun, James C., see Sherman
Callow, Phyllis, 280
Callow, Ridgeway (Reggie), 236, 242
Cameron, Kenneth, 295, 296, 298, 304, 311
Camp Jackson, 96, 97
Camp Wheeler, 114, 118, 339-341, 343, 375
Candler family, 413
Canterbury Tales, 435
Capel, Rose, 138
Carnegie Hall, 141
Carpenter, George, 71
Carr, Lulu B., 94
Carroll, Lewis, 152
Carroll, Nancy, 237
Carter, President Jimmy, 337
Casson, Habenicht (Hebe), 147, 153, 298, 299, 303, 304
Cavendish, Margaret McKenney, 375
Chambers, Robert, 23
Change in the Wind, 414
Chapman, Jim, 465
Charlotte Times Observer, 389
Chestney, Mamie (Mrs. Piercy), 116, 126, 254. 299, 304, 326, 392, 459
Chicago, 149
Chico, 263, 264, 268, 270-272
Children's Hour, 141
Christina (role), 119, 150, 441,
Christmas, Dr. Barbara, 446
Cicero, 403
Citizens Defense Committee, 118, 339
Civitan Club, 305
Claire, Ina, 190, 229, 239
Clemson College, 161
Cline, Ray, 276
Cline, Regina, 52
Cline, Wilfred M., 447
Clune, 248
Cochran Field, 339, 340
Cole, Lois, 159
Coleman, Bill, 308
Coleman Hill (column), 126
Coleman Hill (location in Macon), 152
Coleman, Dr. A. T. , 358
Coleman, Ronald, 147

Collier, Will, 10
Colliers, 248, 313, 361, 460
Columbia University, 105, 126
Come Back, Little Sheba, 397
Confederacy, 134, 189, 217, 218, 391, 398
Confederate Army, 4, 6
Confederate bills, bonds and notes, 7
Confederate Decoration Day, 257
Conn, Charley, 72
Conquest, 443
Cooper, Ann, 135, 142
Cooper, Gary, 147
Cope, Channing, 356
Cordele, Georgia, 150
Cosgrove, Jack, 277
Craig, Jim, 186, 190, 207
Craig's Wife (play), 163
Crane, Fred, 219, 220
Craven, Frank, 156
Crews, Laura Hope, 186, 193, 257, 310, 322
Cripe, Arden, 447, 273
Cross Creek, 129
Cukor, George, 128, 129, 132, 133, 136, 137, 142, 147, 153, 156, 163, 170, 172, 176-179, 181, 183, 185, 187, 197, 199, 200, 213, 220-222, 226, 228, 230, 231, 244, 257, 263, 318, 320, 447-449
Culver City, 171, 215, 231, 296
Cuyler, Colonel Telamon, 253, 254
Cyrano, 236, 237
Daf, 87
Dagwood, 351
Daily Sentinel (Rome, NY), 433
Daniels, Frank, 382
DAR, 360, 361
Darien, Georgia, 139
Dark Town Strutter's Ball, 149
Daugherty, Marshall, 144, 161, 162
David Copperfield, 22, 50
Davenport, Harry, 257
Davis, Bette, 137, 333
Davis, George, 378
Davis, Jefferson, 294, 391
Dawson, Dorothy, 176, 178, 179, 199, 201, 248, 447
Dawson, Mrs. Kenneth, 377
Dawson News, 427
Day, Clarence, 159
de Havilland, Olivia, 183, 184, 230, 238, 240, 247, 248, 278, 282, 308, 310, 313-315, 317, 326, 327, 331-334 376, 430, 447
de Lafayette, Marquis, 114
Dear Abby, 107
Decatur, Georgia, 308
Deets, Charles, 82-87, 89-91, 93, 95, 98, 110
Deighton, Lillian K., 273, 447
Del, see Kenyon
Delco Systems, 8
Dempsey Hotel, 149, 153, 302, 311, 314
Depression, 110, 112, 116, 128, 313, 323, 364, 385, 388
Detroit Free Press, 81
Dickens, Charles, 50, 110
Dinner at Eight, 238
Dixie, 312, 313

Dixon, George, 389
Dixon, Mabel M., 94
Dodd, Lamar, 424
DOS, see Selznick, David O.
Dovedale, 2, 5, 8, 10, 11, 13, 14, 17, 18, 20, 23, 24, 28. 37, 41, 46, 48, 50, 52, 53, 70, 71, 73, 168, 188, 328, 355, 360, 402, 405, 413, 427, 433, 437, 438, 440, 465
Dowdell, James, 360
Dozier, William, 329
Dr. Meade, 257, 258
Dressler, Marie, 238
Drewry, John E., 161
Duke Ellington, 146
Dunwody, Elliot, 136, 147
Durham, Frank, 147, 151, 161
Dutch Tavern, 161
Earhart, Amelia, 434
Earle, Adrienne, 444
Eddie, (see Edwina Nims)
Edwards, Harry Stillwell, 162
Edwards, Lee, 134
Ellis, Marian, (sister of Caroline McCord), 298, 303
Ellis, Mrs. Roland, 138, 145
Ellis, Roland, 126, 136, 138, 131
Elvis, 415
Emery, General A. Robert, 340
Emily Post, 107, 445
Emory University, 73, 413
Enters, Angna, 148
Erwin, Hobe, 136, 137, 173, 230
Erwin, Stuart, 156
Eschmann, Clara H., 428, 485
Esquire, 240
Ethan Frome, 442
Ethridge, Mark, 105, 109, 155, 167, 381
Ethridge, Willie Snow, 168, 281, 389, 419,
Eugenics Registry, 80, 81
Evans, Rex, 263
Every Day's a Holiday, 445
Fairbanks, Douglas, 276, 445
Fairfax, 235
Family Service Agency, 394
Fannie Squeers, 105-107, 109, 135, 166, 186, 244, 353, 394, 405, 428
Farm Bureau, 353
Farmers Club, 357, 360, 361, 395, 463
Farnum, William, 173, 181, 185, 193, 448
Farr, Finis, 324
Faulkner, William, 129
Faye, Alice, 444
Federal Theatre, 176, 181, 198, 213
FFA (see Future Farmers)
Fiddler (radio announcer in Hollywood), 137
Fishback, Margaret, 445
Fisher, Harrison, 23
Fitzgerald, F. Scott, 181, 182, 207, 232
Flamini, Roland, 271, 324
Fleeson, Doris, 375
Fleming, Berry, 445
Fleming, Victor, 236, 242, 244, 247-249, 253, 258, 260, 261, 270, 271, 273, 279, 280, 282, 430, 449
Floyd, Frank, 448,

Forbes, Lou, 224, 227, 241, 258
Forever Ulysses, 444
Forsyte (Saga) family, 235
Fowler, Gene, 137
Fox in the Cloak, 445
Francis, Kay, 198
Frazier, Mrs. (role), 163
Frederickson, Frank, 238, 247, 448
Frederics, John, 237, 254
Fredonia Apartments, 113, 114, 116, 138, 169
Freeman, Mrs., 240
Freeman, Orville, 376
Ft. Benning, 339
Ft. McPherson, 96
Ft. Sumter, 243
Future Farmers (FFA), 350, 353, 463
Gable, Clark, 119, 147, 166, 183, 184, 199, 200, 206, 215, 221, 222, 230, 240, 243, 249, 264, 269, 275, 278-28
308-312, 314, 315, 322, 323, 331, 357, 434
Garbo, Greta, 240, 443
Garrett, O.H. P., 175, 178, 181, 208, 216, 218, 232, 233, 448
George, Senator Walter F. and Mrs., 310
Association of Soil Conservation District Supervisors, 357, 359
Georgia Military College, 72, 363
Georgia Military Institute, 6
Georgia Militia, 6
Georgia Newspaper Hall of Fame, 464, 465
Georgia Normal and Industrial College (GN&IC), 34, 50, 53, 56, 67, 71, 73, 74, 81, 97, 100, 101, 105, 147, 30
360, 396, 400, 418
Georgia Poultry Association, 373
Georgia Press Association, 122, 179, 350, 360, 382
Georgia Press Institute, 122, 123, 157, 350, 406, 433
Georgia Soil Conservation Districts, 365, 371
Georgia Sportsman's Federation, 464
Georgia State College for Women (GSCW), 138, 149, 305, 359, 427
Georgia Tech, 52, 54
Georgia Women of Achievement, 465, 466
Georgian Terrace, 309, 387
Germany, 161, 341
Gershwin, George, 442
Gilbert and Sullivan, 138, 231
Gilbert, John, 186
Gilbert, Leatrice Joy, 186, 200
Gilbert, Leatrice, 186
Ginsberg, Henry, 200, 201, 220-223, 242
Gilpin, John, 308
Gleckler, Robert, 248, 447
Glyn, Elinor, 199
Goldstone, Phil, 275
Gone With The Wind (the book), 122, 131, 132, 134, 137, 142, 153, 159, 229, 230, 242, 259, 261, 323, 324, 32
335-337
Gone With The Wind (the movie), 130-337, 356, 361, 375, 376, 392, 394, 410, 414, 424, 427, 430, 447, 450, 44
Good Buddies, 118
Goodfellows, 343, 394
Goodman, Mrs. Fielder, 359
Gordon, General John Brown, 264
Gordon, Georgia, 53
Gordon, Ruth, 442
Governor's Award, 464
Governor's Mansion, 50, 174

Grand Theatre (Macon), 311
Gray, Gordon, 375
Great Expectations, 22
Green Mansions, 442
Green Pastures, 190, 193, 213, 254, 259
Green, Louise, 144
Griffin, Governor Marvin, 350
Gruenberg, Louis, 442
Guy, Dr. Sam, 413
Hajii Baba, 443
Haley, Margaret, 144
Hall, O. D., 366
Hall, Virginia, 116, 396-398, 402
Haller, Ernest, 423, 448
Halsey, Margaret, 445
Hamilton, Charles, 186, 219, 222,449
Hamp, Johnny, 311
Hanna, Evelyn, 445
Hardy, Cecile Humphrey, 429
Harlem, 209, 210, 442
Harlow, Jean, 227, 239
Harris, Fannie Lou, 135
Harris, Corra, 352
Harris, Joel Chandler, 294, 437
Harris, Lloyd, 135
Harris, Phil, 268
Harris, Roy, 442
Harris, Sam, 443
Hart, Moss, 443
Hartsfield, Mayor William B., 307, 332, 333
Harvard University, 15, 94, 95, 102, 404, 429
Harwell, Richard, 220, 324, 461
Haskell, Mollie, 430
Hastings Daily Tribune, 93
Hastings, Nebraska, 81, 82, 85-88, 90, 93, 94, 101
Hawaii, 111, 114, 394, 400, 404
Hawkins, Frank, 116, 136, 141, 156, 157, 170, 178, 389, 460
Hawkins, Wes, 39
Hawley, Norman R., 409, 410
Hay Fever, 116
Hayden, Julie, 186
Haydn, 141
Hazelhurst, Dr., 422, 425
Head Start Program, 359
Heart of Oaks Books, 22
Hebe, see Casson
Hecht, Ben, 242, 253, 448
Hemingway, Ernest, 128, 400, 423
Henry VII,401
Herald Express, 257
Herbert, Bill, 277
Herrick, Mrs., 384
Herring, Frank and Kat, 155
Herty, Dr. Charles Holmes, 160, 363, 364
Hervey, Harry, 129
Hezekiah, Dovedale employee, 10
Hill, Benjamin Harvey, 4, 424
Hines, Mrs. E. R., 72
Hobbs, James V., 351

Hodges, General Courtney, and Mrs. Hodges, 386, 387
Holt, Mr. and Mrs. Hamilton, 167, 302, 314
Homestead, The, 6, 8
Hooray for What, 155
Horatio at the Bridge, 22, 440
House and Garden, 175
Howard, Katheryn Nimmo, 228, 448
Howard, Leslie,173, 181, 192, 197, 200, 206, 214, 218, 219, 231, 232, 238-243, 247, 264, 281, 314, 322
Howard, Sidney, 175, 178, 232, 233, 256, 259, 260, 263, 269
Hubert, Dr. Terrell E., 31
Hubert, Tippie, see Myrick, Tippie
Huggins, Carl, 366
Humphries, Mrs., 42
Hurst, Paul, 272
Hurt Place, The, 6, 8
Hutchins, Lee, 271
Ibsen, 147
I Lost My Girlish Laughter, 445
Idle Hour Country Club, 334
In Old Kentucky, 179, 182
In Our Time, 423
In the Lion's Mouth, 149
Ingraham, Anna S., 165, 306
Ingram, Conley, 465, 466
Ingram, Nan (see Whitehurst)
Ingram, Silvia, 466
Intermezzo, 269
Ivanhoe, 22
Jacksonville, Florida, 153
James, John, 334, 401, 424, 432
James, Lil Lindsley, 4, 80, 117, 334, 398, 401, 422-425, 432, 465, 466
Jeans, Isabel, 263, 448
Jelks, Albert, 136, 144, 165, 295, 299, 300, 304
Jelks, Doris, 144, 295, 298, 300, 304
Johnson, Hall, 198, 213, 254, 255, 258, 337
Johnson, Walter C. , 358
Jones County, 73
Jones, Jimmy, 389
Jones, John, 116
Jones, Mr., 42
Julius Caesar, 185
Junior League, 139, 309
Kaufman, Evelyn, 207
Kaufman, George S., 443
Kaufman, Gus, 114
Kearney, Bob, 268
Keaton, Buster, 274
Kellogg, Dr. John Harvey, 75, 80
Ken, see Cameron
Kendall, Henry, 151
Kennedy, Frank, 190, 219, 238, 447-449
Kinsey, Dr., 391
Kenyon, Adelbert (Del), 114, 136, 141, 148, 153, 295, 334
Kenyon, Frances (Fran), 114, 136, 141, 148, 153, 154, 206, 295, 298, 300, 334
Keon, Barbara (Bobby), 201, 207, 208, 232, 244, 245, 251, 253, 261, 448
Kern, Hal C., 448
Keyes, Evelyn, 172, 220, 310, 317, 332, 333
Kidd, Culver, 72
King, Cammie, 322, 468

Kirby, Mrs., 444
Kirkpatrick, William S., 228, 231, 257, 264, 448
Kiwanis Club, 305, 314, 316
Knights of the Round Table, 252
Kolenkhov, Boris, 444
Kudzu Kid, 356, 357
Kurtz, Annie Laurie, 154, 171, 175, 177, 180, 182, 192, 202, 257
Kurtz, Wilbur, 147, 154, 175, 177, 180, 184, 202, 205, 206, 234, 246. 309
Lady Bracknell, 117, 119, 424, 441
Lake Sinclair, 401
Lamar, Bonaparte, 408
Lamar, Dorothy (Dolly) Blount, 189, 216, 294, 310, 391
Lamar family, 375, 408
Lamar, Lucius Quintus Cincinnatus, 408
Lamar, Walter, 310
Lamar, Zachariah, 408
Lamb in His Bosom, 140
Lambert, Edward P., 199, 218, 221, 222, 230, 237, 247, 249, 253, 258, 261, 267
Land, Fort, 100
Landon, Alf, 384
Lane, Bruce, 229, 241, 248, 249, 447
Lanier High School for Girls, 102, 105
Latham, Harold, 142
Laughton, Charles, 236, 237
Lawson, Sara, 158
Lawson, Skippy, 465
Lee County, Georgia, 111
Lee House, 375
Lee, Catherine, 433, 465
Lee, General Robert E., 294
Lee, Harry, 445
Lee/Leigh, Rolly, 226, 263, 448
Leigh, Vivien,185, 186, 188, 192, 200, 206, 207, 213, 216, 225-227, 230, 232, 234, 239-241, 247, 249, 263, 264, 269-271, 273, 276-279, 308, 310, 312, 314, 315, 322, 331, 357, 408, 427
Lenox Avenue, 442
Leona, Mrs., 172
Lewis, Margaret Powell, 295, 298-300, 303, 304, 334
Liberty Street, 54, 57, 73, 77, 97, 112, 143
Lidell, J. C., 366
Life in a Tangle, 105
Life with Father, 159
Lincoln, President, 47, 294, 391, 467
Lindberg, Ann Morrow, 445
Lindsley, Dr. Luther C., 299, 364, 406, 413
Lindsley, Lillas Myrick (Mrs. L. C.), 4, 8, 16, 70, 103, 105, 112, 131, 143, 144, 160, 167, 168, 178, 214, 299, 364, 402, 405, 406, 413, 466
Lindsley, Susan, 4, 328-333, 465
Lindsley Three Little Girls, 299, 413
Listen the Wind, 445
Literary Digest, 384
Liston, Mason, 242, 265
Little Cedar Creek, 8
Little Foxes, 128
Little, Arnold W., 133
Llewellyn, 401
Loew's Grand Theater, 306, 307, 309
Lombard, Carole, 228, 308
Long, Margaret, 381
Longfellow, Henry W., 110

Los Angeles Times, 433
Louise (wardrobe), 248
Louisville Times, 389
Luce, Claire, 155
Luther Williams Park, 363
Macedonia, 164
MacMillan Publishing, 158
Macon Chamber of Commerce, 357, 360
Macon Farmers Club, 357, 360, 361, 376, 395, 463
Macon Little Theatre, 50, 116-121, 128, 131, 132, 151, 154-156, 161, 166, 176, 198, 330, 339, 343, 350, 361, 398, 426, 433, 441, 463, 466
Macon News, The, 328, 341, 357, 362, 415, 428, 463
Macon Telegraph, The, 20, 102, 103, 105-116, 131-133, 164, 167, 313, 341, 356, 357, 372, 378, 394, 424, 43 463, 464, 466
Macon Writers' Club, 380
Macon, the dirigible, 110
Madame Curie, 160
Madame X, 443
Mahin, John Lee, 236
Mahone, Perry, 136, 138, 144, 147, 153, 161, 162, 166, 295, 298-300, 303, 304, 311, 326
Maine, the battleship, 47
Maine, the state, 395, 402, 403, 422
Mammy, 136, 160, 173, 175, 177, 190, 191, 193, 200, 206, 208-213, 215, 234, 244-246, 248, 252, 255, 262, 2 267, 272, 278, 331, 336, 337, 459
Manny, 9
Mansion Annex, 50
Marching Through Georgia, 300
Margaret Mitchell of Atlanta, 324
Margaret Mitchell's Gone With The Wind *Letters*, 324, 461
Marquis, Donald, 158
Marse Robert (see also Lee, General Robert E.), 47
Marsh, John, 122, 123, 129, 135, 140-142, 153, 154, 157, 158, 163, 180, 191, 192, 194, 216, 230, 231, 242, 2 253, 254, 257, 259, 272, 323, 324, 358
Marsh, Margaret Mitchell, see Mitchell, Margaret
Marshall Field, 144
Martin, Marcella, 173
Marx, Harpo, 234
Massee, Boots (Jordan, Jr.), 144, 162, 191, 372
Massee, Jordan, Sr., 215, 167
Mattie, Dovedale employee, 10
Mayer, Louis B., 206
Mayer, Mrs. Louis B., 310
McAdoo, Senator, 310
McBride Publishers, 277
McCarthy, Eugene, 424
McCord, Caroline, 297, 298, 304, 334
McCord, Fletcher, 334
McCord, R. A., Sr.,, 310
McCullars, Carson, 129
McDaniel, Hattie, 173, 177, 193, 213, 222, 223, 238, 239, 248, 322
McGee, Marjorie, 138
McGee, Sid, 138, 149
McGibbony, T. H., 366
McKay, Blythe, 138, 147, 148, 153, 154, 165, 166, 295, 298, 301, 304, 334
McLemore, Henry, 340
McQueen, Butterfly, 213, 221, 238, 240, 316, 318, 331
McWhorter, G. E., 366
Mecca, 443
Melanie Room, 172, 173, 174, 177, 178, 181, 190

Mellon, Andrew W., 162
Memory Hill Cemetery, 425, 432
Menzies, William Cameron, 176,179, 184, 220, 221, 236, 237, 238, 242, 250, 261, 270, 276
Mercer University, 326, 423, 424, 426, 430
Mesta, Perle, 375
Meyrick, Sir George, 401
MGM Studios, 147, 206, 260, 305, 306, 308, 313, 314, 319, 326, 328, 329-332, 336, 339
Mice and Men, 155
Michael, Gertrude, 174, 185
Microbe of Love, 71
Middle Georgia Regional Library, 162
Midsummer Night's Dream, 275
Midway, 6-8, 71
Milledgeville, Georgia, 2, 6, 8, 47, 50-54, 56, 70-72, 75, 79, 81, 84, 87, 96-98, 116, 132, 143, 152, 155, 168, 174, 299, 358- 360, 363, 366, 370, 376, 383, 396, 402, 413, 414, 425, 429, 432, 442, 465, 466
Miller, Caroline, 140
Miller, Wallace, 102
Miss America, 249, 315
Miss Mat, Dovedale seamstress, 34-36
Miss X, 173, 175-177, 181, 182, 190
Mississippi, 159,172, 253
Mitchell, Eugene, 135, 140
Mitchell, Margaret/Peggy, 9, 114, 122-126, 129, 131, 133-136, 139-142, 145, 147, 148, 153, 154, 157-159, 163, 170, 178, 180, 191, 215, 223, 224, 229, 231, 232, 238, 240, 242, 251, 255, 256, 264, 269, 294, 307, 311-314, 317, 323-325, 335, 336, 358, 382, 383, 392, 410, 414, 424, 430, 460, 461, 466, 469
Mitchell, Mrs. Martha, 384
Mitchell, Stephens, 324, 326, 330, 334, 410, 435
Mitchell, Thomas, 185, 193, 225, 226
Mobley, Dr. M. D., 359
Monroe, John, 366
Montgomery, Doug, 173
Monticello, 437
Morehouse College, 414
Moore, Zoë Rozar, 144
Morgan, Frank, 237,448
Morgan, Perry, 389
Moultrie, Georgia, 310
Mount Berry Schools, 305
Mr. P. T., see Anderson, Peyton
Mr. W. T., see Anderson, W. T.
Mueller, Bill, 268
Muni, Paul, 442, 443
Munson, Ona, 310, 322
Murphy, Maurice, 449, 186, 220
Murphy, Reg, Tribute to Sue, 328
Murray, George, 444
Murray, Bob, 168
Myrick
Allie, 4, 8-10, 12, 14, 16, 41, 50, 53, 54, 70, 82, 85-87, 100, 111. 126, 139, 140, 144, 257, 350, 376, 395, 400, 401, 402, 404, 413, 416, 417, 422 425, 427, 429, 433, 465
Aunt Lizzie Good, 4, 13, 434
Benjamin Harvey, 4, 13, 47
Betsy, Fullie's daughter, 4, 213, 214
Chan, Fullie's wife, 4, 112, 213
Elizabeth (see Tippie)
Elizabeth Dowdell, 4, 6, 16
Fullillove, 4, 8, 54, 70, 112, 206, 213
Goodwin (Uncle Good), 4, 6, 8, 12, 13, 42
James Dowdell, Jr., 4, 6, 7, 54, 105

James Dowdell, Sr., 4, 6-8, 11,12, 16,17, 21, 24-32, 36, 37, 43, 44, 46, 47, 103, 149, 159, 433, 436
John , 4, 6
Kate, Miss, see Thulia Katherine
Katie, 4, 8, 9, 12, 15, 70, 81, 147, 164, 167, 168, 178, 396, 398, 401, 425
Lillas (see Lindsley)
Lizzie (Aunt Lizzie Good), 4, 13, 436
Martha (Mrs. Stith Parham), 4
Nannaline, 4, 7
Nancy Averette Bryan, 4, 5, 6
Stith Parham, 4, 6-8, 16, 424, 432
Thulia Katherine, 2, 4, 5, 7-9, 11, 15, 19, 53, 54, 69, 70, 103, 112, 168, 432, 437
Tippie, 4, 8, 31, 47, 54, 168, 401, 405, 432
Uncle Ben (see Benjamin Harvey)
Virginia, Fullie's daughter, 4, 214

Myrick Volunteers, 6
Myrick's Mill, 6, 7, 15
Nagel, Conrad, 219
Namath, Joe, 388
Napier, Hamilton, 114
Napier, Skelton, 39
Napier, Viola Rose, 170
Napier's Mill, 39
Napoleon, 443
Nathan, George Jean, 240
National Association of Non-Smokers, 364
National Association of Soil Conservation District Supervisors, 359, 368, 371
National Ballet, 401
National Editorial Association, 368, 372
National Labor Relations Board, 384
Naud, Edna, 235, 400
Nebraska (see also, Hastings), 82, 93, 101, 149
Neil, Edward J., 145
Nelson Road, 8
New York Times, 133, 414
New, Betty, 165, 295
New, Fred, 165, 295, 300, 301
Newcom, James E., 449
Newsome, Johnnie, 111
Newspaper Publishers Association, 358, 361
Nichols Nickleby, 106
Nims, Arthur (Art), 140, 295, 299, 401
Nims, Edwina (Eddie), 116, 140, 147, 163, 295, 296, 299, 304, 401
Niven, David, 323
Normal School of Physical Education, 75, 80, 101
Norris, Bobby, 141, 153
Nunn, Sam, 366, 371
Nunn, Senator Sam, 366, 429
O'Connor, Flannery, 52, 129
O'Connor, Regina (see Cline)
O'Hara, Careen, 172, 261
O'Hara, Ellen, 180, 194, 204, 208, 234, 245-248, 268
O'Hara, Gerald, 173, 179, 181, 185, 193, 203, 209, 222, 225, 226, 228, 248, 249, 467
O'Hara, Scarlett, 136, 147, 159, 171, 172, 175, 177, 181, 184, 191, 192, 194, 201, 203, 204, 208-212, 215, 216, 222, 224, 225, 228, 234, 237, 240, 245, 247, 249, 251, 252, 254, 256-258, 261, 262, 268, 269, 271, 273, 27 310, 315, 325, 326, 335-337, 448
O'Hara, Suellen, 172, 223, 228, 245, 246, 317, 408
O'Neil, Barbara, 247, 248, 268
O'Shea, Daniel T., 165, 169, 172, 187-189, 237, 449

Ocmulgee National Monument, 394
Ocmulgee River, 110, 390, 434
Odom, Crockett, 151
Odom, Mrs., 151
Okefenokee Swamp, 364, 413
Old Man and the Sea, 423
Olivier, Laurence, 239, 241, 247, 277, 278
Our Daily Bread, 359, 360, 460, 463
Our Town, 156
P. T., see Peyton Anderson
Pace, Stephen, 365
Pappy, see Selznick, David O.
Parham, Joe, 357
Parks, M. M., 98
Pasadena, CA, 241, 252
Pasadena Little Theatre School, 198
Pasadena Playhouse, 198
Patterson, Alicia, 125
Patterson, Gene, 384 , 389
Patterson, Isabel, 159
Patterson, Pamela Johnson, 326
Peabody Awards, 161
Peace, Charlie, 386
Pearl Harbor, 339, 342
Penny Wise, 161
Perkerson, Angus, 135
Perkerson, Medora Field, 135
Perry, see Mahone
Persia, 443
Phi Beta Kappa, 76, 126
Philip of Macedonia, 164
Pickford, Mary, 198
Pigeon, Walter, 279
Pilot Club, 305
Platt, Joseph B., 173, 179, 190, 220, 449
Plunkett, Walter, 177, 182, 186, 195, 199, 221, 228, 234-236, 247, 252, 254, 258, 449
Polk, Oscar, 193, 213, 223, 238
Popper, Joe Jr., 128
Popper, Joseph W. Sr., 116, 117, 138
Popper, Marjorie, 147
Pork, 190, 193, 204, 209, 213, 222, 245, 246
Post, Emily, 107, 445
Potato Creek, 8
Powell, Margaret, see Lewis, Margaret Powell
Powell, Mr., 50
POWs, 341, 342
Press Haven, 157
Price and Rationing Board, 343
Price, Will, 176, 181, 185, 191, 193, 197, 198, 208, 230, 263
Princess Pat Regiment, 191
Prinz, Eddie, 449
Prissy, 31, 136, 166, 178, 193, 213, 222, 229, 307, 322, 331, 337
Probes, Dave, 144
Progressive Farmer, 360, 463, 464
Progressive Farmers Club, 376
Public Health Service, 105
Putnam County, Georgia ("Putmon"), 111
Queen Martha (role), 441
Queen Mary, 252

Queen of the May, 249, 440
Quinlan, Robert.(Bob), 116, 136, 138, 144, 148, 153, 154, 162, 165, 295, 298, 300, 304, 311, 334
Rabwin, Marcella, 175, 189, 228, 263
Rawlings, Marjorie Kinnan, 129
Ray (Mr.) (publicity), 189
Ray, Robert, 394, 395
Reader's Digest, 391
Reconstruction, 150, 218, 254, 354
Red Cross, 149, 343
Reay, Nev, 247
Regency Hyatt House, 328
Reid, Wally, 362
Relatively Speaking, 117, 398
Rennahan, Ray, 449
Republic Studios, 274
Republican National Committee, 375
Revolutionary War, 6
Reynolds Square, 162
Rhett, Alicia, 285, 305, 310
Rhinegold, 72
Richardson, Dr., 423
River Place, The, 6
Rivers, Helena, 23
Roaring Twenties, 336
Rob Roy, 22
Robert, Chip, 310
Robert, Mrs., 310
Roberti, Rene, 444
Rockwell Mansion, 6-8, 17
Rodocanachi, C. P., 444
Rogers, Buddy, 198
Rogers, Hazel, 228, 234, 240
Rome, Italy, 325, 400, 402, 403, 405
Rome, NY, 401, 433
Romeo and Juliet, 141
Roosevelt, Eleanor, 158
Roosevelt, Franklin, 111, 339
Roosevelts, 29
Rosa, Miss, 73
Rose, Billy, 142
Rotary Club, 305
Round Oak, Georgia, 73, 74
Roy Harris Pine Tree Symphony, 442
Rozar, Aunt Josie, 143, 144, 168
Rozar, Berry (Mayberry), 143,166, 168, 169, 295, 299, 303, 304
Rozar, Malora, 142, 144, 165, 166, 168, 169, 206, 295, 298, 299, 304
Rozar, Nanette, 168
Run Little Chillun, 194, 198, 213
Rutherford, Ann, 310, 330, 332, 333, 429, 430
Safe Conduct, 445
Sally League, 153
Salute to Yesterday, 137
Salvation Army, 381, 394
Santa Monica, 179, 180, 182, 183, 185, 213, 241, 244
Sara Lou, employee at Dovedale, 9-11, 14
Saturday Evening Post, 23
Savannah, Georgia, 81, 95, 157, 160, 162, 210, 244, 334
Sayers, Jo Ann, actress, 220
Scandals of Clochemerle, 135

Scarlett, Rhett and a Cast of Thousands, 271, 324
Schofield, Harry, 161, 163, 165, 166, 188, 191
Schultz, Harry, 82, 85
Scott, Sir Walter, 110
Scottsboro School, 72
Screenland, 277
Scribner's, 149
Second Quartermaster Regiment, 341
Selznick International Pictures, Inc., 114, 131,171, 187, 215, 242, 296, 313
Selznick, David O. (Pappy/DOS) , 131, 133, 137, 145, 147, 148, 154-157, 169, 171, 173-175,177, 187 189, 191, 192, 195, 201, 203, 208, 220, 222, 223, 226, 228, 232, 234, 236, 242, 249, 251, 254-261, 263-265, 267-269, 271, 273, 277, 305, 307, 308, 312, 314, 323, 331, 336, 357, 361, 430, 467
Shadow and Substance, 155
Shannon, Peggy, 185, 219
Shapiro, Victor M., 244, 264, 265
Sharkey-Stribling fight, 361
Shearer, Norma, 159, 449
Shelburne, Frances and James, 114, 161, 295, 334, 335, 427
Shelton, Marla, 185, 449
Sheppard, I. M., 465
Sherman (James C. Calhoun), 5, 9-11, 18, 26, 71, 72, 422, 437, 440
Sherman, General William T., 5, 217, 253, 293, 354
Shorter, Edward, 310
Sibley, Celestine, 53, 129, 381, 433
Sigma Sigma Psi, 76, 101
Simon Lagree, 229
Singleton, Mary, 323
Sixth Army Corps, 341
Slattery, Emmy, 337
Smith, Ben, 190
Smith, Frances Gordon, 264
Smith, Gertrude (Trawick), 374, 388, 459
Smith, Houser, 118
Smith, Lew, 279
Smith, Taylor, 386
Smitty (owner of Wisteria Restaurant), 388
SMMA, 293-297, 311, 333, 334, 401
Soap Box Derby, 400
Soil Conservation Services Regional Offices, 359
Southern Cultivator, 23, 24, 28
Southern Living, 361
Spain, 145, 400, 402
Sparta Agricultural & Industrial Institute, 164, 165
Sparta, Georgia, 164, 165, 306
Spencer, John Duncan, 383-385
Spiero, Jerry, 137, 151
Spring Creek, 162
Squeers, Fannie (see Fannie Squeers)
Sragow, Michael, 430
St. Johns, Adela Rogers, 324
Stacey, Eric G., 180, 184, 187, 202, 205, 231, 234, 236, 239, 240, 242, 243, 244, 270, 271, 293
Stafford, Jane, 374
Stein, Gertrude, 140
Stella (Tippie's daughter), 146, 401, 425
Stembridge, Bertie, 72
Stephanie "somebody," probably Steffi Duna, 263
Stephens, Alexander, 306, 337, 435
Stepp, Wade, 128
Still, William Grant, 442

Stone, Philip, 129
Strong, Lt. Col. F. K., 97
Struby, Bert, 372
Stuart, Erwin, 156
Stuart, Miss, 172
Stylus Post-Dispatch, 248
Sugar Creek, 111
Summer Place, The, 6
Surgeon General, 95-97
Swan House, 327
Taft, President, 114
Talbotton, Georgia, 147, 154
Tales from Shakespeare (Lamb), 22
Tales of King Arthur's Court, 22
Talladega, Alabama, 174, 185
Tallechet, Margaret, 200
Talmadge, Governor Eugene, 339
Tar Baby, 2, 333
Tara,174, 177, 178, 183, 188, 192, 194, 200, 201, 224, 229, 237, 245, 250, 255, 256, 259, 260, 268, 336, 337,
Tara Ball, 326, 327, 328-333
Tara's Theme, 332
Tarleton, 153, 186, 190, 205, 207, 219, 220 247, 251, 325, 447
Tarver, Jack, 389
Texas, 398, 402, 408 433, 465
The Atlanta Constitution, 356, 357, 389, 409, 433
The Atlanta Journal, 122, 356
The Atlanta Journal-Constitution, 389, 409
The Detroit News, 361
The Editor's Forum, 360, 406
The Georgian, 228, 231
The Life of Emile Zola, 442
The Miser's Dream, 71
The New York Telegram, 391
The New York World, 361, 460
The New Yorker, 149
The New York Evening Post, 159
The Philadelphia Record, 460
The Queen's Husband, 441
The Reporter, 465
The Saturday Review, 324
The Washington Star, 389
Thomas Hardy books, 22
Thomas, Rick, 465
Thomas, Tom, 159, 294, 440
Thomasville, Georgia, 162
Thompson, Tilly, 273, 277, 449
Tifton, Georgia, 86
Tillinghast, David A., 378
Tobacco Road, 141
Tolstoy, 229
Too Much Mustard, 149
Toombs, Robert, 337
Toscanini, 141
Trade Winds, 242
Trader, George Henry, 443
Trawick, Gertrude (see Smith)
Tribble, Edwin, 389
Trojan War, 72
Trotti, Louise and Lamar, 310

Troup, Governor George Michael, 358
Truman, Bess, 374, 375, 434
Truman, Margaret, 374, 375 434
Truman, President Harry, 374, 375, 434
Tupper, Sammy, 135
Turner, Catherine, 98, 99
Turpin, Ben, 385
Twelve Oaks, 131, 202, 233, 245, 248, 252, 253-255, 265, 266, 467
Twiggs County, 6, 381
Twisted Yarn, 157
Tybee, 157
Uncle Peter, 190, 193, 206, 213
Uncle Remus, 71, 72
Uncle Tom (see Tom Thomas)
Uncle Tom's Cabin, 293
Union-Recorder, 24, 71, 72, 358, 440
United Daughters of the Confederacy (UDC), 134, 188, 216, 251, 391
United Press, 276
Universal Studios, 336
University of Georgia, 123, 126, 161, 163, 305, 351, 363, 389
Ursalines, 261
Valhalla, 72
Van Druten, John, 242, 253, 449
Vancouver, 139, 144
Variety, 147, 433
VE Day, 387
Vereen, Mr. and Mrs. Will, 310
Vinegar Tree, 155, 156, 441
Vinson, Chief Justice Fred M., 375
W. T., see Anderson, W. T.
Walaska, Count, 443
Wall Street, 444
War Between the States, 5-7, 48, 111, 131, 245, 254, 333, 354, 391, 437, 467
Warm Springs, 111, 146
Warner Robins Army Air Force Base, 339
Warren, Delmar, 114, 311, 334
Washington University, 7
Washington, D. C., 140, 142, 328, 374, 376, 387, 401, 459
Washington, President George, 103, 360
Water Marvel, 389, 390
Watson, Billy, 465
Weeden, Marie Howard, 459
Welty, Eudora, 129
Wesley, John, 162
Wesleyan College, 117, 128, 395, 465
West, Mae, 243, 445
West, Miss Ruena G., 73
Westminster Abbey, 337
Westmore, Monty, 236, 237, 242, 243, 247, 261, 273-275, 449
Westover Plantation, 131, 248, 402, 405, 406, 413, 414, 425, 462
Wheaton, Ann Williams, 375
Wheeler, Lyle, 173, 449
Whitehurst
  Cincinnatus, 4, 53, 81, 82
  Nan, 4, 81, 82, 143, 359, 402, 465
  Nancy A. Bryan, 4, 5
  Josephine, 4 (see also Rozar)
  Pauline, 53
  Thulia Katherine (see Myrick)

Wilkinson Mayberry, 4
Willa, 4, 11
Zollicoffer, 4, 11

Whitney, John Hay (Jock), 252, 280, 309
Wiggins, Mr., 74
Wilde, Oscar, 424
Wilder, Honey Chile, 163, 191
Wilkerson, Jonas. 204, 248, 317, 337, 447
Wilkes (family), 204, 252
Wilkes, Ashley, 181, 191, 195, 196, 214, 222, 225, 238, 246, 249, 250, 262, 263, 281, 448
Wilkes, Beauregard, 195-197, 229, 273, 274, 337
Wilkes, Jane, 150, 162, 299, 303, 304
Wilkes, Melanie, 136, 172, 183, 191, 195-197, 201, 207, 212, 222, 246, 249, 250, 256, 262, 263, 310, 317, 326, 328, 333, 374, 425
Wilkinson County, 5
William and Mary College, 426
Williams, Beth, 158
Wilson, Eliza, 277
Wilson, Margery, 445
Wilson, Mayor Ed, 424
Winchell, Walter, 127
Winn, Ed, 155
Winner Take Nothing, 423
Winship, North, 326
Winter, Larry, 263, 449
Winterich, John, 136, 146
With Malice toward None, 445
Wolfe, Thomas, 391
Woman of the Year, 360, 463, 464
Women of the Confederacy, 27, 218
Women's League, 305
Women's National Press Club, 360, 374
Wood, Sam, 270, 275
World Bank, 110
World Premiere, 306-311, 317, 326
World War I, 82, 126, 342, 383
World War II, 116, 118, 339, 340, 341, 386, 400, 402, 413, 434
WPA, 158
WSB-TV, 334, 424
Yoch, Florence, 117, 184, 192, 198, 207, 241
You Can't Take It with You, 141, 443
You're a Sweetheart, 444
Young, Andrew, 414
Young, Loretta, 180
Youth's Companion, 14, 23, 47
YWCA, 101
Zola, Emile, 442, 443

www.ingramcontent.com/pod-product-compliance
Lightning Source LLC
Chambersburg PA
CBHW031228090426
42742CB00007B/114

* 9 7 8 1 7 3 3 4 0 4 4 1 9 *